14^{95}

The Encyclopedia Of
GOLF
COLLECTIBLES

A Collector's Identification and Value Guide

by
John M. Olman & Morton W. Olman

Foreword by
Ben Crenshaw

2nd Printing

Distributed by:
OLD GOLF SHOP, INC.
325 W. 5th Street
Cincinnati, Ohio 45202

BOOKS AMERICANA INC
ISBN 0-89689-050-3

Distributed by
CHARLES E. TUTTLE CO., INC.
Rutland, Vermont

DEDICATION:

To the many friendships
made possible through our involvement
in the great game of golf.

ABOUT THE AUTHORS:

MORTON W. OLMAN is known to much of the golfing world as the founder of the Old Golf Shop in Cincinnati, Ohio. A commercial real estate broker and fine amateur golfer, he developed an interest in golf history in the late 1950's. After playing in the British and French Amateur Championships in 1961, Mort became fascinated with the heritage of golf at a time when most golfers were content just playing the game rather than studying its history. He became interested in golf art and began to acquire golf prints as a hobby. As he continued to seek additions to his collection, he realized that there were very few golf prints being offered at the time.

Consequently, Mort formed the Old Golf Shop in 1970 and began by publishing two golf prints. From that small beginning, the shop has grown continually as has the hobby of collecting golf memorabilia, and it is now the largest business of its kind in the world. In addition to handling golf art, Mort and his son Jim, deal in all sorts of antique golf equipment and memorabilia. Many of these collectibles, as well as modern items, are sold to clubs for use as tournament prizes and to galleries, interior designers and gift shops for resale as decorative items. Of course, they regularly do business with collectors and museums. Mort is recognized as one of the most knowledgeable authorities on golf antiquities and spends a considerable amount of time in Great Britain, where the Old Golf Shop is well known.

JOHN M. OLMAN, Mort's son, who by virtue of his family's association with the golfing world, is also very much interested in the history of the game. His interest in golf collectibles started at age twelve when he began to correspond with golf courses throughout the world to request one of their scorecards. By the time he was fifteen, John had constructed a putting green in the front yard of their home, complete with sand trap. A low handicap player like his father, he earned a degree in golf course architecture from the University of Maryland through a specially designed program of study. John has established several businesses including a landscape irrigation company. He enjoys all things pertaining to golf, and in the realm of golf collecting he is particularly interested in books, artwork and antique equipment pertaining to golf courses. John also enjoys researching the finer points of the game's history in old books and periodicals.

Mort and John Olman at the fabled stone bridge at The Old Course, St. Andrews.

PREFACE

Since 1970, when the Old Golf Shop was founded, we have witnessed a tremendous surge in the hobby of golf collecting. There is such a vast assortment of golf related items that each enthusiast has his own unique type of collection. Some collectors search for valuable equipment and artwork made prior to 1900 and have considerable amounts invested in their hobby, while others have simple, but thorough, golf libraries or an accumulation of old wood shafted clubs from the 1920's.

As the Old Golf Shop expanded, customers began to request an illustrated catalog, since they were often unable to visit the showroom or decide on their purchase at a trade exhibit. In 1980, an extensive catalog was published and collectors marvelled at the photos of golf memorabilia and their informative descriptions. The catalog became more than a sales tool; it was a source of information about golf collectibles. Most of the space was devoted to artwork and tournament prizes, with only a small section on clubs, balls and other antique collectibles.

Collectors and others began to request more information about the many types of memorabilia that the Shop regularly sold, but never catalogued. Many of these one-of-a-kind and unusual pieces remained in inventory for only a short while since they were usually sold in a matter of days. Even though we were unable to include these collectibles in the catalog, we had the foresight to photograph them for future reference. As more and more people called and wrote for information on golf memorabilia which they either had or were seeking, it became apparent that somehow all of our information should be assembled into a book.

Once it was decided to proceed with writing a book, we went through the thousands of photos already in our possession and continued to take a few thousand more. We consulted with others knowledgeable on the subject and embarked on a year long task which included further research and eventual compilation of the material that we had gathered. The sharing of information among collectors was vital to us since so much of the history of the manufacturers of golf items has never been documented. Thus the goal of this book was to accumulate all of the previously known facts on golf collectibles, research many of the unknowns, and present the findings in a manner that would assist both experienced and novice collectors, researchers and interested golfers.

The book is divided into fourteen chapters, each dealing with a specific aspect of golf collecting. There are also several alphabetical lists which contain the names of makers, artists, authors and other pertinent information. Some of our findings will be new and enlightening and others might contradict previous writings. We have attempted to be as thorough as possible and have confirmed our facts with recognized experts. If there is ever any supposition on our part, it is noted as such.

There are several dealers of golf related collectibles throughout the world. Some specialize in one aspect, such as clubs, artwork, books or pottery and may handle the golf pieces as an adjunct to another business. When spending substantial sums of money on golf items, it is advisable for the collector to check the reputation of the dealer before making a purchase. As with any type of collecting, fake pieces do exist and the buyer should be wary of a club or print that does not look "just right".

The collector should also be warned that auction estimates and prices realized are not necessarily the true market value of an item. Sometimes a buyer at an auction will pay an exorbitant price for a particular item. This, however, does not necessarily mean that the fair market value goes up immediately. Conversely, an item may be sold for an extremely low price, and this too should not affect its normal value. It is hoped that collectors will become more educated in their hobby by communicating with other collectors and by reading this book prior to investing in valuable pieces of golf memorabilia.

In addition to being an identification guide, this book is also intended to inform the reader of approximate values of golf collectibles. Based on our experience, price ranges have been assigned to items where applicable. These prices are those which a collector should expect to pay a dealer for an article in good condition. The collector should remember that exact pricing of equipment such as clubs and balls is impossible to provide. Millions of these items were produced and much of the work was done by hand. Therefore, identical models may have completely different playing characteristics and their values may vary. Nevertheless, the value ranges shown will be a helpful guide to the collector.

As with all hobbies, when individuals become actively involved, they begin to form many new friendships. The novice collector will usually find that the more experienced collectors are willing to share information and bits of trivia. That sharing of information was necessary for the creation of this *Encyclopedia* and it is hoped that our readers will share their knowledge with us. Any suggestions, corrections or other information which we should consider for future editions should be forwarded to us in writing at: Old Golf Shop, Inc., 325 West Fifth Street, Cincinnati, Ohio, 45202.

THE AUTHORS

FOREWORD

Everyone, at one time or another, collects something. We as golf collectors are very fortunate, indeed, for our heritage has spanned some 500 long and glorious years. Golf is *the* traditionalist's game, having universal appeal to all who come in contact with this wonderful pastime. Therefore, many objects, such as art, books, clubs and other equipment, silver and pottery, reflect a sincere devotion to their subject. These collectibles are so wonderful because, in my mind, they reflect a deep appreciation of golf itself, a game with such a simple proposition, but such a difficult task.

Somehow golf seems to reflect the personality of the player, bringing out his most humanistic behaviors. It is this strange and wonderful result, which happens to everyone who has held a club, that inspires people to write a book, paint a picture, make a club and make it possible for these objects to become golf collectibles.

Exhaustive research to better understand, explore and improve the game of golf has enabled it to reach the level of popularity which it enjoys today. I know that my hobby of golf collecting has helped me to better understand the game, its people, and its historic events. I have approximately 400 golf books which have given me hour upon hour of pure pleasure. I read about the interesting players of the game to learn which of their qualities contributed to their success. I want to know about a particular player's makeup, how he thought himself through a tournament, and how he handled a particular hole in an important event.

I also have a particular passion for golf course architecture, both in learning about its history and in helping to shape its future. As a student and a practitioner of golf course design, I feel compelled to learn about the people who have been involved in the building of golf courses and about the special talents which made some of them so spectacular.

My study of history and architecture books, and also of the many prints and photographs which depict golf course scenes, has been a most pleasurable learning experience. It seems to me that anyone having a genuine interst in golf would naturally try to find out how the revered traditions came into being and how they will be necessary for the continued success of the game. Those that have studied the evolution of golf can see how these time-honored customs live today as colorfully as they appeared on the horizon many years ago.

I would like to thank my good friend, Mort Olman, for giving me the opportunity to contribute to *The Encyclopedia of Golf Collectibles.* He has guided me along in my collecting and has enabled me to meet some wonderful collectors throughout the world.

In closing, it is appropriate that I raise a toast to the golf collectors all over the world . . . for it is their love of the game that we share. My Master's win in 1984 was, for me, a small way of saying "thanks" to them for their devotion to the game and its fine heritage.

Happy Collecting.

Ben D. Crenshaw

Ben Crenshaw

Austin, Texas
September 1984

ACKNOWLEDGEMENTS

This book could not have been completed without the generous assistance of many interested and cooperative people. The Museum and Library of the United States Golf Association was a continual source of information. Janet Seagle, its Curator/Librarian, and collectors Bob Hansen, Pete Georgiady and Bud Dufner provided the direction, consultation and manuscript review which was necessary in order to accomplish this project. Ben Crenshaw took time from his busy schedule to write an inspiring Foreword and also a review of golf architecture books.

This book would have been incomplete without the thousands of photos which enhance the text. Although most of the photography was done by the authors, professional photographers Steve Rindsberg and Bill Lefevor made splendid contributions. Others who were kind enough to provide photographs include: the USGA, *The Cincinnati Enquirer,* The World Golf Hall of Fame, Clayton Adams, Ruffin Beckwith, Henry Cotton, Lawrence Levy, Trevor Yerbury and the British auction houses of Sotheby Parke Bernet, Christie's and Phillips. Pete and Jeff Georgiady supplied the many drawings used in the club chapter, and renowned golf artist Arthur Weaver produced the fine sketches used for the chapter headings. The attractive cover was designed by Becky Lowers.

Several others furnished information and advice, and allowed items from their collections to be photographed. John W. Fischer, an avid collector and good friend, shared his extensive knowledge of golf art and history prior to his recent death. In addition to supplying pertinent information, the following collectors have written articles especially for use in this book and are recognized where these articles appear: Bud Dufner, Ben Crenshaw, Nevin Gibson, Alastair Johnston, Joe Murdoch, George Peper, Janet Seagle and Tom Wishon. Others who helped in their respective areas of expertise were: Jeff August, John Capers, Arthur Colletti, Ray Davis, Jack Dezieck, Frank Hardison, Bert Heizmann, Jim Kaplan, David Kirkwood, Ben Klein, Herb Kretschmar, Bob Kuntz, the London Cigarette Card Co., David Low, Jocelyn Lukins, Millard Mack, Ralph Maltby, Pat Manturi, Robert Perham, Craig Shambeau, Steve Shapiro, John Staver, David Stirk, Harold von Wyl, Larry Ward and Alick Watt.

Dan Alexander, of Books Americana, Inc., was responsible for getting the book to press. His experience with books on collectibles and his appreciation for the popularity of golf memorabilia helped to make this project a satisfying and enjoyable one. Thanks must also be extended to the faceless wonder of modern technology, the computer . . . without which this book could never have been assembled.

Our wives, Lynn and Florence, were a source of support and understanding throughout the researching and writing stages. For it was their continued encouragement which kept the momentum of this project going from beginning to end.

TABLE OF CONTENTS

The Masters, 9th Green.

CHAPTER 1 — GUIDE TO GOLF COLLECTING

The collecting of golf memorabilia is as old as the game itself. Golf collecting started over five hundred years ago when one of the early golfers acquired a new club and set aside one he had been using. As this early golfer accumulated more clubs, he became the first golf collector. Although the identity of this first collector is unknown, he was the first of many golf enthusiasts to save golf items for later use, sale or trade.

It wasn't until 1793 in the third edition of *The Goff,* an early poem on golf, that there was a written mention of a golf collection. It was noted that one of the participants in the match described in the poem had accumulated hundreds of old golf clubs. The next written mention of a golf collection appeared as an advertisement on the back cover of a golf annual in 1866. The ad mentioned that a museum had been opened in the Union Club House in St. Andrews for the purpose of displaying "Old Relics of Golfing Celebrities and other objects of interest in connection with the game." It is thought that this collection became the property of the Royal and Ancient Golf Club of St. Andrews when the two clubs merged in 1877.

By the end of the nineteenth century, there were several substantial golf collections, many of which were displayed at the International Exposition held in 1901 in Glasgow, Scotland. Contributions to the display were made by prominent golfers, golf clubs and golf associations of the period.

In 1910, Harry B. Wood compiled a book called *Golfing Curios and the Like* which was the first comprehensive study of golf memorabilia. Wood, the best known of the early golf collectors, donated his extensive collection to the North Manchester (England) Golf Club, where it remains today. Another important work was done by Cecil Hopkinson who wrote a golf bibliography, *Collecting Golf Books,* in 1938.

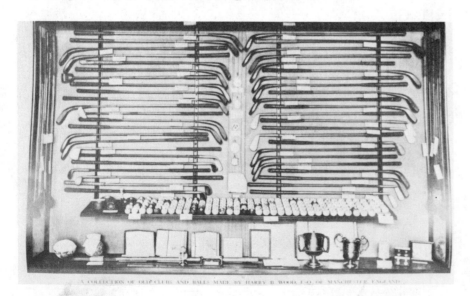

The famous Harry B. Wood Collection, formed in the early twentieth century.

Meanwhile, in America, the United States Golf Association began to acquire golf memorabilia and opened a museum and library at Golf House in 1950 in New York City. In the ensuing years, hundreds of golfers began to form their own collections of clubs, books, artwork and the like. In 1970, The Golf Collectors' Society was created to provide an information exchange for collectors throughout the world. There are now thousands of serious hobbyists with elaborate collections as well as countless others who are fascinated with the heritage of the game and its memorabilia.

1

The most frequently sought after golf collectibles are clubs, books and artwork. Collectors generally make their acquisitions from art and antique dealers, flea markets, auctions, golfers and their families, and of course, by selling and trading with other collectors.

This appeal to book collectors appeared in *Golf* magazine in 1896.

This advertisement dates to 1891. Modern golf collectors would probably trade their entire collection just for a chance to view these early items!

Over the past twenty years, there has been a tremendous growth in the hobby of golf collecting. Golf book collector, Joe Murdoch saw a need for a bibliography and history of the thousands of golf books so he compiled *The Library of Golf*, in 1967. In 1970, Morton W. Olman (a co-author of this Encyclopedia), realized there was an interest for a centralized source for golf art and collectibles, so he established the Old Golf Shop in Cincinnati. There are now a number of dealers throughout the world who deal in golf memorabilia.

Since 1979, the large auction houses in Great Britain have put on sales of sporting items which contain considerable amounts of golf memorabilia. Sotheby's, Christie's and Phillips produce pre-sale catalogs which list all of the lots and show photos of many. The auction firms continue to offer interesting golf treasures, many of which accumulated in attics and cellars from around the world.

The United States Golf Association Museum and Library is situated on a 62 acre estate in Far Hills, New Jersey and is adjacent to the new headquarters building and ball testing facility. The architect of this Georgian Colonial building was John Russell Pope, known also for his designs of government buildings such as the Jefferson Memorial.

The World Golf Hall of Fame and Museum, founded in 1974, is located in Pinehurst, North Carolina. The PGA of America recently acquired the facility and continues to expand the impressive collection.

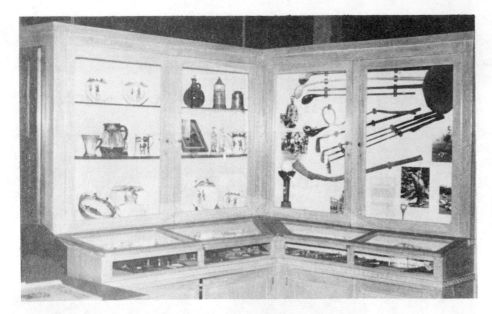

Displays such as this enable visitors to the USGA Museum and Library to comfortably view all types of golf memorabilia.

In addition to the extensive private collections, many golf and country clubs have collections of equipment and trophies on display in their clubhouses. The most impressive public displays of golf collectibles and golf history can be seen at the Museum and Library of the United States Golf Association in Far Hills, New Jersey, the World Golf Hall of Fame and Museum in Pinehurst, North Carolina and the Ralph W. Miller Library and Museum in Industry Hills, California. The Royal and Ancient Golf Club of St. Andrews has a wonderful collection of clubs, books, trophies and other memorabilia, however it may only be viewed by members or by special arrangement. Temporary displays are often set up at golf tournaments, meetings and even banks and other places suitable for public viewing.

Auctioneer Hilary Kay conducts a sale of early golf collectibles at Sotheby's in London.

Phillips auction house recently held a sale in Edinburgh which was comprised entirely of golf clubs, books and other artifacts. The jackets shown are some that were worn by members of the 19th century golfing societies. Bob Gowland can be seen conducting the sale.

THE EVOLUTION OF GOLF FROM THE COLLECTOR'S VIEWPOINT

Hundreds of books have been written about the history of golf, but the true origin of the game has yet to be decided. Toward the end of a long and distinguished career of golf writing, Horace Hutchinson summarized his feelings about early golf as follows: *Learned pens have busied themselves, and unfailingly have blunted themselves, on the History of Golf. They have failed to keep sharp and clear, because immediately they have tried to pierce back into the origins and have found themselves in thick fog.*

In order to avoid the "thick fog", we have dispensed with a lengthy discourse on the origin of golf in favor of the mention of a few minor points. Historians acknowledge that the game is certainly hundreds of years old, but disagree considerably on how it evolved into its present form. Various theories link its beginnings to other club and ball games such as Roman *paganica*, English *cambuca*, French *jeu de mail* and *chole*, and Dutch *het kolven*. The playing of a game resembling golf is evident in Dutch illustrations dating as far back as 1296. Like golf, the *kolven* participants used a club to advance a small ball. However, their game was played in the streets or on frozen rivers and the target was usually a post.

This Dutch game differs considerably from the early golf played in Scotland in which the competitors used several types of clubs to strike a ball over a set course toward a series of holes in the ground, much the same as golfers do today. There are references to Scottish golf dating to 1457 when King James II issued his famous edict in Parliament which forbade the playing of golf in favor of archery practice. Even though the game was outlawed, it was played at intervals over the next 300 years, but not by the masses. There are numerous documents which substantiate the continual existence of the game. By the middle of the eighteenth century, golfing societies had been formed, formal competitions were being staged, and books on golf began to appear.

Throughout this book, it is assumed that golf, as we play it today, had its early beginnings in Scotland. There are many fine books which describe the history of golf in great detail, some of which have been reviewed beginning on page 234. From the standpoint of golf collectibles, our concern is with the evolution of the game since the first golf book was published in 1743. *The Goff* was the first evidence that mankind can become addicted to and obsessed with a game that is like none else. Little did Thomas Mathison know that thousands of books about golf would follow his and that millions of people throughout the world would derive pleasure from the game which he so amusingly described.

Although the game has such a long history, the collector of golf antiquities and memorabilia will find very few items which date before 1800. A smattering of books and prints, along with a small number of clubs and balls, are among the few golf items the collector will come across which date from before the nineteenth century. One of the most interesting areas of golf collecting relates to the clubs and balls used prior to 1850. It was during this era that the balls were made of a leather covering stuffed with feathers. The clubs of this period, which are somewhat difficult to find, were long and graceful with slender wooden heads suitable for striking the somewhat delicate feather ball. These balls took over two hours to make and were quite dependable except when they became wet or were not struck squarely. Iron headed clubs were only used when the ball was in such a bad lie that a wooden club might be broken and then the player risked the chance of severely damaging the feather ball. The early balls and clubs were handcrafted by experienced makers and are prized by collectors and museums today.

Most of the golf at this time was played along the east coast of Scotland in towns such as St. Andrews, Leith, Musselburgh and Bruntsfield and at Blackheath near London. Golf was generally regarded as a pastime for those in high social standing until the 1840's when the professional golfer came into being. Players such as Allan Robertson, Willie Dunn, Jamie Dunn, Willie Park and Tom Morris were known for their great money matches which were in existence long before their first Open Championship was held in 1860. The early professionals made their living by playing these matches, making clubs or balls, tending to the golf course, giving some instruction and caring for the clubhouse.

These great players were admired for their golf skill, but it was not until the end of the nineteenth century that they finally attained a respectable position in the social strata. While Allan Robertson is considered to be the first professional and perhaps the first great player, Tom Morris is credited with being the first professional golfer to be respected and admired by all. Morris provided a tremendous boost for the game of golf in the nineteenth century, just as Palmer and Nicklaus have done in modern times.

Most changes in the game have been a result of improvements to the design of the golf ball. When a ball molded of gutta percha, a hard rubber-like material, was introduced in 1848, golf began a new era. Since this ball was considerably less expensive than the feather ball, many more of the working class started to take up the game. The cost of metal headed clubs was also reduced considerably in the 1860's as the railroad and other industries developed more efficient means to produce iron. The popularity of the game steadily grew and by the late 1880's, the growth was staggering. Golf was spreading to Canada and the United States and new courses continued to be built throughout Great Britain.

Although golf had been played in South Carolina and Georgia in the eighteenth century, it was not until the early 1890's that it began to receive much attention. As in Britain one hundred years earlier, the early American players thought of golf more as a social occasion rather than a competitive sport. The United States Golf Association had its beginning in 1894 and conducted its first championships the following year. Almost all of the golf professionals hired by American golf clubs at the turn of the century were from Scotland. Many of the Scottish pros were hired as club and ball makers by the early U.S. manufacturers like Spalding, MacGregor and B.G.I.

In addition to the spread of golf to the United States, the 1890's saw great improvements in the manufacture of golf equipment. Although the clubs were still made by hand, the makers began to mechanize their facilities with items like drop forges for iron heads and sophisticated lathes for turning the wooden heads. The necks of wooden heads began to be drilled with new boring equipment that became available which enabled the shaft to be inserted into a socket rather than being spliced in the traditional manner. Persimmon soon became the preferred material for wood heads while hickory was standard for the shafts.

Many accessories began to appear as golf patents were applied for by the hundreds. *Golf*, the first golf magazine, began publication in 1890 and featured a column which described many of the new patents. Golf bags and caddy stands were developed to relieve the player of having to carry his clubs under his arm and the golf tee began to appear in various forms.

The most important patent to affect the game was granted in 1899 to Coburn Haskell and Bertram Work for their design of a golf ball with internal windings of elastic thread. Although it took the B.F. Goodrich Company several years to produce a uniform ball, the golf ball revolution was underway. Just as important as the design of the new ball was the machine designed by John Gammeter which would automatically wind the thread. Hundreds of golf ball patents were granted in the United States and Great Britain during the early 1900's and several patent infringement suits appeared in the courts which challenged the licensing of the Haskell patent. Golfers, always willing to try a new idea, continually experimented with the various balls in an effort to improve their scores.

Just prior to the introduction of the Haskell ball, a major event in the history of advertising had taken place. In 1898, Spalding had contracted with Harry Vardon, the British champion, to endorse a gutta percha ball which they would name the Vardon Flyer. This ball and subsequently the Vardon Autograph clubs were the first products to be endorsed by a professional athlete in the manner which is so common today. In 1900, Spalding sent Vardon on a tour of the United States to extol the virtues of their golf equipment. Vardon played seventy-two golf courses during his tour and set many scoring records. Unfortunately, the Haskell invention was soon receiving more publicity than the Vardon Flyer and the ball was soon replaced by the Spalding Wizard, a rubber core ball. Nevertheless, Vardon paved the way for professional golfers and other athletes to endorse not only sporting goods products, but clothing, automobiles, lawn mowers, motor oil and other non-sport commodities.

At the same time as the Haskell ball was being developed, changes in club design were also taking place. The idea of metal shafts was first patented in 1894, but the early shafts were not particularly reliable. It was not until the 1920's that steel shafts began to have a significant impact on the way the game was played. Players and manufacturers argued the merits of both steel and hickory for a period of thirty years. The metal shaft was approved for use in 1925 by the United States Golf Association and in 1929 by the Royal and Ancient Golf Club. The stiff steel shafts eventually changed the swing as golfers learned to use them to their advantage.

As the endorsement of golf equipment by the professionals became commonplace, many of the other golf items of the period were influenced by the amateur players. The *Vanity Fair Magazine* series of illustrations of prominent golfers and other artwork tended to feature the amateur players over the professionals. The items of golf memorabilia which are sought after today features many of the amateur players from the turn of the century such as Horace Hutchinson, Harold Hilton and Chick Evans. Prints, paintings and bronzes glorified the amateur golfer until Bobby Jones became the last to be so honored in the 1920's and 1930's.

As the game continued to grow, golf courses became more sophisticated. Tom Morris was the first of the professional golfers to seriously spend time laying out a course. Later, others became adept at golf course design including James Braid, Willie Dunn Jr., Alister Mackenzie, Willie Park Jr., A. W. Tillinghast, Donald Ross and Charles Blair MacDonald. Under their direction, hundreds of courses were constructed at the turn of the century.

Professional golfers began to organize, and in 1902 the London and County Professional Golfers' Association was formed. Later that year it had 70 members and was renamed the Professional Golfers' Association. The British group was formed mainly as a result of the American influence on the game. They were concerned that the advent of the Haskell ball would lead to the decline of the remolding and repainting business for the golf pro. The Britons were also concerned about their fine players being lured to the United States.

In the United States, informal groups of golf professionals had been formed for the purpose of conducting tournaments, but it was not until 1916 that the Professional Golfers' Association of America was formed. Two employees of the John Wanamaker Company, a golf equipment retailer, realized that an organized group of professionals would be beneficial to the growth of the game and also to the sale of golf equipment. Tom MacNamara, a salesman and fine professional player, and Rodman Wanamaker, the son of the company's owner, invited the prominent players in the United States to play for cash prizes and Wanamaker donated a permanent trophy. An interesting note is that MacNamara's son, Leo, became one of the better known golf collectors in America.

There were 35 charter members of the PGA and Jim Barnes was the winner of the first championship in 1916. Their enthusiastic group encountered a minor setback that year when Chick Evans, an amateur, won the U.S. Open with a record score of 286 which was not bettered until 20 years later. Evans' fine play was not the only thing that concerned the pros. The fact that he frequently played with as few as seven clubs did not encourage the sale of golf clubs.

It was during World War I that golf began its long involvement with charitable organizations. The Red Cross conducted exhibitions and charged admission fees to competitions which often featured the fine women golfers of the period such as Glenna Collett. Admission fees were first charged at the U.S. Open in 1922 at the Skokie Country Club near Chicago. Soon all professional events charged admission fees, with much of the money earmarked for charity, a practice which continues today.

The early golf professionals had generally been regarded as employees of golf or country clubs and often times were not even allowed in the clubhouse. Finally in the 1920's, Walter Hagen was instrumental in changing the image of the golf pro. He was charismatic in addition to being a fine player, and because of his popularity, he was able to command the respect which only Tom Morris had received before him.

In the 1930's there were many changes in golf equipment. The USGA issued several rules changes regarding the size of the ball, and in 1938 the number of clubs a golfer could carry was limited to fourteen. Prior to this time, some players were known to carry over twenty clubs. The use of hickory shafts declined during the decade as steel shafts and matched sets became standard.

The 1940's were dominated by World War II, but the excellent play of golfers like Ben Hogan, Byron Nelson and Sam Snead still made newspaper headlines. Much of the development of golf equipment was halted during the war years. Wooden balls were even used in Great Britain where the traditional rubber ball was not available due to the war effort. The championship golf course at Turnberry, Scotland was converted into a landing strip as were many other courses. In the United States, the popular touring pros played exhibitions and helped to sell war bonds.

Golf continued to be played by increasing numbers of Americans and Hollywood stars began to show off their golf talents. The Bing Crosby Pro-Am Golf Tournament or "Clambake", as it is known, began in 1937 and continues to raise large sums of money for charitable institutions and programs. Crosby and his friend, Bob Hope, made a major contribution to the game by convincing movie and television personalities to promote their charity events.

The most significant modern contribution to the current popularity of the game was the advent of televised golf tournaments in the 1940's. Among the first tournaments to be televised by the networks were the U.S. Open and the Goodall-Palm Beach Championship. The Palm Beach Clothing Company gained publicity by sponsoring their match play tournament and provided clothing to many of the tour players. However, all of the proceeds from the tournament were donated to The Boys' Club. It was also during the late 1940's that colorful sportswear was first introduced. Jimmy Demaret singlehandedly popularized the bold and flashy colors that initially were seen on the golf course, and eventually made their way into everyone's wardrobe.

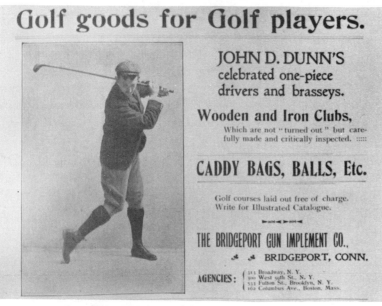

In the 1890's, golf was still at its infancy in America. The Bridgeport Gun Implement Co. (B.G.I.) was so intent upon expanding the popularity of the game that they offered to lay out golf courses free of charge.

In the 1920's, miniature golf was played on rooftops and was later followed by Tom Thumb and Putt Putt layouts. This course did not have any windmills, but it did feature water hazards and bunkers. It was located in New York City at Broadway and 72nd Street.

Television continued to present the game to millions of golfers and potential golfers. In the 1960's, *Shell's Wonderful World of Golf* provided matches between international champions staged at sites throughout the world. The universal appeal of the game became very evident during this fine series which is now being broadcast again on cable television. Television was also responsible for making Arnold Palmer and Jack Nicklaus household names. These men, and the stars who followed, increased the golf industry to a size previously unimaginable. Huge tournament prizes, product endorsements and the increased sale of related products such as books and clothing soon became an international phenomenon.

Television has continued to present the game in a most impressive manner with instant replays, instructional tips and full eighteen hole coverage of the major championships. The video technology now enables instructors to analyze the slow motion swings of their students while they are giving the lessons. The current state of the art is considerably different from the radio broadcasts half a century ago. In 1931, golfers had to be content with the weekly series of radio programs presented by Hillerich & Bradsby and their Grand Slam Golf Clubs. Their advertisement stated: "Into fifteen minutes, each program compresses the thrills and disappointments, the drama, the action and concentration that makes a great golf match great."

Improvements in transportation allowed the idea of golf resorts to prosper as golfers began to plan golf vacations in other parts of the country. As air travel improved more golf resorts were constructed to satisfy the golfers' demands. There were soon hundreds of vacation spots in addition to the old time favorites like Pinehurst, The Breakers, French Lick Springs and The Greenbrier.

Jet travel led to the increased American participation in the British Open and other international events. At the same time, foreign players began to win many of the professional tournaments. These players included Gary Player, Peter Thomson, Robert de Vicenzo, Bob Charles, Bruce Crampton, Tony Jacklin and Bruce Devlin.

Modern golf has also been affected by the space program, specifically in the area of golf club construction. Aluminum, lightweight steel, and graphite shafts in addition to the investment casting of iron heads are all results of the "space age" technologies which we sometimes take for granted. Alan Shepard, commander of the Apollo 14 mission, made golf history in 1971 when he hit a golf ball on the moon with a specially constructed club.

In spite of all the progress of the game which has been discussed in this chapter, the actual playing of golf has changed very little as the rules are basically the same as they were hundreds of years ago. However, the many changes in the world of golfdom have contributed immensely to the continued enjoyment of the game by millions.

Golf certainly has an international flavor, however in 1971, the game found its way to the moon. The "moon club" is now on display at the USGA Golf House in New Jersey.

Television first brought golf viewers across the country in the 1940's. These photos were taken at the 1949 Goodall-Palm Beach Championship in Wykagyl, New York.

BRITISH CITIES OF INTEREST TO GOLF COLLECTORS

Dornoch

Inverness

Aberdeen

Dundee

Perth

Gleneagles

Montrose

St. Andrews

Glasgow

Edinburgh

Troon

Prestwick

Turnberry

FIRTH OF FORTH

Dundee · Carnoustie

Perth

St. Andrews

Crail

Leven · Anstruther

Pittenweem

Dysart · Elie/Earlsferry

Kinghorn

North Berwick

Leith · Gullane

Edinburgh · Musselburgh

IRISH SEA

Lytham-St. Annes

Birkdale

Hoylake

Manchester

Conway

Stoke-on-Trent

Birmingham

NORTH SEA

London

Blackheath

Westward Ho!

Sandwich

ENGLISH CHANNEL

SCALE: 1 inch equals approximately 70 miles

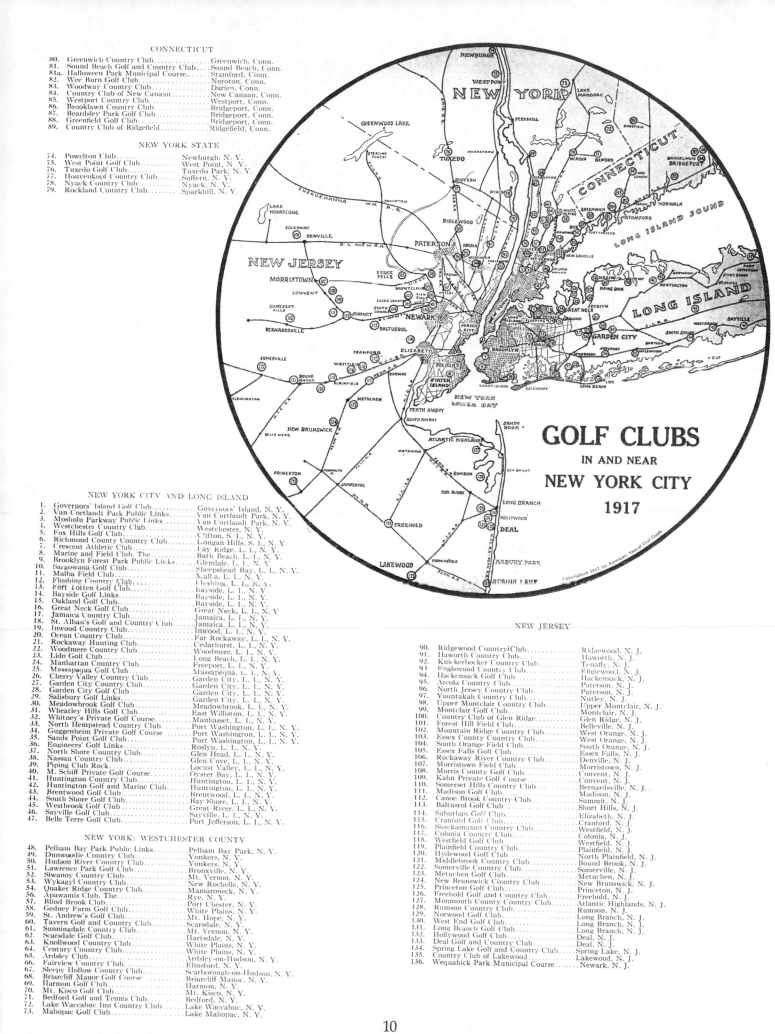

GOLF CLUBS IN AND NEAR NEW YORK CITY 1917

Copyrighted 1917 by American Annual Golf Guide

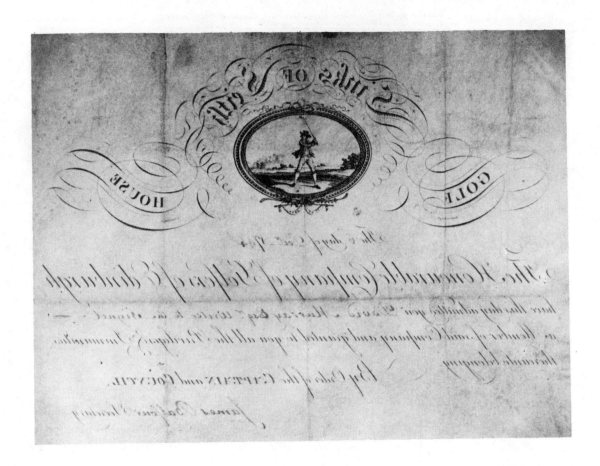

EXCERPT FROM MINUTE OF COUNCIL
26TH MARCH 1800

Read Report from the Magistrates, old Magistrates, and Convener, in consequence of the Remit on the Petition presented by John Gray, Writer to the Signet, *Captain*, Alexander Osborn, Solicitor of the Customs, *Secretary*, and David Murray, Deputy-Clerk of Session, *Treasurer*, of the Honourable the Edinburgh Company of Golfers, for themselves and in name and behalf of the other Members of the said Company, and which petition is of the following tenor:—"Unto the Right Honourable the Lord Provost, Magistrates, and Council of the City of Edinburgh, The Petition of John Gray, Writer to the Signet, *Captain*, Alexander Osborn, Solicitor of the Customs, *Secretary*, and David Murray, Deputy-Clerk of Session, *Treasurer*, of the Honourable the Edinburgh Company of Golfers, for themselves, and in name and behalf of the other Members of the said Company,—Humbly Sheweth, That the Edinburgh Company of Golfers has existed as a Club or Society for these great number of years, and they have occasionally got the aid of Acts of Council for preserving of the Links of Leith in a proper state for their favorite amusement of Golf, They are also Lessees of the Links, and in 1767 obtained a Feu of a piece of Ground adjacent thereto for payment of an Annual Feu-duty, upon which they, at a considerable expence, erected a House and Offices for the accommodation of themselves and workmen connected with the exercise; But not being a legal society or Body Corporate they were under the necessity of holding the Property in name of a trustee—To remedy which, and in order to enable them to manage their Funds and regulate their affairs with proper effect, the present Application is presented. May it therefore please the Right Honourable the Lord Provost, Magistrates, and Council, to grant a Seal of Cause Constituting and Erecting the said Company, and all others who shall hereafter be entered with them, into one Body politic and corporate, or legal Corporation or Society, under the Title and Name of 'THE HONOURABLE THE EDINBURGH COMPANY OF GOLFERS,' And as such and by that name to have a perpetual endurance and succession, so as to entitle your Petitioners and their Successors in office, for the use and behoof of the said Company, to hold Property, real or personal, and with power, with consent of the said Company, at a Meeting upon the first Saturday of any Month, to make Bye-Laws and Regulations for the Management of their Society and Funds; And to be able, in name of their said Captain, Secretary, and Treasurer, for the time being, to sue, plead, and defend, and to be sued and defended in all or any Courts of Justice.—In respect whereof, (Signed) JOHN GRAY, for himself and the other Petitioners."

Although the history of the game extends back hundreds of years, there are very few printed references to golf which date before 1800. This certificate of membership features a drawing by David Allan and was issued by the Honourable Company of Golfers of Edinburgh to David Murray on December 6, 1794. Murray was in the legal profession and was treasurer of the club when they successfully filed a petition with the Magistrates of Edinburgh requesting corporate status. Several references to Murray can be found in the above excerpt from the official minute book which appeared in *Golf: A Royal and Ancient Game* written in 1875 by Robert Clark.

Harry Vardon is recognized as being the first professional athlete to sign a contract with a manufacturer for the endorsement of a product. The Vardon Flyer was introduced in 1899 and the following year, Vardon toured the United States to promote Spalding products and played numerous exhibition matches. This ad was very innovative as compared to others at the turn of the century.

Improvements in transportation led to the spread of golf. This 1926 Pierce Arrow Sports Coupe featured a special compartment for golf clubs.

This text was from a Spalding advertisement in 1902 and refers to their London warehouse which was fully stocked in anticipation of the forthcoming golf season.

The balancing and swingweighting of golf clubs became very scientific in the 1920's. This early swingweight scale was used by clubmakers to assemble a "matched" set of clubs.

CHAPTER 2 — BALLS

The collecting of golf balls is probably the fastest growing segment of golf collecting. Much of the tremendous growth of the game since the middle of the nineteenth century can be attributed to the development of the ball. As the balls became more durable and the prices became lower, golf became affordable to many who had previously shied away from the game. Prior to the 1850's golf balls were constructed of a leather cover which was tightly packed with feathers. These "featheries" were made by skilled makers who could produce no more than four balls per day. Therefore, the lack of mass production, combined with the fragile nature of the feather ball, made the playing of golf affordable only to the wealthy.

In the 1840's, technological advances were being made throughout Great Britain as the world began to become industrialized. During these years, the playing of golf was generally confined to the east coast of Scotland and the ballmakers had a steady clientele. However, a few individuals began to experiment with alternative methods for making golf balls and in 1848 the gutta percha golf ball made its debut. Several men have been credited with initiating the use of the rubber-like substance from the Far East for molding balls suitable for golf.

The gutty balls, as they were called, could be made at a fraction of the cost of the feather ball and were not nearly as fragile. Furthermore, these new balls could be made by relatively unskilled workers. As more golfers began to use the gutty, the clubmakers found that the wooden clubs had to be constructed with thicker necks in order to withstand the impact of the harder ball. The use of iron headed clubs also increased when it was noticed that the gutty could withstand the mishit shots which were often fatal to the feather ball. By the late 1850's, the feather ball was no longer used.

The further development of the gutty, as well as improvements in the production of metal headed clubs throughout the late nineteenth century, resulted in a tremendous expansion of golf throughout Scotland and England and eventually to North America. Many golf courses were constructed throughout this period and many of the golf professionals at these courses were ballmakers and also retailers of gutta percha golf balls made by others. Advertisements featured testimonials from the championship players regarding their favorite ball as the competition among the ballmakers increased.

Less than a decade after Americans began actively playing golf, the next major change in the golf ball took place. Inventors Coburn Haskell and Bertram Work were convinced that a ball with internal windings of rubber thread and an external shell of gutta percha would be superior to the gutty ball. Their research had been carried out at the B.F. Goodrich Company in Akron, Ohio, which had been producing gutta percha balls at the time. Their patent was applied for in 1898 and was granted the following year. The original Haskell balls were far from being perfect and were nicknamed "Bounding Billies" because their results were often unpredictable. After a few years, the perfection of the thread winding machine and an improvement in the design of the cover resulted in a ball which was far superior to the gutty.

Numerous patents for improvements in the golf ball were issued in the United States and Great Britain throughout the early twentieth century. As changes in cover designs and the centers of the balls took place, the sale of golf balls became very competitive. The balls were being produced by the tens of thousands and the small ballmaking firms of the gutty ball era faded out of existence. The new rubber core balls travelled further and the golf courses had to be made longer as had been done fifty years earlier when the gutty ball became popular. The liquid core and dimpled cover soon became standard and from the 1920's, and until the advent of the one-piece rubber ball in the 1960's, very little had changed in the manufacture of golf balls other than several attempts at standardizing their diameter, weight and performance characteristics.

The golf ball may indeed be "mankind's most fascinating sphere," as it was referred to by John Stuart Martin in *The Curious History of the Golf Ball*. Martin's entertaining account of the development of the golf ball from golf's infancy was written in 1968 and reveals many anecdotes about its evolution from the feather ball to the modern rubber core and solid balls. Martin was the first to attempt to present a detailed look at the evolution of the golf ball and his work has been the basis for continued research by others. The remainder of this chapter is devoted to further discussion of the three eras in the history of the golf ball, followed by listings of the hundreds of golf ball brands which the collector may encounter.

The golfers of past eras had a greater respect for the golf ball and other equipment which we now take for granted. It was not uncommon for golfers at the turn of the century to submit poems about their experiences on the course to the various golf periodicals. The poem below was written by J.H. Hayes and appeared in British *Golf Illustrated*.

TO A GOLF BALL

Long ago when first I bought you,
    You were white and fairly round,
And a little gem I thought you,
    Teed upon the teeing ground.

But, alas! The months have vanished,
    And, if I must speak the truth,
They have altogether banished
    The resemblance to your youth.

For I've "pulled" you and I've "sliced" you,
    And you've lain in banks of gorse,
And I've temptingly enticed you
    From the cart-ruts on the course.

So, though quite devoid of beauty,
    I would claim you as a friend
Who has nobly done his duty
    From beginning to the end.

And receive my thanks unsparing,
    That you've heard with dumb assent,
The perhaps too-frequent swearing
    Which I've used though never meant.

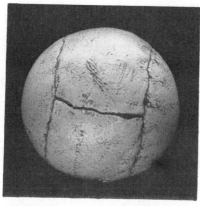

The feather ball in use for a few hundred years up until the early 1850's. Note the smooth seams of the leather cover, a result of fine craftsmanship.

Soon after the smooth gutta percha ball was introduced in 1848, the makers began to hand hammer a pattern into the ball to improve its aerodynamics. This practice continued into the 1870's when the markings were engraved into the ball moulds.

The mesh pattern was one of several patterns commonly used on the gutty balls of the late nineteenth century. Some balls of this period had cork or other substances added to the gutta percha in an effort to improve its performance.

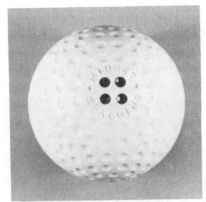

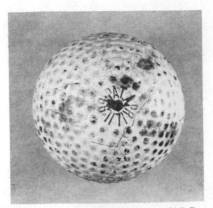

The dimple pattern, which is now the standard for golf ball covers, was first patented in 1905. The design and configuration of the dimples have been improved over the years, but the modern balls appear very much the same as this Spalding ball from over half a century ago.

The Haskell patent was granted by the U.S. Patent Office on April 11, 1899 for a golf ball having a center made of elastic windings and a cover of gutta percha. This patent was the beginning of a new era of ballmaking, for once perfected, the rubber core balls held their shape better and outperformed their predecessors. The ball shown is the Goodrich Haskell made with the bramble marking which was popular on both gutty and rubber core balls. By World War I, all golf balls were made by a method related to the Haskell patent, as the use of the old solid gutty ball was discontinued.

The golf ball industry suffered during World War II when the manufacturers were unable to acquire the necessary rubber materials. Wooden golf balls like this Fleetwood model were used in Great Britain by diehard golfers. The dot on the ball was an indicator necessary for the correct placement of the ball on the tee so that the grain of the wood would be oriented in the proper direction. The frequent splitting of the balls was a minor inconvenience which the golfers endured much the same as the users of the feather balls did a hundred years earlier.

GOLF BALL VALUES

Golf ball values vary considerably due to age, type of construction and maker. Balls which show the least amount of wear generally command the higher values, while those in extremely poor condition will be valued lower than the ranges shown.

FEATHER BALL — pre 1860, with name $1000-2000
FEATHER BALL — pre 1860, without name $400-1200
GUTTY BALL — 1848-1875, hand hammered or smooth $150-800
GUTTY BALL — 1870-1910, molded pattern $30-150
RUBBER CORE BALL — 1898-1915, mint $75-125
RUBBER CORE BALL — 1898-1915, used $20-80
RUBBER CORE BALL — 1916-1930, mint $25-75
RUBBER CORE BALL — 1916-1930, used $10-30
MODERN BALLS — post 1930 .... under $10

FEATHER BALLS

For a few hundred years prior to the 1850's, golf balls had been made of a leather covering stuffed with feathers. The feather ball or "feathery" was a most unique ball and is highly sought after today by collectors. One normally thinks of feathers as being soft, however when the ball is filled with enough feathers to fill a top hat, it becomes quite hard. These balls were made by professional ballmakers who usually had standing orders from the various golfing societies. The making of the balls was not an easy task and a maker's output was only three or four balls per day.

The feathers, usually from the breast of a goose or chicken, were boiled so that they would be easy to manage. After the leather cover was constructed, it was wetted in a solution of alum and water. The feathers were then tightly stuffed into the cover to form the ball and it was allowed to dry. As the drying took place, the feathers expanded and the leather cover contracted. The ball was painted white and was then ready for use. These featheries had fairly good playing qualities, as long as they did not become wet again. The two things which led to most of the failures of the feathery were poorly executed iron shots which would split the cover, and wet weather which would soften the cover and cause it to fall apart.

Most of the golf balls dating from the nineteenth century were made in Scotland and were marked with the maker's name. A majority of the balls still in existence were made by either Allan Robertson, Tom Morris or the Gourlays. The maker's name can best be seen on the balls in mint condition, whereas the early balls were not marked and the heavily used balls have had the names worn off. Almost all ball and club makers marked their work with their last name, however Allan Robertson marked his balls with just "ALLAN". Many fine players were either in business as a ballmaker or were apprenticed to one. Allan Robertson, Tom Morris, Willie Dunn and Jamie Dunn were the most proficient players among the ballmakers.

The makers of golf balls and clubs were a close knit group as evidenced by the marriage of two of the Gourlay women into other families in the golf business. Jean Gourlay was married to Peter McEwan (1781-1836), the fine clubmaker, and later her brother's granddaughter, Isabella, married Willie Dunn's son, Tom (1849-1902). Tom Dunn was a golf course architect and was the father of John Duncan Dunn and Seymour Dunn, all of whom were instrumental in the development of golf in the United States. This is somewhat confusing, but is mentioned so that the reader can realize how small the golfing world was in the eighteenth and nineteenth centuries.

The method of feather ball construction was fairly uniform among the makers, although some variations may exist. The golf collector should be wary of odd looking leather balls since there were other styles similar to golf balls which were used in games such as "fives". These balls were sewn in a much different manner than golf balls and should not be mistaken for one.

The following description of feather ball making has been adapted from an account by H. Thomas Peters in *Reminiscences of Golf and Golfers,* published in 1890. The facts are totally attributable to Mr. Peters, however the text has been modified slightly to make it easier to comprehend.

> *The leather was of untanned bull's hide, two round pieces for the ends and a piece for the middle, being cut to suit the weight wanted. These were properly shaped, after being sufficiently softened, and then were firmly sewn together. A small hole was left through which the feathers might be afterwards inserted. But before stuffing, it was through this little hole that the leather itself had to be turned outside in. This was a difficult operation that resulted in only smooth seams showing on the exterior of the ball.*

> *The skin was then placed in a cup shaped stand and the worker placed the appropriate amount of feathers in the pocket of his apron. The actual stuffing was done with a crutch-handled steel rod, which the maker placed under his arm. And very hard work, I may add, it was. After the ball was tightly packed, the aperture was closed and firmly sewed up. The resultant ball was smooth and only the outside seam was the only one visible. When I say this, I of course refer only to the new balls.*

> *Older balls showed the effects of service with their open seams and feathers outlooking. On a wet day, the water could be seen driven off in showers from a circle of protruding feathers as if from a spray producer. A ball perhaps started as a "twenty-eight" and when wet, ended up as a pounder. Consequently a new one had to be put down at every hole if the match was an important one.*

The balls were made in various diameters and weights and were graded according to their weight in drams. The balls were numbered with their size, however this number soon lost its meaning on a wet day. Most of the balls were made in the 26 to 29 range. Eventually, the numbering would refer to the ball's size rather than its weight, a practice which continued into the twentieth century with the gutta percha and rubber core balls.

In the late 1840's other methods of constructing golf balls were tried and by 1850, balls molded out of gutta percha, a hard rubber substance, were becoming commonplace. The new balls were easier to produce and were much more economically priced. Their affordability enabled many more people to begin playing the game, which had previously been played only by those who could afford the price of the feather balls. Some feather ballmakers such as Allan Robertson resisted the change to the new ball, but prior to his death in 1859, he finally joined other veteran makers in the switch to the production of gutty balls.

Feather ball made by Tom Morris, Sr. Morris learned the ballmaking trade as an apprentice to Allan Robertson, the finest player and ballmaker of the first half of the nineteenth century.

D. M. Gressick feather ball. As with many of the early balls, the maker's stamp is difficult to see. The final closing stitch is shown on this ball which was marked with a size 29.

Feather ball made by John Gourlay. John and his brother, William, took over the ballmaking business of their father and operated as J. & W. Gourlay. William died in 1844, at which time the "W" was dropped from their mark.

16

A BALL COLLECTOR'S DISPLAY: Left: smooth gutty mould with ball. Top row: Wm. Gourlay feather ball (size 25), Allan Robertson feather ball (size 29), Paterson smooth gutty, Allan Robertson hand hammered gutty. Bottow row: Forgan hand hammered gutty, early gutty Eclipse composition ball, Agrippa gutty. Right: Agrippa ball mould (size 27½).

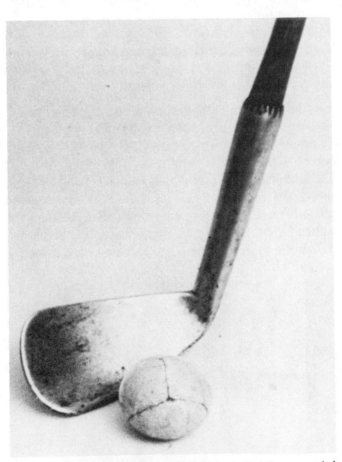

An early nineteenth century iron with feather ball of the same period.

This ball is the same size as a golf ball but is really a "fives" ball used for playing a nineteenth century child's game. It differs from a feathery in that its seams radiate from either end. The stitches are also visible whereas the stitches in a golf ball cover are hidden on the interior.

A collection of early golf balls. Top row: Feather balls by William Gourlay, T. Alexander, Allan Robertson and Tom Morris. Bottom row: Hand hammered gutty by Robert Forgan, feather balls by John Ramsay and David Gressick and a gutty ball marked "McEwan". The McEwans were known as clubmakers and this ball was probably made for them by a ballmaker.

Makers of Feather Balls

The following men are known to have produced feather balls. Examples of some of their works still exist, while evidence of the work of the others has appeared in history books. The birth and death dates of the makers are shown to assist the golf collector in determining the age of a ball, however many of the balls cannot be accurately dated because many of the early makers did not sign their balls. The makers whose works are known to exist have been marked with an asterisk (*).

*ALEXANDER, THOMAS (1803-1841)
Musselburgh
COSGROVE, ALEX (1821-1867)
Musselburgh
DICKSON, ANDREW (1665-1729)
Leith
DICKSON, WILLIAM & THOMAS & JOHN
(circa 1629) Leith
DUNCAN, T. (circa 1722)
St. Andrews
DUNN, JAMIE (1821-1871)
Musselburgh
DUNN, WILLIE (1821-1878)
Musselburgh
GOURLAY SR., DOUGLAS (circa 1780)
Bruntsfield
*GOURLAY, JOHN (1815-1869)
Musselburgh
*GOURLAY, JR., WILLIAM (1813-1844)
Bruntsfield
*GOURLAY, SR., WILLIAM (1778-1836)
Bruntsfield
*GRESSICK, DAVID M. (1821-1871)
Musselburgh
LAW, GEORGE (circa 1770)
St. Andrews
MARSHALL, DAVID (1815-1830)
Leith

MILN, GEORGE (circa 1753)
St. Andrews
MORRIS, SR., TOM (1821-1908)
St. Andrews
PATERSON FAMILY (circa 1620)
*PIRIE, SANDY (circa 1840)
St. Andrews
POTTS, THOMAS (1825-1860)
Perth
*RAMSAY, JOHN (circa 1844)
Musselburgh
*ROBERTSON, ALLAN (1815-1859)
St. Andrews
ROBERTSON, FAMILY OF ALLAN (circa 1720-1836)
St. Andrews
ROBERTSON, GEORGE (circa 1825)
Bruntsfield
ROBERTSON, JAMES (circa 1800)
Leith
*ROBERTSON, WILLIAM (1720-1820)
Leith
RUSSAL, CHARLES (circa 1730)
St. Andrews
*SHARP, JOHN (circa 1850)
Perth
*STEWART, THOMAS (circa 1850)
Musselburgh
TOD, JOHN (circa 1730)
St. Andrews

GUTTA PERCHA BALLS

As the Industrial Revolution progressed in Great Britain, new technology would soon affect the game of golf which had changed little over hundreds of years. Rubber was being used to a great extent in the early nineteenth century for waterproofing and other purposes which included the making of rubber balls. Therefore it was only a matter of time before someone would attempt to substitute this resilient material for the feather stuffed golf ball. Various experiments were performed in the 1840's to create a golf ball out of a rubber like substance and finally gutta percha became the preferred material.

Gutta percha is a milky juice obtained from the Palaquium genus of trees native to Malaysia, India and Ceylon. At the time, it was used for molding tool handles and as a packing material. It would later be used extensively for its insulating properties in the manufacture of electric cable. There are several theories as to who first thought of molding this material into golf balls, but it is generally agreed that the gutta percha golf balls made their entrance into the golfing world in 1848.

The gutta percha was first imported to Britain in the form of thin sheets and later in rope form. The material was heated to make it pliable and was then shaped into a sphere. The early balls were formed by hand, but soon the early makers of the gutta balls were using moulds which were usually machined out of metal. As with the feather ball, these balls were made in several sizes according to weight. The weights usually ranged from 26 to 29 pennyweights and the diameters varied accordingly. The golfers discovered that the balls with their smooth exteriors flew much better after they had been used a while. The hacked up balls definitely had better aerodynamic qualities and in the early 1850's, the ballmakers began to purposely nick up the balls prior to their sale. The caddies would also be given the new balls to play with until they had been sufficiently scarred for use by their original owner. It was also discovered that the balls played better if they aged prior to use. Thus the balls would sometimes sit for over a year before being painted and placed into use.

In order to improve the playing qualities of the balls, the makers began to nick the balls with a chisel-faced hammer or would cut lines in them with a knife. The clubmaking and ballmaking firm of Robert Forgan of St. Andrews is credited with being the first to offer hand hammered balls with a consistently regular pattern. They employed a man who could place from 300 to 320 indentions in a ball in approximately two minutes with exacting precision. By the 1870's, most of the smooth ball moulds had been replaced with ones that would place the markings into the surface during the molding process. Although these new moulds made the job easier, some makers continued to hand hammer balls for their customers.

The hand hammered gutta percha ballmakers who were known to have stamped their names onto the balls were:

Jamie Dunn
Willie Dunn
Robert Forgan
James Gourlay
Tom Morris
Willie Park
Paterson (smooth balls)
Allan Robertson

The golf ball was further improved during the 1870's when materials such as ground up cork, leather and other items began to be incorporated into the pure gutta percha. These balls were thought to have performed better, however pure gutta balls continued to be promoted up until their demise. The composition ball is sometimes referred to as a "gutty" ball while the pure gutta percha ball is called a "gutta". It is almost impossible to discern the difference in the materials, so the names are usually considered to be synonymous. Although the rubber core ball was introduced in 1899, the gutty continued to be used until approximately 1910. Similarly, the use of the feather ball did not cease immediately upon the advent of the gutty ball in 1848.

Perhaps the finest characteristic of the gutta percha golf ball was that it could be remolded when it became scarred from excessive use. Old balls could be traded in for new or remade ones or the golfer could remold them himself. The following article was written by John Duncan Dunn who, with his uncle, Willie Dunn Jr., played a major part in the manufacturing of clubs and balls in the United States at the end of the nineteenth century.

The Remaking of Golf Balls

by John D. Dunn

Originally appearing in American *Golf* magazine in September, 1900

Purchase a can of lye, costing fifteen cents. Half a can of lye in a pail of water will take the paint off six dozen balls in about six hours. Ballmakers use a very strong solution of lye, which they put in an apparatus similar to a washing machine. This brings off the paint in short order and does not injure the gutta percha. Amateurs should stir the balls up in the lye occasionaly.

After the balls have been in the lye about six hours, take them out with a vegetable strainer. Place them in some lukewarm water, and then brush off the old paint with a nail brush.

The balls must now be placed in a pot of water that is almost on the boil. Don't have more or less than half a dozen balls in the pot at one time, and always keep replacing them with others. It is not necessary to let the balls get heated right through. Take a ball out of the pot with a tablespoon and work out the cuts, if any, with your thumb. Roll the ball around in your palms until it is slightly egg-shaped. Do not keep the ball so long in your hands that the outer surface gets cold, or the gutta percha will not take the impression of the marking. Should the balls be sticky in the hands, a little water or linseed oil may be used as a preventive.

When the ball is in the mould squeeze it up in a press. It is not absolutely necessary to have a regular ball press. A book press or vise will do almost as well, and the expedient brings the cost down considerably.

A ball press costs $12 and a mould costs $15. If you can purchase only one mould, size 27 is the one you will find most useful. That size will remake any high grade ball. Of course if you are going into the work extensively you will purchase four moulds, sizes 26, 26½, 27 and 27½. People in the remaking business have them also in the quarters. This not only makes less waste of gutta percha, but you can turn out a better ball when you don't have to crowd a large piece of gutta percha into a small mould. Besides you can remake the balls oftener.

I should advise amateurs to purchase a mould with Ocobo marking, as it seems to be the most popular nowadays. For very little additional cost you can have your initials on the mould. This will save you the trouble of marking your ball before playing in a match, and settles all disputes about ownership.

Allow the ball to remain in the mould about a minute, then put it in a pail of cold water. You can afterwards cut off the "fin" with a sharp knife. On a large scale this is turned off on a machine somewhat like a lathe. The same machine also makes an impression similar to the rest of the marking on the ball. This is not necessary, although it looks better.

The next operation is to paint the balls. This is best done by putting some paint in the palms of one's hands. Rubber gloves may be bought for this work, although they are not nearly so good for the work as the bare skin. The paint does not do any harm and it will wash off easily in warm water. The paint should be put on in four very thin coats. Only the second coat should be rubbed into the marking. After painting, the balls should be stood on a wooden frame to dry.

At some of the large factories, when balls are remade, the old balls are run into a lump and then into a rod. In other words, they are put through part of the process of making new balls.

The Paterson gutty was one of the first smooth balls made in the late 1840's. This is a good example of a gutty ball which is worth as much as, or more than, a feather ball from an earlier period.

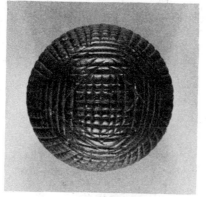

Hand hammered gutty ball, probably made in Forgan's shop in the 1860's. The workmanship on this ball is definitely first class. Many of the gutty balls found today are black as they had never been painted. In later years, the gutta percha was refined so that it was almost white.

The early balls were often crudely hammered and are sometimes in such battered condition that they hardly resemble a golf ball.

The uneven marking on this Tom Morris gutty ball denotes that it was done by hand. Morris began his lengthy career in golf as an apprentice feather ballmaker to Allan Robertson in St. Andrews. They parted ways in 1848 or 1849 following Tom's use of a gutty ball in a match. Allan swore by the feather ball, but he eventually made some of the gutty balls before his death in 1859.

Smooth gutty mold with clamping device, circa 1850.

Popular Agrippa mould with bramble markings.

An Agrippa advertisement from 1901.

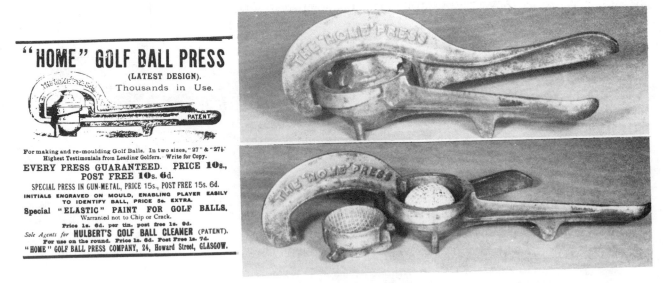

The "Home" golf ball press was very handy for the golfer who liked to remake his own gutty balls.

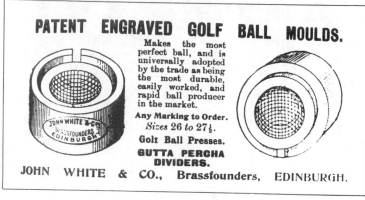

White made several items for the ballmakers of the 1890's.

This gutty ball was made by Allan Robertson late in the 1850's. This type of nicking preceded the criss cross pattern which is seen more often. Robertson was one of the finest feather ballmakers and strongly resisted the introduction of a golf ball which could be molded in a few minutes by an unskilled worker. It had been written that he was so infuriated with the use of the gutty ball that he once bought all of them that he could find in St. Andrews and proceeded to burn them.

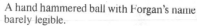

A hand hammered ball with Forgan's name barely legible.

Auchterlonie ball made with a mesh mold circa 1898.

The Vardon Flyer was made by Spalding with a bramble marking. It was highly publicized at the turn of the century, however it was introduced when the sale of gutta percha balls was on the decline and it soon lost its popularity.

This illustration shows a variety of gutta percha golf balls, both hand hammered and mould marked. The bramble marked ball on the right is marked "The Tom Morris" and was probably made by a ball manufacturer for sale in Morris' shop at the turn of the century.

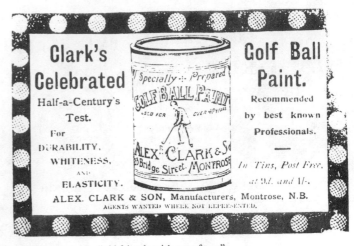
Clark's golf ball paint was available in both white and red in order to make "old friends with new faces".

This photo shows the ballmaking shop of R. Forgan & Sons of St. Andrews. The man on the left continued to produce hand hammered balls for the firm even when the molded markings dominated the market. The worker on the right can be seen applying paint to the balls with his hands. There are two large presses in the foreground for compressing the ball moulds together. Note the balls "seasoning" on the shelves along the walls.

Ashford sold a paint remover in addition to their golf ball paint.

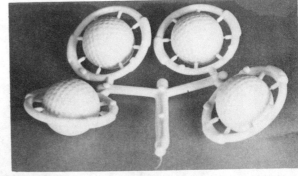

Above: Modern balls are still made in molds as can be seen with these one-piece balls.

Left: There were many ways to paint and dry golf balls. The "Porcupine" and similar homemade racks were the most common methods for ball drying in the latter half of the nineteenth century. Although brushes are shown in these ads, the application of paint by rolling the ball in one's palms gave the best results.

This letter from a Lincoln, Nebraska, golfer
is the GREATEST GOLF BALL ADVERTISEMENT *ever written*

Mr. Charles A. Deklotz and a single Spalding Kro-Flite Ball break
last year's record of 504 holes with a new record of 666 holes!

Lincoln, Nebraska, April 12, 1928

A. G. Spalding & Bros.
New York: — 105 Nassau Street

Gentlemen:

After seeing your ad in the Golfers Magazine, — wherein you guaranteed the Spalding KRO—FLITE for 72 holes — I invested 75c and it was surely the best investment I have ever made in a Golf Ball.

You may wonder why I am bothering you about this particular ball. Well here is the story: I have played 666 holes — 37 rounds — of 18 holes with this particular Ball — my old stand-by as I always call it when playing with the Gang. There is not a cut on this ball. It is true that I have re-painted it several times, as you might know it was bound to lose its whiteness. I made up my mind that I was going to play with this ball until I either cut or lost it. I kept a card in my golf bag pocket and kept track of the number of holes played with it, and the above 666 holes is absolutely correct.

HERE IS THE CROWNING GLORY of the above Ball. This P.M. as the enclosed card will show — which is signed by the other three of the foursome, myself and the Treasurer of the Club — this particular ball pulled the trick of a HOLE in ONE! So I will not be able to tell you or any one else how many more holes that the ball might have gone without cutting — as I am placing this ball on a pension. I am mounting it in a round glass paper weight to use on my desk. No doubt that I may have to answer a lot of questions why the Golf Ball on my desk — but will gladly do so when not too busy. I thought that it would be of interest to you to know the number of holes played with one of your balls.

Very truly yours,

Chas A. Deklotz

649th HOLE	650th HOLE	651st HOLE	652nd HOLE	653rd HOLE	654th HOLE	655th HOLE	656th HOLE	657th HOLE	658th HOLE	659th HOLE	660th HOLE	661st HOLE	662nd HOLE	663rd HOLE	664th HOLE	665th HOLE	666th HOLE
NO 1	NO 2	NO. 3	NO. 4	NO. 5	NO. 6	NO. 7	NO. 8	NO. 9	NO. 10	NO. 11	NO. 12	NO. 13	NO. 14	NO. 15	NO. 16	NO. 17	NO. 18
6	2	5	4	4	5	5		1	5	4	5	4	4	4	5	5

A N D   T H E   6 5 8 TH   H O L E   W A S   A   H O L E - I N - O N E !

Spalding
KRO-FLITE
each 75 *cents*

NOTE: All golf professionals, all sports dealers, all Spalding stores sell Kro-Flite.

© 1928, A. G. S. & B.

The golf ball business was highly competitive during the early part of this century and every manufacturer claimed their ball to be the most durable. This Spalding magazine advertisement was typical of the advertising during this period in golf history.

RUBBER CORE BALLS

The modern golf ball is a direct descendent of the rubber core ball developed in 1898 in Akron, Ohio. Coburn Haskell, a wealthy sportsman originally from New England, combined forces with Bertram Work of the B.F. Goodrich Company and developed an idea for a golf ball having a center of rubber thread wound under tension. They thought that their concept would produce a golf ball with a liveliness not attainable with the hard gutta percha ball in use at the time. Goodrich had already been in the golf ball business for a few years, both making gutties and selling gutta percha to other makers.

Haskell applied for a patent in 1898 for their invention and it was granted the following year. The early Haskell balls were hand wound and then covered with gutta percha which was molded in a mesh pattern. When the patent was applied for, the two men were not sure how they would make their new ball in large quantities, but they gave John Gammeter, an engineer at Goodrich, the responsibility of designing a ball winding machine. Finally in 1900, Gammeter received a patent for his thread winding device and the balls were then produced by the thousands. They were so lively on the golf course that they were soon nicknamed "Bounding Billies." The most significant feature of the wound ball over the gutty was that poorly struck shots would travel a great length, an occurance which was not the case with the "dead" gutty.

The early Haskell balls were considered to be a novelty and players would buy a few to try out. Although the balls travelled farther than the gutties, they had a tendency to "duck and dart" out of control. Goodrich was determined to solve this problem, but one of their customers saved them the expense. The original balls which came onto the market had a mesh patterned cover like many of the gutty balls of the period and could easily be mistaken for one. James Foulis, professional at the Chicago Golf Club, did this one day as he was remolding some old gutty balls and proceeded to mold a Haskell with the pebble-like bramble exterior characteristic of the Agrippa ball. When Foulis played with this remade Haskell, he was astonished with the way he was able to control the ball and was so intrigued that he proceeded to cut it open for inspection. To his surprise, he had been unknowingly playing with a Haskell ball and from then on the mesh pattern was abandoned and all Haskells were made with the bramble cover. This was a most important improvement as the ball would soon become the standard of the industry.

Goodrich formed a subsidiary called the Haskell Golf Ball Company and began to allow other ballmakers to manufacturer the rubber core balls under a licensing agreement. The first licensees in the early 1900's were A. G. Spalding & Bros., The Kempshall Manufacturing Company, The Worthington Ball Company, and The St. Mungo Manufacturing Company of Glasgow, Scotland. Balls made under the Haskell patent began to appear in Great Britain in 1901, but were scorned by skeptics who thought that the new balls would make the game too easy. In 1902, Sandy Herd became the first to win the British Open with a Haskell ball and did so by using the same ball for the entire 72 holes. His ball was quite tattered and had the elastic threads showing through the cover for the final nine holes. It has been written that he was the only player in the field to use the new ball, but his victory was instrumental in the new ball becoming popular overseas.

Even though Goodrich had secured both American and British patents for the Haskell ball, some of the British companies began to manufacture their own versions of the ball. In 1905, Goodrich filed a patent infringement suit against Hutchison, Main & Co. of Glasgow in an attempt to put an end to the unauthorized use of their patent. In a well publicized case, the Haskell patent was declared void in Great Britain on the grounds that it was not a novel idea. As a result of the decision, many companies began to produce rubber core balls in Great Britain, while the American balls were still subject to the Haskell patent. There were attempts to sell the British made balls in the United States, however the Haskell Golf Ball Co. was effective in thwarting the effort.

The rubber core balls made up the majority of the golf ball sales by 1910 as improvements continued to be made. In 1905, William Taylor, an Englishman, patented the dimple method of golf ball marking claiming a better flying ball. Spalding immediately bought the American rights to the patent and began to make the dimpled balls in 1909. Until Taylor's patent expired in the 1920's, the makers produced many types of ball markings. However, the dimple was far superior to the others and by 1930, it was the industry standard. The small ball makers eventually dropped out of the marketplace as large companies like St. Mungo and Spalding dominated the industry. In 1935, St. Mungo was making 32 different makes of balls and was shipping 900 dozen balls per day!

The other significant improvement was the incorporation of an uncompressible liquid into the center of the ball. In America, Eleazer Kempshall had been experimenting with water filled capsules as early as 1902, and, as a result of his patents, received royalties for all liquid core balls sold from 1902 until 1919. The Kempshall Company was subsequently bought by the St. Mungo Manufacturing Company in 1910. There were other later patents such as the one by Frank Mingay of Scotland which were based on Kempshall's original idea. Other improvements for golf balls were developed and hundreds of patents were granted, but the concept of the dimpled cover combined with a liquid center became the mainstay of the industry until the one-piece rubber ball was developed in the mid 1960's.

Prior to 1921, there was no standard size for the golf ball. From the days of the feathery, the balls were made in varying combinations of size and weight. Numbers such as "27½" and "28" appeared on balls to designate their size, a carryover from the feather ball and gutty ball eras. Many of the large, lightweight balls actually floated in water and were appropriately called "floaters." Players would choose a ball for play depending on the wind, temperature and the course which they were playing. The idea of a ball's hardness or compression was introduced in 1915 and, that too, was also taken into account when selecting a ball for play.

The following are the major changes in golf ball characteristics that have been made by the United States Golf Association:

1921 - Weight not greater than 1.62 ounces and diameter not less than 1.62 inches. (British "small ball")

1931 - Weight not greater than 1.55 ounces and diameter not less than 1.68 inches.

1932 - Weight not greater than 1.62 ounces and diameter not less than 1.68 inches. (Current U.S. size)

The British continued to use the "small" 1.62-1.62 ball exclusively until 1968 when the British PGA began to experiment with the larger American ball which the American professionals had mastered so well. The proponents of the change felt that the British golfers would never play as well as their American counterparts if they did not master the larger ball which was harder to control in the wind. The major opponents of the large ball were the traditionalists and the British ball manufacturers who did not want to induce competition with the large American companies. The British professionals adopted the new ball, however the Royal and Ancient officials were not so quick to act. They finally made the large ball mandatory for the British Open Championship in 1974. The larger ball continued to become more universal in use and since January of 1983, has been acceptable for use in competitons sanctioned by the R & A. The small percentage of players still using the small ball are primarily from Scotland.

One of the popular aspects of golf ball collecting is the area of logo balls. These collectors focus their efforts on acquiring balls imprinted with the name or logo of companies, organizations, colleges, groups and individuals. Thousands of these balls have been produced by the golf ball manufacturers for use as gifts and advertising. Personalized balls have even been ordered by several Presidents of the United States.

Early ball winding machine at the Silvertown Company in London.

After their patent for the rubber core ball was declared void in Great Britain in 1905, Haskell tried to keep the British imitations of their ball from being imported into the United States.

Haskell Golf Ball Patent

622.834. BALL. Bertram G. Work, Akron, and Coburn Haskell, Cleveland, Ohio. Filed Aug. 9, 1898. Serial No. 688,152. (No Model)

To all whom it may concern:

Be it known that we, BERTRAM G. WORK, residing at Akron, in the county of Summit, and COBURN HASKELL, residing at Cleveland, in the county of Cuyahoga, State of Ohio, citizens of the United States, have invented a new and useful Improvement in Balls, of which the following is a specification.

Our invention is in the nature of an improved ball for use more especially in the game of golf, though it may be used in other games where a ball of similar properties is desired.

Our object is to provide a ball for the above purposes which shall possess the essential qualities of lightness and durability and which shall also have the property of being comparatively non-resilient under the moderate impacts incident to its use, but highly resilient under the stronger impacts.

We accomplish the objects sought by making the main body of the core of rubber thread wound under tension into spherical form and providing the same with an adequately-thick covering of gutta-percha or one of its substitutes, such as balata gum, the covering possessing the attributes, comparatively speaking, of inelasticity, toughness, hardness and lightness.

The invention is illustrated in the accompanying drawings, in which—

Figure 1 is a view of the interior of the ball; Figs. 2 and 3, interior views of the two halves of the outer shell or covering laid open; Fig. 4, an outer view of the elastic core employed; Fig. 5, a section taken on line 5 of Fig. 1; and Fig. 6, a view, partly in section, of a modified form of the elastic core, showing the rubber thread, from which it is made, as wound upon a central core-section of gutta-percha or the like.

The preferred manner of making the ball is by winding a rubber thread *t* upon itself, under a tension approximating the elastic limit, to produce a spherical core A and covering this core with a gutta-percha shell of adequate thickness. The preferred method of applying the inclosing shell is by wrapping or inclosing the core in one or more sheets of gutta-percha suitably cut and previously heated sufficiently to give it a certain degree of plasticity, as by dipping it in boiling water, and then placing the core thus wrapped in a mold and subjecting the whole to sufficient pressure to form it to the exact shape desired, which shape is retained on cooling; but the shell may be produced by any other method which may be found practicable. The shell thus formed to be effective must be of such thickness as to remain comparatively rigid under the moderate impacts to which the ball is subjected, as in the case of light blows with the golf-club or on striking the earth, but to yield under the more violent impacts, as in "driving," whereby the force is brought to bear upon the elastic core.

B is the complete ball, and B¹ B² the halves of the comparatively unyielding shell which receives the elastic core. A. The exterior surface of the ball may be roughened, as shown in Fig. 1, by using a mold having intersecting ridges on its inner surface.

Fig. 5 shows a complete half-section of the ball, the core being shown as made simply by winding a rubber thread upon itself to form a sphere.

Fig. 6 shows the rubber winding inclosing a small central core-section C, which may be of any suitable material serving to facilitate the winding and, if desired, to regulate to some extent the weight of the ball.

It is an essential feature of the construction that the core shall closely fill the interior of the shell and desirable that the core be confined therein under some compression.

A core produced by winding a rubber thread under high tension into spherical form possesses a remarkably high degree of elasticity coupled with high rigidity in the sense of resistance to deformation, which imparts to the ball the property of very great resilience. As the result of the described construction, therefore, our golf ball has exceptionally high driving qualities owing to the fact that the impact of a golf-club is capable of distorting it through the shell by reason of the adequate flexibility of the latter and little tendency to bound by reason of the fact that little, if any, distortion takes place upon contact with the ground. The highest resistance to change in form, therefore, is attained when the thread is at all parts of the ball under a tension close to the elastic limit, tending to maintain a perfect sphere, whereby the slightest distortion is resisted by approximately the full strength of the material, and the effect is enhanced by the close environment of the elastic body within the comparatively unyielding shell.

In the appended claims the term "elastic core" is meant to cover that portion of the ball included within the outer shell and composed wholly or mainly of rubber thread, while the term "gutta-percha shell" is intended as limiting the claims wherein it is employed to gutta-percha or one of its substitutes, such as the one mentioned above.

What we claim as new, and desire to secure by Letters Patent, is —

1. A golf-ball, comprising a core composed wholly or in part of rubber thread wound under high tension, and a gutta-percha inclosing shell for the core, of such thickness as to give it the required rigidity, substantially as described.

2. A golf-ball comprising a central core-section of relatively non-elastic material, rubber thread wound thereon under tension, and an inclosing shell of gutta-percha, of such thickness as to give it the required rigidity, substantially as described.

BERTRAM G. WORK.
COBURN HASKELL.

In presence of—
R. T. Spencer
D. W. Lee

No. 622,834.

Patented Apr. 11, 1899.

B. G. WORK & C. HASKELL.

BALL.

(Application filed Aug. 9, 1898.)

(No Model.)

Fig. 1.

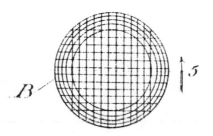

B

5

Fig. 2.

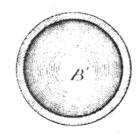

B'

Fig. 3.

B²

Fig. 6.

C

A

Fig. 4.

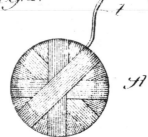

t

A

Fig. 5.

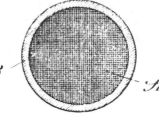

B

A

Witnesses:

Chas E Guylord.
Sub. B. Pitts

Inventors:
Bertram G. Work,
Coburn Haskell,
By Dyrenforth & Dyrenforth,
Attys.

MAJOR GUTTA PERCHA AND RUBBER CORE GOLF BALLMAKERS PRIOR TO 1940

The following makers and their respective brands are most important to the collector and to the history of the game. The balls names are usually listed under the name of their original maker and not under the name of an agent or retailer. It was common for golf equipment manufacturers to advertise a particular brand of ball and the inference was that they were the maker of the ball. This was not always the case.

There are many ball names which do not appear below, but instead have been included on the alphabetical list of ball names. The dates sown are those believed to be the first actual use or advertisement of the balls. Descriptive adjectives such as colors are placed after the ball name. For example: "Dot, red" instead of "red Dot". The names of the balls are generally shown as they actually appear on the ball.

The "G" and "R" designations stand for Gutta percha or Rubber core construction.

ACUSHNET - New Bedford, Massachusetts

PGA Championship	R	1936
Pro	R	1932
Ray, Blue	R	1934
Ray, Gold	R	1934
Super	R	1934
Titleist	R	1939

AGRIPPA GOLF BALL CO. - Coventry, England

Agrippa	G	1896
Agrippa No. 2	G	1898

ALAN HERBERT & GREENING - London

Dot, 38 green	R	1909
Dot, 38 red	R	1909

ALLIED GOLF CO.

Allied 162	R	1922
Mercury	R	1922

ANDERSON, ANDERSON & ANDERSON LTD. - London

Anderson	G	1898
Anderson White	G	1898
Varsity	G	1898
Varsity White	G	1898

Varsity gutta percha ball.

ARGUS GOLF BALL AND REQUISITES MFG. CO. - London

Argus Bramble 27½	G	1902
Argus, Special	G	1902

ARMY & NAVY STORES - London

Army & Navy C.S.L. Driver	R
Army & Navy C.S.L. Furlong	R
Army & Navy C.S.L. No. 1	R
Army & Navy C.S.L. No. 2	R

ASSOCIATED GOLFERS INC.

Darby Flyer	R	1910

AVON INDIA RUBBER CO. - Melksham, Wilts, England

Avon	R	1910
Avon Junior	R	1910
Avon Rifled	R	1910

AYRES LTD., F.H. - London

International	G	1893
Olympic	R	1911
Supreme	R	1907
Vaile	G	

The "Vaile" had a most unusual pattern.

B.G.I. - Bridgeport, Connecticut

Champion Flier	G	1901
New BGI	G	1901
Opresto, The	G	1901
Thistle	G	

BAKER & BENNETT - New York

Goose, Gray	R	1927

BETTORUS LTD. - London

Bettorus	R	1912
Joyce	R	1912

BIRD & ETHERINGTON - London

Bird, The	R	1913
Bird, Wee	R	1914
Birdeth, The	R	1913

BOSTON BELTING CO. - Boston

Forsyth	G	1899

The Forsyth was one of several gutta percha balls made in the United States.

BROWNING - U.S.A.

King Dimple	R	1926
King Mesh	R	1926

BRYNE, F.A. - Birmingham, England

Elect 09	R	1909

BURKE GOLF CO. - Newark, Ohio

Browning KI	R	1935
Burke 50-50	R	1928
Commander	R	1935
Forespot	R	1935
Lady Burke	R	

BUTCHART-NICHOLLS - Glenbrook, Connecticut

Autograph	R	
Butchart S	R	1923
Custom	R	1918

CAPON HEATON & CO. LTD. - Birmingham, England

Capon Heaton	R	1909
Ring, Black	R	1914
Ring, Blue	R	1914
Ring, Green	R	1914
Ring, Red	R	1914
Ring, Yellow	R	1913
Sunbeam	R	1914
Zeppelin	R	1909

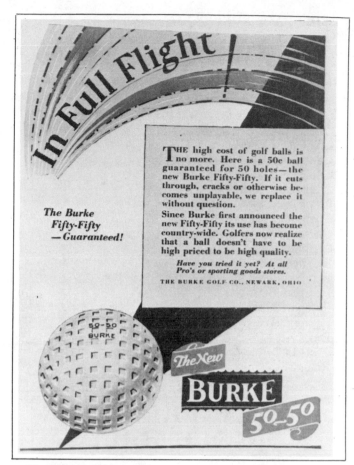

The Burke 50-50 was considered to be a low priced ball at 50 cents in 1928.

CLAN GOLF CLUB CO. -

Clan	G	1893

CLARK, J & D - Musselburgh

Musselburgh	G	1898

Above: Harry Vardon liked the Musselburgh ball enough to use it in winning the 1898 British Open, but soon signed an endorsement contract with Spalding to promote the heralded Vardon Flycr.

Right: Musselburgh ball.

CLYDESDALE RUBBER CO. - Glasgow		
C	G	1894

COCHRANE & CO. J.P. - Edinburgh

Ace (Gelatine Center)	R	1907
Ace, New	R	1901
Challenger	R	1908
Challenger (Red)	R	1908
Challenger 26½	R	1912
Challenger King	R	
Challenger XL	R	1921
Challenger, Floating	R	1913
Challenger, R & A	R	1914
Challenger, Star	R	1907
Cochrane Challenger	R	1904
Cochrane's Patent	R	
Cochrane's Rex	G	
Dot, Yellow	R	
Paragon (St. Andrews)	G	1900
Paragon (Bramble)	G	1900
Paragon (Hoylake)	G	1900
Paragon (Westward Ho)	G	1900
Pro, New	R	1901
Profs Ball (Red Dot)	R	1901
Regina	R	1913

Cochrane named its Paragon patterns after British golf courses.

Cochrane's Patent rubber core ball.

COUNTY CHEMICAL CO. (CHEMICO) - Birmingham, England

Bob	R	1913
Chemico Triumph	R	1914
Comet	R	1911
DeLuxe	R	1913
Popular	R	1913
Special	R	1913
Stella	R	1911

CRAIGPARK ELECTRIC CABLE CO. - Glasgow

Climax	R	1909
Craigpark	R	1909
Craigpark Special	R	1909
Express (Dimpled)	R	1908
Flyer, White	R	1914
Mono	R	1913
Scoto	R	1908

CROMBIE & SMITH - Edinburgh

Cromith, The	R	1912
Dormy	R	1912

CUPPLES -

Pro	R	1926
Rhino	R	1926
Trophy	R	1926

CURRIE & CO., WILLIAM - Edinburgh

Eclipse	G	1877
Star	G	1890

Currie's Eclipse was patented in 1877 and was the first of the composite balls, being made of a blend of India rubber, cork, leather and other items.

DAVIDSON RUBBER CO. - Boston

Davidson	G	1901

DUNLOP TIRE & RUBBER CO. -
Birmingham and New York

30	R	1918
Dunlop 162	R	1921
Dunlop 4	R	1907
Dunlop, Ball, The	R	
Dunlop England 5 5	R	
Dunlop Floater	R	1915
Dunlop Gold Cup	R	1934
Dunlop Junior	R	1909
Dunlop Maxfli (Black)	R	
Dunlop Maxfli (Blue)	R	1922
Dunlop No. 31	R	1915
Dunlop Orange Spot	R	1909
Dunlop Warwick	R	
Dunlop, The	R	
Dunlop, The New	R	1914
Manor Junior	R	1914
Manor, Red	R	
Manor, The	R	1914
Nimble	R	1914
No. 29	R	1912
No. 31	R	
V	R	
Vac	R	1918

Typical Dunlop rubber core ball from the 1920's.

DUNN, WILLIE, SR. - London and Musselburgh

Dunn, W.	G	1850

EDINA GOLF BALL MANUF. CO. LTD. - Edinburgh

Dux	R	1907
Ensign	R	1908
Ensign, Red	R	1908
Homer	R	1907
Knock Out	R	1908
Silkor	R	1907

FORGAN, R. & SON - St. Andrews

Acleva	G	1901
Forgan	G	1901

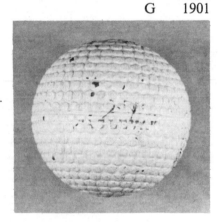

The "Acleva" stamp is barely visible on this ball.

Dunlop grossly mis-calculated their figures when they ran this advertisement. Six million golf balls would only be a fraction of the size of the ball shown.

FORTH RUBBER CO. - England

Bullet	G	1899

GOLF BALLS, LTC. - Hammersmith, Scotland

Dot, Red	R	1909
Star, Black	R	1908

GOLF BALL VALUES

Golf ball values vary considerably due to age, type of construction and maker. Balls which show the least amount of wear generally command the higher values, while those in extremely poor condition will be valued lower than the ranges shown.

GUTTY BALL — 1848-1875, hand hammered or smooth $150-800
GUTTY BALL — 1870-1910, molded pattern $30-150
RUBBER CORE BALL — 1898-1915, mint $75-125
RUBBER CORE BALL — 1898-1915, used $20-80
RUBBER CORE BALL — 1916-1930, mint $25-75
RUBBER CORE BALL — 1916-1930, used $10-30
MODERN BALLS — post 1930 . . . . under $10

The "G" and "R" designations stand for Gutta percha or Rubber core construction.

GOODRICH, B.F. - Akron, Ohio

Bantam	R	1912
Bunny	R	1911
Comet	R	1912
Final	R	1913
Haskell	R	1898
Haskell Bramble	R	
Haskell Match	R	1899
Haskell Mesh	R	1902
Haskell No. 10	R	1904
Haskell Royal	R	1909
Haskell Streak	R	1909
Haskell, Regular	R	1904
Jack Rabbit	R	1911
Meteor	R	1912
Moose	R	1912
Scotty	R	1913
Silvertown	R	1926
Stag	R	1912
Streak	R	1909
Tournament	R	1907
Whiz	R	1908

Haskell Bramble.

The Goodrich Tournament was one of the first dimpled balls in 1907.

1898 1898 1898 Goodrich Golf Balls.

Pure Gutta Percha.

Seasoned 1 Year and Over.

Good Color. - Clean Cut.

Endorsed by Golfers every-where. For sale by dealers or will send direct.

GOODRICH

... MANUFACTURED BY ...

The B. F. Goodrich Company,
Akron, Ohio.

BRANCHES:

NEW YORK - 66-68 Reade Street.   CHICAGO - 141 Lake Street.

SAN FRANCISCO - 35 New Montgomery Street.

Goodrich was in the gutta percha ball business before they got involved with the Haskell ball.

GOODRICH SERVICE COVERS THE MAP

Goodrich golf balls could be purchased at their service stations located across the country as shown on this 1912 map.

The original Haskell rubber core golf ball.

GOLF BALL VALUES

Golf ball values vary considerably due to age, type of construction and maker. Balls which show the least amount of wear generally command the higher values, while those in extremely poor condition will be valued lower than the ranges shown.

GUTTY BALL — 1848-1875, hand hammered or smooth $150-800
GUTTY BALL — 1870-1910, molded pattern $30-150
RUBBER CORE BALL — 1898-1915, mint $75-125
RUBBER CORE BALL — 1898-1915, used $20-80
RUBBER CORE BALL — 1916-1930, mint $25-75
RUBBER CORE BALL — 1916-1930, used $10-30
MODERN BALLS — post 1930 .... under $10

The "G" and "R" designations stand for Gutta percha or Rubber core construction.

GOODYEAR TIRE & RUBBER CO. - Akron, Ohio

Arrow	R	1902
Dollar	R	1910
Pneumatic, The	R	1905
Silk Pneumatic	R	1907

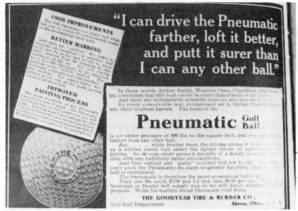

The Pneumatic and later the Silk Pneumatic balls claimed superior durability, however these balls were known to explode for no apparent reason.

Pneumatic compressed air ball.

GOURLAY, JOHN - Scotland

Gourlay, J.	G

GRAVITATOR GOLF BALL CO., THE - London

Gravitator Flyer, The	R	1909
Gravitator, The	R	1907

GRESSICK, DAVID - Scotland

Unmarked	G	1850

GUTTA PERCHA CO. - London

A1 (Red)	G	1894
A1 (Black)	G	1894
A1 Special	G	1893
Alpha	G	1898
Eltham	G	1899
Eureka	G	1898
Eureka, The New	G	

HALLEY, J.B. - London

Halley's Ball	R	1912
Ocobo	G	1894
Ocobo	R	1914
Tom Tit	R	1911

Original gutta percha version of The Ocobo.

Later rubber core ball also named "Ocobo". This ball is known for its oversized flat bramble markings. It was also made with dimples of the same style.

HARLEQUIN BALL & SPORTS CO.

- Ascot
- Dot & Dash
- Harlequin, Super
- Spot, Red

Super Harlequin rubber core ball.

HASKELL GOLF BALL CO.
See: GOODRICH

HELSBY CO., THE - Helsby, Scotland

Dot, New Green	R	1909
Dot, Red	R	1909
Helsby National	G	
Link, The	R	1913
Mersey, The	R	1910

HENLEY'S TELEGRAPH WORKS CO · LTD., W.T. - London

Henley	G	1895
Henley B	G	1900
Melfort	G	1896
Musselburgh	G	1896
Why Not	R	1911

The following description of the Henley ball appeared in a golf magazine when the ball was introduced in 1895:

The ball is different from other balls on the market, inasmuch as the nicking is entirely on novel lines. It is grooved in a series of rings, divided into compartments and curiously interwoven with the happiest effect to the eye, as well as utility in scoring the longest flight. The name "Henley" is printed on two sides of the ball, and this, with its novelty above described, prevents a player from taking refuge in the well-worn excuse attached to playing the wrong ball — namely, that he did not know the one from the other, owing to their similarity of nicking, though coming from the factory of different makers.

Indented Marking   *Bramble Marking*
Made by W.T. Henley's Telegraph Works Co., Ltd., London, Eng.

"WHY NOT" Your Golf Ball?

Dependable—that's the word. Dependable for long, long distance from the tee. Dependable on the approach, dependable for its nice balance—its accurate molding.

One "Why Not" Ball is exactly like another—for every ball is tested and guaranteed for far flight and absolute accuracy. "Hit it *right* and you know it goes right."

Ask your Professional for the "*Why Not*" Tested Ball or send direct to us. Your satisfaction is guaranteed.

Price $10 per dozen; 85c. each; weight 30 dwt.

SUCCESSORS OF

SAM'L BUCKLEY & CO.
(OF LONDON AND NEW YORK) LTD.

16 East 33rd St.   *Sole Agents*   New York City

This Why Not advertisement was typical of the ads of the period in that the golfer could purchase balls directly from the manufacturer rather than through a golf professional. Henley was one of the first companies to mechanically test every ball before shipment.

HENRY, ALEXANDER - Edinburgh

Rifled Ball	R	1903

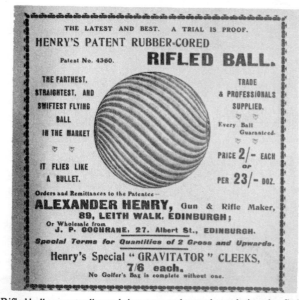

THE LATEST AND BEST.   A TRIAL IS PROOF.

HENLEY'S PATENT RUBBER-CORED RIFLED BALL.

Patent No. 4360.

THE FARTHEST, STRAIGHTEST, AND SWIFTEST FLYING BALL IN THE MARKET

IT FLIES LIKE A BULLET.

TRADE & PROFESSIONALS SUPPLIED.

Every Ball Guaranteed.

PRICE **2/-** EACH or PER **23/-** DOZ.

Orders and Remittances to the Patentee—

ALEXANDER HENRY, Gun & Rifle Maker, 89, LEITH WALK, EDINBURGH;
Or Wholesale from J. P. COCHRANE, 27, Albert St., EDINBURGH.

Special Terms for Quantities of 2 Gross and Upwards.

Henry's Special "GRAVITATOR" CLEEKS, 7/6 each.

No Golfer's Bag is complete without one.

The Rifled ball was actually made by a gun maker and was designed to fly "like a bullet."

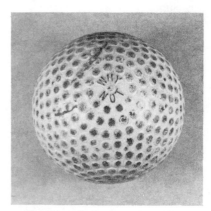

Why Not ball with bramble marking.

HERD, ALEX - Huddersfield, Scotland

Fixby		G	1898

HOLMAC - New York

5-5		R	1923
Aero		R	1921
Beldam		R	1921
Belgrave		R	1921
Corona		R	1921
Crow		R	1921
Dart, Blue		R	1921
Dart, The		R	
HM		R	1923
JH		R	1921

HUNTER, RAMSAY - Sandwich, England

Hunter		G	1892

HUNTER'S SPECIAL GOLF BALL
Is certainly the Best Ball on the Market.

OPINIONS.

MR. JOHN BALL, Jun., says : " He never played with a better.'
MR. H. H. HILTON says : " They fly well and keep exceptionally true."
MR. F. A. FAIRLIE says : " They are excellent balls."
MR. S. MURE-FERGUSSON says : " They cannot be beat."
MR. LESLIE M. BALFOUR says : " He found them admirable."
MR. A. D. BLYTH says : " No one could wish for a finer ball."
MR. A. M. ROSS recommends them as one of the best.
MR. GREGOR MCGREGOR says : " They are beautifully moulded."

HUNDREDS OF TESTIMONIALS.

Made of the Finest Black Gutta Percha, and, as seen from the above
Testimonials, they are used by all the leading players, and on all greens.

12s. per Doz., Post Free.

Only to be had from

MR. RAMSAY HUNTER, Golf Club and Ball Maker, Sandwich, KENT.
Messrs. JNO. WISDEN & Co., 21, Cranbourne St., Leicester Sq., LONDON, W.C.

These testimonials from 1893 for Hunter's ball were primarily from amateur golfers. John Ball and Leslie Balfour are quoted referring to a "He". It seems that Hunter may have been writing these testimonials himself.

HUNTINGTON MANUFACTURING CO. - U.S.A.

Goose, Gray		R	1923
Jack Rabbit		R	1923

SPRINGVALE AND SPRINGVALE-RAMPANT GOLF BALLS (Patented).

These Balls are the BEST in the Market. BECAUSE

SPRINGVALE
SOLID
14/-
per dozen.

They are the longest-driving Balls in existence.
They are the ONLY Balls that CANNOT BE HACKED or SPLIT.
For approaching and putting they are unequalled.
They are by far the most ECONOMICAL Balls, lasting many times longer than all others, whether Gutta or Rubber-Cored, and CAN BE RE-MADE.

Springvale-
RAMPANT
(CORED)
20/-
per dozen.

Manufactured by **HUTCHISON, MAIN & CO.,**

Telegraphic Address :
"Springvale, Glasgow."

COWLAIRS, GLASGOW.

The Springvale series of balls were marked "S'VALE" since their name was too long. At the turn of the century, Hutchison Main was sued for patent infringement by Goodrich, the makers of the Haskell ball. Goodrich ended up losing the rights to their patent in Great Britain, but were still protected in the United States where they had licensing arrangements with several manufacturers.

HUTCHISON MAIN & CO. - Glasgow

Kite, Golden		R	1905
S'Vale (Springvale)		R	1903
S'Vale Eagle		R	1905
S'Vale Falcon		R	1907
S'Vale Hawk		R	1905
S'Vale Kite		R	1905
S'Vale Rampant		R	1903

HYDE IMPERIAL RUBBER CO. - Cheshire, Scotland

Woodley Flier		G	1898

THE "WOODLEY" FLIER
(Fully Seasoned)
IS ALL THE RAGE.
PRICE LIST ON APPLICATION.

The Hyde Imperial Rubber Co., Ltd.
WOODLEY, CHESHIRE.

The Woodley Flier was "all the rage" in 1898. For some unknown reason, some makers used "flier" and others used "flyer".

IMPROVED GOLF BALLS CO. LTD. - London

Arcadia		R	
Auchterlonie Flyer			1903
Elastine		R	1904
Flipoot		G	1902
I.G.B.		R	1907
Jellicore		R	1907
Ortogo		R	1902
Ortogo Singer		R	
Skor			
Star, White		R	1907
Vulcan, White		R	1907

The Improved Golf Balls Company was innovative in their methods of applying covers to both gutty and rubber core balls. They were the suppliers to both the King and the Prince of Wales.
The Ortogo Singer actually contained a small revolving ball in the center of its gutta percha covering.
The Skor ball was essentially a gutty ball but had several rubber covers to help it retain its shape and durability.

JOHNSON, FRANK A. - London

Mail	G	1901
Pin	R	1909
Snipe	R	1909
Tee	R	1909

KEMPSHALL MANUFACTURING CO. -
Arlington, New Jersey

Crescent, Gold	R	1909
Crescent, Gold Flat	R	1909
Bramble		
Flyer	R	1903
Kempshall Flyer	R	1902
Kempshall Flyer Click	R	1904
Kempshall League	R	1903
Non Skid	R	1909
Six Pole Bramble	R	1909

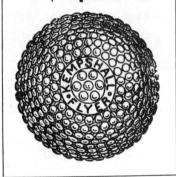

As its name implies, this Kempshall Flyer had "click", a feature which is now taken for granted with modern golf balls.

Left and bottom: The Kempshall Flyer was one of the many British balls designed along the lines of the Haskell patent. This ball was introduced in 1902 and as the ad says is "protected by over 100 patents". Mr. Kempshall, an American, had been granted hundreds of patents for golf balls in the early twentieth century. Kempshall was eventually bought out by the St. Mungo Manufacturing Co.

KROYDON CO. - Maplewood, New Jersey

Flying K	R	1926
Kroydon	R	1910
Steel Center	R	

LEE & UNDERHILL - U.S.A.

Diamond, White & Black		1909

LEE CO., HARRY C. - New York

Flyer, White	R	1922
Maxim	R	1923
Mono	R	1922
O.K.D.	R	1922
P.D.Q.	R	1921

LEHMANN & CO., R. - London

Bogey	R	1912
Zenith	R	1912
Zenith Orb	R	

LEITH GOLF BALL CO. - Leith, Scotland
Persevere

LEYLAND & BIRMINGHAM RUBBER CO., LTD.

Leyland Birco	R	1908
Leyland Flier	R	1908

LOWNE & CO., DONALD - London

Farsure 27½	G	1899
Farsure Bramble	G	1899
Farsure Grooved	G	1899
Farsure Meteor	G	1905
Farsure, New	G	
Lowne's Special	G	1902

This advertisement from 1900 mentions Lowne's practice of marking ball boxes with the date of moulding and painting. This was important to the buyer since the balls had to be well seasoned prior to play.

LUNN & CO. - London

Balfour	R	1890

MacGREGOR GOLF CO. - Dayton, Ohio

1.62 30 Mesh	R	1921
259	R	
31	R	1919
Dry Ice Center	R	1935
Dubble Cover	R	1936
Duralite	R	1928
Master	R	1922

MacLEND-MERRITT - U.S.A.

Avon Deluxe	R	

MARTINS-BIRMINGHAM LTD. -
Birmingham, England

Hex	R	
High Tensioned Rubber Core	R	
Martins' Tube Core	R	1905
Martins' Flyers	R	
Martins' Nipper	R	
Marzo	R	1908
Pluto	R	1913
Tube Core	R	1907
Zodiac	R	1909
Zodiac Pearl	R	
Zome	R	1908
Zome One	R	1924

Martins made their balls with a seamless process.

Martins' High Tensioned Rubber Core ball.

"ZODIAC WINS"

1910
AMATEUR CHAMPIONSHIP AT HOYLAKE.

WE HAVE THE HONOUR TO ANNOUNCE THAT

The WINNER of the CHAMPIONSHIP PLAYED WITH A "ZODIAC"
ALSO
The "ZODIAC" was played by the FINALISTS.

2/- and an old "Zodiac" purchases a new "ZODIAC."

MARTINS-BIRMINGHAM, Ltd., Golf Ball Makers, BIRMINGHAM.

By 1910, the manufacturers were no longer using the names of amateur golfers as endorsements. However, advertisements such as this were common. For those who cannot remember, John Ball was the winner of this championship.

McDAID, MARTIN - Edinburgh

Active, The	R	1914
Corona	R	1911
Eaglet	R	1914
Iris	R	
Pimpernil	R	1911
Radio, The	R	1911
Scarlet Runner	R	1914
Scarlet Sikh, New	R	

METROPOLITAN GOLF BALL CO. - London

Opal	R	1914
Pal	R	1913

MIDLAND RUBBER CO. LTD. - Birmingham, England

Aero M	R	1914
Aero Small	R	1914
Aero, The	R	1910
Ajax	R	1912
Ajax Bramble	R	1914
Ajax Special	R	1910
Bramble	R	1914
M Recessed	R	1913
Nimble Bob	R	1914

MILLAR, W. - Glasgow

Micro Special, The	G	1901

MILLER & TAYLOR - Glasgow

Little Model, The	R	1911
Spot, Black	R	1913
Spot, Green	R	1913
Spot, Superior Brown	R	1914

NORTH BRITISH RUBBER CO. LTD. Edinburgh

Chick	R	1913
Chick, Big	R	1912
Chick, Bramble	R	1914
Chick, Dimple	R	1914
Chick, The Diamond	R	1913
Click, Super	R	1919
Clincher, The	R	1913
Clincher Cross	R	1913
Hawk, The New	R	1913
Hi Spot	R	1912
Kite, The New	R	1912
N.B. Twin Dot	R	1912
Osprey, The	R	1913
ST	R	1936
Superflite (Blue)	R	1926

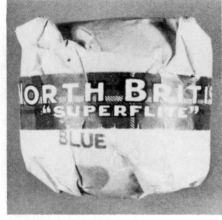

Superflite golf ball in its original wrapper.

ORME CO., THE - London

Orme	R	1913

PADON, A & D - Edinburgh

Allaway	R	1904

PARK & SON, WM. - Musselburgh

Dispatch	G	
Royal	G	1896
Times	G	
Wm. Park	G	1890

PATERSON - Scotland

Paterson's New Composite	G	1848

PATRICK, ALEX - Leven, Scotland

Honour, The	R	1911
Patrick	G	

PAXTON, PETER - Musselburgh & London

Bramble	G	
Distant	G	1896
English	G	1892
Furzedown	G	1898
Gladstone	G	1898
Perfection	G	1892
Re-Made	G	1896
Sirdar	G	1900

PENFOLD

Penfold 75	R	1935
Penfold Floater	R	1934
Penfold Hearts	R	1930

PERFECT GOLF BALL CO.

Perfect	R	1905

RAWLINGS MFG. CO. - St. Louis

Play-Off	R	

Above two photos: Paxton was a clubmaker, ballmaker and professional. He also retailed balls for Henley's. It is interesting to see that he advertised that he purchased his gutta percha from the Silvertown Company, a competitor in the ball business.

REACH, A.J. - Philadelphia

Eagle	R	1929
Paramont A & B Mesh & Dimple	R	1915
Paramont C & F	R	1917
Whippets	R	1915

REDFERN'S RUBBER WORKS LTD. - Manchester, England

Favorite	R	1912
Mercury	R	1912
O.K.	R	1912
Wonder	R	1912

ROBERTSON, ALLAN - St. Andrews

Allan	G	1851

ROGER, JAMES H. - Glasgow

Jonny, The	R	1912

RUBASTIC LTD. - Southall, Scotland		
Chancellor	R	1913
Commodore	R	1913
Dictator	R	1913
General	R	1913
Skipper	R	1913
White Prince	R	

SCOTTISH GOLF BALL MFG. CO. LTD. - Edinburgh		
Conqueror	R	1912
D.D.	R	
King Conqueror	R	1913
Lunar, The	R	1912
Student	R	
Victor, New	R	

SCOTTISH INDIA RUBBER CO. - Glasgow		
Advert	G	1896
Jim	G	1894
Maxim	G	1896
Scottish	G	1894
Victor	G	1895

SEAMAN MANUFACTURING CO. - Milwaukee		
Bogey, The	R	1905

SEARS ROEBUCK & CO. - Chicago		
Higgins Autograph, J.C.	R	

SELFRIDGE'S - London		
Grip, The	R	1910

SHARP, JOHN - Musselburgh		
Sharp	G	1850

SILVERTOWN CO. - London		
Granton		
Lynx	G	1902
Lynx	R	1915
Pentland	R	1909
Silver Black Dot Mesh	R	1913
Silver King	R	1911
Silver King 1	R	1932
Silver King (Black Dot)	R	1913
Silver King Face	R	1918
Silver King HV	R	1920
Silver King Plus	R	1934
Silver Prince	R	
Silvertown Bramble	G	1900
Silvertown No. 4	G	1888
Silvertown No. 5	G	1898
Silvertown No. 9	G	1906
Silvertown Snippet	G	
Silvertown, New	G	1904
Silviator	G	
Sovereign	R	
Stoughton	R	

The early Lynx gutty ball had no name markings on it, which makes it quite difficult for the collector to know if he has one. The Lynx ball shown here is the later rubber core model and not the ball referred to in the above ad.

The Silvertown Co's
NEW BALL
THE
"SILVER KING"

Its flight, both off Wood and Iron Clubs, is excellent.

The most remarkable feature of the ball is the fact that it retains its resiliency and life for a most unusually long period, and keeps its shape.

STOCKED BY ALL PROFESSIONALS.

ALLOWANCE FOR OLD BALLS.

An allowance of 6d. each will be made by your professional for used "SILVER KING" Balls, provided a like number of new balls is purchased in exchange.

Made by
The Silvertown Co., 106, Cannon St., London, E.C.
Works: Silvertown, London, E.

Silvertown was actually offering a trade-in allowance for old balls.

The Silvertown gutty was a well made and popular ball in the 1890's.

This Silvertown ball appears to be brand new, but is approximately 50 years old and has never been used.

SLAZENGER & SONS - New York & London

Boodie	G	1900
Challenger	R	1916
Cross, Green	R	1913
Cross, Red	R	1909
L.P.H.	G	1900
Slazenger	G	1892
Slazenger	R	1904
Truflite	G	1900
Xpres	G	1900

Slazenger's in New York was an importer of golf equipment in the 1890's. The prices in this ad are most amusing. The gutty balls were made in Britain, aged for eighteen months, and were shipped to America where they retailed for $3.75 per dozen. One wonders where the profit was made. The cost of a driver was about five times that of a single ball. This ratio has increased considerably over the years.

SPALDING & BROS., A. G. -
London & Chicopee Falls, Massachusetts

Air-Flite	R	1936
Baby	R	1899
Birds Eye	R	1909
Black and White	R	1909
Black and White Dimple	R	1910
Blue Dot	R	1908
Bramble	G	1901
Bullet Honor	R	1916
Cinch	R	1914
Clinker, Black		
Corker	R	1914
Cross, Black	R	1909
Dimple	R	1908
Dimple, Baby	R	1916
Dimple, Domino	R	1912
Dimple, Midget	R	1912
Dimple, Red and Black	R	1910
Dimple, The	R	1909
Domino Dimple	R	1912
Domino, Orange	R	1916
Dot, Red and Black	R	1910
Dyna Flite	R	
English Midget Dimple	R	1915

SPALDING & BROS., A.G. (cont.)

Fairfield	R	
Glory	R	1914
Glory Dimple	R	1908
Glory Dimple (Blue Dot)	R	1907
Glory Dimple (Red Dot)	R	1907
Glory Dimple (White Dot)	R	1907
Glory Dimple Floater	R	1922
Honor	R	1908
Kro-Flite Dimple	R	1922
Kro-Flite Mesh	R	1920
Midget	R	
Needled	R	1937
Nimble	R	
Olympic Rebuilt	R	1943
PGA Championship	R	1926
Spalding 50	R	1919
Spalding 60	R	1920
Spalding Blue Circle	R	1910
Spalding Bob	R	1907
Spalding Bramble	G	1901
Spalding Dot (Red Dot)	R	1906
Spalding Executive	R	1954
Spalding Floater	R	1917
Spalding Floater	R	1921
Spalding No. 1		
Spalding No. 1		
Spalding Practice	G	1898
Spalding White Bramble	R	1907
Spalding White	R	1905
Spalding White (Black Dot)	R	1907
Spalding White (Red Dot)	R	1907
Spalding White (With Click)	R	1906
Spalding Wizard	R	1903
Starflite	R	
Thirty and Forty	R	1917
Topflite	R	1932
Vardon Flyer	G	1899
White Dot	R	1908
Witch	R	1916

Spalding gutty ball, circa 1895.

The Vardon Flyer gutty ball, introduced in 1899.

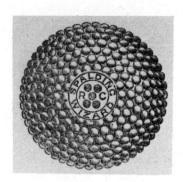

The Wizard was one of Spalding's first rubber cored balls. It was introduced in 1903 and was redesigned in 1904 so that it had "click". Much to Spalding's dismay, the new ball fell apart during play and their fine reputation was being damaged. They decided to return to making the old style ball which "left the club like a ghost in the night" and even offered to exchange the good balls for the bad ones.

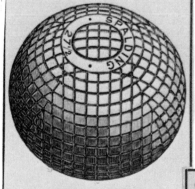
These models were the standard gutta percha balls which were offered by Spalding in the mid 1890's.

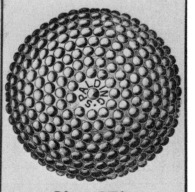

The
many victories won
with the
Spalding Ball
in
1927

★ *...again recommend its use during 1928 by all golfers* ★
to whom a trophy is something worth striving for

HERE ARE SOME OF THE 1927 TOURNAMENTS WON WITH SPALDING GOLF BALLS

INTERNATIONAL CHAMPIONSHIPS

U. S. OPEN GOLF CHAMPIONSHIP
BRITISH OPEN CHAMPIONSHIP
U. S. AMATEUR CHAMPIONSHIP
CANADIAN OPEN GOLF CHAMPIONSHIP
CANADIAN AMATEUR CHAMPIONSHIP
FRENCH AMATEUR GOLF CHAMPIONSHIP
DUTCH OPEN GOLF CHAMPIONSHIP
BELGIAN OPEN GOLF CHAMPIONSHIP
AUSTRALIAN OPEN GOLF CHAMPIONSHIP
U. S. WOMEN'S CHAMPIONSHIP
CANADIAN LADIES' OPEN CHAMPIONSHIP
CANADIAN LADIES' CLOSED CHAMPIONSHIP

NATIONAL CHAMPIONSHIPS

U. S. PUBLIC LINKS GOLF CHAMPIONSHIP
SOUTHERN OPEN GOLF CHAMPIONSHIP
NORTH AND SOUTH OPEN GOLF CHAMPIONSHIP
NORTH AND SOUTH AMATEUR CHAMPIONSHIP

CANADIAN CHAMPIONSHIPS

ALBERTA OPEN GOLF CHAMPIONSHIPS
ALBERTA AMATEUR CHAMPIONSHIP
ALBERTA LADIES' CHAMPIONSHIP
PROVINCE OF QUEBEC OPEN GOLF CHAMPIONSHIP
PROVINCE OF QUEBEC AMATEUR CHAMPIONSHIP
MARITIME AMATEUR GOLF CHAMPIONSHIPS
MARITIME PROFESSIONAL CHAMPIONSHIPS

WESTERN CANADIAN AMATEUR CHAMPIONSHIP
WESTERN CANADIAN OPEN CHAMPIONSHIP
WESTERN CANADIAN PROFESSIONAL CHAMPIONSHIP
MANITOBA AMATEUR GOLF CHAMPIONSHIP

SECTIONAL CHAMPIONSHIPS

SOUTHERN CALIFORNIA OPEN CHAMPIONSHIP
WOMEN'S WESTERN CHAMPIONSHIP
UPPER PENINSULA OF MICHIGAN CHAMPIONSHIP
LONG ISLAND OPEN GOLF CHAMPIONSHIP
WESTERN AMATEUR GOLF CHAMPIONSHIP
CENTRAL OHIO GOLF CHAMPIONSHIP
TRANS-MISSISSIPPI GOLF CHAMPIONSHIP

STATE CHAMPIONSHIPS

OREGON OPEN CHAMPIONSHIP
CALIFORNIA STATE CHAMPIONSHIP
WASHINGTON STATE GOLF CHAMPIONSHIP
OHIO STATE OPEN GOLF CHAMPIONSHIP
ILLINOIS PROFESSIONAL CHAMPIONSHIP
NEW JERSEY OPEN GOLF CHAMPIONSHIP
PENNSYLVANIA OPEN CHAMPIONSHIP

LOCAL CHAMPIONSHIPS

METROPOLITAN OPEN GOLF CHAMPIONSHIP
PHILADELPHIA OPEN GOLF CHAMPIONSHIP
ST. LOUIS DISTRICT GOLF CHAMPIONSHIP
WOMEN'S GOLF CHAMPIONSHIP OF ST. LOUIS

★

SPALDING GOLF BALLS

A.G. Spalding & Bros.

Spalding compiled an excellent record of tournament victories int he 1920's. In addition to their fine record in 1927, Spalding balls were used in winning 32 out of the 36 championships of the U.S. Open, British Open and British Amateur from 1913 through 1927.

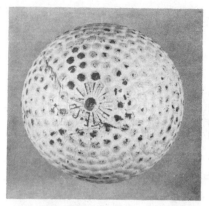

The Spalding White rubber core ball was first marketed in 1905 and was later offered in several styles.

RED HONOR

It Happened Again—AS USUAL

At the Red Cross Tournament held at the White Marsh Valley Golf Club, Chestnut Hill, Pa., which took the place of the Open Championship ordinarily held, Jock Hutchison won with a Red Honor.

There are ten different Spalding Balls in the 1917 line—including also the famous Baby Dimple and new Witch Dimple.

Let us suggest the proper ball for you. Tell us how and where you play, and we shall be glad to do so.

Descriptive golf ball booklet on request

A. G. SPALDING & BROS.
Stores in all large cities

Spalding had ten different balls in their 1917 line.

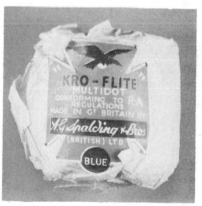

The Kro-Flite was first manufactured in the 1920's and eventually became one of Spalding's most popular brands of equipment. It was a standard practice for golf balls to be individually wrapped, possibly a marketing gimmick to justify their relatively high prices.

ENDORSED by the Professional Golfers Association of America

The Fact

that the P.G.A. golf ball bears the imprint of the initials of the Professional Golfers Association signifies conclusively that it has passed the most exacting playing tests imaginable.

The PGA endorsement was a program in which the manufacturer contributed to the PGA Benevolent Fund based upon the sales of the endorsed product. In 1927 alone, the fund earned $82,000 primarily from the sale of 23,000 dozen golf balls.

GOLF BALL VALUES

Golf ball values vary considerably due to age, type of construction and maker. Balls which show the least amount of wear generally command the higher values, while those in extremely poor condition will be valued lower than the ranges shown.

GUTTY BALL — 1848-1875, hand hammered or smooth $150-800
GUTTY BALL — 1870-1910, molded pattern $30-150
RUBBER CORE BALL — 1898-1915, mint $75-125
RUBBER CORE BALL — 1898-1915, used $20-80
RUBBER CORE BALL — 1916-1930, mint $25-75
RUBBER CORE BALL — 1916-1930, used $10-30
MODERN BALLS — post 1930 .... under $10

The "G" and "R" designations stand for Gutta percha or Rubber core construction.

ST. ANDREWS GOLF CO. LTD. - Glasgow

Scottish King	R	1914

ST. MUNGO MFG. CO. -
Newark, New Jersey & Glasgow

Admiral	R	1907
Arlington	R	1903
Captain	R	1906
Colonel 27 Dimple	R	1919
Colonel 29 Dimple	R	1919
Colonel 30 Dimple	R	1919
Colonel 31 Dimple	R	1919
Colonel Click Dimple	R	1915
Colonel, 26½	R	1911
Colonel, 27	R	1914
Colonel, 29	R	1914
Colonel, 31	R	1914
Colonel, Arch	R	1912
Colonel, Blue Click	R	1925
Colonel, Bramble	R	1910
Colonel, Click	R	1910
Colonel, Crescent	R	1912
Colonel, FS Ballbearing	R	1916
Colonel, Green Star	R	1912
Colonel, Heavy	R	1914
Colonel, Little Bramble	R	1911
Colonel, Little Crescent	R	1910
Colonel, Patent	R	1909

ST. MUNGO MFG. CO. (cont.)

Colonel, Perfect	R	1935
Colonel, Plus	R	1914
Colonel, Red Star	R	1912
Colonel, The	R	1905
Colonel, White	R	1910
Corporal	R	1906
Fast N Slow	R	1902
Fife	R	1900
Floater	R	1912
Floater Little Bramble	R	1911
Flyer	R	1902
Haskell, Scotch	R	1904
Judge, The	R	1910
Karifar	R	
League	R	1903
Major	R	1912
One Up	R	1900
Oswald	R	1909
St. Mungo Water Core	R	1911
St. Mungo, New	R	1901

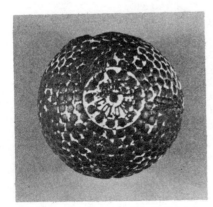

COLONEL GOLF BALLS

SUNKEN MARKING

F & S Colonel, Small Size, Non-Floater, $1.00 Each, $12.00 Doz.
Colonel 31, Small Size, Non-Floater   Arch Colonel, Small Size, Non-Floater
Colonel 29, Medium Size, Non-Floater   Crescent (Red) Full Size, Floater
Colonel 27, Full Size, Floater   65c Each, $7.50 Doz.
75c Each, $9.00 Doz.

BRAMBLE MARKING

Colonel 31, Small Size, Non-Floater, 65c Each, $7.50 Doz.
Red and Blue Crescent Colonel, Full Size, Floater—Non-Floater, 50c Each, $6.00 Doz.

ST. MUNGO MANUFACTURING COMPANY OF AMERICA
121-123 SYLVAN AVENUE, NEWARK, N. J.

NEW YORK   BOSTON   PHILADELPHIA   CHICAGO   SAN FRANCISCO
36 Warren Street 143 Federal Street 1201 Chestnut Street 36 So. State Street 46 Kearny Street

St. Mungo offered a complete line of balls as this 1912 ad shows. Their top of the line ball cost $1.00 before World I. If inflation is taken into account, it becomes apparent how expensive golf balls used to be.

One of the original Colonel balls from the early twentieth century.

STOUGHTON RUBBER CO. - Boston

Stoughton	R	1902

The Stoughton was an early rubber core ball made in Boston which was sold by various golf retailers.

STOW-WOODWARD

Banner	R	1933
Burbank	R	1935
Champion	R	1933
Dorchester	R	1933
Whip	R	1933

TAYLOR, ALEX - New York

3TO	R	1920
Ace	R	1920
Imp	R	1920
Mesh	R	1920

TELEGRAPH MANUFACTURING CO. LTD. - Helsby, Scotland

Helsby	G	1898

THORNTON & CO. - Edinburgh

Flying Scotsman	G	
Match, The	G	1896
Thornton	G	1896

U.S. ROYAL (U.S. RUBBER CO.) - New York

30-X	R	1921
444	R	1930
Electronic	R	
Fairway	R	1923
Nobby	R	1917
Pro Royal	R	1932
Special	R	
Spun Latex	R	1936
Tiger	R	1930
True Blue	R	1934

Royal produced many brands of balls, mostly with dimpled pattern.

UNIO GOLF BALL CO. - Glasgow		
Field	R	1911
Royal	R	1911
Success, New	R	1911
Traveller	R	1911
Traveller, Little	R	1911

VIPER GOLF BALL CO. - London		
Viper	G	1901
Viper Bramble	G	1901

WANAMAKER CO., JOHN - New York		
Diana	R	1921
Flash, Blue	R	1916
Flash, Long	R	1927
Flash, Red	R	1917
Flash, Yellow	R	1917
Mystery	R	1921
Super Radio	R	1921
Taplow	R	1916
Wonder	R	1923

WILSON SPORTING GOODS CO. - Chicago		
Cheerio	R	1928
Crest	R	1926
Dura-Dist	R	1928
Flag Hi	R	1934
Hol-Hi	R	1928
Hol-Hi 1.68	R	1930
Hol-Hi Thin Cover	R	1933
Hutchison	R	
K-28	R	1939
Pinehurst	R	1922
R-34	R	1922
Round Up	R	1934
Sam Snead 100	R	
Sarazen 50	R	1934
Sarazen Autograph	R	
Snead Blue Ridge	R	
Staff	R	
Success	R	1919
W	R	1918
Walker Cup	R	
Wilson Bramble	R	

WHITMAN & BARNES MFG. CO. - Akron, Ohio		
Diamond	G	1900
Norka	G	1900
Willie Dunn's Stars and Stripes	G	1900

The best design for a golf ball exterior definitely appeared on the ball aptly named Willie Dunn's Stars and Stripes. Dunn's family was very instrumental in the development of golf and Willie Junior, for whom this ball was named, was a pioneer of golf in America at the turn of the century.

Not only did the Crest have a "click", but "in a split second it's but a tiny white speck on the horizon."

GOLF BALL VALUES

Golf ball values vary considerably due to age, type of construction and maker. Balls which show the least amount of wear generally command the higher values, while those in extremely poor condition will be valued lower than the ranges shown.

GUTTY BALL — 1848-1875, hand hammered or smooth $150-800
GUTTY BALL — 1870-1910, molded pattern $30-150
RUBBER CORE BALL — 1898-1915, mint $75-125
RUBBER CORE BALL — 1898-1915, used $20-80
RUBBER CORE BALL — 1916-1930, mint $25-75
RUBBER CORE BALL — 1916-1930, used $10-30
MODERN BALLS — post 1930 . . . . under $10
      The "G" and "R" designations stand for Gutta percha or Rubber core construction.

color-
means fewer lost golf balls

the greatest sensation since Haskell made wound balls

KEEP your eye on the ball—and what a differ-ence it makes if you don't. Now Wilson has made it easy by originating colored golf balls. Play the new Oriole-Orange or Canary-Yellow and you will be amazed how easy it is to follow this simple, fundamental rule of the game.

Brilliant-dominant color rays cause the attention to focus on the ball and stay focused during a shot—spank it for a long one—way down the fairway—the sweetest little drive you ever shot and still the color holds your eye. A bright, scintillating sphere of color—flashing location signals to you from great distances—you just can't lose sight of it.

The Hol-Hi and Dura-Dist are available in both colors

The Hol-Hi is the toughest distance ball ever made—$1 each, $10.75 per doz. The Dura-Dist, guaranteed for 72 holes, is a glutton for punishment and gives an excellent account of itself in performance—75c each, $9 per doz.

Ask your Pro or Dealer

CANARY — ORIOLE
another
Wilson
scoop

WILSON-WESTERN SPORTING GOODS CO.
NEW YORK CHICAGO SAN FRANCISCO

Wilson first introduced colored golf balls in 1928. The idea was not very popular at that time, however in 1981 they began to market a colored version of the Wilson Staff ball and now colored balls are responsible for almost forty per cent of the total golf ball sales.

WISDEN, JOHN - London

Rocket	G	1902

WOOD-MILNE, LTD. - Preston, England

Chief, White	R	1914
Club	R	1913
Dot, Green	R	1911
Eclipse, The	R	1913
Kiddy	R	1911
Lady	R	1911
Special	R	1911

WORTHINGTON RUBBER CO. Elyria, Ohio

Ace	R	1914
Beauty, Black	R	1930
Bird, Blue	R	1923
Champion No. 2	R	1905
Champion No. 7	R	1905
Crown	R	1914
Deuce	R	1914
Diamond A	R	1914
Diamond King	R	1911
Diamond Ring	R	
Diamond Stud	R	
Diamond, Black	R	
Dice	R	1938
King B	R	1914
Lady Champion	R	1905
Marvel	R	1923
Mystery	R	1919
PGA	R	1923
Queen B	R	
Scotty	R	1913
Seamless Champion	R	1905
Standard	R	1903
Sweet Shot	R	1933
Tommy Armour	R	1936
Trey	R	1914
Wiffie Cox	R	1916
Worthington	R	1919
Worthington White	R	1909

WRIGHT & DITSON - Boston

19	R	1922
29	R	1919
31	R	1919
75 Floater	R	1920
Acme		
Birdie	R	1916
Bisk	R	1916
Bullet	R	1926
Circle (Black)	R	1920
Circle (Blue)	R	1912
Circle (Green)	R	1909
Circle (Purple)	R	1912
Circle (Red)	R	1912
Circle Floater (Orange & Black)	R	1913
Dormie	G	1900
Eagle	R	1911
Lynx Style	R	1912
National Floater	R	1916
Record	R	1927
Record WD	R	1928
Victor	R	1919
Victor 30	R	1921
Wright & Ditson	G	1900
Wright-Ditson Bramble	R	1912
Wright-Ditson Selected	G	1898

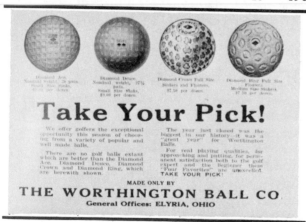

The names of Worthington balls sounded like a deck of playing cards.

YEOMAN, WILLIAM -
Wheathamstead, England and St. Andrews

Bramble, Black	G	1900
Flying Fox	G	1900
Swipe, The	G	1900

YOUNG CO., L.A. - Detroit

Hagen	R	1930
Hagen Honey Boy	R	1933

The Exhibition ball resembled many other gutties of the 1890's.

The Nova was a large sized rubber core ball which floated on water due to its light weight.

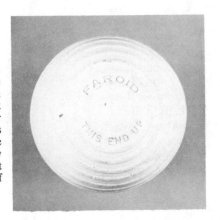

The Faroid golf ball had unique ridges and had to be teed in a certain manner in order to perform correctly. It may have worked fine for teeing off, but one wonders what happened when the player had to play fairway and approach shots without rearranging the position of the ball.

GUTTA PERCHA AND RUBBER CORE GOLF BALLS MADE PRIOR TO 1940

Listed alphabetically by ball name.

The following is an alphabetical listing of golf ball names and their respective makers. A list of makers and their brands is also included in this chapter. Descriptive adjectives such as colors are placed after the name. For example: "Dot, Red" instead of "Red Dot". The names of the balls are generally shown as they actually appear on the ball.

BALL NAME	MAKER	BALL NAME	MAKER
1.62 30 Mesh	MacGregor Golf Co.	Active, The	McDaid, Martin
19	Wright & Ditson	Adams A1	Adams Golf Ball Co.
259	MacGregor Golf Co.	Admiral	St. Mungo Mfg. Co.
29	Wright & Ditson	Advert	Scottish India Rubber Co.
30	Dunlop Tire & Rubber Co.	Aero M	Midland Rubber Co. Ltd.
30-X	U.S. Royal	Aero Small	Midland Rubber Co. Ltd.
31	MacGregor Golf Co.	Aero, The	Midland Rubber Co. Ltd.
31	Wright & Ditson	Agrippa	Agrippa Golf Ball Co.
3T0	Taylor, Alex	Agrippa No. 2	Agrippa Golf Ball Co.
444	U.S. Royal	Air-Flite	Spalding & Bros., A.G.
5-5	Holmac	Ajax	Midland Rubber Co. Ltd.
75 Floater	Wright & Ditson	Ajax Bramble	Midland Rubber Co. Ltd.
A1 (Black)	Gutta Percha Co.	Ajax Special	Midland Rubber Co. Ltd.
A1 (Red)	Gutta Percha Co.	Alexandra	
A1 Special	Gutta Percha Co.	Allan	Robertson, Allan
Ace	Taylor, Alex	Allaway	Padon, A & D
Ace	Northington Rubber Co.	Allied 162	Allied Golf Co.
Ace (Gelatine Center)	Cochrane & Co., J.P.	Alpha	Gutta Percha Co.
Ace, New	Cochrane & Co., J.P.	Alpine, The	
Acleva	Forgan, R. & Son	Anderson	Anderson, Anderson & Anderson Ltd.
Acme	Wright & Ditson	Anderson White	Anderson, Anderson & Anderson Ltd.

BALL NAME	MAKER	BALL NAME	MAKER
Arcadia	Improved Golf Balls Co.	Browning KI	Burke Golf Co.
Aero	Holmac	Bruce Core	
Argus Bramble 27½	Argus Golf Ball and Requisites Mfg. Co.	Bullet	Forth Rubber Co.
Argus, Special	Argus Golf Ball and Requisites Mfg. Co.	Bullet Honor	Spalding & Bros., A.G.
Ariel	George Borgfeldt	Bullet	Wright & Ditson
Arlington	St. Mungo Mfg. Co.	Bunny	Goodrich Co., B.F.
Armstrong	Armstrong Tires	Burbank	Stow-Woodward
Army & Navy C.S.L. Driver	Army & Navy Stores	Burke 50-50	Burke Golf Co.
Army & Navy C.S.L. Furlong	Army & Navy Stores	Butchart S	Butchart-Nicholls
Army & Navy C.S.L. No. 1	Army & Navy Stores	C	Clydesdale Rubber Co.
Army & Navy C.S.L. No. 2	Army & Navy Stores	Camden, The	
Arrow	Goodyear Tire & Rubber Co.	Camperdown	
Ascot	Harlequin Ball & Sports Co.	Capon Heaton	Capon Heaton & Co. Ltd.
Athletae		Captain	St. Mungo Mfg. Co.
Atlantic Flyer		Carstairs	Carstairs
Atlas		Cestrian	
Atomic		Challenger	Cochrane & Co., J.P.
Auchterlonie Flyer	Improved Golf Balls Co.	Challenger	Slazenger & Sons
Auchterlonie St. Andrews		Challenger 26½	Cochrane & Co., J.P.
Autograph	Butchart-Nicholls	Challenger King	Cochrane & Co., J.P.
Avon	Avon India Rubber Co.	Challenger XL	Cochrane & Co., J.P.
Avon Deluxe	MacLend-Merritt	Challenger, Floating	Cochrane & Co., J.P.
Avon Junior	Avon India Rubber Co.	Challenger, R & A	Cochrane & Co., J.P.
Avon Rifled	Avon India Rubber Co.	Challenger, Red	Cochrane & Co., J.P.
Baby	Spalding & Bros., A.G.	Challenger, Star	Cochrane & Co., J.P.
Balfour	Lunn & Co.	Champion	Stow-Woodward
Banner	Stow-Woodward	Champion Flier	B.G.I.
Bantam	Goodrich Co., B.F.	Champion No. 2	Worthington Rubber Co.
Baylun		Champion No. 7	Worthington Rubber Co.
Be-Up		Chancellor	Rubastic Ltd.
Be-Up Dimple		Cheerio	Wilson Sporting Goods Co.
Beauty, Black	Worthington Rubber Co.	Chemico Triumph	County Chemical Co. (Chemico)
Beldam	Holmac	Chick	North British Rubber Co. Ltd.
Belgrave	Holmac	Chick, Big	North British Rubber Co. Ltd.
Bettorus	Bettorus Ltd.	Chick, Bramble	North British Rubber Co. Ltd.
Bird, Blue	Worthington Rubber Co.	Chick, Dimple	North British Rubber Co. Ltd.
Bird, The	Bird & Etherington	Chick, The Diamond	North British Rubber Co. Ltd.
Bird, Wee	Bird & Etherington	Chief, White	Wood-Milne, Ltd.
Birdeth, The	Bird & Etherington	Cinch	Spalding & Bros., A.G.
Birdie	Wright & Ditson	Circle (Black)	Wright & Ditson
Birds Eye	Spalding & Bros., A. G.	Circle (Blue)	Wright & Ditson
Bisk	Wright & Ditson	Circle (Green)	Wright & Ditson
Black and White	Spalding & Bros., A.G.	Circle (Purple)	Wright & Ditson
Black and White Dimple	Spalding & Bros., A.G.	Circle (Red)	Wright & Ditson
Blue Dot	Spalding & Bros., A.G.	Circle Floater (Orange & Black)	Wright & Ditson
Bob	County Chemical Co. (Chemico)	Clan	Clan Golf Club Co.
Bogey	Lehmann & Co., Ltd., R.	Click, Super	North British Rubber Co. Ltd.
Bogey, The	Seaman Manufacturing Co.	Climax	Craigpark Electric Cable Co.
Boodie	Slazenger & Sons	Clincher Cross	North British Rubber Co. Ltd.
Bramble	Midland Rubber Co. Ltd.	Clincher, The	North British Rubber Co. Ltd.
Bramble	Paxton, Peter	Clinker, Black	Spalding & Bros., A.G.
Bramble	Spalding & Bros., A.G.	Club	Wood-Milne, Ltd.
Bramble, Black	Yeoman, William	Cochrane Challenger	Cochrane & Co., J.P.
Brand		Cochrane's Patent	Cochrane & Co., J.P.
Bristol		Cochrane's Rex	Cochrane & Co., J.P.
		Cock of the Walk	
		Colonel 27 Dimple	St. Mungo Mfg. Co.
		Colonel 29 Dimple	St. Mungo Mfg. Co.

BALL NAME	MAKER	BALL NAME	MAKER
Colonel 30 Dimple	St. Mungo Mfg. Co.	Diamond Ring	Worthington Rubber Co.
Colonel 31 Dimple	St. Mungo Mfg. Co.	Diamond Stud	Worthington Rubber Co.
Colonel Click Dimple	St. Mungo Mfg. Co.	Diamond Black	Worthington Rubber Co.
Colonel 26½	St. Mungo Mfg. Co.	Diamond, White &	
Colonel 27	St. Mungo Mfg. Co.	Black	Lee & Underhill
Colonel, 29	St. Mungo Mfg. Co.	Diana	Wanamaker Co., John
Colonel, 31	St. Mungo Mfg. Co.	Dice	Worthington Rubber Co.
Colonel, Arch	St. Mungo Mfg. Co.	Dickson-Edinburgh	
Colonel, Blue Click	St. Mungo Mfg. Co.	Dictator	Rubastic Ltd.
Colonel, Bramble	St. Mungo Mfg. Co.	Dimple	Spalding & Bros., A.G.
Colonel, Click	St. Mungo Mfg. Co.	Dimple, Baby	Spalding & Bros., A.G.
Colonel, Crescent	St. Mungo Mfg. Co.	Dimple, Domino	Spalding & Bros., A.G.
Colonel, FS Ballbearing	St. Mungo Mfg. Co.	Dimple, Midget	Spalding & Bros., A.G.
Colonel, Green Star	St. Mungo Mfg. Co.	Dimple, Red and Black	Spalding & Bros., A.G.
Colonel, Heavy	St. Mungo Mfg. Co.	Dimple, The	Spalding & Bros., A.G.
Colonel, Little Bramble	St. Mungo Mfg. Co.	Dispatch	Park & Son, Wm.
Colonel, Little Crescent	St. Mungo Mfg. Co.	Distant	Paxton, Peter
Colonel, Patent	St. Mungo Mfg. Co.	Dollar	Goodyear Tire & Rubber Co.
Colonel, Perfect	St. Mungo Mfg. Co.	Domino Dimple	Spalding & Bros., A.G.
Colonel, Plus	St. Mungo Mfg. Co.	Domino, Orange	Spalding & Bros., A.G.
Colonel, Red Star	St. Mungo Mfg. Co.	Done-It, The	
Colonel, The	St. Mungo Mfg. Co.	Dorchester	Stow-Woodward
Colonel, White	St. Mungo Mfg. Co.	Dormie	Wright & Ditson
Comet	County Chemical Co. (Chemico)	Dormy	Crombie & Smith
Comet	Goodrich Co., B.F.	Dot & Dash	Harlequin Ball & Sports Co.
Commander	Burke Golf Co.	Dot, 38 Green	Alan Herbert & Greening
Commodore	Rubastic Ltd.	Dot, 38 Red	Alan Herbert & Greening
Compass Top Hole		Dot, Green	Wood-Milne, Ltd.
Conqueror	Scottish Golf Ball Mfg. Co. Ltd.	Dot, New Green	Helsby Co., The
Corker	Spalding & Bros., A.G.	Dot, Red	Golf Balls Ltd.
Cornet, Gold		Dot, Red	Helsby Co., The
Corona	Holmac	Dot, Red	Spalding & Bros., A.G.
Corona	McDaid, Martin	Dot, Red and Black	Spalding & Bros., A.G.
Corporal	St. Mungo Mfg. Co.	Dot, Yellow	Cochrane & Co., J.P.
Craigpark	Craigpark Electric Cable Co.	Double Duty 75	
Craigpark Special	Craigpark Electric Cable Co.	Dry Ice Center	MacGregor Golf Co.
Crescent, Gold	Kempshall Manufacturing Co.	Dubble Cover	MacGregor Golf Co.
Crescent, Gold Flat		Dunlop 162	Dunlop Tire & Rubber Co.
Bramble	Kempshall Manufacturing Co.	Dunlop 4	Dunlop Tire & Rubber Co.
Crest	Wilson Sporting Goods Co.	Dunlop Ball, The	Dunlop Tire & Rubber Co.
Cromith, The	Crombie & Smith	Dunlop England 5 5	Dunlop Tire & Rubber Co.
Cross, Black	Spalding & Bros., A.G.	Dunlop Foater	Dunlop Tire & Rubber Co.
Cross, Green	Slazenger & Sons	Dunlop Gold Cup	Dunlop Tire & Rubber Co.
Cross, Red	Slazenger & Sons	Dunlop Junior	Dunlop Tire & Rubber Co.
Crow	Holmac	Dunlop Maxfli (Black)	Dunlop Tire & Rubber Co.
Crown	Worthington Rubber Co.	Dunlop Maxfli (Blue)	Dunlop Tire & Rubber Co.
Custom	Butchart-Nicholls	Dunlop No. 31	Dunlop Tire & Rubber Co.
D.C.		Dunlop Orange Spot	Dunlop Tire & Rubber Co.
D.D.	Scottish Golf Ball Mfg. Co. Ltd.	Dunlop Warwick	Dunlop Tire & Rubber Co.
Daisy		Dunlop, The	Dunlop Tire & Rubber Co.
Darby Flyer	Associated Golfers Inc.	Dunlop, The New	Dunlop Tire & Rubber Co.
Dart, Blue	Holmac	Dunn, W.	Dunn, Willie Sr.
Dart, The	Holmac	Dura-Dist	Wilson Sporting Goods Co.
Davidson	Davidson Rubber Co.	Duralite	MacGregor Golf Co.
DeLuxe	County Chemical Co. (Chemico)	Dux	Edina Golf Ball Manuf. Co. Ltd.
Deuce	Worthington Rubber Co.	Dyna Flite	Spalding & Bros., A.G.
Diamond	Whitman & Barnes Mfg. Co.	E. Ray - Ganton	Edward Ray
Diamond A	Worthington Rubber Co.	Eagle	Reach, A.J.
Diamond King	Worthington Rubber Co.		

BALL NAME	MAKER	BALL NAME	MAKER
Eagle	Wright & Ditson	Furzedown	Paxton, Peter
Eaglet	McDaid, Martin	G. McHardy Special	
Eclipse	Currie & Co., William	Gem	
Eclipse, The	Wood-Milne, Ltd.	General	Rubastic Ltd.
Edinburgh		Gipsy	
Elastine	Improved Golf Balls Co.	Gladstone	Paxton, Peter
Elect 09	Byrne, F. A.	Globe	
Electronic	U.S. Royal	Glory	Spalding & Bros., A.G.
Eltham	Gutta Percha Co.	Glory Dimple	Spalding & Bros., A.G.
Endura		Glory Dimple	Spalding & Bros., A.G.
English	Paxton, Peter	Glory Dimple (Red Dot)	Spalding & Bros., A.G.
English Midget Dimple	Spalding & Bros., A.G.	Glory Dimple (White Dot)	Spalding & Bros., A.G.
Ensign	Edina Golf Ball Manuf. Co. Ltd.	Glory Dimple (Blue Dot)	Spalding & Bros., A.G.
Ensign, Red	Edina Golf Ball Manuf. Co. Ltd.	Glory Dimple Floater	Spalding & Bros., A.G.
Eureka	Gutta Percha Co.	Golf Bounder	
Eureka, The New	Gutta Percha Co.	Golfcraft	
Excello, The		Golfrite	
Exhibition		Goose, Gray	Baker & Bennett
Express (Dimpled)	Craigpark Electric Cable Co.	Goose, Gray	Huntington Manufacturing Co.
Fairfield	Spalding & Bros., A.G.	Gourlay, John	Bourlay, John
Fairway	U.S. Royal	Grand Slam Poweramic	
Falcon		Granton	Silvertown Co.
Far and Sure		Gravitator Flyer, The	Gravitator Golf Ball Co., The
Faroid		Gravitator, The	Gravitator Golf Ball Co., The
Farsure 27½	Lowne & Co., Donald	Grip, The	Selfridge's
Farsure Bramble	Lowne & Co., Donald	Gyroscope	Sperry
Farsure Grooved	Lowne & Co., Donald	Hagen	Young Co., L.A.
Farsure Meteor	Lowne & Co., Donald	Hagen Honey Boy	Young Co., L.A.
Farsure, New	Lowne & Co., Donald	Halley's Ball	Halley, J.B.
Fast N Slow	St. Mungo Mfg. Co.	Harlequin	Harlequin Ball & Sports Co.
Favourite	Redfern's Rubber Works Ltd.	Harlequin, Super	Harlequin Ball & Sports Co.
Fernie's Gem		Haskell	Goodrich Co., B.F.
Field	Unio Golf Ball Co.	Haskell Bramble	Goodrich Co., B.F.
Field Marshall Deluxe		Haskell Match	Goodrich Co., B.F.
Fife	St. Mungo Mfg. Co.	Haskell Mesh	Goodrich Co., B.F.
Final	Goodrich Co., B.F.	Haskell No. 10	Goodrich Co., B.F.
Fixby	Herd, Alex	Haskell Remade	Wayne Ball Co.
Flag Hi	Wilson Sporting Goods Co.	Haskell Royal	Goodrich Co., B.F.
Flash, Blue	Wanamaker Co., John	Haskell Streak	Goodrich Co., B.F.
Flash, Long	Wanamaker Co., John	Haskell, Regular	Goodrich Co., B.F.
Flash, Red	Wanamaker Co., John	Haskell, Scotch	St. Mungo Mfg. Co.
Flash, Yellow	Wanamaker Co., John	Haskin's 27½	
Flipoot	Improved Golf Balls Co.	Hawk, The New	North British Rubber Co. Ltd.
Floater	St. Mungo Mfg. Co.	Heather, White	
Floater Little Bramble	St. Mungo Mfg. Co.	Helsby	Telegraph Manufacturing Co. Ltd.
Flyer	Kempshall Manufacturing Co.	Helsby National	Helsby Co., The
Flyer	St. Mungo Mfg. Co.	Henley	Henley's Telegraphic Works Co. Ltd.
Flyer, White	Craigpark Electric Cable Co.	Henley B	Henley's Telegraphic Works Co. Ltd.
Flyer, White	Johnson, Joey	Hex	Martins-Birmingham Ltd.
Flyer, White	Lee Co., Harry C.	Hi Spot	North British Rubber Co. Ltd.
Flying Fox	Yeoman, William	Higgins Autograph, J.C.	Sears Roebuck & Co.
Flying K	Kroydon Co.	High Tensioned Rubber Core	Martins-Birmingham Ltd.
Flying Scotsman	Thornton & Co.	HM	Holmac
Forespot	Burke Golf Co.		
Forgan	Forgan, R. & Son		
Formby			
Forsyth	Boston Belting Co.		
Frost's Dormie			
Furlong			

BALL NAME	MAKER
Hol-Hi	Wilson Sporting Goods Co.
Hol-Hi 1.68	Wilson Sporting Goods Co.
Hol-Hi Thin Cover	Wilson Sporting Goods Co.
Homer	Edina Golf Ball Manuf. Co. Ltd.
Honor	Spalding & Bros., A.G.
Honour, The	Patrick, Alex
Hopper, The	
Hoylake	
Hunter	Hunter, Ramsay
Hutchison	Wilson Sporting Goods Co.
I.B.R. Co.	
I.G.B.	Improved Golf Balls Co.
Imp	Taylor, Alex
Imperial	Davega
Improved	
International	Ayres Ltd., F.H.
Iris	McDaid, Martin
Jack Rabbit	Goodrich Co., B.F.
Jack Rabbit	Huntington Manufacturing Co.
Jebob	
Jellicore	Improved Golf Balls Co.
JH	Holmac
Jim	Scottish India Rubber Co.
Jimmy Crane	A.M.C.
Johnnie Ball, The	
Jonny, The	Roger, James H.
Joyce	Bettorus Ltd.
Judge, The	St. Mungo Mfg. Co.
K-28	Wilson Sporting Goods Co.
Karifar	St. Mungo Mfg. Co.
Kempshall Flyer	Kempshall Manufacturing Co.
Kempshall Flyer Click	Kempshall Manufacturing Co.
Kempshall League	Kempshall Manufacturing Co.
Kiddy	Wood-Milne, Ltd.
King B	Worthington Rubber Co.
King Conqueror	Scottish Golf Ball Mfg. Co. Ltd.
King Dimple	Browning
King Mesh	Browning
Kite, Golden	Hutchison, Main & Co.
Kite, The New	North British Rubber Co. Ltd.
Knock Out	Edina Golf Ball Manuf. Co. Ltd.
Kro-Flite Dimple	Spalding & Bros., A.G.
Kro-Flite Mesh	Spalding & Bros., A.G.
Kroydon	Kroydon Co.
L.P.H.	Slazenger & Sons
Lady	Wood-Milne, Ltd.
Lady Burke	Burke Golf Co.
Lady Champion	Worthington Rubber Co.
League	St. Mungo Mfg. Co.
Leyland Birco	Leyland & Birmingham Rubber Co.
Leyland Flier	Leyland & Birmingham Rubber Co.
Link, The	Helsby Co., The
Lion	
Little Model, The	Miller & Taylor
Lowne's Special	Lowne & Co., Donald
Luck Repaired	Luck Golf Ball Co.
Lunar, The	Scottish Golf Ball Mfg. Co. Ltd.
Lynx	Silvertown Co.
Lynx Style	Wright & Ditson

BALL NAME	MAKER
M Recessed	Midland Rubber Co. Ltd.
Mail	Johnson, Frank A.
Major	St. Mungo Mfg. Co.
Manor Junior	Dunlop Tire & Rubber Co.
Manor, Red	Dunlop Tire & Rubber Co.
Manor, The	Dunlop Tire & Rubber Co.
Maponite	
Martins' Flyers	Martins-Birmingham Ltd.
Martins' Nipper	Martins-Birmingham Ltd.
Martins' Tube Core	Martins-Birmingham Ltd.
Marvel	Worthington Rubber Co.
Marzo	Martins-Birmingham Ltd.
Master	MacGregor Golf Co.
Matabie	
Match, The	Thornton & Co.
Maxim	Lee Co., Harry C.
Maxim	Scottish India Rubber Co.
McIntosh	
Melfort	Henley's Telegraphic Works Co. Ltd.,
Melville	
Mercury	Allied Golf Co.
Mercury	Redfern's Rubber Works Ltd.
Mersey, The	Helsby Co., The
Mesh	Taylor, Alex
Meteor	Goodrich Co., B.F.
Midget	Spalding & Bros., A.G.
Mirco Special	Millar, W.
Mitchell	
Mono	Craigpark Electric Cable Co.
Mono	Lee Co., Harry C.
Moose	Goodrich Co., B.F.
Mungay's Liquid Core	
Musselburgh	Clark, J & D
Mystery	Wanamaker Co., John
Mystery	Worthington Rubber Co.
N.B. Twin Dot	North British Rubber Co. Ltd.
National Floater	Wright & Ditson
Needled	Spalding & Bros., A.G.
New BGI	B.G.I.
Newton's Flyer	
Nimble	Dunlop Tire & Rubber Co.
Nimble	Spalding & Bros., A.G.
Nimble Bob	Midland Rubber Co. Ltd.
No. 29	Dunlop Tire & Rubber Co.
No. 31	Dunlop Tire & Rubber Co.
Nobby	U.S. Royal
Non Skid	Kempshall Manufacturing Co.
Norka	Whitman & Barnes Mfg. Co.
Nova	
O.K.	Redfern's Rubber Works Ltd.
O.K.D.	Lee Co., Harry C.
Ocobo	Halley, J.B.
Olympian	
Olympic	Ayres Ltd., F.H.
One Up	St. Mungo Mfg. Co.
Opal	Metropolitan Golf Ball Co.
Opresto, The	B.G.I.
Orient, The	
Orme	Orme Co., The

BALL NAME	MAKER	BALL NAME	MAKER
Ortogo	Improved Golf Balls Co.	Ring, Black	Capon Heaton & Co. Ltd.
Ortogo Singer	Improved Golf Balls Co.	Ring, Blue	Capon Heaton & Co. Ltd.
Orton		Ring, Green	Capon Heaton & Co. Ltd.
Osprey, The	North British Rubber Co. Ltd.	Ring, Red	Capon Heaton & Co. Ltd.
Oswald	St. Mungo Mfg. Co.	Ring, Yellow	Capon Heaton & Co. Ltd.
P.D.Q.	Lee Co., Harry C.	Rocket	Wisden, John
P.R.E.S.		Rompo	
Pal	Metropolitan Golf Ball Co.	Round Up	Wilson Sporting Goods Co.
Par King		Royal	Park & Son, Wm.
Paragon		Royal	Unio Golf Ball Co.
Paragon (Bramble)	Cochrane & Co., J.P.	Royce	
Paragon (Hoylake)	Cochrane & Co., J.P.	S'Vale (Springvale)	Hutchison, Main & Co.
Paragon (St. Andrews)	Cochrane & Co., J.P.	S'Vale Eagle	Hutchison, Main & Co.
Paragon (Westward Ho)	Cochrane & Co., J.P.	S'Vale Flacon	Hutchison, Main & Co.
Paramont A & B Mesh		S'Vale Hawk	Hutchison, Main & Co.
& Dimple	Reach, A.J.	S'Vale Kite	Hutchison, Main & Co.
Paramont C & F	Reach, A.J.	S'Vale Rampant	Hutchison, Main & Co.
Paterson	Paterson	S. 27½	
Patrick	Patrick, Alex	Sam Snead 100	Wilson Sporting Goods Co.
Penfold 75	Penfold	Sandy Horne	
Penfold Floater	Penfold	Sarazen 50	Wilson Sporting Goods. Co.
Penfold Hearts	Penfold	Sarazen Autograph	Wilson Sporting Goods Co.
Pentland	Silvertown Co.	Scarlet Runner	McDaid, Martin
Perfect	Perfect Golf Ball Co.	Scarlet Sikh, New	McDaid, Martin
Perfection	Paxton, Peter	Scoto	Criagpark Electric Cable Co.
Persevere	Leith Golf Ball Co.	Scottish	Scottish India Rubber Co.
PGA	Worthington Rubber Co.	Scottish King	St. Andrews Golf Co. Ltd.
PGA Championship	Acushnet	Scotty	Goodrich Co., B.F.
PGA Championship	Spalding & Bros., A.G.	Scotty	Worthington Rubber Co.
Philpot		Scout	British & Colonial
Phoenix 27½		Seamless Champion	Worthington Rubber Co.
Pimpernil	McDaid, Martin	Sexton, The	
Pin	Johnson, Frank A	Sharp	Sharp, John
Pinehurst	Wilson Sporting Goods Co.	Siemens	
Play-Off	Rawlings	Silk Pneumatic	Goodyear Tire & Rubber Co.
Pluto	Martins-Birmingham Ltd.	Silkor	Edina Golf Ball Manuf. Co. Ltd.
Pneumatic, The	Goodyear Tire & Robber Co.	Silver Black Dot Mesh	Silvertown Co.
Popular	County Chemical Co. (Chemico)	Silver King	Silvertown Co.
Practice	Spalding & Bros., A.G.	Silver King (Black Dot)	Silvertown Co.
Prestwick		Silver King 1	Silvertown Co.
Pro	Acushnet	Silver King Face	Silvertown Co.
Pro	Cupples	Silver King HV	Silvertown Co.
Pro Royal	U.S. Royal	Silver King Plus	Silvertown Co.
Pro, New	Cochrane & Co., J.P.	Silver Prince	Silvertown Co.
Professional		Silvertown	Goodrich Co., B.F.
Profs Ball - Red Dot	Cochrane & Co., J.P.	Silvertown Bramble	Silvertown Co.
Pulford 27½		Silvertown No. 4	Silvertown Co.
Queen B	Worthington Rubber Co.	Silvertown No. 5	Silvertown Co.
R-34	Wilson Sporting Goods Co.	Silvertown No. 9	Silvertown Co.
Radio, The	McDaid Martin	Silvertown Snippet	Silvertown Co.
Ram		Silvertown, New	Silvertown Co.
Ray, Blue	Acushnet	Silviator	Silvertown Co.
Ray, Gold	Acushnet	Sidar	Paxton, Peter
Re-Made	Paxton, Peter	Six Pole Bramble	Kempshall Manufacturing Co.
Record	Wright & Ditson	Skipper	Rubastic Ltd.
Record WD	Wright & Ditson	Skor	Improved Golf Balls Co.
Regina	Cochrane & Co., J.P.	Slazenger	Slazenger & Sons
Rhino	Cupples	Slazenger	Slazenger & Sons
Rifled Ball	Henry, Alexander	Snead Blue Ridge	Wilson Sporting Goods Co.

BALL NAME	MAKER	BALL NAME	MAKER
Snipe	Johnson, Frank A.	Supreme	Ayres Ltd., F.H.
Sovereign	Silvertown Co.	Sweet Shot	Worthington Rubber Co.
Spalding 50	Spalding & Bros., A.G.	Swipe, The	Yeoman, William
Spalding 60	Spalding & Bros., A.G.	Tam O'Shanter	
Spalding Blue Circle	Spalding & Bros., A.G.	Taplow	Wanamaker Co., John
Spalding Bob	Spalding & Bros., A.G.	Taylor's Winner	
Spalding Bramble	Spalding & Bros., A.G.	Tee	Johnson, Frank A.
Spalding Dot (Red Dot)	Spalding & Bros., A.G.	Thirty and Forty	Spalding & Bros., A.G.
Spalding Executive	Spalding & Bros., A.G.	Thistle	B.G.I.
Spalding Floater	Spalding & Bros., A.G.	Thistle, Scotch	
Spalding Floater	Spalding & Bros., A.G.	Thompson Agrippa	
Spalding No. 1	Spalding & Bros., A.G.	Thornton	Thornton & Co.
Spalding No. 2	Spalding & Bros., A.G.	Tiger	U.S. Royal
Spalding Practice	Spalding & Bros., A.G.	Times	Park & Son, Wm.
Spalding White Bramble	Spalding & Bros., A.G.	Titleist	Acushnet
Spalding White	Spalding & Bros., A.G.	Tom Morris, The	
Spalding White (Black Dot)	Spalding & Bros., A.G.	Tom Tit	Halley, J.B.
Spalding White (Red Dot)	Spalding & Bros., A.G.	Tommy Armour	Worthington Rubber Co.
		Topflite	Spalding & Bros., A.G.
Spalding White (With Click)	Spalding & Bros., A.G.	Tournament	Goodrich Co., B.F.
Spalding Wizard	Spalding & Bros., A.G.	Traveller	Unio Golf Ball Co.
Special	County Chemical Co. (Chemico)	Traveller, Little	Unio Golf Ball Co.
Special	U.S. Royal	Trey	Worthington Rubber Co.
Special	Wood-Milne, Ltd.	Trophy	Cupples
Spot, Black	Miller & Taylor	True Blue	U.S. Royal
Spot, Green	Miller & Taylor	Truflite	Slazenger & Sons
Spot, Red	Harlequin Balal & Sports Co.	Tube Core	Martins-Birmingham Ltd.
Spot, Superior Brown	Miller & Taylor	Tucker's Crypt	
Spun Latex	U.S. Royal	Unique	
ST	North British Rubber Co. Ltd.	V	Dunlop Tire & Rubber Co.
St. Mungo Water Core	St. Mungo Mfg. Co.	VAC	Dunlop Tire & Rubber Co.
St. Mungo, New	St. Mungo Mfg. Co.	Vaile	Ayres Ltd., F.H.
St. Nicholas	W & R	Vardon Flyer	Spalding & Bros., A.G.
Staff	Wilson Sporting Goods Co.	Varsity White	Anderson, Anderson & Anderson Ltd.
Stag	Goodrich Go., B.F.	Varsity White	Anderson, Anderson & Anderson Ltd.
Standard	Worthington Rubber Co.	Victor	Scottish India Rubber Co.
Star	Currie & Co., William	Victor	Wright & Ditson
Star Flyer		Victor 30	Wright & Ditson
Star, Black	Golf Balls Ltd.	Victor, New	Scottish Golf Ball Mfg. Co. Ltd.
Star, White	Improved Golf Balls Co.	Viper	Viper Golf Ball Co.
Starflite	Spalding & Bros., A.G.	Viper Bramble	Viper Golf Ball Co.
Steel Center	Kroydon Co.	Vulcan, White	Improved Golf Balls Co.
Stella	County Chemical Co. (Chemico)	W	Wilson Sporting Goods Co.
Steven		Walker Cup	Wilson Sporting Goods Co.
Stoughton	Silvertown Co.	Warwick	
Stoughton	Stoughton Rubber Co.	Wembly	
Stranahan	MacGregor Golf Co.	Whip	Stow-Woodward
Streak	Goodrich Co., B.F.	Whippets	Reach, A.J.
Student	Scottish Golf Ball Mfg. Co. Ltd.	White Dot	Spalding & Bros., A.G.
Sturrock, The		White Prince	Rubastic Ltd.
Success	Wilson Sporting Goods Co.	Whiz	Goodrich Co., B.F.
Success, New	Unio Golf Ball Co.	Why Not	Henley's Telegraphic Works Co. Ltd.,
Sunbeam	Capon Heaton & Co. Ltd.	Wicklow Rebuilt	
Super	Acushnet	Wiffie Cox	Worthington Rubber Co.
Super Radio	Wanamaker Co., John	Willie Dunn's Stars and Stripes	Whitman & Barnes Mfg. Co.
Super Whippet		Wilson Bramble	Wilson Sporting Goods Co.
Superflite (Blue)	North British Rubber Co. Ltd.	Winchester Duac	
		Witch	Spalding & Bros., A.G.

BALL NAME	MAKER		BALL NAME	MAKER
Wm. Park	Park & Son, Wm.		Wyatt	
Wonder	Redfern's Rubber Works Ltd.		Xpres	Slazenger & Sons
Wonder	Wanamaker Co., John		Zenith	Lehmann & Co., Ltd., R.
Woodley Flier	Hyde Imperial Rubber Co.		Zenith Orb	Lehmann & Co., Ltd., R.
Worthington	Worthington Rubber Co.		Zeppelin	Capon Heaton & Co. Ltd.
Worthington White	Worthington Rubber Co.		Zodiac	Martins-Birmingham Ltd.
Wright & Ditson	Wright & Ditson		Zodiac Pearl	Martins-Birmingham Ltd.
Wright-Ditson Selected	Wright & Ditson		Zome	Martins-Birmingham Ltd.
Wright-Ditson Bramble	Wright & Ditson		Zome One	Martins-Birmingham Ltd.

Several Presidents of the United States have had specially marked golf balls made as souvenirs for their golfing friends. The unsigned ball was issued during the Carter term, as he was not a golfer like the other three.

CHAPTER 3 — CLUBS

Golf clubs are by far the most sought after items in the hobby of golf collecting. Much of the fascination with old golf clubs is due to the close relationship of the golfer with his clubs. When on the course, the golfer will go for hours without losing contact with his clubs. For when he is not swinging at a ball, his clubs are either on his shoulder or within arm's reach.

The collector enjoys holding, swinging or just looking at clubs of earlier times. There is a nostalgic bit of history behind the collectible clubs and each collector thrives upon it in his own particular way. Some seek out clubs from a particular era, while others look for clubs made with a certain feature or those made by a particular maker.

Old golf clubs have personalities to which the modern day collector can relate. A fancier of early wooden clubs made in the nineteenth century is usually a student of the golf history of that period. He can admire a long nose putter made in the late 1840's and imagine how Allan Robertson may have used a similar one to putt the feather ball in a match against one of the Dunn brothers. Similarly, a collector of wooden shafted clubs marvels at the skill of Bobby Jones and how he mastered the use of the hickory shaft.

The history of the game, the talents of the clubmakers, and the thrill of acquiring good clubs combine to make golf club collecting a hobby of immense pleasure and satisfaction. This chapter is designed both to educate the novice collector and also to enhance the knowledge of the experienced collector. A list of all important makers and sellers of collectible clubs is presented, followed by detailed information about the makers and their clubs.

Club Categories Used In This Chapter

LN = LONG NOSE WOODS: PRE 1890

Long nose woods were used during the era of the feather ball and during most of the gutta percha ball era. These hand crafted clubs have long curving faces, a poured lead backweight, a piece of horn on the leading edge of the sole, and large leather grips on the wood shafts.

VALUE: $200 to $1000 (some over $2000)

Long Nose Wood

Early Iron

EI = EARLY IRONS: PRE 1890

Early irons were hand forged by makers with blacksmithing experience and were not always marked with the maker's name. They have large hosels and are often concave in the hitting area.

VALUE: $100 to $1000 (some over $2000)

SH = SCARED, SOCKET HEAD AND SIMILAR WOODS: 1890-1915

The scared head clubs of this period were shorter in head length and had much thicker necks than the long nose clubs. Most of the early clubs with drilled necks did not have the soleplates that later clubs would possess. One piece clubs, early aluminum headed clubs, and those with forked and other unusual means of splicing are included in this category.

VALUE: One piece wood: $600 to $1000 (some $1400)
     Scared head: $50 to $125 (some $300)
     Aluminum Head: $75 to $250
     Early socket head: $10 to $30 (some $50)

Scared Head

Machine Age Iron

MI = MACHINE AGE IRONS: 1890-1920

When the mechanized method of drop forging was developed, the manufacture of iron headed clubs greatly increased. These irons are finely finished and are stamped with the names or marks of the makers and sellers. Most were not chrome plated, even though some makers were doing this at the turn of the century. The earlier clubs of this period had smooth faces without markings.

VALUE: Smooth face, 1890-1905: $15 to $100 (some $150)
     Marked face: $5 to $20 (some $50)

WS = OTHER WOOD SHAFTED CLUBS: PRE 1935

There are many wood shafted clubs which do not fit into the above categories. These are the clubs which appeared in matched sets of the 1920's and 1930's. They were stamped with club names or were numbered similar to modern clubs. The iron heads were chrome plated and were marked with information about their being "matched" or "harmonized".

VALUE: Numbered irons: $3 to $15 (some $50)
     Matched iron sets: $50 to $100 (some $200)
     Woods: $3 to $10 (some $20)
     Matched wood sets: $15 to $30 (some $60)

Wood Shaft

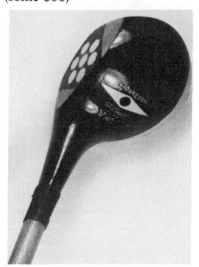

Wood Shaft

Steel Shaft

SS = STEEL SHAFTED CLUBS: 1915-1945

The only collectible steel shafted clubs made prior to 1945 are the ones with unusual shafts and faces. Of the thousands of clubs which make up this category, only a few have any value.
VALUE: $1 to $15 (some over $50)

CC = CLASSIC CLUBS: POST 1945

Of the clubs manufactured after 1945, only a select few are considered to be classics. These clubs are highly collectible for both display purposes and for use on the golf course. Some of the other modern steel shafted clubs may be semi-classic due to their high quality and playability, however the rest of the clubs of this period are classified as simply "used clubs."
VALUE: Drivers: $100 to $300
       Wood sets: $250 to $600 (some over $900)
       Iron sets: $150 to $250 (some over $500)
       Wedges: $50 to $150
       Putters: $50 to $250 (some over $500)

The values shown above for golf clubs are ranges for typical examples in good condition. The upper end of the price range applies to unique clubs, special patented clubs and to those which are of important historic value. Clubs in very poor condition will be valued lower than the prices shown. The reader should be reminded that millions of wood shafted golf clubs have been made and that only a small percentage are considered to be valuable.

The authors are greatly indebted to Pete Georgiady and Bob Hansen for their assistance in compiling the sections in this chapter on wood shafted and long nose clubs. The resources and knowledge of these two club collectors provided valuable information concerning the history of the clubmakers.

BRIEF GLOSSARY OF GOLF CLUB TERMS

ADJUSTABLE HEAD

Several companies have devised metal clubheads with a method for varying the loft. In theory, the golfer could use one of these clubs for an entire round. These clubs were deemed illegal in 1956 when the United States Golf Association ruled that the player could not change the playing characteristics of a club during a round.

ANTI-SHANK

These clubs had unusual bent hosels designed to eliminate lateral shots. They were popular from 1890's through the 1920's using either the Smith or Fairlie patents.

CLEEK

A long faced iron headed club with little loft in which the upper and lower edges of the face run almost parallel to each other. Other irons of the wood shaft era are sometimes incorrectly referred to as cleeks.

FAIRLIE PATENT

Fairlie invented an anti-shank iron which had the leading edge of the club ahead of the hosel.

FORGED

The method by which bars of iron were formed into clubheads through a heating and hammering process. Prior to the 1890's, heads were hand forged on an anvil with a hammer, while almost all later clubs were made with a mechanized drop forge.

HORN

A piece of ram's horn commonly affixed to the sole at the leading edge of the early wooden headed clubs to prevent wear or damage. In later years, the horn was replaced with vulcanite or other synthetic material. Eventually, this practice was discontinued as face inserts and metal soleplates became standard.

HOSEL

The upright portion of an iron headed club into which the shaft is inserted. A metal pin is usually inserted through the walls of the hosel in order to secure the shaft in place.

INSERT

A material which was inlaid into the striking area of a wooden headed club, for extra protection or for repair of the clubface.

IRON

Obviously denotes a metal headed blade type club, but specifically refers to the primitive iron head clubs prior to 1830 which were called "irons" by the early players.

JIGGER

A general purpose club often used for chipping onto the green made with the loft of a four or five iron.

LISTING (or RIND)

The fabric or paper material applied under the outer layer of the grip in order to build up thickness.

NICKING

The knurled or indented area on an early iron club around the top of the hosel for the purpose of preventing the wooden shaft from turning. By 1910, the markings were purely ornamental.

PUTTING CLEEK

A lofted blade putter.

RUT IRON (or RUT NIBLICK)

A small headed iron similar to the earlier track iron. See: TRACK IRON.

SAMMY

A round back pitching club from the wood shaft era similar to the jigger.

SCARE (or SPLICE)

The angled joint used to join the shaft to the head on early woods prior to the advent of the socket head.

SEELY PATENT

This patent featured strap-like extensions from an iron head which were fastened to the shaft rather than using a conventional hosel.

SMITH PATENT

The Smith anti-shank patented iron featured a bent hosel configured so that the golfer had no way to hit the ball in the socket.

SOCKET

Usually refers to the drilled hole of a wooden headed club into which the shaft is inserted. On an iron club, this features is the hosel. Also refers to the area on an iron clubhead between the hosel and the face.

SPLICE

See SCARE

SPRING FACE IRON

These irons had a thin steel face and cavity behind the hitting area for the purpose of giving a greater rebound to the ball.

TRACK IRON (or RUTTER)

A small headed iron used for extracting the ball from a wheel track or similar bad lie. These early irons had extremely small faces with disproportionately large hosels. By 1885, the heads became larger and were referred to as a rut iron or rut niblick.

WARRANTED HAND FORGED

A phrase often found on 20th century iron clubs which usually were not entirely hand made, since true hand forging was not commonly used after the 1890's.

WHIPPING

The twine or thread wrapped spirally around the joint of a wooden headed club to help secure the shaft to the head. Whipping was also used to hold the ends of a wrapped leather grip in place and for repairs to split wooden shafts.

The following is an amusing description of a wooden club written by Sir W. G. Simpson in 1887 in his most enjoyable book, *The Art of Golf*.

Nearly everyone carries a play club, an instrument consisting of many parts. It has no legs, but a shaft instead. It has, however, a toe. Its toe is at the end of its face, close to its nose, which is not on its face. Although it has no body, it has a sole. It has a neck, a head and clubs also have horns. They always have a whipping, but this has nothing to do directly with striking the ball. There is little expression in the face of a club. It is usually wooden; sometimes, however, it has a leather face. Clubs, without being clothed, occasionally have lead buttons, but never have any button-holes. Clubs' heads are some black, some yellow, but colour is not due to any racial difference. From this description it will be easy to understand, without a diagram, what a club is like.

INTRODUCTION TO CLUB MAKERS LIST

The following list of clubmakers is a comprehensive index of known clubmakers and also those individuals or companies responsible for the sale of substantial numbers of golf clubs. Golf history books, periodicals, lists of club collections, consultations with club collectors, and the authors' research enabled this list to be formed.

Any golf club dating before 1950 was probably made by or sold by one of these firms. An astonishing fact is that fewer than ten of the 500 + makers on the list were responsible for making over eighty per cent of the clubs sold during this period.

Excluded from the list are the names of over 400 golf professionals and others who, at one time or another, might have stamped their names on the heads of clubs which they had purchased from someone else. The section in this chapter on maker's marks explains how to identify some of the actual makers of clubs which may also bear a club professional's name. The reader will find that some of the makers on the list were also professionals, but are included due to their prominence as players, clubmakers or club designers.

GUIDE TO THE COLUMNS ON THE MASTER LIST

MAKER — This term refers to clubmakers, club assemblers, manufacturers, prominent retailers and golf professionals particularly known for their sale of golf clubs. **The names of the many golf professionals who sold clubs which bore their name but were made by others have generally been excluded from the list.**

LOCATION — The place or places where the maker produced the majority of his clubs. Many of the makers held positions at several clubs throughout their career or had more than one retail location.

CATEGORY — Each maker produced clubs which could be classified into one or more of the following classifications:

LN = Long Nosed: pre 1890
 EI = Early Irons: pre 1890
SH = Scared or early Socket Head, and other woods: 1890-1915
MI = Machine age Irons: 1890-1920
WS = Other Wood Shafted clubs: pre 1935
 SS = Steel Shafted clubs: 1915-1945
CC = Classic Clubs: post 1945

LIST — The makers of most interest to the collector are listed alphabetically in greater detail on one of four areas of this chapter. If one of the following designations appears by a maker's name, the reader may consult one of the following lists:

1 = Long Nose Woods: pre 1890	See page 72
2 = Early Iron: pre 1890	See page 83
3 = Wood Shafted Clubs: 1890-1935	See page 97
4 = Classic Clubs: post 1915	See page 128

MASTER LIST OF CLUBMAKERS AND SELLERS

LIST	MAKER	LOCATION	CATEGORY	LIST	MAKER	LOCATION	CATEGORY
	Abercrombie & Fitch Co.	New York & Chicago	WS, SS	1	Allan, John	Preswick & Westward Ho!	LN
	Abraham & Straus, Inc.	New York	WS, SS		Allied Golf Company	Chicago	WS, SS
	Acme Golf Co.	Glasgow	WS, SS		Allinone Adjustable Club Corp.	San Francisco	SS
	Acushnet	New Bedford, MA	CC		Altman & Co., B.	New York	WS
	Adam, John	Leven	LN		Alverson Sales Co.	Bloomington, IL	WS
	Adams, David	Glasgow	MI	3	Ampco	Milwaukee	WS
	Adamson, Jimmy	Duddington	WS		Anderson & Blythe	St. Andrews	WS, MI
	Adjustable Golf Club Co.		WS	3	Anderson & Gourlay	St. Andrews	MI
	Aitken, Alex	Gullane	SH, WS	3	Anderson & Sons, D.	St. Andrews	MI
	Aitken, John	Portrush, Ireland	SH				

LIST	MAKER	LOCATION	CATEGORY	LIST	MAKER	LOCATION	CATEGORY
	Anderson & Sons, Robert	St. Andrews & Edinburgh	MI		Barnes, Jim	New York	WS
3	Anderson, Alex	Anstruther	MI		Batley, James	London	WS
3	Anderson, Anderson & Anderson Ltd.	London	MI		Bayonne Casting Co.	New Jersey	WS
1	Anderson, David, Jr.	St. Andrews	LN	4	Beckley Ralston Co.	Chicago	WS, SS
1	Anderson, David, Sr.	St. Andrews	LN	1	Beetson	London	LN
	Anderson, J.H.	Edinburgh	WS	1	Bell, Frank		LN
2,3	Anderson, James	Anstruther	EI, MI		Benetfink Co.	London	WS
1	Anderson, James (Jamie)	St. Andrews	LN		Berry, Jack Co.	London	WS
	Anderson, James R.	Grandmere	WS	1	Beveridge, James	St. Andrews & New York	LN
3	Anderson, Joe	Perth	MI		Bishop and Gourlay	Edinburgh	WS
	Anderson, Willie	London & St. Andrews	SH, MI		Bishop and Hendry	Leith	WS
	Andrews, Bob	Perth	LN		Bisset, Andrew	North Berwick	WS
	Anson, J.T.		WS		Black, John	Carnoustie & California	WS
	Arden	New York	WS	3	Blaisdell, Fred	London	MI
1,3	Army & Navy Stores, Ltd.	London	LN, MI, SS		Bradbeer, A.R.	Barnham and Berrow	WS
	Arroflite	Baltimore	WS		Bradbeer, Charles	Hendon, Middlesex	WS
3	Ashford, W. & G.	Birmingham	MI	3	Bradbeer, James	London	MI
	Ashland Mfg. Co.	Chicago	WS	3	Braddell & Son, Joseph	Belfast	MI
	Atco - (See Taylor & Co., Alex)				Braid, James	Walton Heath	SH, MI
3	Auchterlonie & Crosthwaite	St. Andrews	MI		Braid, William	St. Andrews	MI
3	Auchterlonie, D & W	St. Andrews	MI, WS	3	Brand, Charles	Carnoustie	MI
1	Auchterlonie, David	St. Andrews	LN		Braw Laddie Golf Co.	Oakland, CA	WS, SS
	Auchterlonie, Laurie	St. Andrews	SS	3	Breeze, G. Brodie	Glasgow	MI
3	Auchterlonie, Tom	St. Andrews	WS, SS		Breitenbach, William F.	Philadelphia	WS
1	Auchterlonie, Willie	St. Andrews	LN		Bretson and Brews	South Africa	WS
	Auld, Robert	Dunbar	WS		Bridgeport Athletic Mfg. Co.	Jersey City, NJ	SH, WS
	Aveston, Willie	Northampton	WS		Bridgeport Gun Implement - (See BGI)		
1,3	Ayres, F. H.	London	LN, MI, WS		Brine Co., James W.	Boston and Cambridge	SH, MI
3	B.G.I.	Bridgeport, CT	SH, MI	4	Bristol	Melrose Park, IL	SS, CC
	Bailey and Izett	Philadelphia	SS		Bristol-Horton Mfg. Co.	Connecticut	SS
1	Bailey, Andrew	Edinburgh	LN	1	Brodie, Robert	Anstruther	EI
	Bain, Colin	Edinburgh	WS	3	Brodie & Sons, R.	Anstruther	MI, WS
1	Ballantyne	London	LN	3	Brougham, Reginald	London	MI
1	Ballantyne, William, Jr.	Leith	LN		Brown & Smart	Chicago	MI
1	Ballantyne, William, Sr.	Leith	LN		Brown, George Daniel	St. Andrews	LN
	Ballingalls	Edinburgh	SH		Buchanan, John & Co.	Edinburgh	SH, MI
	Baltimore Putter Co.	Baltimore	WS	3	Buhrke Co., R.H.	Chicago	WS
1	Baptie, Thomas	St. Andrews	LN		Bullock's	Los Angeles	WS
				3,4	Burke Golf Co.	Newark, OH	WS, SS, CC

LIST	MAKER	LOCATION	CATEGORY	LIST	MAKER	LOCATION	CATEGORY
	Burke Golf-Ten Co.	Newark, OH	WS	3	Condie, Robert	St. Andrews	MI
3	Bussey and Co., George	London	MI		Cook, Ray	San Antonio, TX	CC
	Butchart Co., Cuthbert S.	London & Rye, NY & Glennbrook, CT	SH, WS, SS	1	Cossar, David	Leith	LN
1	Butchart, John	Carnoustie	LN	1	Cossar, Simon	Leith	LN
3	Butchart-Nicholls Co.	Glenbrook, CT	WS, SS		Cowan Co.	Sunderland	WS
	Byrnes, Eugene	Carmel, CA	WS	3	Craigie, J and W	Montrose	MI
	Caird, Adam	Hexham, England	MI	3	Crawford, McGregor and Canby (see MacGregor)	Dayton, OH	SH, MI
	Campbell, Colin	Leith	LN		Crighton, J & R	Carnoustie	WS
3	Cann and Taylor	London & New Jersey	MI, SH	4	Crisman, Otey	Selma, AL	CC
	Capitol Golf Co.	London	SS		Croke, Jack	Chicago	WS
	Cargills	Glasgow	WS		Crosthwaite and Lorimer	St. Andrews	SH, MI
	Carr, Jack	Finchley	WS		Crowley, James	Elie and Earlsferry	LN
2,3	Carrick, F & A	Musselburgh	EI, MI		Cumberland Hickory Co.	Nashville, TN	WS
3	Carruthers, Thomas	Edinburgh	MI		Cunningham, W.	Edinburgh	SH, MI
	Carson Pirie Scott & Co.	Chicago	WS, SS		Cupples Co.	St. Louis	WS
	Carstairs	Leven	SH, WS, SS		Curtis, H. L.	Bournemouth	SH, WS
	Castle Golf Club Co.	London	WS, SS		Cuthbertson, William	Leith	LN
	Catlin, A.	Wheathampstead	WS	1	Dalgleish, Joseph	Nairn	LN
	Cawsey, Harry	Skegness	WS		Dalrymple, David	St. Andrews	SH, MI
	Clephane, David	Leith	LN		Dargie, Bert	Memphis	SS
	Clephane, John	Leith	LN		Dargo, J. H.	Edinburgh	MI
	Chestney, H.R.	Burnham	WS		Davega	New York	WS
3	Clan Golf Club Co.	London & Scotland	MI	1	Davidson, Robert	Montrose	LN
3	Clark, J and D	Musselburgh	MI		Davis, W. F.	Newport, RI	SH
	Clucas, J.	Bamford	WS	1	Day, Walter D.	Musselburgh	LN
	Coburn, George	West Bromwich	WS		Dayton, Co., The	Minneapolis	WS, SS
3	Cochrane's Ltd.	Edinburgh	MI		Denholm, A.	Hove	WS
1	Cockburn	London	LN	1	Denholm, David	Edinburgh	LN
	Cogswell and Harribon	London	WS		Dick, David	St. Andrews	LN
	Collins, Richard	Leith	LN	1	Dickson, Alexander	Edinburgh	LN
	Collins, Willie	Long Island & Staten Island	SH, MI	1	Dickson, Andrew	Leith	LN
	Colt Golf Co.	New York	WS, SS	3	Dickson, J. & A.	Edinburgh	MI
	Coltart, Alex	Perth	SH	1	Dickson, John	Leith	LN
	Coltart, Frank	Perth	SH, MI	1	Dickson, John	Edinburgh	LN
	Colver Golf Co.	Dallas	WS		Doig, R.	Musselburgh	MI
	Comb, Thomas	Edinburgh	LN		Doleman, Frank	Edinburgh & Musselburgh	SH, MI
3	Compagnie Brunswick Francais, La	London & Paris	MI		Donaldson Mfg. Co., Ltd.	Glasgow	WS, SS
	Comston, Archie	Manchester	WS	1	Donaldson	London	LN
				3	Donaldson, James	Glasgow	MI

LIST	MAKER	LOCATION	CATEGORY
1	Dow, Robert	Montrose	LN
3	Draper & Maynard Co.	Plymouth, NH	WS
	Dubow Co., J.A.	Chicago	WS
	Duncan, George	Cheshire	WS
	Dunlop	Greenville, SC	SS
1	Dunn, Jamie	North Berwick & Blackheath	LN
	Dunn, John Duncan	New York	SH
	Dunn, Seymour	New York	SH
1	Dunn, Thomas	Wimbledon & Musselburgh	LN
1	Dunn, W. and J.		LN
	Dunn, Willie, Jr.	Musselburgh	SH, MI
1	Dunn, Willie, Sr.	North Berwick & Blackheath	LN
	Duo-Set Golf Co.		WS
	East, J. Victor	England & USA	WS, SS
	Ebb Golf Co.	Bristol, CT	WS
	Faith Mfg. Co.	Chicago	WS
	Far and Sure Golf Club Co.	Edinburgh	SH, MI
1	Fergie, Willie	Edinburgh	LN
	Feltham's		SH, MI
1	Ferguson, Bob	Musselburgh	LN
	Fernie, Peter	Ipswich	SH, MI
1	Fernie, Willie	Dumfries & Troon	LN, SH, MI
	Filene's Sons Co., Wm.	Boston	WS
	Findlay, Alexander H.	U.S.	MI
	First Flight	Chattanooga, Tenn.	SS
	Fletcher, W.	Luton, Torquay	WS
1, 3	Forgan & Son, Ltd., Robert	St. Andrews	LN, SH, EI, MI, WS
1,3	Forgan, Andrew	Glasgow	LN, SH, MI
1,3	Forrester, George	Elie & Earlsferry	LN, SH, MI
	Forrester, James	Earlsferry	SH, MI
	Forth Rubber Company	Edinburgh	MI
	Fortnum & Mason	London	WS
	Foster Brothers	Ashbourne, England	WS
	Foulis, James and David	Chicago	MI
1	Frier, William	Edinburgh	LN
	Fulford, H.	Hawksworth, Yorks	WS
	Gadd, George	Wrexham	WS
3	Galloway, Thomas	Pittenweem	MI
	Gassiat, Jean	Chantilly & Biarritz, France	WS

LIST	MAKER	LOCATION	CATEGORY
	Gemmell, F.	Edinburgh	MI
	General Electric	Long Island	SS
1,3	Gibson, Charles	Musselburgh & Westward Ho!	LN, SH, MI
3	Gibson, William	Kinghorn	MI, WS
	Gilchrist, Alex	Blackheath	WS, SS
	Gimbel's	New York	WS
	Glasgow Golf Company	Glasgow	MI
	Globe-Union Mfg. Co.	Milwaukee	SS
	Goldsmith Sons Co., P.	Cincinnati	WS, SS
	Golf Company	St. Andrews	SH, MI
	Golf Depot	Edinburgh	WS
	Golf Engineering Co.	Newton, MA	WS
3	Golf Goods Mfg. Co.	Binghampton, NY	SH, MI
	Golf Shop	Chicago	MI, WS
	Golf Specialty Mfg. Co.	Baltimore	WS
	Goodrich	Multiple locations	WS
	Goudie and Co., James T.	Edinburgh	MI
3	Gourlay, James Jr.	Carnoustie	MI
3	Gourlay, James Sr.	Carnoustie	MI
	Gourlay, Walter	St. Andrews	MI
	Grand Leader	St. Louis	MI
	Grant Co., W.T.	New York	WS
	Gray & Co., E.	Cambridge	SH, MI
	Gray & Co., H.J.	London	SH, MI
2, 3	Gray, John	Prestwick	EI, MI
3	Great Lakes Golf Co.	Milwaukee	WS, SS
	Greig, Alexander	St. Andrews	LN
	Grondahl, Joseph	New York	SS
	Grosse Ile Putter Co.	Detroit	WS, SS
	Hackbarth, Otto	Cincinnati	MI
4	Hagen, Walter — (See Young, L.A.)	Detroit	SS WS
3	Halley & Co., James B.	London	MI, WS
	Harrod's	London	WS
3	Harrower, Thomas	Carnoustie	MI
	Hartley & Graham Co. — (See BGI)	New York	SH, MI
3	Hemming's Golf Co.	Redditch, Worcestershire	MI
3	Hendry and Bishop	Edinburgh & Leith	MI
	Henry, Hugh	Rye, Sussex	WS

LIST	MAKER	LOCATION	CATEGORY
	Hepburn, Jas.	New York	WS
	Herd and Herd	Chicago	SH, MI
	Herd and Yeoman	Chicago	MI, WS
	Herd, Alex	London & St. Andrews	WS
	Herd, David	Littlestone on Sea	WS
3	Hewitt, Walter Reynolds	Carnoustie	MI
	Hiatt & Co.	Birmingham	MI
	Hill, John	Warlingham	WS
3,4	Hillerich & Bradsby Co.	Louisville, KY	WS, SS, CC
	Hills, Percy	Manchester	SH, MI
4	Hogan Co., Ben	Fort Worth, TX	CC
	Holmac, Inc.	New York	WS
1	Hood, Thomas	Musselburgh & Dublin	LN, SH
	Hooker, E.A.	London	SH, MI
	Horne & Co., Joseph	Pittsburgh	WS
	Horton Mfg. Co.	Bristol, CT	WS, SS
	Horton, Chester	Chicago	WS
	Horton, Waverly	Chicago	WS
	Hunt Mfg.	Westboro, MA	MI
1	Hunter, Charlie	Prestwick	LN
	Hutchings, W.	Derby	WS
1	Hutchison, James H.	North Berwick	LN, MI
	Ife, A.J.	Tilford, The Hague	MI
	Illini	Springfield, IL	WS
	Imperial Golf Co.	Sunderland, England	MI
	Indestro Mfg. Co.	Chicago	WS
	Izett, George	Philadelphia	CC
1	Jackson, A.	St. Andrews	LN
1	Jackson, John	Perth	LN
	Jarvis and White	Chicago	WS
	Jeffries, Walter	Saunton & Birmingham	MI
3	Johnson Ltd., Frank A.	London	MI
	Johnson, Claude		WS
	Johnstone Brothers	Tayport	WS
	Jordan Marsh Co.	Boston	WS, SS
	Kaufmanns, (The Big Store)	Los Angeles	WS
	Kenny, Dan	Kirkudbright	WS
	Kilrymont Golf Club Mfg.	St. Andrews	SH, MI
	King, Irving	Shreveport, LA	CC

LIST	MAKER	LOCATION	CATEGORY
	Kirk, R.W.	Wallasey	SH, WS
1	Kirk, Robert, Jr.	Blackheath & St. Andrews	LN
1	Kirk, Robert, Sr.	St. Andrews	LN
	Kismet		WS
	Klin Bros. Golf Mfg. Co.	Homewood, IL	WS
	Klin-McGill Golf Co.	Valparaiso, IN	WS
	Kraeuter Golf Co.	Newark, NJ	WS
3	Kroydon Co.	Maplewood, NJ	**WS, SS**
	Laclede Brassworks	St. Louis, MO	WS
	Lamb, Henry	Royal Wimbledon	SH
1	Lang, Bennett	Perth	LN
	Lard, Allan		SS
	Lee & Underhill	New York	WS
3	Lee, Harry C.	New York	MI, WS
	Leslie and Co., R. & W.	Chicago	SH, MI
3	Letters and Co., John	Glasgow	MI, WS, SS
3	Leyland & Birmingham Rubber Co.	Birmingham & Glasgow	WS
	Lillywhite Frowd and Co., J.	London	SH, MI
	Littledale, N.	Houghton, MI	WS
1	Lloyd, Joseph	Hoylake & Pau, France	LN
	Logan, Hugh	Wimbledon	SH, MI
	Low and Hughes	New York	WS
	Low, David	St. Andrews	MI
	Lowe and Campbell	Chicago	WS
3	Lumleys, Ltd.	Glasgow	MI
	Lunn and Company	London	MI
	Lytton and Sons, Henry C.	Chicago	MI, WS
	Mac and Mac	Oak Park, IL	WS
	MacDonald	Musselburgh	WS
3,4	MacGregor Golf Co.	Dayton & Cincinnati	SH, MI, WS, SS, CC
	Mackay, D.	North Berwick	WS
	MacKenzie, T & G	Edinburgh	WS
	Macy & Co. Inc., R.H.	Riverside, NY	WS
	Manderson, Alexander	Dunbar	LN
	Manton and Co.	Calcutta	MI
	Mark Cross	New York	MI, WS

66

LIST	MAKER	LOCATION	CATEGORY	LIST	MAKER	LOCATION	CATEGORY
	Marling & Smith	Aberdeen	WS		Neaves, Charles	Leven & Lossiemouth	MI
	Martin Adjustable Club Co.		WS, SS		Neilson, Alexander	Leith	LN
	Martin and Kirkaldy	Edinburgh	MI		Neilson, R.	Musselburgh	MI
	Martin, R.B.	Edinburgh & Kirkaldy	WS		Neilson, Robert	Leith	LN
1	Martin, Robert	St. Andrews	LN		New York Sporting Goods Co.	New York	MI, WS
	Maxwell, Robert	North Berwick	WS	2,3	Nicoll, George	Leven	EI, MI, WS
1	Mayne, William	Edinburgh	LN		Nicolson Bros.	Anstruther	MI
	Mayo, Charles	Walton on Thames & New Jersey	WS	3	Nicolson, D.	Pittenweem	MI
	McDaid, Martin	Edinburgh	SH		North British Rubber Co., Ltd.	Edinburgh & Toronto	MI, WS
1	McDonald, Walter 'Watty'	St. Andrews & Perth	LN		Northwestern Golf Co.	Chicago	SS
1	McEwan, Douglas #1	Bruntsfield	LN		Novak Club	San Francisco	SS
	McEwan, Douglas #2	Musselburgh	SH, MI		Ogg, Willie	Worchester, MA	WS, SS
1	McEwan, James	Musselburgh & Edinburgh	LN, MI		Oke, J. H.	Sutton Coldfield	WS
1	McEwan, Peter #1	Bruntsfield	LN	3	Oke, W. G.	London	MI
1	McEwan, Peter #2	Musselburgh	LN	4	Palmer Company, Arnold	Chattanooga, TN	CC
	McEwan, Stewart	Pittsburgh	MI	3	Park & Son, W.	Musselburgh	MI
	McEwan, W.	Formby & Pittsburgh	SH, MI	1	Park, Mungo	Musselburgh	LN
	McGill Mfg. Co.	Valparaiso, IN	WS, SS	1,3	Park, Willie, Jr.	Musselburgh	LN, SH, MI
	McGregor, John	St. Andrews	SH, MI	1,3	Park, Willie, Sr.	Musselburgh	LN, EI
	McPherson, J.	Troon	MI		Parker, William	Carnoustie	MI
3	Millar, Charles L.	Glasgow	SH, MI	1,3	Patrick, Alex	Leven	LN, SH, MI, WS
	Mills, Sir William	Sunderland	MI, WS		Patrick, D.M.	Leven	MI, SH
	Miln, Henry D.	St. Andrews	LN	1	Patrick, John	Leven & Edinburgh	LN
	Mitchell and Ness	Philadelphia	WS		Paxton, James	Musselburgh & London	SH, MI
	Mitchells	Manchester	MI, WS	1	Paxton, Peter	Musselburgh & London	LN, SH, MI
	Montgomery Ward	Chicago	WS, SS		Penna Co., Toney	Jupiter, FL	SS, CC
1	Morris, George D.	St. Andrews	LN		Penney, Co., The J.C.	New York	WS, SS
1	Morris, J.O.F. (Jamie)	St. Andrews	LN		Pett, James	St. Andrews	LN
1	Morris, John (Jack)	St. Andrews & London & Liverpool	LN		PGA of America	Endorsed certain brands of clubs	
1	Morris, Tom, Jr.	St. Andrews	LN	1	Philp, Hugh	St. Andrews	LN
1,3	Morris, Tom, Sr.	St. Andrews	LN, MI		Ping	Arizona	SS
	Mules	Penarth, Wales	WS		Pirie, Alex	Glasgow	WS
1	Munro, Alexander	Aberdeen	LN		Playgolf, Inc.	Cleveland	WS
	Munro, J.	Wimbledon	WS	1	Poke	London	LN
	Murray, J.	Pitlochry	WS		Pope, W. R.	Chorlton	WS
	Murrie and Son	Methven, Scotland	MI				
	National Department Stores, Inc.	New York	WS, SS				

LIST	MAKER	LOCATION	CATEGORY	LIST	MAKER	LOCATION	CATEGORY
	Premier Golf Co.	Glasgow	WS	3	Sherlock, James	Oxford	MI
	Professional Golf Co.	Toronto	WS		Simmons Hardware Co.	St. Louis	MI, WS
	Pryde, Robert D.	New Haven, CT	WS		Simplex	London	SH
	Ram	Melrose Park, IL	SS		Simpson, Andrew	Aberdeen	WS
	Ramsbottom	Manchester	MI	1	Simpson, Archie	Carnoustie & Aberdeen	LN
	Randall, John	Bromley	WS	3	Simpson, J. & A.	Carnoustie & Edinburgh	SH, MI
	Rangefiner-Rapier	Glasgow	WS	1,3	Simpson, Robert	Carnoustie	LN, SH, MI
	Rawlings Mfg. Co.	St. Louis	SS	3	Slazenger and Son	London	SH, MI
	Rea, W.	Antrim, N. Ireland	WS	3	Slazenger Corp., Frank L.	London & New York	MI, WS, SS
3	Reach Co., A.J.	Philadelphia	WS		Smethwick Golf Co.	Birmingham	MI
	Renouf, T.G.	Manchester	MI, WS		Smith Sports Co., W.P.	London	WS
	Rigden, Francis E.	Garden City, NY	WS		Smith, E.	Halifax, England	MI
3	Ritchie, W.L.	London	MI		Smith, Kenneth	Kansas City, MO	SS
	Roberts Hughes Co.	Egypt	MI		Smith, MacDonald	Carnoustie	WS
	Robertson, Peter	Oakmont and Yahnundasis	WS		Somerville, Andrew	Dunbar	SH
	Robson, Fred	Bexhill	WS	3,4	Spalding & Bros., A.G.	Dysart & London & Chicopee, MA	SH, MI, WS SS, CC
	Rodwell Ltd., Chas. H.	London	WS	3	Spence & Gourlay	St. Andrews	MI
	Rollins & Parker	Redditch	MI, WS	3	Spence, James	St. Andrews	MI
	Ross & Sons, Wm.	Glasgow	MI, WS		Sports and Games Association	London	WS
	Royal Mfg. Co.	Toledo & Bowling Green	WS, SS		Sportsman's Emporium	Glasgow	WS
	Rustless Golf Club Co. (R.G.C. Co.)	Chicago	WS		Sprague & Co., C.S.	Boston	WS
1	Sandison, Ludovic	Aberdeen	LN	3	St. Andrew Golf Co.	Dunfermline and Glasgow	MI
	Saunders, Fred	London	WS	3	Stadium Golf Co.	London	WS
	Sayers & Sons, Bernard	Glasgow	WS, SS	3	Standard Golf Co. (Mills)	Sunderland	MI, WS
1, 3	Sayers, Bernard (Ben), Sr.	North Berwick	LN, MI		Stellite Golf Co.	Kokomo	WS
	Sayers, George T.	Merion, PA	WS		Stewart, Peter	Perth	SH
	Schavolite	New York	SS	3	Stewart, Tom, Jr.	St. Andrews	MI
	Schnectady Golf Club Co.	Schnectady, NY	WS	3	Stewart, Tom, Sr.	St. Andrews	EI
	Schmelzer Arms Co.	Kansas City, MO	WS	1	Strath, Andrew	Prestwick & St. Andrews	LN
	Schoverling Daly and Gales	New York	SH, WS	1	Strath, David	North Berwick	LN
	Schwartz, F.A.O.	New York	WS	1	Strath, George	St. Andrews & Troon & Brooklyn	LN
1,3	Scott, Andrew Herd	Elie & Earlsferry	LN, SH, MI		Streamline Co.	St. Louis	SS
	Scottish Golf Club Mfg. Co.	Edinburgh	MI		Stuart, John G.	Montrose & London	WS
	Sears Roebuck	Chicago	MI, WS		Swilcan Golf Co.	St. Andrews	SS
	Shakespeare	Columbia, SC	SS		Tait, Alexander	Musselburgh	MI
	Shaler Co., The	Milwaukee	WS, SS		Tait, David	St. Andrews	MI
	Shapleigh Hardware Co.	St. Louis	WS, SS				
1	Sharpe, Archibald	London	LN				
3	Shepherd, Alex	Iverness	MI				

LIST	MAKER	LOCATION	CATEGORY	LIST	MAKER	LOCATION	CATEGORY
	Tait, T.	Leven	MI	3	White, Jack	Sunningdale & North Berwick	MI, WS
	Taylor and Co., Alex	New York	WS, SS	2,3	White, Robert	St. Andrews & Cincinnati	EI, MI
	Tedder, W.	Nottingham	WS		Whiting, Samuel	Rotherham	WS
	Teen and Co., A.	London	SH, MI, WS		Williams and Co., J.H.	Brooklyn	MI
	Thistle Golf Co.	Glasgow	MI		Williamson, Tom	Nottingham	WS
	Thistle Putter Co.	New York	WS		Wilson & Co., Thomas E.	Chicago	WS, SS
	Thompson, Jamie	St. Andrews	WS	3,4	Wilson - Western	Chicago	WS, SS
	Thomson, Alex	Norbury	WS	3,4	Wilson Sporting Goods Co.	River Grove, IL	SS, CC
3	Thornton and Co., Ltd.	Edinburgh	MI	1	Wilson, James	St. Andrews	LN
	Tingey, Albert	St. Andrews & Watford	SH, WS	2,3	Wilson, Robert	St. Andrews	EI, MI
	Tollifson, A.C.	Lake Geneva, WI	MI	3	Wilson, Robert Black (R.B.)	St. Andrews	MI
	Toogood, A.H.	Chingford	WS	3	Wilson, William Christie	Hereford	MI
	Toogood, Walter	Ilkley	WS	2,3	Wilson, Willie	St. Andrews	EI, MI
3	Tooley and Sons, A.	London	MI		Wimbar Inc.	New York	WS
	Tru-Aim Manufacturing Co.	Chicago	WS	3	Winton & Co., William	Montrose	MI
	Tryon Jr. & Co., Edward K.	Philadelphia	SH, MI	3	Winton, James	Montrose	MI
	Tucker, Willie	New York	SH, MI		Wisden, John	London	SH, MI
	Tyler, Ralph G.	Muncie, IN & Cleveland	WS, SS	3,4	Wright & Ditson Co.	Boston	MI, WS, SS, CC
	U.S. Golf Mfg. Co.	Westfield, MA	WS, SS		Wynne, Philip	Mitcham	WS
	Union Golf Co.	Nashville	WS		Yeoman, William	St. Andrews & Chicago	MI
3	Urquhart's Ltd.	Edinburgh	MI		Yonkers Sporting Goods Co.	New York	WS
	Velaney	Chicago	MI		Youds, J.	Chislehurst	WS
	Venters, Jack	St. Andrews	WS	3	Young Co., L.A.	Detroit	WS, SS
3	Vickers, Ltd.	Sheffield	WS				
	Victor Sporting Goods Co.	Springfield, MA	SH, MI, WS				
	Von Lehrke and Antoine	Chicago	WS				
	Von Lengerke and Detmold	New York	WS				
	Vulcan Golf Co.	Portsmouth, OH	WS				
1	Walker, James	Edinburgh	LN				
	Walker, Thomas	St. Andrews	LN				
	Wannamaker Co., John	Philadelphia & New York	WS				
	Watt, James	North Berwick	MI				
	Watt, William	Perth	MI				
	Way, W.H. (Bert)	Detroit & Cleveland	MI				
	Webster, Harry	Salt Lake City	WS				
	Weir, A.N.	Aberdeen	WS				
	Wellington-Stone	Chicago	WS				
	Western Auto Supply	Los Angeles	WS, SS				

LN = Long Nosed: pre 1890
EI = Early Irons: pre 1890
SH = Scared or early Socket Head, and other woods: 1890-1915
MI = Machine age Irons: 1890-1920
WS = Other Wood Shafted clubs: pre 1935
SS = Steel Shafted clubs: 1915-1945
CC = Classic Clubs: post 1945

1 = Long Nose Woods: pre 1890 — See page 72
2 = Early Iron: pre 1890 — See page 83
3 = Wood Shafted Clubs: 1890-1935 — See page 97
4 = Classic Clubs: post 1915 — See page 128

LONG NOSE CLUBS

The earliest of the wooden headed golf clubs are known as long nose clubs. From the middle of the fifteenth century, through the feather ball era, to the late 1880's, this club design prevailed. It was the development of the gutta percha golf ball about 1850 that caused the gradual demise of these long, slender, shallow-faced clubs and initiated an evolution in clubmaking which led to the more compact design of the 1890's and beyond. While examples of the very old clubs are difficult to locate, there are enough in museums and private collections to learn about their nature and manufacture.

The heads of the clubs were made of wood from the apple, pear, thorn and beech trees. The wood was cut to align the grain with the bend in the neck of the club which was to be shaped. The heads, with their hooked faces, generally measured 5" in length, 2" in width, and 1" in depth. The back side of the head was hollowed out to accept lead for added weight. At the lower edge of the clubface, a 3" to 3½" strip of ram's horn was installed to protect the leading edge of clubhead from damage. In the neck of the club, the heel was cut on an angle to form a long surface suitable for splicing to the shaft. In the latter part of the nineteenth century, the clubheads were made in the same fashion, but the heads were much shorter in length. These are referred to as semi-long nose clubs and should not be confused with the pre 1890 woods discussed in this section.

Some of the early clubs have had an insert of hard material applied to the clubface. During this period the wooden clubs were not made with inserts, so the appearance of one usually signifies a repair to the face due to damage from play. These inserts were made of oil soaked leather, wood, horn and sometimes gutta percha. The colors of the clubheads range from black to various shades of brown. This is due to the different types of wood used, the finish which was applied, and exposure to the elements. The old finishes were usually resinous varnishes which darkened with age.

The shafts on these clubs were shaped with hand tools from several varieties of wood which included ash, greenheart, redheart, purpleheart, hazelwood, lancewood and hickory. Hickory proved to be the most suitable due to its superior playing qualities and abundance. The shaft was fitted to the head by means of a scare (or splice) joint. The head and shaft were shaped to matching angles so that when the joint was made, the clubhead would appear as a natural extension of the shaft. The completed scare was made secure with a bit of glue and then was whipped with pitch coated twine for added strength and protection. Finally, the head and scare were given a coat of varnish.

The grip was then carefully applied. First, a band of woolen material called a listing or rind was wrapped down the shaft to a length of 10 to 14 inches. It was held in place by applying pitch to the shaft before a carefully prepared length of sheepskin or other soft leather was wrapped on and secured with a few wraps of whipping twine. The grips on these long nose clubs were large in diameter by today's standards and the leather had a soft texture.

During the feather ball era, most golf shots were played with some type of wooden club. The few iron clubs in use were generally cumbersome in nature and were used only to extract the delicate feathery from the toughest of lies, or to play a shot which might severely damage a wooden headed club. The clubmakers fashioned several types of long nose clubs, each capable of producing a variety of shots. The better players had superior shotmaking skills which enabled them to manipulate the ball in a manner much different than the modern player with his matched set of clubs.

PLAY CLUBS or DRIVERS were equal to the number one wood in use today. Their shafts were long and tapering with lengths of up to 45". (Modern drivers measure 43".) They generally had little, if any, loft applied to the face. The GRASSED DRIVER was similar in nature, but had a bit more loft.

There were several clubs known for their scooping ability. They were the LONG SPOON, MID SPOON, SHORT SPOON, BAFFING SPOON, and WOODEN NIBLICK. The aforementioned clubs are listed in descending order by length of shot which they were capable of producing. As the loft increased on the various spoons, the shaft also became shorter as with modern clubs. The short spoon and wooden niblick also had stiffer shafts than the longer clubs. While the baffing spoon was considered the "shortest" spoon for general play, players also carried the wooden niblick which had a shorter head and was designed to extract the ball from the more difficult lies. By 1850, the wooden niblick had been replaced by the iron headed track iron.

Another type of wooden niblick appeared circa 1880. Clubmakers were looking for improvements in club design which would help the games of the increasing number of golfers. This new club, called a BRASSIE, resembled a long spoon, but had a stiffer shaft, more loft, and a shorter head. The most important improvement was the addition of a full brass soleplate which afforded desirable protection to the clubhead. Soon, every player carried one.

The final type long nose clubs which need to be discussed are the putters. The three styles were the DRIVING PUTTER, APPROACH PUTTER and GREEN PUTTER. The driving putter was a short stiff shafted club for hitting medium length shots into the wind. The approach putter resembled a putter for use on the green except that it had more loft and was intended for low run-up approaches.

The green putter had an upright lie and and was about 36" long. As the name implies, it serves the same purpose as the modern putter. The head was slightly shorter than many of the other long nose clubs and was noticeably heavier. While there were many examples of fine craftsmanship evident in the long nose clubs which still exist today, there are surprising few well designed and balanced putters.

The clubmakers responsible for producing these early woods were from one of two distinctly different backgrounds. The CRAFTSMAN was experienced as a cabinetmaker, wheelwright, bowmaker, fishing rod maker, or similar occupation. These makers had little to do with the playing of golf other than their clubmaking businesses. The more notable craftsmen were Hugh Philp, the McEwan family, Robert Forgan, J. Jackson, Alexander Patrick and James Wilson.

The other type of clubmaker was the PROFESSIONAL. The professional golfer in the eighteenth century had many responsibilities and in addition to playing in matches and tournaments, they were also greenkeepers, custodians and instructors. As a sideline, they would make wooden clubs. Some of the professionals who also excelled at clubmaking were Willie Park, Sr., Willie and Jamie Dunn and the Morris family.

Most of the clubmakers would stamp their name on their clubs before their sale, however this was probably not done on the very early clubs. An exception to this theory would be one of the very old wooden clubs on display at the Troon Golf Club in Scotland. This club was marked with a design and was one of several ancient clubs found in a boarded up cupboard along with a newspaper dated 1741. Whether or not the design was made by the clubmaker or user is not known. The collector should be aware that quite a few of the men referred to in history books as clubmakers were actually employees of clubmakers and did not make and sell clubs on their own. The following list includes all persons who were either bona fide clubmakers, or in the judgement of the authors, deserve to be included because of their historical significance.

Many of the early clubmakers were also professional golfers and frequently competed in challenge matches among themselves. Starting with the Open Championship in 1860, stroke play tournaments became more commonplace. The players shown here were the entrants in a tournament held on the Leith Links on May 17, 1867. From Left: Jamie Dunn, George Morris, Alexander Greig, Andrew Strath, David Park, Willie Dunn, "Old Tom" Morris, "Young Tom" Morris (rear), Bob Kirk, Willie Dow, Jamie Anderson.

This group of well known players participated in a tournament held at Troon Golf Club on August 26 and 27, 1886 to celebrate the opening of the new clubhouse.
Standing back row: George Strath, Jamie Anderson, Willie Park Jr., Peter Fernie, Dr. Highet (club secretary).
Second row, standing: Bob Kirk, Douglas McEwan, James Boyd, Bob Dow, Charles Thomson, Willie Campbell (seated).
Center, standing: J.O.F. Morris, "Old Tom" Morris.
Left group, seated, back row: Willie Anderson, David Leitch. Front row: Bob Simpson, Davie Ayton, Jack Simpson, A. Somerville, Ben Sayers, Willie Dunn, Bob Martin (lying down).
Right group seated: Davie Grant, James Mair, A. Monaghan, Wm. Cosgrove, Archie Simpson, J. Ferguson, Bob Ferguson (behind the club).

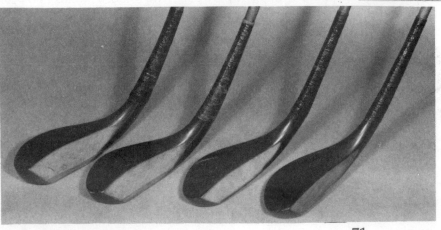

Set of clubs made by Hugh Philp in 1840.

"Old Fiery" was a well known caddy in the 19th century. He is best remembered for his association with Willie Park Jr.

Several types of grips were used on the early clubs:

#1: Grip made entirely of listing, with no leather.

#2: Experimental shaft made by a fishing rod maker.

#3: The most common of the grips seen on long nose clubs. The whipping along the length of the grip is occasionally seen.

#4: This grip was actually wrapped around the shaft and sewn in place.

This closeup of a Forgan play club clearly shows the horn, scare and whipping.

LIST #1 — LONG NOSE WOODS (LN DESIGNATION)

ALLAN, JOHN (1848-   )

Prestwick & Westward Ho! (Professional)

Produced Long Nose Clubs: 1867-1890. Stamped with: "J. Allan"

Allan is recognized for his durable, well made clubs.

ANDERSON, DAVID, JR. (1847-1912)

St. Andrews (Craftsman)

Produced Long Nose Clubs: 1875-1890. Stamped with "D. Anderson"

He operated a firm circa 1892 as D. Anderson & Sons with his five sons.

Anderson club made towards the end of the long nose club era. (David Anderson, Jr.)

'Old Da' with his familiar snack cart on the Old Course at St. Andrews. (David Anderson, Sr.)

ANDERSON, DAVID. SR. (1821-1901)

  St. Andrews (Professional)

  Produced Long Nose Clubs: 1845-1875. Stamped with: "D. Anderson"

  Known as 'Old Da', he was a ballmaker and also keeper of the green at St. Andrews for the four years during the 1850's prior to the return of Tom Morris. Anderson is believed to have been responsible for the double green concept at the Old Course. He was the father of David and Jamie and was a common figure around St. Andrews for many years. Most of the clubs marked "D. Anderson" were made by Junior as Old Da was not a serious clubmaker.

ANDERSON, JAMES (JAMIE) (1842-1905)

  St. Andrews (Professional)

  Produced Long Nose Clubs: 1865-1890. Stamped with: "J. Anderson"

  Jamie was the Open Champion in 1877, 1878 and 1879. He was the eldest son of Old Da and operated his business as J. Anderson & Sons. His son, James, continued on in business with David Blythe after his death.

ARMY & NAVY STORES LTD.

  London (Retailer)

  Produced Long Nose Clubs: 1870-1890. Stamped with: "Army & Navy"

  A retailer of golf equipment including long nosed clubs made by Forgan.

AUCHTERLONIE, DAVID (1865-   )

  St. Andrews (Craftsman)

  David was in partnership with his brother, Willie. He probably made some long nose clubs after working as an apprentice to Forgan.

AUCHTERLONIE, WILLIE (1873-1963)

  St. Andrews (Professional)

  Willie originally was an apprentice in Robert Forgan's clubmaking shop and probably learned the craft of long nose clubmaking there. After winning the Open in 1893, he left Forgan and started making clubs on his own. In 1895 Crosthwaite joined him and they started the firm of Auchterlonie & Crosthwaite. Then in 1897, when Crosthwaite left the firm to start up Crosthwaite & Lorimer, the firm of D. & W. Auchterlonie was established with his brother, David.

  There is an example of a long nose club which was probably made by Willie, however it was possibly made as a replacement.

AYRES, F. & H.

  London (Retailer)

  Produced Long Nose Clubs: 1880-1890. Stamped with "F. H. Ayres"

  They were sporting goods retailers who offered a line of golf items which were probably made by other firms and marked with their name.

BAILEY, ANDREW

  Edinburgh (Craftsman)

  Produced Long Nose Clubs: 1735.

  A letter dated June 20, 1735 makes reference to the purchase of clubs from Bailey at Bruntsfield Links.

BALLANTYNE

  London (Craftsman)

  Produced Long Nose Clubs: 1815-1817.

  He was employed by the Blackheath Golf Club as both a clubmaker and caretaker and probably did not mark his clubs.

BALLANTYNE, WILLIAM SR. (1793-1845)

  Leith and Musselburgh (Craftsman)

  Produced Long Nose Clubs: 1818-1845. Stamped with "Ballantyne"

  Ballantyne was a clubmaker to the Company of Edinburgh Golfers and the Thistle Club from 1818-1834 and then moved to Musselburgh.

BALLANTYNE, WILLIAM JR. (1826-1851)

  Musselburgh (Craftsman)

  Produced Long Nose Clubs: 1843-1851. Stamped with: "Ballantyne"

  He took over his father's business and then died shortly thereafter.

BAPTIE, THOMAS (1861-   )

St. Andrews (Craftsman)

Produced Long Nose Clubs: 1880-1890.

Baptie was employed by Forgan and probably made clubs under his own name.

BEETSON

London (Craftsman)

Produced Long Nose Clubs: Circa 1823.

Beetson was employed by the Blackheath Golf Club as a clubmaker and caretaker.

BELL, FRANK

(Professional)

Produced Long Nose Clubs: 1840-1890. Stamped with "F. Bell"

Only a few clubs by Bell exist, one of which is on display at the USGA Museum and Library.

BEVERIDGE, JAMES (1852-1899)

St. Andrews (Professional)

Produced Long Nose Clubs: 1870-1890. Stamped with: "J. Beveridge"

He learned the trade from Tom Morris. A competitive golfer, he emigrated to the United States and Shinnecock Hills G.C. in 1894.

BUTCHART, JOHN (1854-   )

Carnoustie (Craftsman)

Produced Long Nose Clubs: 1875-1890. Stamped with "Butchart"

Clubs by Butchart exist today and appear to be well designed and constructed.

COCKBURN

London (Craftsman)

Produced Long Nose Clubs: 1817-1823.

He was employed by the Blackheath Golf Club as a clubmaker and caretaker.

COSSAR, DAVID (1788-1816)

Leith (Craftsman)

Produced Long Nose Clubs: 1810-1816. Stamped with "D. Cossar"

David was the son of Simon who carried on his father's business.

COSSAR, SIMON (1766-1811)

Leith (Craftsman)

Produced Long Nose Clubs: 1785-1811. Stamped with: "S. Cossar"

Cossar was one of the earliest clubmakers whose clubs exist today.

DALGLEISH, JOSEPH (1860-   )

Nairn (Professional)

Produced Long Nose Clubs: 1880. Stamped with: "J. Dagleish"

Dalgleish primarily made semi-long nose clubs, however he was in business at the very end of the long nose era.

DAVIDSON, ROBERT (1801-1875)

Montrose (Craftsman)

Produced Long Nose Clubs: 1825-1870. Stamped with: "R. Davidson"

He was one of the better clubmakers of the feathery period.

DAY, WALTER D. (1837-   )

Edinburgh (Craftsman)

Produced Long Nose Clubs: 1860-1890. Stamped with: "W. D. Day"

Day was a craftsman who continued his trade by making socket headed clubs in the 20th century.

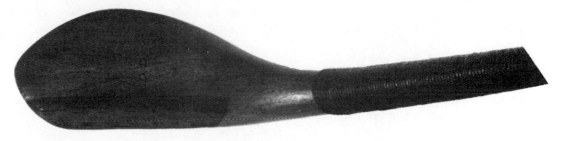

Mid Spoon made by W. D. Day and later repaired with a leather insert.

DENHOLM, DAVID (-1820)
>Edinburgh (Craftsman)
>Produced Long Nose Clubs: 1809-1920.
>>Denholm was the clubmaker to The Burgess Company of Golfers from 1809-1820.

DICKSON, ALEXANDER (1861-1926)
>Edinburgh (Craftsman)
>Produced Long Nose Clubs: 1883-1890. Stamped with: "J & A Dickson"
>>He was in business with his brother, John.

DICKSON, ANDREW (1665-1753)
>Leith (Craftsman)
>Produced Long Nose Clubs: 1690-1753. Stamped with: "A.D."
>>There is conflicting information as to whether this was the Dickson who forecaddied for James II, Duke of York hundreds of years ago. It is assumed that clubs marked 'A.D.' can be attributed to Dickson, however this cannot be confirmed.

DICKSON, JOHN (1710-1755)
>Leith (Craftsman)
>Produced Long Nose Clubs: 1730-1755.
>>One of the many Dicksons reported to have made clubs.

DICKSON, JOHN
>Edinburgh (Craftsman)
>Produced Long Nose Clubs: 1880-1890. Stamped with: "J & A. Dickson"
>>He was in business with his brother, Alexander.

DONALDSON
>London (Craftsman)
>Produced Long Nose Clubs: 1800-1815.
>>Donaldson was employed by the Blackheath Golf Club as a clubmaker and caretaker.

DOW, ROBERT (1832-1909)
>Montrose (Professional)
>Produced Long Nose Clubs: 1850-1890. Stamped with: "R. Dow"
>>Dow was quite active in match play competition and was also the Keeper of the Green at Royal Albert Club.

DUNN, JAMIE (1821-1871)
>Musselburgh and London (Professional)
>Produced Long Nose Clubs: 1840-1871. Stamped with: "J. Dunn" or W & J Dunn"
>See Willie Dunn.

DUNN, THOMAS (1849-1902)
>Musselburgh, Wimbledon & Other (Professional)
>Produced Long Nose Clubs: 1870-1890. Stamped with: "T. Dunn"
>>The son of Willie, Tom crafted well designed clubs. He later became a golf course architect and was responsible for the design of over 130 courses worldwide.

DUNN, WILLIE, SR. (1821-1878)
>Musselburgh and London (Professional)
>Produced Long Nose Clubs: 1840-1878. Stamped with: "WM. Dunn" or "W & J Dunn"
>>The Dunns were golf professionals, famous for their playing prowess, and were first ballmakers to W & J Gourlay in Musselburgh. They also made clubs with their own mark. Willie moved to Blackheath in 1851, where they used the mark, "W & J Dunn".

FERGIE, WILLIE (1856-1924)
>Edinburgh (Craftsman)
>Produced Long Nose Clubs: 1875-1890. Stamped with: "Fergie"
>>Fergie also had a later mark in an oval shape.

FERGUSON, ROBERT (1846-1915)

Edinburgh (Professional)

Produced Long Nose Clubs: 1865-1890. Stamped with: "R. Ferguson"

He was Open Champion in 1880, 1881, 1882 and lost the 1883 championship in an 18 hole playoff with Willie Fernie. Ferguson was also the Keeper of theGreen at the Musselburgh Links.

FERNIE, WILLIE (1858-1924)

Dumfries & Arder & Troon (Professional)

Produced Long Nose Clubs: 1878-1890. Stamped with: "W. Fernie"

Willie was a fine clubmaker and one of five golfing brothers.

FORGAN, ANDREW (1868-1890)

Perth & Glasgow (Professional)

Produced Long Nose Clubs: 1868-1890. Stamped with: "A. Forgan"

The younger brother of Robert Forgan, Andrew was the Keeper of the Green at the Royal Perth Golfing Society. He moved to Glasgow in 1882 to open a clubmaking shop.

FORGAN, ROBERT (1824-1900)

St. Andrews (Craftsman)

Produced Long Nose Clubs: 1856-1890. Stamped with: "R. Forgan" until 1863 when he added the Prince of Wales Plume.

Forgan began as an apprentice to his uncle, Hugh Philp, and took over the business in 1856. He prolonged the fine clubmaking tradition of Philp and was appointed the official clubmaker to the Prince of Wales (later King Edward VII) in 1863. When the prince became king, Forgan changed his mark to the crown.

FORRESTER, GEORGE (1847-1930)

Elie and Earlsferry (Craftsman)

Produced Long Nose Clubs: 1860-1890. Stamped with: "G. Forrester"

While he did make long nosc clubs early in his career, Forrester's real fame came after the turn of the century as a socket head clubmaker.

FRIER, WILLIAM (1842-   )

Edinburgh (Craftsman)

Produced Long Nose Clubs: circa 1860.

Very little information can be found about Frier, except that examples of his work do exist.

GIBSON, CHARLES (1864-1937)

Musselburgh (Craftsman)

Produced Long Nose Clubs: 1882-1890. Stamped with: "C. Gibson"

Gibson began his career as an apprentice to Willie Dunn, Sr. at North Berwick. From 1888 until 1937, he was employed as professional and clubmaker at Royal North Devon Golf Club at Westward Ho! Gibson was considered a master clubmaker.

HOOD, THOMAS (1843-1909)

Musselburgh (Craftsman)

Produced Long Nose Clubs: 1865-1890. Stamped with: "T. Hood"

Hood used several stamps throughout his career, the most noteworth being in large script. His clubs were made to high standards.

HUNTER, CHARLIE (1837-1921)

Prestwick (Professional)

Produced Long Nose Clubs: 1860-1890. Stamped with: "C. Hunter"

Hunter took over as professional at Prestwick after Old Tom Morris returned to St. Andrews. Hunter's son was married to Tom Morris' daughter.

HUTCHISON, JAMES H. (1847-1912)

North Berwick (Craftsman)

Produced Long Nose Clubs: 1860-1890. Stamped with: "Hutchison"

Hutchison is best known for his later successes as a maker of patent clubs in the early 20th century.

JACKSON, A.

St. Andrews (Craftsman)

Produced Long Nose Clubs: 1875-1890. Stamped with: "A. Jackson"

Jackson received his early training from Tom Morris and made only a small quantity of clubs with his own stamp.

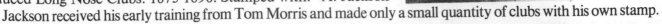

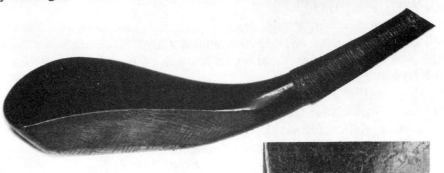

Short Spoon made by John Jackson.

JACKSON, JOHN (1805-1878)

Perth (Craftsman)

Produced Long Nose Clubs: 1825-1872. Stamped with: "Jackson"

Jackson's early clubs were unusually large in size. He was a superb craftsman comparable to Hugh Philp and Douglas McEwan.

KIRK, ROBERT, JR. (1845-1886)

St. Andrews and London (Professional)

Kirk was a noted player who was the open runner-up to young Tom Morris in 1870 and to Jamie Anderson in 1878, both of whom were three time winners.

KIRK, ROBERT, SR. (1810-1891)

St. Andrews (Craftsman)

Produced Long Nose Clubs: 1840-1890. Stamped with: "R. Kirk"

There is little information available on Kirk except the inclusion of his name in several directories of the mid 1800's.

LANG, BENNETT (1849-1913)

Perth (Craftsman)

Produced Long Nose Clubs: 1868-1890. Stamped with: "B. Lang"

Ben Lang worked under Tom Morris, Jamie Anderson, Douglas McEwan, Mungo Park, Alexander Patrick, Robert Forgan and Willie Fernie. He was a superb craftsman and was known to duplicate the work of others.

LLOYD, JOSEPH

Hoylake and Pau, France (Professional)

Lloyd was the first professional at the popular Pau Resort in the south of France. He was the winner of the third U.S. Open Championship in 1897.

MARTIN, ROBERT (1855-1917)

St. Andrews (Professional)

Produced Long Nose Clubs: 1880-1890.

Martin, the Open Champion in 1876 and 1885, made clubs in the shop of Tom Morris. He played in numerous challenge matches in the 1870's and 1880's.

MAYNE, WILLIAM

Edinburgh (Craftsman)

Produced Long Nose Clubs: 1600.

Mayne was appointed Bower, Spearmaker and Clubmaker to King James I according to C.B. Clapcott, a golf historian of the early 20th century.

McDONALD, WALTER (WATTY) (1836-   )

Perth and St. Andrews (Craftsman)

Produced Long Nose Clubs: 1856-1890. Stamped with: "W. McDonald"

He learned the trade in St. Andrews and went to Perth by 1867. He produced well made clubs in the style of the master craftsman of the feathery period.

THE OLDEST BUSINESS IN THE TRADE.

EST. 1770.

D. McEWAN & SON.

Golf Club & Ball Makers,

MUSSELBURGH,

SCOTLAND.

Simple and straightforward, this McEwan ad tells it all.

J. Mc EWAN.

McEWAN, JAMES   (1747-1800)

Bruntsfield (Craftsman)

Produced Long Nose Clubs: 1770-1800. Stamped with: "J. McEwan" and a Thistle

He founded the family clubmaking business in 1770 which continued for five generations. James was a joiner and cartwright by trade. All of his clubs bore a thistle stamp above his name making him one of the few makers to have decorative marks at the time.

McEWAN, PETER #1 (1781-1836)

Bruntsfield (Craftsman)

Produced Long Nose Clubs: 1800-1836. Stamped with: "McEwan"

Peter continued James McEwan's (his father) business and removed his father's initial from the mark. The thistle stamp was still used, but not with any regularity. By the 1820's, he was known to have had three apprentices.

McEWAN, DOUGLAS #1 (1809-1886)

Bruntsfield and Musselburgh (Craftsman)

Produced Long Nose Clubs: 1836-1886. Stamped with: "McEwan"

Douglas moved the family business to Musselburgh in 1847 following the shift of golfing activities to that locale. He was the son of Peter and is recognized as one of the finest clubmakers of all time, along with Philp and Jackson.

McEWAN, PETER #2 (1834-1895)

Musselburgh (Craftsman)

Produced Long Nose Clubs: 1855-1890. Stamped with: "McEwan"

Peter was the son of Douglas, grandson of Peter, and great grandson of James. As the game expanded, so did his staff. However, in the 1880's, he was reluctant to follow the trend toward mechanization.

MORRIS, GEORGE D. (1819-1888)

St. Andrews (Professional)

Produced Long Nose Clubs: 1840-1863. Stamped with: "G. Morris"

George was the older brother of Old Tom and often his partner in early matches. He went to Carnoustie to make clubs, but left the golf business in 1863 to work for W & R Chambers, an Edinburgh publisher. There are not very many examples of his work.

Jamie Morris is seen with his father, Old Tom, in their shop in the late 1890's. Note the gutty balls 'seasoning' on the shelf.

MORRIS, J.O.F. (JAMIE) (1856-1906)

St. Andrews (Professional)

Produced Long Nose Clubs: 1875-1890. Stamped with: "T. Morris"

Jamie was the son of Old Tom and produced clubs under his father's mark.

MORRIS, JOHN (JACK)

St. Andrews and Liverpool (Professional)

Produced Long Nose Clubs: 1869-1890. Stamped with: "J. Morris"

Jack was the son of George and nephew of Old Tom. He was the first professional at Hoylake, a position he held for 60 years while producing many clubs.

MORRIS, TOM, JR. (1851-1875)

St. Andrews (Professional)

No examples are known, but Young Tom probably worked in his father's shop. He was the first to win three successive Open Championships in 1868, 1869 and 1870. He made the use of lofted irons popular and died at the early age of 24 of a broken heart after his wife's death.

MORRIS, TOM, SR. (1821-1908)

St. Andrews and Prestwick (Professional)

Produced Long Nose Clubs: 1845-1890. Stamped with: "T. Morris"

Old Tom began as a ballmaker under Allan Robertson, became a greenkeeper, clubmaker and outstanding player. Open Champion in 1861, 1862, 1864 and 1867. Morris opened his clubmaking business in St. Andrews in 1867, employed several workers and made many fine clubs!

MUNRO, ALEXANDER (1796-1847)

Aberdeen (Craftsman)

Produced Long Nose Clubs: 1820-1847. Stamped with: "A. Munro"

Munro was a maker of fishing rods and golf clubs. Not all of his clubs may have been stamped as few examples exist, one being at the World Golf Hall of Fame in Pinehurst, North Carolina.

PARK, MUNGO (1860-1904)

Musselburgh (Professional)

Produced Long Nose Clubs: 1860-1890. Stamped with: "M. Park"

The younger brother of Willie Park, Sr., Mungo traveled the seas in his younger years. His fame as a golfer was his win in the 1874 Open Championship. He had a newphew also named Mungo who worked with Willie, Jr. in New York City.

PARK, WILLIE, JR. (1864-1925)

Musselburgh & Edinburgh (Professional)

Produced Long Nose Clubs: 1884-1890. Stamped with: "Wm. Park"

Willie Jr. was a maker of both woods and cleeks. He is credited with the development of the Bulger Driver and the mesh pattern for the golf ball. He bacame a golf course designer and opened retail golf shops in London, Edinburgh and New York.

Willie Park, Sr. poses with the Open Championship Belt.

PARK, WILLIE, SR. (1834-1903)

Musselburgh (Professional)

Produced Long Nose Clubs: 1855-1890. Stamped with: "Wm. Park"

Willie won the first Open Championship in 1860 and also in 1863, 1866 and 1875. His early clubs were stamped 'W. Park'.

PATRICK, ALEXANDER (1845-1832)

Leven (Craftsman)

Produced Long Nose Clubs: 1866-1890. Stamped with: "A. Patrick"

Alexander was the son of John and took over the family business upon his father's death. He built solid, sturdy clubs.

PATRICK, JOHN (1820-1866)

Leven (Craftsman)

Produced Long Nose Clubs: 1840-1866. Stamped with: "J. Patrick"

Patrick's business was as a carpenter and cabinetmaker and began making golf clubs as a sideline.

PAXTON, PETER (1859-   )

Musselburgh (Professional)

Produced Long Nose Clubs: 1880-1890. Stamped with: "P. Paxton"

Paxton learned to make clubs under Tom Hood and then prospered as both a clubmaker and ballmaker.

After Philp's death, his nephew Robert Forgan assumed directorship of the business and stamped clubs with both of their names for a short period of time.

PHILP, HUGH (1782-1856)

St. Andrews (Craftsman)

Produced Long Nose Clubs: 1810-1856. Stamped with: "H. Philp"

Philp was possibly the finest craftsman of wood clubs. His designs and finish served as models for others to follow. His clubs became highly collectible soon after his death. Several makers were known to have made Philp forgeries.

POKE
  London (Craftsman)
  Produced Long Nose Clubs: circa 1823.
  Poke was employed by the Blackheath Golf Club as a clubmaker and caretaker.

SANDISON, LUDOVIC (1825-1884)
  Aberdeen (Craftsman)
  Produced Long Nose Clubs: 1845-1884. Stamped with: "Sandison"
  Little information is available on Sandison except that his clubs do exist. He probably took over the business of Alexander Munro as clubs have been seen with both names.

SAYERS, BERNARD (BEN) (1857-1924)
  North Berwick (Professional)
  Produced Long Nose Clubs: 1877-1890. Stamped with: "B. Sayers"
  Sayers was both a fine player and an outstanding teacher of the game. He flourished as a ballmaker and club-maker at the turn of the century.

SCOTT, ANDREW HERD (1875-   )
  Elie & Earlsferry (Craftsman)
  Produced Long Nose Clubs: 1890.
  While Scott did not produce many long nose clubs, he was a noted pioneer in the modern methods of clubmaking.

SHARPE, ARCHIBALD
  London (Craftsman)
  Produced Long Nose Clubs: 1823-1834.
  Sharpe was employed by the Blackheath Golf Club as a clubmaker and caretaker.

SIMPSON, ARCHIE (1866-   )
  Carnoustie (Professional)
  Produced Long Nose Clubs: 1885-1890. Stamped with: "A. Simpson"
  Archie was one of six brothers who participated in professional golf events. He was twice runner-up in the Open Championship and worked with his brother, Robert, until the mid 1890's. He then went into business for himself.

SIMPSON, ROBERT (1862-1923)
  Carnoustie (Professional)
  Produced Long Nose Clubs: 1880-1890. Stamped with: "R. Simpson"
  Known for his fine playing ability, Robert became a clubmaker and was instrumental in the development of the Bulger type club.

STRATH, ANDREW (1836-1868)
  St. Andrews (Professional)
  Produced Long Nose Clubs: 1856-1868. Stamped with: "A. Strath"
  Winner of the Open Championship in 1865, Strath learned clubmaking from Robert Forgan while with Hugh Philp.

STRATH, DAVID (1840-1879)
  St. Andrews (Professional)
  Produced Long Nose Clubs: 1860-1879. Stamped with: "D. Strath"
  Like his brother Andrew, David was a fine player. He was one of a few who could compete on the same level as 'Young Tom' Morris. Strath was associated with the strangest finish in British Open history. In 1876, he was tied with Bob Martin after the completion of play but refused to participate in a playoff. It seems that he was irritated with the manner in which the Rules Committee handled a possible rules infraction. Three years later, he died an untimely death after sailing to Australia.

STRATH, GEORGE
  St. Andrews & Troon (Professional)
  Produced Long Nose Clubs: 1870-1890. Stamped with: "G. Strath"
  While George was not an outstanding player, he was the first professional at Troon in 1881. He later emigrated to Brooklyn, New York.

WALKER, JAMES
  Edinburgh (Craftsman)
  Produced Long Nose Clubs: 1875-1890. Stamped with: "J. Walker"
  Walker's clubs can be found in only a few collections.

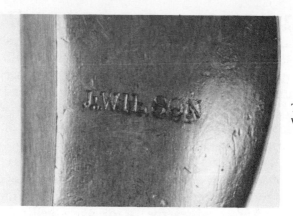

This Wilson club was stamped with two different size stamps.

WILSON, JAMES (1803-1866)
St. Andrews (Craftsman)

Produced Long Nose Clubs: 1845-1866. Stamped with: "J. Wilson"

Wilson was employed by Hugh Philp from 1845 to 1852. When he realized that Robert Forgan would soon take over Philp's business, Wilson opened up his own shop. He made beautiful clubs and probably forged a few with Philp's mark along the way.

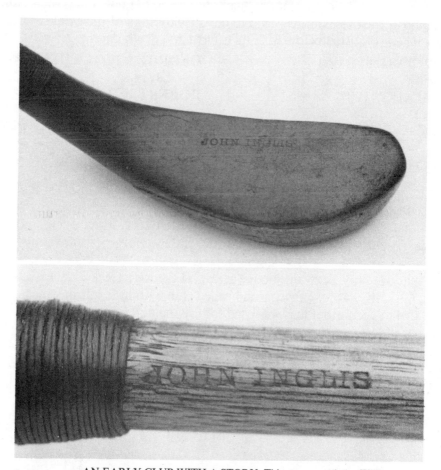

AN EARLY CLUB WITH A STORY: This spoon, made by Willie Park, belonged to John Inglis, a popular Scottish golfing figure. He was the Lord Justice General of Scotland and in 1877, was Captain of the Royal and Ancient Golf Club. Several references are made to Inglis in Tulloch's *Life of Tom Morris*. He gave the dedication at the erection of the often photographed tombstone of Young Tom Morris in St. Andrews in 1878.

LIST #2 — EARLY IRONS (EI DESIGNATION)

Golfers in earlier times did not use metal headed clubs for their approach shots in the manner in which we do so today. Prior to the 1850's, the golf ball was made of a stitched hide stuffed with feathers and was quite susceptible to damage. Iron headed clubs were only used as a last resort to hit a ball out of a wheel track or similar bad lie. Since a poorly hit iron shot would destroy the feather ball, golfers preferred to use a wooden headed club whenever possible. It was common for a player of that era to carry several wooden clubs and only one or two iron clubs with him. Finally, when the more durable gutta percha ball was introduced in 1848, the irons became more popular and eventually the golfer would carry three to four times as many irons as woods as is common today.

The reference to an early iron headed club in this book means that it was entirely hand made prior to the 1890's. After this date, most of the hosels were drilled and several other mechanized operations made the mass production of iron heads possible. The making of an early iron was a lengthy process requiring the skills of a blacksmith.

Starting with a bar of iron, the maker would heat the bar to make it malleable and would proceed to hammer out the shape on his anvil. The part which was to become the hosel was hammered flat and wrapped around a mandril to form a socket for the insertion of a wood shaft. The remainder of the bar was then bent to the correct lie and through heating, more hammering, and a final filing, a single head was created. On some heads the hosel and blade were formed separately and were then fused together. Usually the older irons were more crude than the ones made in the latter part of the nineteenth century. The sometimes deep hand nicking around the end of the hosel helped to hold the shaft in place along with a pin inserted through the hosel. On many of the early irons, the seam along the hosel is visible.

Most of the makers prior to 1850 were primarily blacksmiths and did not stamp their names on the clubhead. In the years that followed, some of the blacksmiths began to devote almost all of their time to iron clubmaking. The men known to have been clubmakers are listed below with their birth and death dates.

JAMES ANDERSON (1845-1895)
Anstruther, Fife
ROBERT BRODIE (1837-1907)
Anstruther
F. & A. CARRICK
Musselburgh
JOHN GRAY (1824-1904)
Prestwick

GEORGE NICOLL (1861-1945)
Leven
ROBERT WHITE (1857-   )
St. Andrews
ROBERT WILSON (1845-1906)
St. Andrews
WILLIE WILSON
St. Andrews

In addition to making clubs under their own name these makers would provide heads to the wooden head clubmakers for shafting and sale to golfers. Some of the clubmakers who sold these early irons, but did not actually make them, are Tom Morris, the McEwans, A. Patrick and Robert Forgan. Several examples of irons stamped with the names of these makers exist today.

The early irons were made in only a few distinctive styles. These were cleeks, track irons, sand irons, lofting irons and just plain "irons". The CLEEK was long faced iron headed club with little loft in which the upper and lower edges of the face run almost parallel to each other and was used for driving and other long shots. The LOFTER often had a concave face and was similar in loft to a modern five iron. The lofter was used for approach shots. The SAND IRON was a lofted iron with a large heavy head used for play from bunkers in the early 19th century. The TRACK IRON was a small headed iron used for extracting the ball from a wheel track or similar bad lie. These early irons had extremely small heads with disproportionately large hosels. By 1885, the heads became larger and were referred to as a rut iron or rut niblick.

This old iron, by an unknown blacksmith, dates to the late eighteenth century.

An early cleek used from the 1830's to the 1850's.

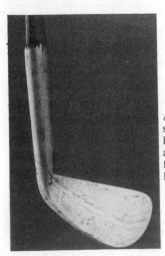

A seam can be seen on this hand-forged iron as a result of the forming of the hosel.

Willie Wilson was one of the early ironmakers who produced fine clubs in the latter part of the 19th century. This club was retailed by Peter Paxton in the 1880's.

This Carrick cleek from the 1870's was used with the gutty balls of the period. It exhibits the Carrick mark which is believed to have been the first mark used by a cleekmaker, probably in the 1850's. They also stamped clubs with "F & A Carrick, Musselburgh".

This concave faced iron was designed for use in the feather ball era.

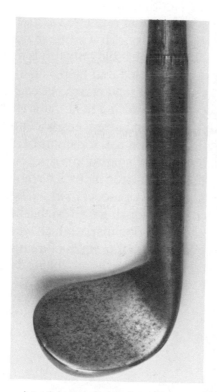

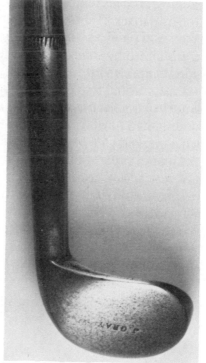

A track iron crafted by John Gray in the 1850's. This small headed club was used for hitting the ball out of cart tracks and similar depressions.

WOOD SHAFTED CLUBS (1890-1935)
Iron Headed Clubs

In the 1890's, the process of drop forging was developed. Until this time iron golf club heads had been made entirely by hand by heating the iron and hammering out the head on an anvil. The drop forging method still required heating and a small amount of hand hammering, but most of the work was performed by the drop hammer. A set of dies was made with the cavity forming the rough shape of the iron head. After an iron bar was prepared and heated, it was inserted into the die where it was formed by many impacts of the heavy mechanical hammer. The larger makers had several men heating iron bars at their forge in preparation for forming by the hammerman who was situated in the middle of the shop. Following the forging, the heads were finished on a grinding wheel. All of the irons eventually had drilled hosels rather than formed ones. The collector should be aware that most clubs marked "hand forged" are really drop forged as true hand forged clubs were made without mechanized machinery. The early hand forged clubs were not stamped as such since they could only have been made by hand.

One of the more fascinating aspects of Scottish irons is the logo mark that was often applied to the back of the club by the maker. In the beginning, when irons were still forged by blacksmiths, the maker's name usually did not appear on the clubhead. As the sport of golf became more popular, the craft cleekmaking evolved and the makers began to mark the iron heads with an identification mark. For some, the maker's name sufficed as his mark, but others preferred to use a symbol or design.

As the game grew in popularity, the ironmakers began to make clubs for players or dealers who would then market them. It was at this time that they began to be called cleekmakers. The clubs were frequently stamped with both the name of the seller and the mark of the maker. In most cases both these marks were applied by the maker during the process of finishing the clubhead. The heads were then shafted and gripped by the retailer or were sold fully assembled to him by the maker.

Tom Stewart produced most of his clubs in this manner. All of Stewart's clubs, with the exception of some of his older serpent marked ladies clubs, bore his famous pipe mark which he later registered as his protected trade mark. Some of those irons also carried the oval mark "T. Stewart, Maker, St. Andrews". However a majority were stamped with the names of professionals, makers and retailers who sold his product. Stewart sold only heads for shafting, so the shaft and grip on Stewart clubs were assembled by someone else. Stewart advertised that he would arrange for his iron heads to be shafted by other St. Andrews makers for his customers or he would send crates of heads for assembly later.

In time, the iron club makers would trade on their success by advertising their mark as their identity. This caused other manufacturers to follow the notables of the club making business and invent easily identifiable marks for their clubs as well. All through the wood shafted heyday of 1910 to 1930, most clubs had some sort of mark to catch the eye of the buyer and suggest that such a marked club was one of quality and craftsmanship.

Besides the true maker's marks, other similar marks can be found on iron clubs. The more prolific makers manufactured various grades of clubs which they distinguished by brand marks or model marks. They would also make private lines for professionals with a private brand mark unique to that professional. Retail establishments and importers would have their clubs marked in a similar way. Some makers even had inspection marks which were not intended to be identified by the public but served to grade clubs during the finishing process. Examples of all these types of club marks are shown in this section along with the identity of the maker or professional, the approximate dates of the mark's usage and brief background information.

Workshop of D. Anderson & Sons in St. Andrews.

The well equipped golf shop at the Pelham (New York) Country Club in 1925 where Jim Barnes, the first winner of the PGA Championship, was the professional for a number of years.

View of the forge area of Tom Stewart's shop in St. Andrews. Note the iron bars being prepared for the drop hammer.

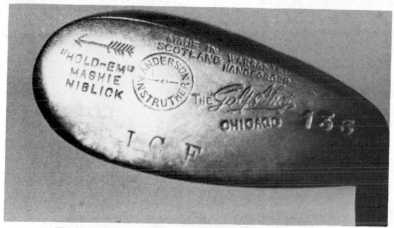

This iron exhibits the many types of marks which were used: makers name, makers mark, retailers name, owners initials, club name, model number.

Wood Headed Clubs

The design of wooden clubheads began to change considerably in the 1880's when the neck of the club became thicker and the length of the clubhead was gradually made shorter. First there was the semi-long nose club and then the bulger concept came into being. By 1890 the long nose club was being phased out because of these improvements in playability.

These clubs varied greatly in appearance from the long nose woods which had been in use for well over a hundred years prior to the 1890's. Club faces were beginning to receive different treatments as inserts and convex bulges started to be used. As mechnization entered the clubmaking trade, heads were shaped on lathes and were finished by hand rather than being entirely handmade as in the earlier years.

The head continued to be joined to the shaft by means of a scare or spliced joint. Soon makers such as George Forrester began to develop the socket joint which is still used today. The socket was drilled into the head and then the shaft was glued in place and finally whipped. The necks of the clubs became slender and more rounded than the earlier oval shape of the scared head clubs. Although Walter Hagen and others were using scared head woods well into the teens, the socket heads were dominating the market at the beginning of this century.

Other methods of joining the head to the shaft were being tested in the 1890's before the socket joint became the preferred method. Variations of the traditional splice appeared in the form of forked and other interlocking types of joints such as the Scott and Smith patents. As the clubmaking business became more competitive, many of the makers tried to develop a better type of clubhead. Durable persimmon was introduced in the mid 1890's and when the rubber core ball came into being at the turn of the century, it became the preferred material for wooden heads. Competing with persimmon was the aluminum headed club made popular by the Standard Golf Company. Their Mills model clubs were popular on both sides of the Atlantic.

One of the most fascinating types of clubs during this period was the one piece wood. These clubs normally resembled the other compact heads being made at the time, except that they had no whipping. Willie Dunn, Jr. and his nephew, John Duncan Dunn, were reponsible for the popularity of these clubs first in Great Britain. The one piece clubs became available in the United States when the Dunns arrived to set up business and subsequently worked for BGI, Spalding and MacGregor. Although these clubs were produced from approximately 1894 to 1902, there are several theories as to how these clubs were actually made.

It is generally thought that the one piece clubs were made from a long piece of lumber which was steamed at one end to render it pliable so that it could be bent like a golf club. When the wood had assumed its shape, it was then shaped by hand. Another theory is that the wood was harvested from shrubs growing on a steep slope. These large shrubs had branches which naturally formed the general shape of a golf club. A third theory is that the entire club was sawed from a length of lumber approximately four inches square and four feet long and then was shaped to an exact form. This last method appears to be the most time consuming and wasteful of the theories.

Regardless of how they were made, the one piece club is truly a collector's item today. The following names have been seen on one piece clubs: Dunn's Patent, Willie Dunn, Dunn & Son, R. Forgan & Son, Lilywhite, BGI, Slazenger, Webb, G. G. Nieman, Spalding, MacGregor and J. Hagen. It is not known whether any of the clubs were made by any makers other than the Dunns, since they may have marked their clubs with any number of names.

Other than the increased use of face inserts and metal soleplates, the shape and general design of the wood headed clubs changed little through the remainder of the wood shaft era.

The Sweny patent from 1896 utilized a method for attaching the shaft to the top of the head.

Simplex made wood shafted clubs with this odd shaped head in the 1890's. This is a putter although a full set was produced. A select group of golfers enthusiastically used these clubs until they were eventually outlawed.

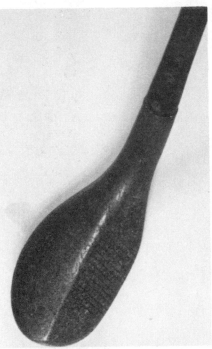

An aluminum head pitching mashie made by the Standard Golf Company of Sunderland, England. They produced an entire line of Mills design putters and fairway clubs beginning in 1896.

Slazenger sold many ordinary looking socket head woods. This model was introduced in 1913.

One of the crazy innovations in clubmaking at the turn of the century was this spliced head putter equipped with rollers. It was patented by T.H.B. Black in 1902 in Great Britain.

A semi long nose one piece driver made by BGI in the United States. This was probably a model since all other one piece clubs were of a compact design.

One of several styles of one piece clubs made by the Dunns. This club was made in England and was patented in 1894.

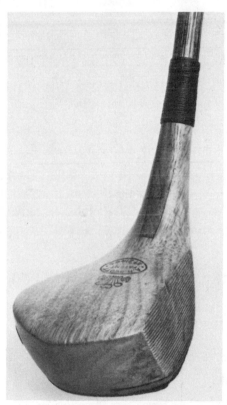

This wood by A. H. Scott was patented in 1895 and featured a forked type of splice.

This aluminum head driver has an insert molded of gutta percha. It is marked Spalding, but was not known to be a production model.

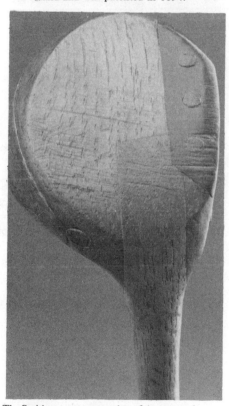

The Smith patent was another of the unusual methods of securing the head to the shaft.

Scott heavily advertised his new style of club.

One of the early matched sets of woods, made by D. M. Patrick of Leven in the semi-long nose style.

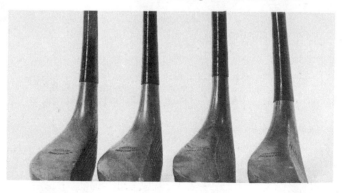

Horton's was one of several patented woods in the early 1920's.

Master model used on a lathe for the mass production of duplicate clubheads.

Golf Club Names

The number of golf clubs and the idea of a matched set of irons was discussed as early as 1903 by John Low in *Concerning Golf*. The players prior to the twentieth century relied heavily on wooden headed clubs. More irons with varying lofts began to appear and by the 1920's, players would carry twice as many irons as woods. The clubs were given names which were later used in conjunction with and eventually replaced with the numbering system currently in use. By the late 1940's the number system was used exclusively by the manufacturers.

ORIGINAL NAME	MODERN EQUIVALENT	ORIGINAL NAME	MODERN EQUIVALENT
Driver	1 Wood	Mid Mashie	3 Iron
Brassie	2 Wood	Mashie Iron	4 Iron
Spoon	3 Wood	Mashie	5 Iron
Driving Cleek	1 Iron	Spade Mashie	6 Iron
Driving Iron	1 Iron	Mashie Niblick	7 Iron
Mid Iron	2 Iron	Niblick	8-9 Iron

Wilson manufactured these early matched clubs with wooden shafts. The sole of this iron was marked "1 - 180 TO 200 YARDS" to assist the golfer in club selection.

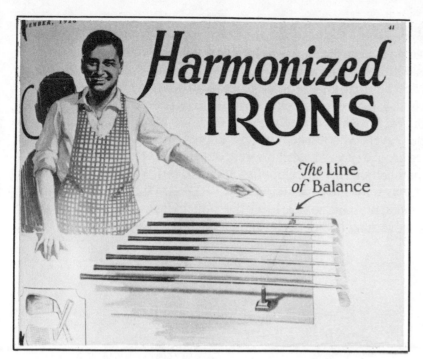

MacGregor ad promoting their matched sets of 1926.

Gene Sarazen displays the set of clubs he was using in 1928.

Iron Head Face Markings

Prior to 1900, the vast majority of iron clubs had no face markings or scorings. It was common for caddies to carry emery cloth to clean the light rust off the clubheads. Often the emery cloth was used to create a cross grain pattern at the club's "sweet spot". In the 1890's, hand punched dots began to appear on the clubface in order to increase the amount of backspin, and by 1905 many patterns had been devised. The three most common face markings were hyphen, dot punch and the line scoring which still prevails today. Smooth face irons were rarely used after 1910, but some continued to be offered in the catalogs of club manufacturers for the players who resisted the new improvements.

One group of collectible face markings is the deep groove type. These clubs were designed to create an extra amount of backspin to enable the golfer to better control his approach shots. These clubs first appeared in 1914 and Jock Hutchison won the 1921 British Open with them. Soon thereafter they were outlawed and by 1925 they were no longer manufactured. Other irons were made with either concave or convex faces, the most notable being the Walter Hagen concave sand wedge. Eventually these clubs were also ruled illegal by the governing bodies of the game.

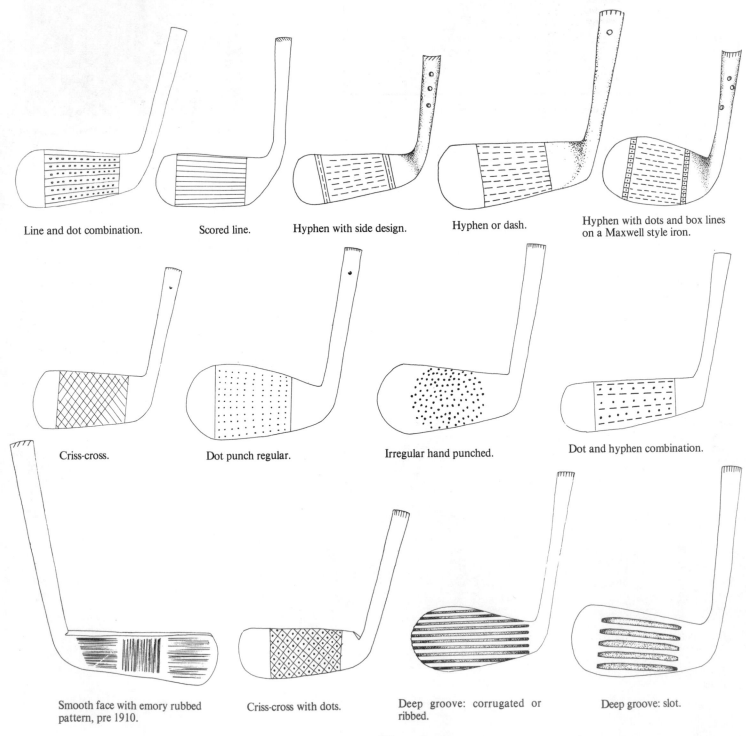

Line and dot combination.

Scored line.

Hyphen with side design.

Hyphen or dash.

Hyphen with dots and box lines on a Maxwell style iron.

Criss-cross.

Dot punch regular.

Irregular hand punched.

Dot and hyphen combination.

Smooth face with emory rubbed pattern, pre 1910.

Criss-cross with dots.

Deep groove: corrugated or ribbed.

Deep groove: slot.

Deep grooved Backspin mashie made by MacGregor.

Iron Head Shapes

There were only a few different shapes for irons until the 1890's when the use of irons became more common and clubmakers began to experiment with various designs. Some of the more common shapes in use from 1890 to the 1920's are illustrated.

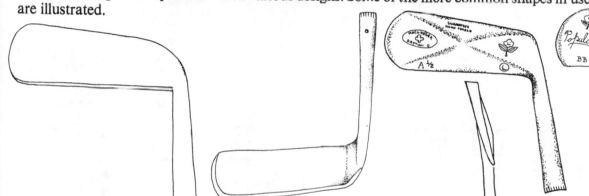

Standard blade.

Bent blade putter (circa 1895).

Diamond back — supposedly originated by Anderson of Anstruther.

Mussel back — resembles a mussel shell.

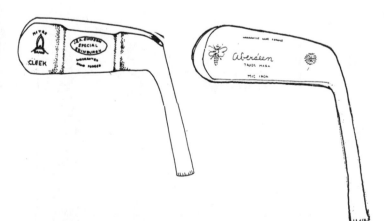
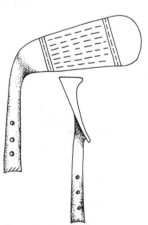
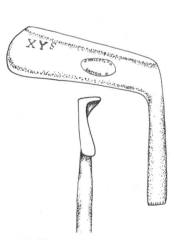

Carruthers style - hosel drilled all the way through the head. Patented by T. Carruthers of Edinburgh in 1891. Note the short hosel.

Round back — several styles exist including a slightly rounded back.

Flanged sole (weighted sole) — sometimes with Maxwell style drilled holes in hosel.

Duoflange — with weighted top and bottom as in this MacGregor Model 90 putter.

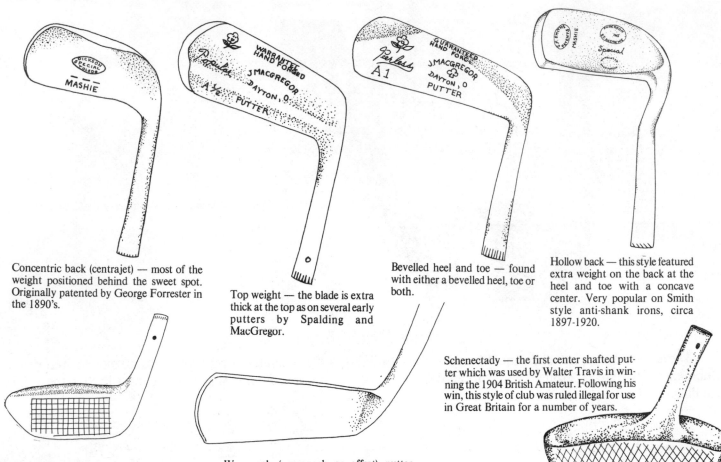

Concentric back (centrajet) — most of the weight positioned behind the sweet spot. Originally patented by George Forrester in the 1890's.

Top weight — the blade is extra thick at the top as on several early putters by Spalding and MacGregor.

Bevelled heel and toe — found with either a bevelled heel, toe or both.

Hollow back — this style featured extra weight on the back at the heel and toe with a concave center. Very popular on Smith style anti-shank irons, circa 1897-1920.

Schenectady — the first center shafted putter which was used by Walter Travis in winning the 1904 British Amateur. Following his win, this style of club was ruled illegal for use in Great Britain for a number of years.

Mallet head — normally found on putters made of wood or aluminum.

Wry neck (gooseneck or offset) putter. Patented by Willie Park Jr. in 1894.

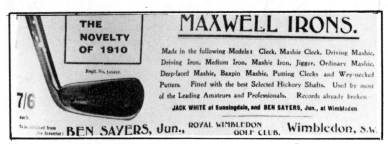

The Maxwell style hosel had holes drilled in it in order to take position of more weight behind the hitting area. Wilson and others perfected this principle many years later.

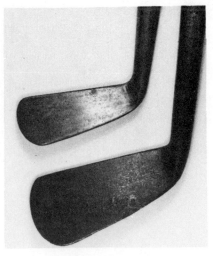

Junior size clubs compared to standard size. A child's club was even smaller than the junior, but was more of a toy.

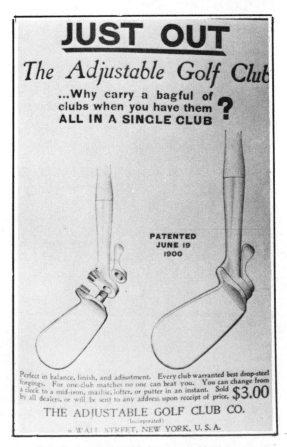

One of several adjustable irons available at the turn of the century.

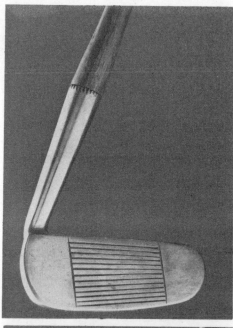

A 1930's version of the Basakwerd putter which has been popular in recent years.

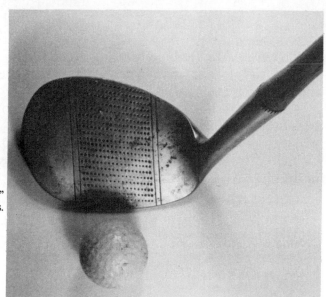

Several models of "giant niblicks" were manufactured in the 1920's.

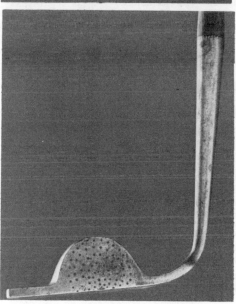

Unusual shaped putter made by Gibson of Kinghorn. The user had no problem locating the "sweet spot".

The Otto Hackbarth is one of the many collectible putters with odd shapes.

Thomson was an innovator with his mussel back irons and metallic faced woods.

Club Parts Suppliers

Advertisements in the 1890's were directed toward the clubmakers and disclosed much about the materials and processes which were used at the time. Many of the makers and almost all of the club professionals had their wood heads delivered to them ready for finishing and shafting. Iron heads were also supplied in various stages, with the larger companies operating their own forges.

It is interesting to note that by the twentieth century most of the wooden items were imported to the British Isles from the United States. It was common for hickory and persimmon logs to be shipped from the U.S. to Scotland where they would be cut, dried and turned into shafts and heads by a lumber mill. A clubmaker could buy these rough components from his supplier and finish them into golf clubs which he would then retail or sell through an agent. Many of the clubs were then exported back to America.

MACHINE-TURNED HEADS
(To any Pattern).

Turned Shafts in all Woods Hickory (first and second qualities), Greenheart, Lancewood, and Washaba.

Beech Blocks, cut to any shape. Largest stock of seasoned woods.

C. SPINKS,

The first to introduce machinery in the manfacture of Golf Club Material.

Factory: Pirrie St., LEITH, N.B.

Important to Golf Club Makers.

Large stock of all woods always on hand. Turned shafts in Hickory (1st, 2nd, and 3rd quality), Greenheart, Washaba and Lancewood, Beech, etc. Blocks cut to shape.

SPINKS, *Golf Material Factory*,

PIRRIE STREET, LEITH, N.B.

Two ads from C. Spinks

TO CLUB MAKERS.
Timber for Handles and Heads a Speciality.

HICKORY
GREENHEART
LEMON WOOD
LANCEWOOD
PURPLEHEART
IRONHEART
BULLET WOOD
WASHABA

} Turned for Irons or Drivers or in Square.

HEADS IN BEECH, HORNBEAM, Etc:

APPLY TO

REMER, NOWELL & CO., LIMITED,
Timber Importers and Manufacturers,

168, Boundary Street, Liverpool.

Telegrams: TALLYHO, LIVERPOOL. Telephone, 1,817.

This English timber company offered a large variety of woods to the clubmaker.

GOLF CLUB BLOCKS,

From wood grown in a high district, very hard, the young wood having the appearance of hornbeam, **36**s. per gross; 1¼ in. face, **24**s. per gross. Hickory shafts, **30**s. per gross.

FRANCIS S. STEWART, 5, Burlington Street, Leith.

Francis S. Stewart wanted everyone to know that his clubheads came from trees grown on high ground, a desirable quality.

Quarter of a Million Golf Shafts.

WE have just received from America the above quantity of second-growth Hickory Shafts, in splendid condition, and which we offer to Golf Club manufacturers at a very attractive price, with discounts running from 2½% to 20%, according to the quantity taken.

The minimum amount for which we will receive an order is 1,000 and the maximum 10,000.

Write for particulars—

A. G. SPALDING & BROS.,
53, 54, 55, Fetter Lane, London, E.C.
Factory—Putney Wharf, S.W.

To all readers of "Golf Illustrated" our 1907 Illustrated Catalogue (No. 18 of all Golf Requisites will be sent Post Free on request.

By 1907, golf shafts were claiming a sizable portion of the American hickory harvest as evidenced by this ad.

R. CONDIE, ST. ANDREWS, N.B.,

The leading Golf Cleek and Iron Manufacturer to the trade, has always on hand a large stock of well FORGED heads of best material and workmanship. Engraved Golf Ball Moulds, newest pattern, also supplied.

PRICES ON APPLICATION.

Robert Condie, the famous cleekmaker, was willing to sell his hand forged heads to others for final assembly.

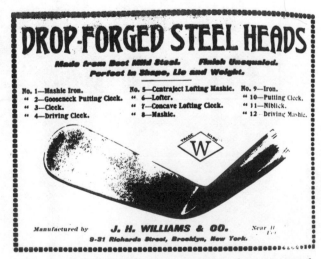

DROP-FORGED STEEL HEADS
Made from Best Mild Steel.   Finish Unequaled.
Perfect in Shape, Lie and Weight.

No. 1—Mashie Iron.
" 2—Gooseneck Putting Cleek.
" 3—Cleek.
" 4—Driving Cleek.

No. 5—Contraject Lofting Mashie.
" 6—Lofter.
" 7—Concave Lofting Cleek.
" 8—Mashie.

No. 9—Iron.
" 10—Putting Cleek.
" 11—Niblick.
" 12—Driving Mashie.

Manufactured by **J. H. WILLIAMS & CO.**
9-31 Richards Street, Brooklyn, New York.

These numbers are merely catalog numbers and are not part of the numbering system we use today. One might wonder for whom their heads may have been "perfect in shape, lie and weight".

Soft Steel Heads.
☞ TO THE TRADE ONLY.

Every One Tested and Guaranteed,
Full Price Lists on Application.

Heads of all kinds **Nickel-plated**, only **3d.** each extra. These are in great demand by players, especially ladies, and require no cleaning.

SOLE MAKER:—
JOHN COCHRANE,
44, KIRKGATE, LEITH.

Apparently the women golfers of the early 1900's were quite fond of nickel plated iron heads.

95

Paxton was one of the few makers who made clubheads from oak. In addition to being a clubmaker, he sold all kinds of golf related supplies.

This ad for D. Mackay from 1908 illustrates the highly competitive nature of the clubmaking business at that time.

LIST #3 — WOOD SHAFTED CLUBS (1890-1935)
(SH, MI, WS DESIGNATION

AMPCO GOLF CO.
Milwaukee

 AMPCO   Mark in use: 1926-1933

The Ampco Golf Co. started business in 1926 and manufacured sets of "Ampco" and "Gold Eagle" irons which were made from a unique rustproof bronze alloy. When polished, they are very handsome clubs but unfortunately for Ampco, they are more popular in club collections today than they were on the course in their day.

ANDERSON & SONS, D.
St. Andrews

Mark in use: 1923-1926

David Anderson Jr. (1847-1912) ran the firm with his five sons. He was the son of the famous David "Old Da" Anderson (1821-1901). The company was in business from 1895 until 1926.

D. ANDERSON & SONS,
Professional Golf Club and Ball Makers,
ST. ANDREWS, N.B.
Anderson's Special Mashie, **6/6** each. Anderson's Special Iron Putter, **6/6** each
HUGH KIRKALDY, Ex-Champion, says :—
" I have tried your special Putter, and can strongly recommend it to Golfers."
London Agents: **JOHN WISDEN & Co., 21, Cranbourne St., W.C.**
SHIPPERS AND THE TRADE SUPPLIED.   SEND FOR LIST.

Like many of the Scottish makers, Anderson had sales agents in England.

This Anderson club was forged by Millar circa 1900.

ANDERSON & GOURLAY
St. Andrews

Mark in use: 1925 +

ANDERSON, ALEX
Anstruther, Fife

Mark in use: 1895-1910

Alex was one of the largest manufacturers, working well into the 1930's. He inherited the business of Anderson & Son from his father, James Anderson in the late 1800's. They are known as the "Andersons of Anstruther" and should not be confused with the other Andersons in the golf trade. This is his earliest mark.

Mark in use: 1910-1930

This is a replica of the mark used by his father, James. It can be distinguished from his father's earlier mark by its larger size (5/8" diameter). It was in use after his first mark was abandoned.

〉〉〉〉〉〉⟶   Mark in use: 1908 +

The "Arrow" mark was also used by other clubmaking firms usually in combination with the word "Accurate". Anderson's clubs were marked only with the plain arrow which always pointed to the toe of the iron.

ANDERSON, ANDERSON & ANDERSON, LTD.
London   1900-1910.   Mark in use: 1900-1910

These Andersons were retail golf and India rubber merchants with a family tie to the Andersons of Anstruther.

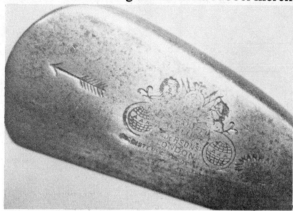

Iron club made by Alex Anderson of Anstruther, Scotland and sold by Andersons of London.

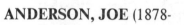

ANDERSON, JAMES (1845-1895)
Anstruther, Fife   Mark in use: 1880 -

James was a well known cleekmaker in the last third of the 19th century. He was not related to the Andersons of St. Andrews with the same name: Jamie, the Open champion and Jamie's son, James. The diameter of his mark is ½" and should not be mistaken for the similar, but larger, one later used by his son, Alex.

ANDERSON, JOE (1878-   )
Perth

The "OK" mark appeared in several different versions from 1910 to 1930.

Another of the "OK" marks in use from 1925.

ARMY AND NAVY STORES, LTD.
London

Officially titled the Army and Navy Co-Operative Society, Ltd., it was and still is a general purpose department store. For a while before the turn of the century, they made their own clubs with the help of young James Braid.

ASHFORD, W. & G.
Birmingham

Ashford was one of the early makers of golf bags and handled a full line of golf equipment. This is their "Foxhead" mark which was used from 1893 to 1897.

Mark in use: 1896-1897

This mark was used on Ashford's "Fore Flags" clubs. The company was short lived, going out of business before 1900.

AUCHTERLONIE & CROSTHWAITE
St. Andrews

This was the firm of Willie Auchterlonie and A. W. Crosthwaite that began business in 1895. In 1897 Crosthwaite dropped out of the firm and Willie changed the name to D. & W. Auchterlonie to recognize his brother David, who probably was already involved in the business before this change.

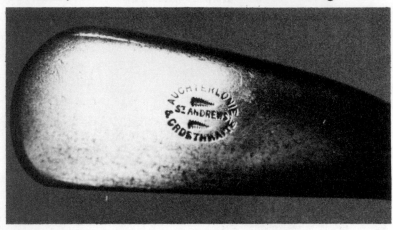

Clubhead forged by Condie for Auchterlonie & Crosthwaite.

AUCHTERLONIE, D. & W.
St. Andrews

The successor firm to Auchterlonie & Crosthwaite, David (1865-   ) and Willie (1873-1963) became a well known source for golf equipment in St. Andrews. Their brother, Laurence (1868-   ), who won the 1902 U.S. Open, was not associated with the firm.

Willie's son, Laurie (1904-   ), is the current proprietor of the business which continues to hand craft clubs under the "Mastercraft" label. As was his father, Laurie is the honorary professional to the Royal and Ancient Golf Club.

D. & W. AUCHTERLONIE,
(W. AUCHTERLONIE, Open Champion, 1893.)
GOLF CLUB SPECIALISTS AND BALL MAKERS,
Albany Place, St. ANDREWS.
Auchterlonie's Special Registered Approaching Cleek kept in Stock, price 6s. 6d.
Agents : LONDON--JOHN WISDEN & Co., 21, Cranbourne Street.
MANCHESTER--ALEC. WATSON, 85, Oxford Street.
DUBLIN--J. W. ELVERY & Co., 46, Lower Sackville Street.
NEW YORK--C. C. BARTLEY, 58, Warren Street.

Willie Auchterlonie's Open Championship victory played a key part in his advertising.

Willie Auchterlonie poses in front of his original shop on Albany Street in St. Andrews.

AUCHTERLONIE, TOM
St. Andrews

Tom set up business in 1919 and became a supplier of all kinds of golf equipment. His son, Eric, joined the firm in 1928 and currently runs their busy shop in St. Andrews.

AYRES, F. H.
London

Although Ayres manufactured golf items and games as early as the 1880's, their "Maltese Cross" mark was not used until about 1910. The company was established in 1810 and was eventually bought out by Slazenger.

B.G.I. Co. (Bridgeport Gun Implement)
Bridgeport, CT

One of the few American golf companies founded prior to 1900, B.G.I. was run by John Duncan Dunn and his uncle Willie Dunn Jr. B.G.I. had been in the firearms business before it sold golf clubs, but by 1897 they were known to have offered golf equipment in their catalogs and showrooms.

B.G.I. irons were forged by the J.H. Williams Company of Brooklyn, N.Y. and many can be found with a small hosel mark of a "W" in a diamond outline. Of all the B.G.I. clubs, probably the best known was Willie Dunn's famous patented one piece driver with the head and shaft made out of a single piece of wood. They also sold clubs made by other makers such as the early Mills aluminum clubs from England and Sprague putters. B.G.I. stopped selling golf clubs in about 1906 for unknown reasons.

The mark of the "Rampant Lion" shown here was registered by Willie Dunn in the 1890's and can be found stamped on some of his one-piece clubs. In later years similar lion marks were found on irons by MacGregor, Burke, Wright and Ditson and Charles Brand.

B.G.I. was quite proud of their one piece clubs.

Williams made irons for BGI and also sold to other for shafting and resale.

Willie Dunn was actually in business on his own in America before joining up with B.G.I.

B.G.I. was a sales agent for the Sprague Patent Putter. This club featured a ball and socket arrangement which allowed the player to easily reposition the angle of the clubhead.

BLAISDELL, FRED
London
    This mark was sold as the "Black Star" from 1908 until 1910.

BRADBEER, JAMES (1879-   )
London
    Bradbeer was a well known professional and clubmaker at various clubs in London and made use of this "Jay Bee" symbol from 1905 until 1935.

BRADELL & SON, JOSEPH   Mark in use: 1895-1905
Belfast
    The Braddells are best known for their high quality aluminum drivers although they also made wood and iron headed clubs. The "Shamrock" mark was also used on the shaft below the grip. In 1900 they advertised that their club with a bent beech head was "without a doubt the highest quality club on the market".

Braddell's aluminum headed clubs featured leather inserts.

Mark in use: 1910-1922

BRAND, CHARLES (1849-1922)
Carnoustie
    Brand began making clubs in the 1890's and was a well known golfing figure in Carnoustie. This "Rampant Lion" was used by several clubmakers in America, but only by Brand in Great Britain.

BREEZE, G. BRODIE
Glasgow
    Breeze sold all sorts of golf items including cups and flags for putting greens. The "Royal Crown" mark appeared later in his career, probably in 1910.

BRODIE & SON, ROBERT (1858-1943) & (1880-1963)

Anstruther

Mark in use: 1911-1925

The original Robert Brodie, a blacksmith and clubmaker of the nineteenth century, was the father and grandfather of the owners of this firm. These Brodies were primarily retailers of golf equipment who probably did some club assembly work. This "triangle" mark is usually found in conjunction with a maker's cleekmark. (See page 83.)

BROUGHAM, REGINALD

London

Brougham was one of the earliest makers of aluminum clubs and was only in business for a short time circa 1895.

Brougham's "Reduction in Price" offers must have been indicative of the lack of acceptance for their innovative clubs.

BUHRKE CO., R.H.

Chicago

Mark in use: 1920 +

R. H. Buhrke was a tool company that entered the golf club business in the mid 1920's. Their "Burr-Key Bilt" brand name was a phonetic pronunciation of the company name. Buhrke's quality was typical of mass produced club making. Some of their heads were actually purchased from Wilson Sporting Goods in Chicago.

Many of the clubs which can be easily found are the "Burr-Key Bilt", "Medalist", and "Finalist" lines. One interesting model was the "Classic" line of irons in which a circular brass plug was inserted in the club face at the sweet spot. The Buhrke Company still exists in Chicago, however they no longer deal in golf equipment.

BURKE GOLF CO.

Newark, Ohio

The Burke Golf Co. was founded in 1910 by William Burke and originally produced buggy whips and golf shafts. The ownership of the company has changed several times and in 1945 the name became Burke Golf, Inc. In more recent years, Faultless and Rawlings have each been owners of the Newark facilities. Burke used dozens of marks, however the ones shown above were most popular circa 1915.

Older Burke catalogs show that the company made and sold a wide variety of golf items besides golf clubs. They first were a maker of golf balls, but then supplied through the Worthington Company of Cleveland. Burke also imported Mills Aluminum Putter heads from England and Nicoll Iron Heads from Scotland which they then shafted in Newark.

Their lines included popular models such as the "Golfrite", "A-2", "Elite", "Columbia Special" and "Smith" irons and the "End Grain" driver.

The following poem appeared with these Burke advertisements for their sand clubs.

Sunshine or shadow
Fair wind or gust
If the rough don't get you
The sand traps must.

The Grand Canyon at the Green
Height is desired — not much distance. Use the Burke Sherwood Niblick No. S-10, a successful "shovel."

The Cross Pits
Grand Prize Mashie Niblick No. 9, slightly goose-neck, with deep face; built to give safe outs and generous distances.

The Shallow Fairway Trap
Burke Mashie Niblick No. 38 gives both safety and distance. A fairly heavy club, narrow face.

The Shallow, Sloping-Sided Trap
Try Burke Grand Prize Putter No. 19 to run up the slope. A plain back, long blade, putting cleek. It runs up nicely.

The Yawning Chasm
Use Grand Prize Niblick No. 23. A medium club — medium length blade, medium depth face, medium weight.

BUSSEY AND CO., GEORGE
    London
        Bussey was an innovative maker, manufacturer and retailer. He used this mark from 1890 to 1910.

BUTCHART-NICHOLLS CO.   Mark in use: 1920's
    Glenbrook, CT
        This company was an outgrowth of Cuthbert S. Butchart's Golf Works in the mid 1920's. Their chief claim to fame was the large number of clubs they sold with shafts of laminated bamboo or a combination of laminated bamboo and hickory. Butchart was a transplanted Scotsman with a fine reputation as a clubmaker and professional golfer.

CANN AND TAYLOR
Winchester & Richmond (London) & Asbury Park, NJ

Mark in use: 1895-1930

J. H. Taylor (1871-1963) was best known for his fine British Open play, having been both a five time winner and a five time runner-up. His fine reputation enabled his clubmaking partnership with George Cann to become a successful one. His signature is stamped on most of the clubs.

This was known as the "Fliweel" mark which was used between 1895 and 1930.

FLIWEEL

J. H. TAYLOR, Champion Golfer, 1894 & 1895.

J. H. TAYLOR'S Registered Putter, as used by him during the two recent Championships, 6s. 6d.   None genuine unless stamped with TAYLOR's name.   Fac-similes of TAYLOR's Mashie.

CANN & TAYLOR,
Golf Club and Ball Makers,
WINCHESTER, HANTS.

Agents:—THE LANCASHIRE GOLF CO., MANCHESTER.
Scotch Agents:—TWEEDIE, GRIEVE & Co., EDINBURGH.

Cann & Taylor began business in England and later opened a branch in New Jersey.

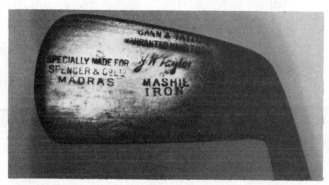

Cann & Taylor mashie iron which was exported for sale in India, where there were quite a few British golfers.

CARRICK, F. & A.
Musselburgh

Mark in use: mid 1850's +

Francis and Archibald Carrick were early makers who were blacksmiths and toolmakers by trade. They started forging heads in the first half of the 19th century and continued their golf trade until the early 1900's. Their "Cross" mark did not appear on their earlier irons which were stamped with just "Carrick". (See page 83.)

CARRUTHERS, THOMAS
Edinburgh

Carruthers invented the drilled hosel cleek in 1891 which later was copied by many makers.

T. CARRUTHERS,
WHOLESALE
Golf Club Manufacturer,
5, GILLESPIE PLACE,
EDINBURGH.
Works: Bruntsfield Links.
WHOLESALE and EXPORT ORDERS.
Terms on Application.

THE LONGEST
DRIVING CLEEK
in the
WORLD.
All other kinds also on the same principle.

Carruthers claimed to have "the longest driving cleek in the world"

CLAN GOLF CLUB CO.
London

This early company brought clubs from Scotland south to London which were stamped with a version of the "Thistle" mark during the period 1890-1895. These clubs should not be confused with the Spalding "Clan" model.

CLARK, J. & D.
Musselburgh

Clark produced fine clubs for only a short time in the 1890's. One early advertisement infers that their iron heads were made by Willie Park, Jr. whose business was located nearby, although examples of heads made by Condie have been seen.

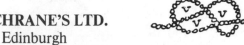

COCHRANE'S LTD.
Edinburgh

Marks in use: 1915-1939

J. P. Cochrane was originally in the ball business in 1906, later entering the club market. His marks were the "Bowline Knot", the "Knight" and a monogram.

COMPAGNE BRUNSWICK FRANCAIS SOCIETY ANONYME, LA
London & Paris

Mark in use: 1922 +

This French company undoubtedly tried to get in on the golf boom in England and France following World War I.

CONDIE, ROBERT (1863-1823)
St. Andrews

Mark in use: 1890-1936

Condie was one of the better known cleekmakers of St. Andrews who had a reputation for handmade quality, having learned the trade from James Anderson of Anstruther. Condie traveled to the United States in the 1890's to learn of the much talked about methods which the Americans were using for drop forging heads. He was very much impressed with the mass production capabilities of the modern facilities, but his experience as a fine player and his knowledge of clubmaking prompted him to continue hand forging iron heads.

The firm was operated as R. Condie & Sons Ltd. after World War I and was eventually taken over by Robert's son, George B. Condie. Some historians feel that MacGregor imitated Condie's "Rose" mark.

Mark in use: 1894-1898

The "Fern" mark appears in two forms: one frond and two fronds and was used only for a short while.

CRAIGIE, J. & W.
Montrose, Forfarshire

John (1854-1928) and William (1859-1936) ran a small firm which produced a limited quantity of well made clubs which bore the "Rifle" symbol from 1895 to 1925.

DICKSON, J. & A.
Edinburgh

This Dickson firm operated from 1890 to 1914, apparently following other family members in the business.

DONALDSON, JAMES
Glasgow

The "Rangefinder" mark in use: 1920-1930.

Mark in use: 1920 +

DRAPER AND MAYNARD CO.
Plymouth, N.H.

A general sporting goods company which added golf clubs to its line about 1920. Their clubs are well **made**, not overly common, and easily recognized by its "Dog" mark which can be found in several forms.

Mark in use: 1893-1897

FORGAN, ANDREW (1846-1926)
Glasgow

The younger brother of Robert Forgan, Andrew made clubs for only a short time using a "Tree" mark, **but** still continued in the golf business as a retailer of golfing items.

FORGAN & SONS, LTD., ROBERT (1824-1900)
St. Andrews

Mark in use: 1880's-1901

Forgan became clubmaker to HRH the Prince of Wales in 1863 and used the prince's plume of three **feathers** as his mark. He was primarily a wooden clubmaker and is thought to have assembled and sold iron clubs as **early** as the 1860's.

Mark in use: 1901-1908

Used the "King's Crown" mark when the prince became King Edward. A son, Thomas (1853-1906), took **over** the firm after his father's death in 1900.

Left: Forgan's shop and staff at the turn of the century. Even his building displayed the Prince of Wales plume.

Right: Robert Forgan poses in his clubmaking shop with his son, Thomas, in the late 1890's.

Forgan's name still remains imbedded in the sidewalk where their shop existed for years at St. Andrews.

FORRESTER, GEORGE (1847-1930)

Elie & Earlsferry

Forrester is credited with being one of the first to make socket headed woods in the late 1890's. He also patented the "concentric" iron which had additional weight behind the sweet spot. Forrester ran his business from 1887 until his death in 1930.

One of Forrester's early socket headed woods.

GALLOWAY, T. - See NICOLSON, D.

Mark in use: 1910-1925

GIBSON, CHARLES (1860-   )

Westward Ho!

Gibson was a fine player as well as clubmaker. This is the "Rampant Stallion" mark. He was the professional at the Royal North Devon Golf Club and had four sons who were also professionals at courses throughout the world.

The "Phoenix" brand by Gibson, first used in 1920.

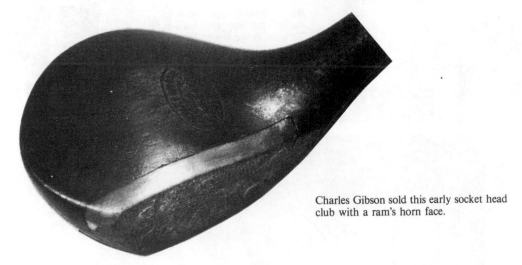

Charles Gibson sold this early socket head club with a ram's horn face.

GIBSON, WILLIAM (1868-1921)

Kinghorn, Fife   Mark in use: 1895-1930

"Gibson of Kinghorn" supplied heads to many makers and professionals. His "Outline Star" mark was registered in 1906 although he started using it when he began his business in the 1890's.

Mark in use: 1930 +

The "Deep Struck Star" mark replaced the outline star.

Mark in use: 1920 +

Gibson was acknowledged as the world's largest maker of golf clubs at one time and made many brands of his own including one which featured the "Hunting Horn".

Mark in use: 1920 +

This mark was for Gibson's "Fife Golf Company" brand.

GRAMPIAN RANGE   Mark in use: 1925 +

Another of Gibson's private brands named after the Grampian mountain range in Scotland.

Mark in use: 1925 +

The "Crusader" brand was yet another of Gibson's different lines.

GOLF GOODS MANUFACTURING CO.

Binghampton, New York

Willie Tucker had an association with this company, but almost nothing else is known about this very early American producer of golf club supplies. They manufactured both wood and iron heads for a short time in the mid 1890's and then either closed or sold out to another firm. Their clubs were well made in the old Scottish fashion and are very rare. Some were stamped by the professionals who performed the final assembly.

GOURLAY, JAMES (SR. AND JR.)

Carnoustie

The Gourlay family made clubs for many years. Both father and son were named James. Their mark was the "anchor". They also forged many heads for Robert Simpson and other makers.

Mark in use: 1905-1920   Mark in use: 1905-1920   Mark in use: 1910 +

"Crescent Moon and Star"   A variation of the "Crescent Moon" Mark.   Gourlay's "Horseshoe" brand mark.

GRAY, JOHN (1824-1904)
Prestwick

Gray was one of the earliest known cleekmakers using several different stamps with his name between 1850 and 1880. He was not related to E. Gray & Co. of Cambridge, a sporting goods firm in the early 20th century. (See page 83.)

GREAT LAKES GOLF CO.
Milwaukee, WI

Mark in use: 1925 +

A small manufacturer of clubs, Great Lakes originally was called the Morehead Company when it began clubmaking circa 1920. They changed their name to Great Lakes in 1924.

While they did not produce high quality, professional grade clubs, some of their lines are of interest to collectors. One was a wood shafted set bearing the name of Tommy Armour made long before the great Scottish player was associated with MacGregor.

HALLEY & CO., JAMES B.
London

Halley's was a retailer and relative latecomer to the golf business. They sold other lines prior to introducing their own "Praymid" brand in 1926.

Mark in use: 1926 +

The "Shell" brand. Besides selling golf clubs, Halley sold many brands of golf balls and other equipment.

"Crossed Swords" in use: 1923 +.

"Circle H" Mark in use: 1923 +

HARROWER, THOMAS
Carnoustie

Harrower ran a small business which produced fine quality clubs with the "Heart" mark beginning in 1910.

TRADE MARK.

HEMMINGS GOLF CO.
Redditch, Worcestershire

Thomas Hemming was only in business as a clubmaker for a year or two using the "Lion on Crown" mark circa 1907.

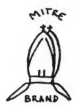

HENDRY AND BISHOP
Edinburgh & Leith

"Mitre Brand" clubs were first produced about 1910, however the actual words were not added to the stamp until 1926. In 1929, the company was restructured as "Hendry & Bishop (1929) Ltd." and began to expand their wholesale business worldwide.

HEWITT, WALTER REYNOLDS (1862-1940)
Carnoustie

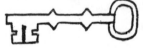

Hewitt ran a small clubmaking shop and marked his clubs with a "Heart and Arrow" from 1896 to 1915.

HILLERICH AND BRADSBY CO.
Louisville, Kentucky

"H & B" today produces fine golf clubs in their "Citation" line, but when they first entered the market prior to World War I, however they did not compete in the quality market. They have always been better known for their famous Louisville Slugger Baseball Bats and general line of sporting goods. In recent years, the golf plant has moved across the Ohio River to Jeffersonville, Indiana. Earliest Hillerich and Bradsby clubs date from about 1915 though most commonly they are from the mid 1920's.

JOHNSON LTD., FRANK A.
London   Mark in use: 1900-1911

Another small clubmaking shop which closed up after Johnson's death in 1911. Their mark was a "key".

KROYDON CO.
Newark, New Jersey   *"Kroydon"*

Not much is known about the original Kroydon Co. except that it first started doing business in Maplewood, N.J. about 1919 and moved to Newark shortly thereafter. In more recent times, Kroydon was purchased by the Ram Golf Company.

Kroydon iron sets came with many unusual face scorings like the "J" series with its circular golf ball pattern and the "U-5" with its unique brickwork design. Other Kroydon irons can be identified by their blade angles (such as 40 degrees stamped on the sole of the mashie club).

LEE, HARRY C.
New York   Marks in use: 1908-1930

While not a clubmaker, Lee imported a great number of clubs to America for his retail stores and marked them with an "acorn".

LETTERS AND CO., JOHN
Glasgow   1923-1960's.

Letters is still in business and formerly was named Letters Logan & Co. This marke was used from 1923 through the 1960s.

LEYLAND & BIRMINGHAM RUBBER CO.
Birmingham

This was a large manufacturing company which originally entered the golf business as a maker of golf bags. They were the first to use the zip fastener on golf bags. Their "bear" mark was first used in 1920.

LUMLEYS, LTD.
Glasgow

Mark in use: 1927 +

Lumleys was a retail establishment which had their own mark and brand of clubs: The Scottish Champion.

MacGREGOR
Dayton, Ohio

See page 131 for more information on MacGregor.

Willie Dunn, Jr. left B.G.I. to run the MacGregor operation, where he stayed for only one year.

MILLAR, CHARLES L.
Glasgow

Mark in use: 1905-1910

Millar started his business in 1895 and primarily used a "Thistle" mark. He was a prolific, but little known, cleekmaker who also produced and sold two private brands under the names of Glasgow Golf Co. and Thistle Golf Co.

1910 +   1915 +   1910 +

MORRIS, TOM, SR. (1821-1908)
St. Andrews
Mark in use: 1915 +

This mark was initiated after Old Tom's death and was used through the 1940's by the firm which still bears the Morris name today. The heads were forged by Stewart and sometimes sold by Brodie of Anstruther.

This ad refers to woods as being either ordinary or socket. Socket heads eventually became the ordinary ones.

Morris' shop did not make iron clubs in the early years. This one was sold to them by the firm of Robert Brodie & Son.

NICOLL, GEORGE (1861-1945)
Leven
Mark in use: 1898-1903

George Nicoll began forging iron heads in 1881 and the firm continued under family supervision until 1982. His son, Robert (1884-1946), ran the firm in later years. This was their earliest "hand" mark. Prior to using the hand mark, the irons were stamped "G. Nicoll, Leven". (See page 83.)

Mark in use: 1905-1910

The "hand" mark was not registered until 1924, but Nicoll claimed continuous usage since 1898.

Mark in use: 1910 +

Another version of the "hand" which appears in ten different forms. In the United States, Burke and Spalding also hand marks which were never registered.

Mark in use: 1910-1920

Another version of the "hand" which appeared on many of the irons which Nicoll exported to the Burke Golf Company in Newark, Ohio.

1925 +

By this time there were several lines including: Able, Clinker, Recorder, Zenith, Precision, Viking and the Indicator, which was one of the first matched sets of irons.

NICOLSON, D. (1864-1900)

Mark in use: 1890-1900

Pittenweem, Fife

    Nicolson was so proud of his gold medal exhibit at the Edinburgh Exhibition of 1890 that he began to stamp his clubs with a reference to the medal. Upon his death in 1900, the business was continued by T. Galloway until 1915. Galloway marked clubs with the stamp, "Successor to D. Nicolson".

OKE, W. G. (1892-   )

London

    Oke was a clubmaker and professional at a number of London area golf clubs and first used an "oak tree" mark in 1923.

PARK, WILLIE, JR. (1864-1925)

Musselburgh

    The son of the famous golfer of the 1860's and 1870's, Willie used his two Open victories and family heritage to embark on a long career of clubmaking, golf course design and golf writing. As in the early days of marking clubs, Park stamped his name and not a symbol during the years 1885-1915. Park was in business with his father, Willie (1834-1903) as W. Park & Son.

    Park's "Wry Necked" putter, patented in 1894, was popular in both Britain and the United States. Park claimed constant use by outstanding players such as John Ball, Harry Vardon, Willie Fernie, A. J. Balfour, Robert Maxwell, Ben Sayers, Sandy Herd and Jack White.

Park's mark.

Contrary to Park's claim, not all good golfers can make good clubs! However, he was certainly correct when referring to himself.

PATRICK, ALEX (1845-1930)

Leven & Wimbledon

    A family business concern since 1847, Patrick used this "spur" mark in the twentieth century between 1905 and 1915.

WEL MADE REGD.

    This "Wel Made" mark shows a figure of a woman at a water well and was used from 1920 to 1925. Patrick also had a mark with the initial "P" which he used circa 1915.

1915.   WARRANTED P FORGED

The Patricks were originally long nose wood makers and eventually began to sell balls and irons.

REACH CO., A. J.
Philadelphia

Mark in use: 1915-1935

Reach was already a famous sporting goods retailer by the time they started selling golf clubs around 1905. Most clubs found today date from 1918-1930. The company was owned by Spalding and many of the Reach club heads were made by Spalding in styles very similar to the Spalding line.

RITCHIE, W. L.
London

WLR Brand

Mark in use: 1920 +

Ritchie was the professional at the Addington Golf Club in Croydon and used the "Scottish Bluebell" as the mark on his private brand. In a 1929 advertisement, Ritchie claimed that all of his clubs were handmade and that each is personally examined by him prior to sale. He also claimed to have the largest clubmaking shop in England which was run by a golf professional.

SAYERS, BERNARD (BEN) SR. (1857-1924)
North Berwick

Mark in use: 1920 +

Sayers was a famous player, instructor and clubmaker. He started out in the golf business as a gutty ballmaker in the 1880's in Musselburgh before entering the clubmaking business in North Berwick. He was later joined by his son, Ben, who greatly increased the output of the firm. Ben is easily recognized in old photographs due to his short stature and magnificent mustache. This is his "Robin" mark.

Shipping Department at the Ben Sayers Company in the early 1930s.

SCOTT, ANDREW HERD
Elie, Fife

Mark in use: 1902-1910

Scott succeeded Forgan as clubmaker to HRH the Prince of Wales following the coronation of Edward VII. This earned him the right to use the plume cyper of the prince.

Mark in use: 1911-1925

Upon the coronation of George V in 1911, Scott became clubmaker to the king. He devised a "Crown" mark with a lion which differed from Forgan's "royal" mark.

SHEPHERD, ALEX
Iverness
   Shepherd's mark was none other than a "shepherd's crook" which he began using in 1915.

 Mark in use: 1900-1912

SHERLOCK, JAMES (1875-   )
Oxford
   Sherlock was an English professional best known for his time at the Oxford University Golf Course. His mark actually spells "Oxford" in a roundabout way. He also held professional positions at the Stoke Poges and Hunstanton Clubs in England.

SIMPSON, J. & A.
Edinburgh
   Archie and Jack, the 1880 Open champion, ran this firm from 1900 to 1915. Archie held numerous positions throughout Great Britain before moving to the United States.

SIMPSON, ROBERT (1862-1923)
Carnoustie
   One of six golfing brothers, Robert started the family business in 1885.

Simpson was one of the early makers to electro-plate iron heads as mentioned in this ad from 1903.

SLAZENGER AND SON (Also called FRANK L. SLAZENGER CO.) Mark in use: 1895-1900
London & New York
   This London based sporting goods firm had its own brand of wood shafted clubs for only a short time. Most of their clubs can be found with Stewart or Condie cleekmarks, although some were made by Nicoll and Gibson.
   In 1913 they were claiming that they were "The oldest golf house in the United States". Slazenger is still in the sporting goods business today.

SPALDING & BROS., A. G.

London & Dysart, Scotland & New York & Chicopee, Massachusetts

See page 131 for more information about Spalding.

Spalding began in London and later started a second works in Dysart. This is their "anvil" mark.

The "tong" brand was first produced in Scotland in 1915.

The "hammer" forged irons were manufactured in London beginning in 1910.

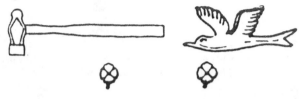

Some of Spalding's American marks.

The mark on the left is similar to the American one on the right except for the "Made in Gt. Britain" portion of the mark. The British mark was in use: 1902-1908.

The spring face concept was a clever idea, although it never performed satisfactorily.

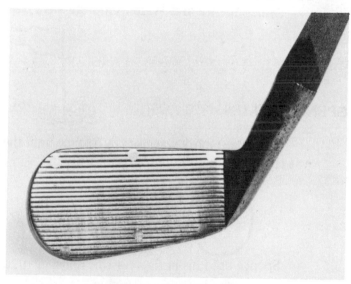

Spalding spring face club model.

This "Calamity Jane" model is a reproduction of Bobby Jones' famous putter.

This is "Calamity Jane I" which is in the possession of the Augusta National Golf Club. The club was made by Condie for William Winton, who sold clubs in the Acton area of London before going into the clubmaking business in Montrose. Jones had a copy made of the original worn putter in 1924 and used it through 1930 in winning 12 of his 13 major championships. This putter, "Calamity Jane II" is on display at the USGA Museum. It should also be noted that Jones had six more copies made by Spalding in 1926 which he gave to friends.

116

Spalding "Medal" putter.

Spalding introduced the Cran Cleek with its wood insert in the late 1890's.

Only a few sets of Jones model irons were specially made with wooden shafts, while thousands were produced with steel shafts.

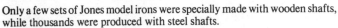

SPENCE & GOURLAY   Mark in use: circa 1920
   St. Andrews
   James Spence and Walter Gourlay were partners in this firm.

SPENCE, JAMES (1870-1929)   Mark in use: 1920-1926
   St. Andrews
   This "flag" mark was used by Spence until the firm was bought out by Forgan in 1926. Thereafter, the mark was then used in conjunction with Forgan's.

   Spence used his initials for this mark in 1920.

ST. ANDREW GOLF CO.
   Glasgow & Dunfermline
   This company used the "Ogg-Mented" version of designing balanced sets of clubs which was invented by Willie Ogg. Denny Shute used St. Andrew clubs in winning the 1933 British Open. Other players using these clubs in the 1930's were Gene Sarazen and Johnny Farrell. Their "stag" mark was in use from 1910 until 1925, while the "sun" mark was first used in 1925.

STADIUM GOLF CO.
   London
   Heads were specifically forged for Stadium by the Gourlays. This "anchor" mark was put into use in 1925.

STANDARD GOLF CO.
Sunderland

William Mills was known for over 40 models of aluminum putters and fairway clubs. He began in 1895 by making aluminum copies of long nose wooden putters such as Hugh Kirkaldy's famous Philp putter.

An early Mills putter.

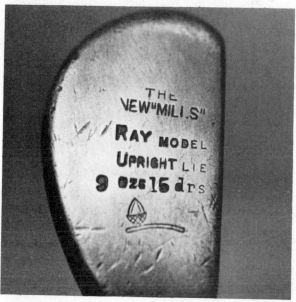

A Mills putter made for resale by the Harry C. Lee Company of New York (Acorn mark). All Mills putters were marked with both the head weight and lie specifications.

STEWART, TOM
St. Andrews

 Mark in use: 1893-1905

Tom Stewart, Jr. (1861-1931) learned clubmaking from his father and also from Robert White. Their firm is one of the better known of the early clubmakers and their output of clubs over the years reached into the millions. His earliest mark was the plain "pipe" to which was added in 1905, the phrase "T.S.St. A. REG. TRADEMARK."

Stewart used the "serpent" mark to designate ladies or juvenile clubs between 1895 and 1905.

This Stewart iron was made for the Tom Morris shop and was stamped with both the "Serpent" and an "L" to indicate that it was a ladies club.

ST. ANDREWS
X
REG. TRADE MARK

This unusual mark was used on clubs which were shipped to Australia circa 1915.

This was a secondary mark which was used to denote an imperfect, but usable, clubhead.

R.T.J   F.O.
             R.T.J.

These secondary marks were used in 1931 to advertise the fact that Bobby Jones won the Open Championship with irons forged by Stewart. The "F.O." indicates that Francis Ouimet was also a patron of Stewart.

Stewart's "RTJ" model was produced in 1931 without the authorization of Bobby Jones.

An "F.O. R.T.J." iron made by Stewart and sold by Yeoman's of Chicago

Entrance to the Stewart shop as it looked in 1942.

THORNTON AND CO., LTD.
Edinburgh
    Thornton was in the India rubber business and had a long history of selling golf items. This mark designated their own brand beginning in 1925.

TOOLEY AND SONS, A.
  London
      Tooley was a professional who had his own private mark circa 1920.

URQUHART'S, LTD.
  Edinburgh
      The Urquhart family pioneered the adjustable club and used this mark from 1892 to 1906.

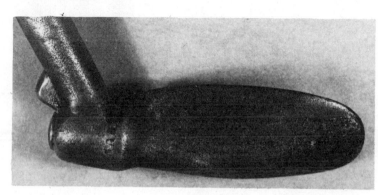

Urquhart adjustable club. The "U" mark usually appears towards the toe on the back of the club.

VICKER'S LTD. Mark in use: 1925 +
  Sheffield

WHITE, JACK (1873-1949)   Mark in use: 1905-1910
  London & Gullane
      White was an excellent player and won the Open Championship in 1904. The "Sun" mark is attributed to his position as professional to the Sunningdale Golf Club outside of London. White was the maker of the woods used by Bobby Jones in winning the Grand Slam in 1930.

       Mark in use: 1910-1930

      In the mid 1930's, White retired from Sunningdale and returned to Gullane, his hometown in Scotland, where he opened a new factory. His business was the only industry located in this small village which has many fine golf courses, including Gullane and Muirfield.
      This is the later, more common design of White's "Sun" mark.

WHITE, ROBERT (1857-   )
  St. Andrews
      White made iron heads in Scotland before moving to the U.S. in the early 1890's where he took part in the formation of the McGregor Golf Company. It is thought that young Tom Stewart was apprenticed to him in the early 1890's.   (See page 83.)

White produced fine irons in St. Andrews before emigrating to the United States.

WILSON, ROBERT (1845-1906)
St. Andrews

Wilson was an early cleekmaker and therefore many of his irons have no markings. He did have a stamp with his name in an oval pattern and is thought to have also marked clubs with a bent nail. (See page 83.)

WILSON, ROBERT BLACK
St. Andrews

Known as "Buff", Wilson was a popular St. Andrews character who made clubs from 1890 to 1910 and also held golf professional positions in England and America. He should not be confused with Robert Wilson, an earlier St. Andrews clubmaker.

Buff Wilson was one of the first makers to export clubs not only to America, but also to New Zealand.

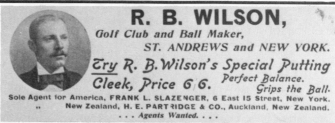

R. B. WILSON,
Golf Club and Ball Maker,
ST. ANDREWS and NEW YORK.
Try R. B. Wilson's Special Putting
Cleek, Price 6 6. Perfect Balance.
Grips the Ball.
Sole Agent for America, FRANK L. SLAZENGER, 6 East 15 Street, New York.
" New Zealand, H. E. PARTRIDGE & CO., Auckland, New Zealand.
. . . Agents Wanted. . . .

WILSON SPORTING GOODS COMPANY
River Grove, Illinois
See page 132 for more information on Wilson.

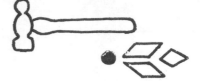

WILSON, WILLIAM CHRISTIE
Hereford

Mark on a private line of clubs in use: 1925 +

WILSON, WILLIE
St. Andrews

Mark in use: 1885-1895

Wilson was from the old line of St. Andrews clubmakers and also stamped irons with his name. (See page 83.)

WINTON, JAMES & WILLIAM
London & Montrose

This family of clubmakers had several separate businesses which were later combined as Wm. Winton & Co. They produced a large volume of their "diamond" brand clubs from 1900 to 1939.

For some unknown reason, all of the marks were stamped on the toe of this Winton iron.

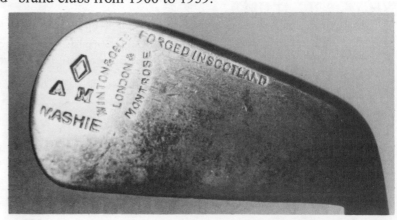

WRIGHT & DITSON CO.

Boston

    The Wright and Ditson Co. was an early sporting goods retailer. While their early history is not very clear, it is known that they were part of the Spalding organization as early as 1900. In the mid 1890's they sold imported Scottish clubs before manufacturing their own lines.

ST. ANDREWS

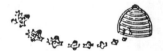

Mark in use: 1920-1930

    One of the most famous lines of Wright and Ditson clubs was their "St. Andrews" model. These are often confused by novice collectors for Scottish clubs.

Mark in use: 1912 +

Another common brand was the "One-Shot", marked by an arm holding a shot glass.

Mark in use: 1915-1930

The "Bee Line" model. **BEE-LINE**

A popular player at the turn of the century, Findlay had a line of clubs made by Wright & Ditson.

122

YOUNG CO., L. A.
Detroit

Mark in use: 1927 +

This company was founded by Leonard Young in the late 1920's and capitalized on the fame of Walter Hagen by manufacturing lines of Hagen clubs exclusively. In 1930, Young was promoting a "compact blade" style of irons which was popularized again in the 1970's.

The best known Hagen club and the most collectible is the concave faced sand iron popularized by Hagen in 1929 and subsequently banned in 1931. The L. A. Young Company was later purchased by Wilson Sporting Goods who continues to run the division as the Walter Hagen Company.

...for Christmas

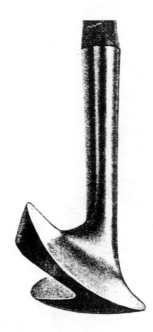

...the
Walter Hagen Sand Wedge

This year there need be no last minute hurry and scurry, no vain searching for a suitable gift—the Walter Hagen Sand Wedge makes the selection easy. For experts—for novices—this club is a welcome addition to the golfer's bag. Sand traps, bunkers, thick rough—these are the bugbears on any golf course, and the golfer who can overcome these difficulties with the least trouble is the one who is hard to beat. Many clubs have been designed and improved to aid your game, but in the Walter Hagen Sand Wedge we find the first really perfect trouble club. With the Sand Wedge the difficult explosion shot from bunkers becomes amazingly simplified. The sole helps the club go through instead of stopping at the impact with deep or hard sand —and the 20 ounces of weight aids in slashing through all manner of trouble. A marvelous club in bunkers and sand traps—an excellent aid in approaching from mud or tall grass—the Walter Hagen Sand Wedge has been enthusiastically received by the country's outstanding golfers. For anyone who plays golf—for any-

one who is going to play—the Walter Hagen Sand Wedge is an ideal Christmas gift. This club—at $12.00—is available at the leading dealers in sporting goods or from your professional.

THE 1.68 WALTER HAGEN GOLF BALL has been improved. By a gift of these balls you will remove for someone a little of the uncertainty from a very uncertain game. The new construction insures maximum carry as well as absolute accuracy in the air and on the greens. For anyone desiring the best in the large ball, the Hagen Ball is the logical answer. The 1.68 Walter Hagen Golf Ball—75c.

A GIFT NOW OF WALTER HAGEN CLUBS is very timely. Though a sensation this year with the small ball these clubs were designed primarily to meet the requirements of the new 1.68 balls. Woods with large deep-faced heads—the famous Walter Hagen "Compact Blade" irons —these clubs will more than ever prove their superiority this year. Give Hagen clubs and insure to the recipient the enjoyment which comes from using the equipment of champions.

THE L. A. YOUNG CO., DETROIT
Makers of Walter Hagen Golf Equipment
Canadian Distributors: HARGRAFT BROS., LTD., Toronto

L.A. Young heavily promoted the popular, but eventually illegal, concave faced sand club.

STEEL SHAFTED CLUBS
The Introduction of Steel Shafts

Following hundreds of years of making golf clubs with wooden shafts, steel shafted clubs were finally accepted as the preferred style in the late 1930's. Prior to this acceptance of metal shafted clubs, the most noteworthy occurences in the evolution of clubmaking had been the introduction of mechanization and mass production to clubmaking in the late nineteenth century, the drilling of the clubhead for shaft insertion, and the idea of matched sets of clubs.

As early as 1894, a British patent was granted for the design of a solid steel shaft. Unfortunately the technology needed for the proper manufacture of the idea did not exist at the time and the idea was soon forgotten. Around 1905, inventors in the United States and Great Britain began experimenting with metal shafts again. These shafts were tubular and sometimes had spiral or straight grooves, or other unusual seams. However, metal shafted clubs which were somewhat reliable were not introduced to the golfing market until the 1920's.

None of these metal shafted clubs had been designated legal for play in this country until they were approved by the United States Golf Association in 1925. It was not until 1929 that the Royal and Ancient Golf Club of St. Andrews finally legalized the new shafts for use in the rest of the golfing world. It should be noted that substantial numbers of the steel shafted clubs were in use prior to these dates even though they were not approved for official use.

Although many styles of steel shafts came on the market, the golfing masses were generally satisfied with the hickory ones to which they were accustomed. In 1929, the Horton Manufacturing Company tried to lure golfers away from hickory by introducing their Bristol Torsion shaft which had a pronounced seam running down its length. They claimed that this innovation was "the only shaft that duplicates the feel of fine hickory". It was in 1927 that True Temper patented a shaft with the step method of tapering which eventually became the standard for the golf club industry. It is this shaft, with, subsequent improvements, that continues to be used most often today.

There continued to be much publicity aimed at informing the golfer of the advantages of steel over hickory, such as economy, consistency of flex, availability of materials and the resistance to warping. However acceptance was not immediate and throughout the 1930's, the major golf manufacturers offered the customer the option of purchasing their new models with the old hickory or the new steel shafts. Some of the players who were reluctant to change were correct in their loyalty to hickory, because it was not until after World War II that the steel shafts were consistently manufactured to exacting standards. The last time a major American championship was won with hickory shafts was in 1936 when Johnny Fischer won the U.S. Amateur.

Following the universal acceptance of the steel shafted golf club, there was a period of approximately twenty years when there were no major improvements in the club design other than the introduction of stainless steel forgings. Of course, there continued to be minor advances in manufacturing and appearance. Endorsements by touring professionals proliferated as manufacturers heavily advertising their products in the post war era.

Further Improvements In The Shaft

By the early 1950's all of the club manufacturers were using quality steel shafts. Painting, sheathing and wood graining were several of the treatments that had been applied to the shaft, but chroming became the preferred method for rust prevention. Always looking for improvements, the club designers continued to experiment with other materials for shafts.

In the late 1950's, fiberglass shafts were marketed by Golfcraft, Shakespeare and Burke. These colored shafts were not very popular even though they were heavily promoted by Gary Player. The shafts were not known to have improved anyone's game, however when used by a very skillful player, they were capable of winning the U.S. Open. Dick Mayer used fiberglass shafts in 1957 and Player used them to win his 1965 title. Mayer's win with these innovative shafts was noteworthy because twenty-six years earlier, at the same Inverness Country Club, another new type of shaft was used to win the Open. In 1931, Billy Burke had become the first player to win the Open with steel shafted clubs!

As fiberglass was declining in popularity in the mid 1960's, aluminum shafts were offered to golfers. This was the first true lightweight shaft and proved to be a fine feature for the average player. Unfortunately aluminum shafts were not endorsed by the touring pros and their sales subsequently declined. Arnold Palmer, then promoting his own club manufacturing company, did win some tour events using the aluminum shafts. However, aluminum was soon overshadowed by the new lightweight steel alloys of the late 1960's and graphite shafts of the 1970's.

Changes In Iron ClubHeads

The basic club head shape changed little since the early 1900's. Many techniques from the turn of the century often reappeared in later years as "revolutionary new breakthroughs". Some of these concepts were: perimeter weighting, drilled through hosels, short hosels, offset heads and contoured soles. In the 1960's club designers began to apply space age technology to enlarge the "sweet spot" in order to improve the results of mishit shots.

The most noteworthy of these new clubs were the Ping and Confidence irons which were noticeably non-traditional in appearance. Golfers soon accepted these clubs and were very pleased with the improvement in their games. These clubs and similar models which soon followed were made by a process known as investment casting. Simply stated, the heads were formed by pouring molten steel into very exact molds which resulted in a head almost ready for shafting. This method is still in use today along with the traditional method of forging which requires mechanical hammering, grinding and many finishing steps. The lower startup cost and labor saving techique of investment casting has enabled dozens of clubmakers to start up production within the last fifteen to twenty years. Unfortunately poor designs and improper marketing have caused many of the small firms to go out of business.

While the cast heads have certainly earned their place in the golf market, the forged heads have traditionally been preferred by the better players who prefer their "feel". The cast clubs have dominated the golf scene in recent years, but the forged heads are currently enjoying a renewed popularity with the trend toward the classic look of the 1960's.

Changes In Wood Clubheads

The most significant changes in wood head designs in the steel shaft era have been the standard inclusion of an insert in the hitting area, improved methods of weighting and the use of laminated heads. Wilson introduced their Strata Bloc head in 1941 which was constructed of thin sheets of maple glued together in a manner similar to plywood. This laminated head was designed to be more durable and less expensive than the traditional persimmon heads. It took about twenty years for the head to be totally successful since the gluing process was not totally perfected until the 1960's. The laminated maple heads currently being produced are actually stronger and more reliable than the persimmon heads, but for nostalgic or psychological reasons, many players prefer the non-laminated ones.

The most popular of the innovative clubs being sold today is the metal headed "wood". While they have been in use since the late nineteenth century, only recently have the manufacturers been able to reproduce the feel and playing qualities of the traditional wooden clubs. Other heads are also being made of graphite and similar materials.

Classic Clubs

In the early 1970's, a new category of golf clubs became popular. Once referred to as merely "old clubs", the term classic now denotes those clubs with exceptional looks or playability which were made from the late 1930's through the mid 1960's. When the large number of investment cast and nontraditional looking clubs began to dominate the golf market in the 1970's, the better pros and amateurs were wanting clubs like the ones "in the good old days". As the touring pros started to play with these "used" clubs, they quickly gained in popularity and became collector's items.

As the following list shows, MacGregor dominates the classic club field. Models like the famous Tommy Armour series, designers like Toney Penna and a huge advisory staff of golf professionals assisted MacGregor in surpassing all other manufacturers in the creation of timeless golf club styles. These clubs of a past era are now the models for the clubs of the 1980's which are better constructed and balanced, but still resemble the originals. Other notable collectible classics include Bristol putters and the wedges and putters made by Wilson.

The classic club market has had its ups and downs over the last decade. There are a number of dealers throughout the country, many of which sell clubs on the phone and through the mail. Because these clubs are not that old, many golfers collect them for use on the course, while others collect for the pleasure of owning and displaying their classics. Most of the playable classics tend to be the woods, wedges and putters. Generally the better players prefer to play with modern irons because of their superior shafts and weight distribution.

Collectors who are new to the field of classic clubs should be wary of fake clubs and should realize that two clubs of the same model may vary greatly in value. Since all of these clubs had their final grinding and finishing steps performed by hand, each has its own feel, loft, lie and other playing characteristics. Because of these variables, the appearance of Tommy Armour's name on a golf club does not automatically signify that it is a valuable classic club. The restoration and refinishing can also greatly affect the value of a club, so the collector must take all of this into account when buying or selling a classic club.

There are several books which will greatly assist the classic club enthusiast. *Classic Golf Clubs, A Pictorial Guide* by Joe Clement does a fine job of explaining the characteristics of hundreds of clubs. Tom Wishon has recently compiled *The Golf Club Price Guide* for use by golf professionals and classic club collectors. This detailed guide contains trade-in values and identification information for golf clubs manufactured since 1950. Jim Kaplan, owner of Vintage Golf in Glencoe, Illinois, has reproduced the golf club catalogs issued during the classic era for three of the largest manufacturers: MacGregor, Wilson and Hillerich & Bradsby. All of these books are an immense help to the collector for the identification and dating of classic clubs.

CLASSIC CLUB VALUES

Prices of classic golf clubs have fluctuated considerably over the years and will probably continue to do so as various clubs are made popular by the players on the professional tour. The following prices are those which a collector would be expected to pay to a dealer for **true** classic clubs in playable condition. Older playable clubs which are not considered classics are valued considerably less. Clubs in poor shape or those which have been improperly restored may be worth only a fraction of their potential value.

DRIVERS	$100 to 300
WOOD SETS	250 to 600 (some over $900)
IRON SETS	150 to 250 (some over $500)
WEDGES	50 to 150
PUTTERS	50 to 250 (some over $500)

During the late 1920's, some shafts were constructed of a combination of materials. This one was made of bamboo, hickory and steel.

Gary Player was an advocate of fiberglass shafts in the 1960's.

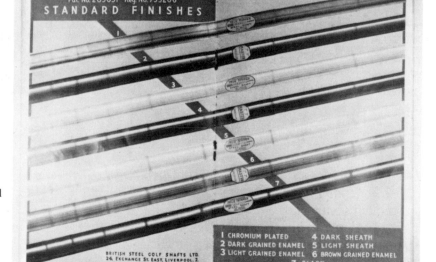

For a period of time True Temper manufactured steel shafts with seven different finishes.

126

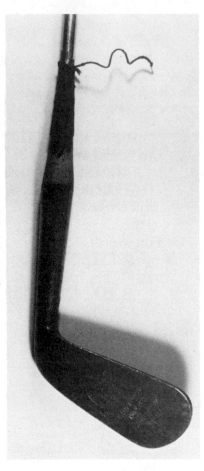

As the steel shaft became more popular, club manufacturers found theselves overstocked with ironheads made for the larger diameter wooden shaft. To reduce their inventory, bushings such as this were devised so that the thin steel shaft could be used with the older heads. This conversion was used only on the economy grade models.

The Horton Manufacturing Company was a pioneer in the steel shaft industry with their Bristol shaft.

Few collectors realize that R. Forgan & Sons, the historic clubmaking firm in St. Andrews, also made Tommy Armour putters. Their agreement with the famous Scottish golfer entitled them to use his name for marketing purposes everywhere except the United States.

The Streamliner golf club, with its bullet shaped head, was patented in the early 1930's. The company was eventually sold to MacGregor in 1938, who produced the model for only a few more years.

Set of removable head clubs. The single shaft inserts quickly and securely into one of the several heads.

LIST #4 — CLASSIC CLUBS (CC DESIGNATION)
Listing of Some of the More Desirable Classic Clubs

ARNOLD PALMER COMPANY

Chattanooga, Tennessee

ARNOLD PALMER PERSONAL PUTTER: This putter was designed by Palmer after he left Wilson in the 1960's along the lines of other classic flange putters. This club should not be confused with the earlier Palmer models made by Wilson.

BEN HOGAN

Fort Worth, Texas

SPEED SLOT WOODS: The Hogan persimmon woods of the 1960's were well made and many are quite playable today. They have no real collector value.

EQUALIZER WEDGE: These pitching wedges have appeared on some classic club lists even though they are valued under $50.

BRISTOL

Melrose Park, Illinois

Bristol manufactured all types of golf clubs, but collectors and players are mainly interested in their line of end shafted flange putters made in the late 1950's, and early 1960's. Bristol putters are probably the most sought after of the classic putters with some of the models selling for over $1000. Much of their appeal results from their use by tour players such as Jack Nicklaus. Some of the models are identical in design, but have different markings. George Low was the designer of these clubs which are all fine putters.

George Low Sportsmen 600
George Low Wizard 600
Melrose Park Wizard 600
Wizard 600
Tropicana
Greenbriar

BURKE GOLF CO.

Newark, Ohio

SAV-A-SHOT PUTTERS: These putters were available in both blade and offset mallet head styles.

SAV-A-SHOT BLASTER: This early wedge was one of the first with a large flanged sole. The face has dots rather than conventional scoring.

HILLERICH & BRADSBY CO.

Louisville, Kentucky

POWER BILT CITATION WOODS: These woods with their characteristic brass backweight are known for their normally shallow faces, which are preferred by many golfers. They also offered a deep face driver model which is a desirable club. These well designed clubs are not true classics, but are still desirable.

MacGREGOR

Dayton and Cincinnati

MacGregor has produced more clubs which are now considered classics than any other manufacturer. Since the late 1930's, they were innovative both in design and marketing. Their advisory staff has included golf greats such as Tommy Armour, Ben Hogan, Byron Nelson, Jimmy Demaret, Louise Suggs and Jack Nicklaus. Many of their innovations were cosmetic rather than structural, such as their various insert designs for wooden clubs.

MacGregor actively promoted their Custom Department which would tailor clubs for the discerning golfer. Many of these custom clubs made by craftsmen like John Huggins are commanding the highest prices in the classic market today. It should be mentioned that many of the Armour and other models are not true classic clubs due to shape, lie and other considerations. Because of this, club buyers should consult with an expert before paying large sums of money for MacGregor clubs.

The most noteworthy of the collectible MacGregor clubs are listed below.

WOODS: Tommy Armour 945 Eye-O-Matic, Tommy Armour 693, Tommy Armour M85 Eye-O-Matic, and Ben Hogan model.

IRONS: "VIP by Nicklaus" models from 1966-1967.

WEDGES: VIP and D.S. models.

PUTTERS: Tommy Armour putters, both the older green shafted and the Ironmaster models IM and IMG.

From 1935 until 1967, Tommy Armour's name was placed on thousands of the numerous putter models offered by MacGregor. Because of the variations in the offset and head shape of this flanged putter, a golfer usually could find one to suit his game. In 1968 Armour's name was dropped, however the Ironmaster insignia continues to be used today.

MacGregor Tommy Armour woods dominate the classic club field.

MacGregor woods were made with several special types of inserts: Eye-o-matic, Keyhole and Velocitized. These inserts had many variations in color and shape which can be extremely confusing. This driver was produced from 1958 to 1960 and has the Velocitized insert which actually had dowels forming the three dots. The alignment arrow at the top of the insert was another of MacGregor's many innovations.

The Tommy Armour 945 iron was introduced in 1953 and is one of the fine playable classics. To the casual observer many models of the Armour irons look alike, but it is the little variations that intrigue the classic club enthusiast.

The FC4000 model iron has the patented "Recessed Weight" design which was meant to centralize the head weight behind the sweet spot. It did not prove to be as popular as the traditional Armour blade. The "FC" designation on the club referred to the flame ceramic treatment which would darken the scored area of the clubface for cosmetic reasons.

As with all MacGregor clubs, there were many styles from which to choose. This Armour 11 iron is a Colokrom model 156 which was first sold in 1957. The Colokrom models introduced in 1955, featured exposed copper plating in the scored area of the clubface. This was primarily an alignment aid, however MacGregor claimed that the plating would enable "the club head to literally 'grab' the ball and throw it accurately toward the cup."

SPALDING

Chicopee, Massachusetts

CASH-IN PUTTERS: The Cash-In model was produced by Spalding beginning in the 1930's. The early ones are recognized by their extremely long grips and sheathed steel shafts. As time progressed, the putter was modernized, but still featured the same center shafted blade. There were several varying styles including brass, chromed and stainless steel heads; chromed or colored sheath shafts; and, rocker or rounded soles. There were thousands of these clubs made and prices are generally under $40, depending on age, style and condition.

OTHER PUTTERS: The HB, HBA and the wooden shafted Blue Chip putters are considered to be collectible classics and are valued higher than the Cash-In. The TPM putters of the late 1960's which were individually hand finished are also desirable.

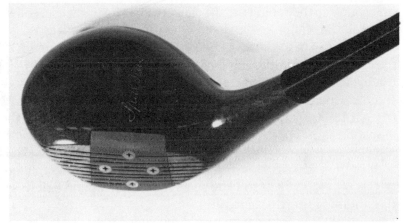

Spalding's Cash-In putter has been a favorite for many years since it was first marketed in the late 1930's. The earlier shafts had a colored sheathing and the heads have been made in chromed steel, stainless steel and brass. It is not considered to be a valuable club because of the great numbers produced, but still is used by many players.

An attractive, but not necessarily classic, Spalding driver from the 1950's.

WALTER HAGEN

Detroit

Hagen wedges and the Cascade putter are the most notable of their classic clubs.

WILSON SPORTING GOODS

River Grove, Illinois

PUTTERS: Wilson produced many fine flange type putters over the years as evidenced by the many in use on the professional golf circuit. The most desirable models are the "Designed by Arnold Palmer", the 8802 and the 8813.

WEDGES: Wilson was a pioneer in the design of the modern wedge in the 1930's. The R-20, R-60, R-90 and Helen Hicks models have enjoyed great popularity in the last decade, but tend to be lower in value in present times.

IRONS: The Wilson Staff irons manufactured between 1958 and 1974 are some of the playable classic irons which are being collected.

Top: Manufactured since the 1930's, the early "R" series wedges by Wilson are very popular among better golfers. The R-20 and R-90 were made with either scored or dot punched faces and are the most frequently seen models. Because of their popularity, Wilson began to offer a reproduction version of the R-90 in 1975, complete with the brown painted shaft.

Bottom: This is the original Wilson 8802 putter and should not be confused with the later reproduction which actually is stamped with the word "original". The 8802 was sold with either a chrome head or a black head. The Arnold Palmer model is very similar to this model but is usually worth more to collectors.

Left: Wilson's Staff model from the fifties and sixties are also popular with the classic club collector. This Top Notch model was introduced in 1954 and discontinued for the 1956 season when the Fluid-Feel model with its drilled through hosel was introduced.

WRIGHT & DITSON

Boston

The Spalding HB and HBA models were also sold under the Wright & Ditson name.

MAJOR GOLF MANUFACTURERS
A. G. Spalding & Bros.
London; Dysart, Scotland; New York; Chicopee Falls, Massachusetts

Spalding existed for several decades in the United States before beginning to offer golf equipment in their line of sporting goods. Their interest in golf began in 1892 when Julian Curtiss was sent to Scotland to purchase leather for use in making footballs. According to the two versions of the story, Curtiss purchased five hundred dollars worth of golf equipment either due to his interest in the game or as a result of having had too much to drink at the tavern. The company was not very impressed with his acquisition since golf was not a common game, so he took the clubs to his home in Greenwich, Connecticut for storage. Shortly thereafter, Curtiss and his brother got some friends together to help lay out a five hole golf course so they could use the clubs and balls. Meanwhile, golf was gaining in popularity in America and Spalding decided to recall the equipment and subsequently began to advertise golf items in their 1893 catalog of sporting goods.

Spalding began making golf clubs in the United States in the mid 1890's and in Britain shortly thereafter. One of the original manufacturing facilities was in Morristown, New Jersey and in 1898 they introduced the Morristown line of clubs to augment their earlier "The Spalding" line. Also about this time, Spalding designer James Cran patented the famous wood faced iron club popularly known as the Cran Cleek.

In 1898, Spalding signed a contract with Harry Vardon, the British Open Champion, for the purpose of endorsing a Spalding gutta percha golf ball which they called the Vardon Flyer. In doing so, Vardon became the first professional athlete to receive money for promoting a product. He won the 1900 U.S. Open with this ball and then conducted an exhibition tour of the United States to promote the Vardon Autograph model clubs and the Vardon Flyer balls. Spalding's timing of this promotion was too late since the rubber wound ball was rapidly gaining in popularity and the Vardon Flyer was discontinued shortly thereafter.

In 1904, Spalding won a gold medal for their display of sporting goods at the Louisiana Purchase Exposition. To celebrate this award, they introduced their Gold Medal line in 1905 and continued to make these models until 1919. They were also having great success with the Wizard golf ball and their version of the dimpled ball which was introduced in 1909.

Spalding continued to be a major manufacturer of golf clubs and balls. The most successful of their clubs were the Kro-Flite matched woods and irons, of which millions were produced. They were introduced in the late 1920's along with the popular Thistle, Symetric, Dundee and Firebrand lines of clubs.

Spanning the hickory to steel shaft transition was the Robert T. Jones autograph line of clubs which for a number of years were the finest balanced clubs available. Following his retirement from competition in the 1930's, Jones became an advisor to the company. Spalding has continued to be a successful club manufacturer and has also greatly affected the golf ball business with the development and sale of their Top Flite brand.

MacGregor
Dayton, and later Cincinnati and Georgia

The MacGregor Golf Company was originally known as the Crawford, McGregor & Canby Company which was an offshoot of the Dayton Shoe Last Company. It is believed that Robert White, the famous St. Andrews clubmaker, applied the mechanized woodworking techniques used in the shoe last factory in Dayton, Ohio to the turning of wooden golf club heads. The company's first catalog was produced in 1898 at a time when Willie Dunn, earlier with B.G.I., spent a year with MacGregor. The company grew very rapidly due to the export of hundreds of thousands of wooden golf heads to Scottish makers.

By 1910 the company was producing a full line of golfing requisites including bags and golf course maintenance supplies. They even built a company golf course in Dayton for employee recreation and the testing of new equipment.

The reason for the difference in the spelling of "McGregor" as in the original company name and "MacGregor", the Scottish version of the name which appeared on the clubs, is somewhat unclear. It was probably part of a marketing scheme to appease the many Scottish golf professionals making their living in the United States and as a gimmick to give character to their line of golf equipment. Clubs were even stamped "J. MacGregor" which was either a fictitious name or referred to John MacGregor, who had once worked for the St. Andrews clubmaking firm of Robert Forgan & Son.

The most common of the many models from the hickory era are the Par, Peerless, Pilot and economy grade Edgemont lines. In the years prior to it being illegal, they produced over 20 models of the famous Bakspin iron with its deep grooved scoring.

Tommy Armour was a fine Scottish player and teacher who was working at the Medinah Country Club in Chicago when he was hired by MacGregor in 1935. He brought his assistant, Toney Penna, with him and together they designed clubs such as the famous Tommy Armour oil hardened woods, Silver Scot irons and Ironmaster putters which were the standards of the industry for decades. Their clubs of the 1950's and 1960's are now sought after by classic club collectors.

MacGregor has always been masterful at marketing golf products. Their Advisory Staff of tour players and club professionals has had many outstanding players including Byron Nelson, Ben Hogan, Jimmy Demaret, Bob Toski, Louise Suggs, Jack Nicklaus, Tom Weiskopf, Ben Crenshaw, Johnny Miller and Tom Watson. The company is still a major force in the golf world even though it has experienced several changes in ownership. The present owner and long time user of MacGregor products is Jack Nicklaus.

Wilson Sporting Goods Company
Chicago and River Grove, Illinois

The Wilson Sporting Goods Company dates back to 1914 when the Thomas E. Wilson Company was formed by the Ashland Manufacturing Co. of Chicago. Ashland was a large company involved in several meat packing and meat by-product ventures. The new Wilson Company grew quickly and soon became one of the largest sporting goods firms in the country. In 1923, they merged with the Western Sporting Goods Co. and the company name was changed to Wilson-Western Sporting Goods Co. They continued to offer a full line of athletic equipment and by 1931, the use of the Western name was discontinued in favor of the present name, the Wilson Sporting Goods Company. Throughout the 1940's they acquired many small companies which produced sports related items such as uniforms and leather goods. As this expansion continued, they needed larger quarters and relocated to the Chicago suburb of River Grove.

Many of the companies which Wilson took over had some golf items, but it was not until 1944 that they purchased a major golf manufacturer. The L.A. Young Company, with their popular Walter Hagen line, became part of the Wilson empire. This division is now known as the Walter Hagen Company and continues to be operated at a separate facility in Grand Rapids, Michigan.

The Hagen Company had its start in 1922 when Hagen formed the Walter Hagen Golf Products Corporation in Longwood, Florida with two partners. Hagen had been using Spalding clubs since 1915 and had unsuccessfully tried to arrange a lucrative contract for his endorsement. Soon after commencing production, he found out that the humid Florida climate was not conducive to the golf club business. The hickory shafts which they were using would dry out and shrink when shipped to less humid regions of the country. This resulted in loose clubheads and numerous complaints, a problem which Hagen solved by selling out in 1925. The new owner was L.A. Young, a wealthy man from Detroit, who was then the country's largest manufacturer of automobile springs. Hagen continued on with the company as a club designer and was instrumental in the development of the wedge. Eventually the company moved to Grand Rapids, where it remains today.

Wilson's aggressiveness in the business world was also evident in the marketing of their golf equipment. In 1925, they formed an Advisory Staff of professional golfers which would play a large part in their advertising. Their early Staff included many noteworthy players such as Gene Sarazen, Sam Snead, Ben Hogan, Walter Hagen, Lloyd Mangrum, Cary Middlecoff, Patty Berg and Babe Zaharias. In the modern era, Arnold Palmer, Billy Casper, Hale Irwin, Jerry Pate, Andy Bean and Tom Kite have continued the fine Wilson tradition. Wilson named several models after these players and even called their top line clubs the "Wilson Staff" model.

Wilson was one of the first makers to feature matched sets of clubs and have always offered a full line of clubs and accessories. Their most notable club feature has been the Strata-Bloc laminated wood clubhead which was introduced in 1941. Other club manufacturers were offering laminated heads during the 1940's and 1950's, but none promoted them like Wilson. While makers like MacGregor were focusing much of their design efforts on the appearance of their clubs, Wilson was concentrating on the mechanical aspects. In an effort to rearrange the clubhead weight, they designed a drilled through hosel which was first offered in their 1956 catalog. The Wilson "fluid feel" hosel was a much refined version of the earlier Carruthers cleek developed in the 1890's.

Until 1967, Wilson had always been a subsidiary of a large meat packing concern. In one of their rare instances of sharing the resources of the various divisions, they packaged tennis balls in a large can originally designed for lard. Generally, the divisions kept to themselves. Since the late 1960's Wilson has been owned by several conglomerates, including PEPSICO, Inc. As always, they continue to be a dominant force in the realm of sporting goods.

CHAPTER 4 — OTHER EQUIPMENT

This chapter is intended to give the reader an overview of various types of golf equipment which may exist other than clubs and balls. Items such as tees, club carriers, shoes and other accessories have been important in contributing to the current level of enjoyment which the game provides. Many of these innovations were introduced in the 1890's at a time when golf was experiencing a surge of popularity in Great Britain and was in its infancy in America. Some of this equipment can be of substantial value such as the early caddy stands which range in value from $200 to $600. Other items, such as tees, may not be worth very much, but nevertheless are fun to study and collect.

The wooden golf tee in use today is generally taken for granted by millions of golfers. Few realize that the peg type tee was not universal in use until the 1940's. From the earliest days of golf until the end of the nineteenth century, golfers would form a tee with a small mound of sand or dirt taken from the bottom of the hole on the green. Throughout this period, the player would tee off from the "green" within a few yards from the hole, so the cup was a convenient place from which to acquire the sand. In the mid 1890's, an area next to the green was built for the purpose of teeing off on the next hole. These small teeing areas have since evolved into the large teeing grounds which we make use of today.

Beginning in the late nineteenth century, buckets of sand or "tee boxes" were placed at the teeing areas as a convenient source of sand. For many years the player would often have his caddy form his tee out of the sand. By the late 1890's, small wooden or metal moulds were used to shape the moistened sand to a prescribed height. As golfers became more inventive, rubber or wooden pegs came into use, thus avoiding the messy task of molding the sand. Some of the pegs were tethered with a string so that they would not be lost, while others were made in the form of a small stand or disposable cardboard cylinder. Teeing devices are a fascinating area of golf collectibles because of the many styles which have resulted from the dozens of patents which have been granted over the years.

Hard to find items of early golf equipment include articles of golf clothing and the early instructional aids. The red golfing jackets worn in the nineteenth century sometimes appear in the British auctions and command prices of several hundreds of dollars. Unfortunately, many of the instructional or practice aids can only be admired by the collector through advertisements, since these gimmicks rarely performed correctly and were eventually discarded.

The illustrations which follow will give the reader a general overview of the multitude of golf collectibles which exist. Since these items vary greatly in availability and popularity with the collector, price ranges cannot be established.

133

In 1891, Currie was referring to the golf bag as a "carrier."

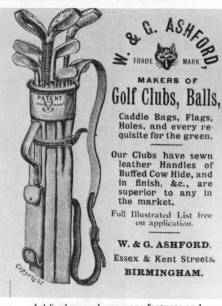

Ashford was a large manufacturer and supplier of all types of golf equipment.

These ball holders were a clever idea in 1927 and can still be found today.

Osmond's Patent caddie stand was designed so that the legs automatically extended when the bag was set down. The patent was awarded in 1893.

The Bussey caddy stand was one of several which had folding legs in the mid 1890's.

The Rover caddie of the late 1890's was the forerunner of the modern day trolley. Since there was no handle for trailing the unit behind the player, it must have been somewhat cumbersome. The small hard wheels probably led to early failure of the device which is why few remain today.

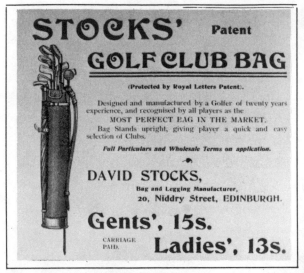

STOCKS' Patent
GOLF CLUB BAG

(Protected by Royal Letters Patent).

Designed and manufactured by a Golfer of twenty years experience, and recognised by all players as the
MOST PERFECT BAG IN THE MARKET.
Bag Stands upright, giving player a quick and easy selection of Clubs.

Full Particulars and Wholesale Terms on application.

DAVID STOCKS,
Bag and Legging Manufacturer,
20, Niddry Street, EDINBURGH.

Gents', 15s.
CARRIAGE PAID.
Ladies', 13s.

Stocks was one of the first to offer golf bags in either a gents or a ladies style. He also included an umbrella holder on this patented bag which featured a metal stake for holding it upright.

This cane has a spear like tip for easy insertion into the turf and a bent brass rod on which to lean the clubs. This item was used in the late 19th century at a time when clubs were loosely carried under the arm.

This caddie stand with a wooden handle was a version of Osmond's Patent.

TEES

ALEXANDER'S "TEE MOULD"
(PATENT).

This little contrivance will recommend itself to Golfers on account of its simplicity in use, uniformity in shape of TEE made, and saving in Sand. Can be obtained of Messrs.

F. H. AYRES & CO., LONDON,
The Stores, and all Golfing Outfitters.

Alexander's tee mould was simple and had no moving parts.

RANSOME'S DOUBLE GOLF TEE STAMP.

In Polished Brass. A splendid thing for making a sand tee. Accurate and quick. Everyone should use it.

TESTIMONIAL.—"I am greatly pleased with the stamp you sent me, and shall advise all my golfing friends to get one."

Professionals and Dealers should apply for Terms.

PRICE, ONE SHILLING.
Of all Dealers. Sample sent Post Free on Approval.
J. E. RANSOME, Holme Wood, IPSWICH.

Ransome's considered their sand mould to be a "stamp". The profile shows that the golfer had a choice of two teeing heights.

GREENWOOD'S Patent
GOLF TEE MOULD.

No. 561725.

FIG. 1.   FIG. 2.

The only PERFECT GOLF TEE MOULD ever invented, Simplicity itself.

Any Caddie can work it. Makes perfect Moulds—always same height—thus ensuring consistent driving. The of this Tee Mould keeps hands clean and free from grit. **Fig. 1** shows the manner in which Mould is filled. **Fig. 2** shows the Mould in the act of discharging.

Made in 3 sizes, 1 - each.

The following Testimonials have been received: J. L. WANKLYN, Esq., M.P., on behalf of the R. A. J. BALFOUR, M.P., and himself, says :—" It is an ingenious invention, and will prove invaluable in the hands inexperienced Caddie." G. HERBERT BLACKBURN, Esq., Hon. Sec. of the Bradford Golf Club, writes on behalf CRESSWELL, Esq., Captain of the Bradford Golf Club, and himself :—" My Caddie used mine in the memorable some (opening of the Bradford Golf Club's new Links), and it answered its purpose very well." E. A. LASSEN, Yorkshire Amateur Champion, writes :—" I have tried the Golf Tee Maker, and it answers its purpose admir EDITOR OF "GOLF NOTES," *Bradford Observer*, says :—" The apparatus is substantial and well adapted to its purp

Special Terms quoted to Golf Professionals and Wholesale Dealers.
☞ Patentee : JOHN A. GREENWOOD, 21, Swaine Street, BRADFORD.

The Greenwood tee mould actually ejected the sand.

THE NEW "VICTOR" PATENT RUBBER GOLF TEE.

The *Field* says: "For simplicity of adjustment and durability, the Tee CANNOT BE EQUALLED BY ANY OTHER PATENT."

PRICE

4/-

Per Dozen.

Liberal Discount to the Trade.

TO BE HAD FROM ALL LEADING STORES, SPORTS, ATHLETIC AND RUBBER DEPOTS THROUGHOUT THE WORLD OR DIRECT FROM

SOLE AGENTS FOR ENGLAND, WALES, AND IRELAND:

ANDERSON, ANDERSON, & ANDERSON, Ltd.,

India Rubber and Waterproof Manufacturers,

35, ST. PAUL'S CHURCHYARD, LONDON, E.C.

An early peg style tee molded of hard rubber.

A New and Better Tee

YOU CAN PLAY EVERY HOLE IN PAR

or you can dub a round—but there is one sure thing—you cannot locate a better nor more useful tee than

RITE TEE

TRADE MARK

A tee and a pencil combination indispensable to every golfer. 18 for 25c red or yellow. A score card on every box. If your Pro or dealer is sold out, use the coupon.

WIMO SPECIALTY CO., Inc.
Hudson Falls
New York

WIMO SPECIALTY CO., Inc.
Hudson Falls, N.Y.
Enclosed find 25c for one box of { red { yellow } tees.

NAME ....
ADDRESS ....
CLUB ....

Every tee a pencil

Possibly the most ingenious tee ever produced - a combination tee and pencil.

First at Oakmont

As in other clubs throughout the country

A check-up of the tees used by the 142 star golfers competing for championship honors at Oakmont showed Morley Yello Tees away in the lead.

In the 1927 U.S. Open at Oakmont Country Club, 81 of the 142 players were using the Yello tee. During this era, pro golfers actually would endorse tee brands.

The popular Bobby tees sometimes came in a little packet which contained a scorecard and advertising such as this one from a ball bearing company.

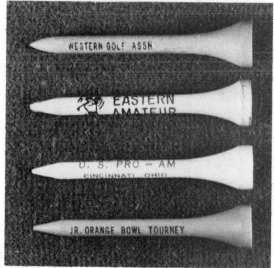

Imprinted advertising tees like these have been in use for years.

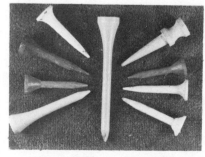

Several styles of wooden tees are shown. Before the generic golf tee was established, golfers actually purchased tees by brand name.

Some tees were actually imprinted on the top.

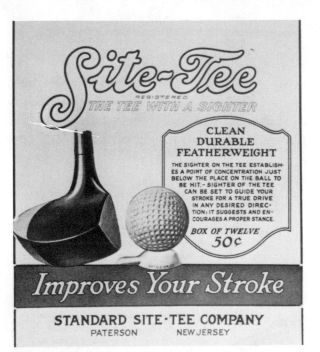

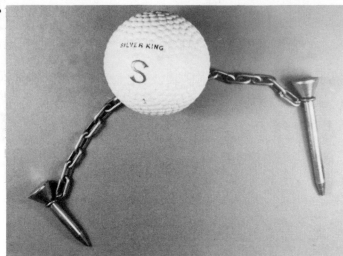

This sterling silver tethered tee gave the golfer a choice of heights and also a touch of class.

The Site-Tee, patented in 1925, was designed to aid the golfer's alignment.

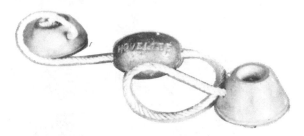

The best thing about the Noveltee is its name.

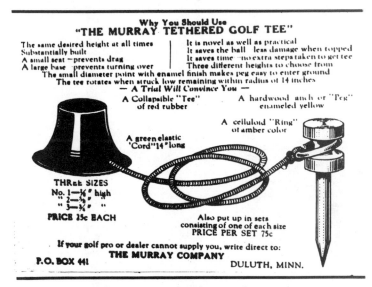

Murray informs us that one of the features of the tethered tee is that "it saves time".

This rubber tee was made by Spalding in the 1920's.

Parlor Putters were indoor practice devices for the upper class golfer in the early 20th century. These elaborately decorated stands were made of painted cast iron or chrome plated brass.

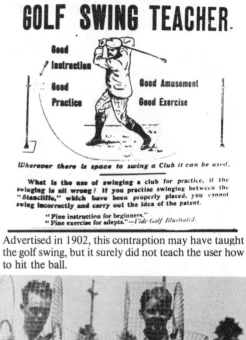

Advertised in 1902, this contraption may have taught the golf swing, but it surely did not teach the user how to hit the ball.

This device was obviously intended to cure a sway. One wonders if this gentleman actually took his aid with him on the golf course.

In an indirect way, these driving range ball pickers are classified as practice aids. The gentleman on the left is shown at the Milan (Italy) Golf Club, while the two boys on the right are Americans. Apparently the Milan picker was not too concerned with frontal protection.

Similar in function to the wiffle ball, these practice balls were made of wool.

This putting cup allows the ball to enter by rolling over the spring and then keeps it captive.

These tethered practice balls from 1906 were among the first of many to be sold in later years.

The Swingmaster was a weighted device used for loosening up the golfers muscles before play.

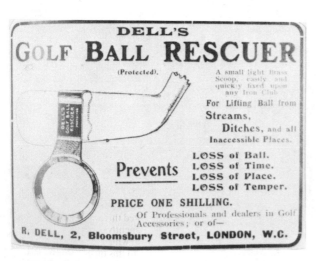

This ball rescuer from the early 20th century is a convenient gadget which, as the ad says, "prevents loss of temper". These clip-on units are now being made of plastic instead of brass.

This swing analyzer somehow recorded the swing while allowing the golfer to actually hit a "non-captive" ball. This is a good example of a device which is probably now extinct because it did not perform well and was eventually discarded by the user.

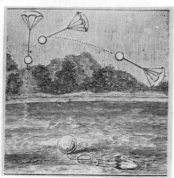
This ad contains what may be the most ludicrous claim in golf advertising: a rubber tip for the golf club grip that "positively adds yards to your shots".

Right: The Folda Fairway is a captive ball shot analyzer which was sold in the 1940's. After hitting the ball, the distance is measured and the rope is captured in the comb device seen on the top left of the unit. This comb has markings which show the user the direction of the shot.

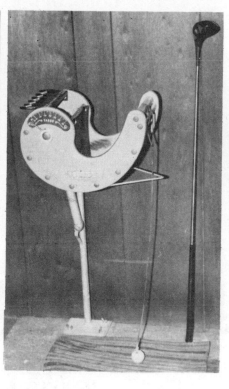

" PARACHUTE "

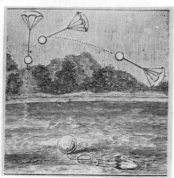

GOLF BALL.

For restricting the flight of the Ball, and enabling Golfers to practise in confined spaces.
EVERY PLAYER SHOULD POSSESS ONE.
PRICES: Complete with Compo. Ball, 1s. 6d.; Gutta Ball, 2s. Superior, with central aperture for regulating distance of flight. 3s. Postage, 3d.
Illustrated Golf List and Full Sports Catalogue Free by Post.

J. JAQUES & SON,
102, Hatton Garden, E.C.

The Parachute practice ball makes an amusing addition to a golf collection. This model was made in the early 1890's.

GOLF COURSE ITEMS

For years, these special rakes were used to create the characteristic furrows in the many sand traps at Oakmont Country Club outside Pittsburgh. After the holding of several major championships under these unique conditions, the practice was discontinued.

Sand containers such as this were common golf course fixtures until the wooden peg became the preferred method of teeing the ball. The bucket on the top contained water for moistening the sand.

George C. Bussey & Co., an English sporting goods manufacturer, developed this improved hole liner in 1894. The holes had been equipped with metal liners for several years prior to this time, but the flagstick would always lean to the side. This model provided both a means for keeping the flagstick upright and also kept the ball from falling in the dirt at the bottom of the hole.

In 1895, an inventor named Dalziel patented this adjustable rubber teeing device which was designed to be permanently set in the ground. This invention coincides with the time period in which separate teeing areas on the golf course came into being. Prior to this time, the golfer would tee off from a prescribed distance from the hole on the green just completed, usually two clublengths.

140

GOLF COURSE ITEMS

PATENT GOLF TEEING STAND.

Some of its Advantages.

Perfect Tee and Perfect Stance in all weathers.

Cheap to buy and cheap to keep up.

Great economy in up-keep of Green.

Will last for months without attention.

Don't be afraid of getting down to your ball, as it is impossible to break your club.

Makes driving more certain, as it is impossible to cut under ball.

Rising, hanging, or level Tee, as required.

Tee on wood or matting, according to taste (wood recommended).

For Price & Particulars, apply to G. COMBE, Castle Lane Place, Belfast.

Patentee and Sole Maker.

This teeing stand was developed in 1895 and in various forms found its way to the 20th century driving range.

BOGEY HOLE CUTTER,
And Putting Tins.
(Cole's Patents.)

"*GOLF*" *says*—
"A Boon and a blessing"

PETER PAXTON says—
"Most satisfactory."

J. H. TAYLOR says—
"Very ingenious."

BEN SAYERS says—
"Really excellent."

H. VARDON says—
"The Bogey Tin is the best I have ever seen. A good thing."

Particulars from
H. PATTISSON,
55, Killieser Avenue,
STREATHAM HILL, S.W.

Most of the early holes were cut with a knife although mechanical hole cutters were in use as early as 1829. In 1894, the diameter was standardized at 4¼ inches and many hole making devices were made available to the greenkeepers. Cole was granted a patent for his cutter in 1897 and received several fine endorsements.

GOLF CLOTHING

This overshoe was designed by Alfred Schacht, a member of The Royal Blackheath Club in the late 19th century. He thought that "city gentlemen" would save time and trouble by not having to change their boots when out for a quick round of golf.

DONALDSON & SON'S
Celebrated
ST. ANDREWS Golfing Shoes
For Ladies and Gentlemen.

C. DONALDSON & SON, Sole Manufacturers.
163, South Street, St. Andrews.

Donaldson's golf shoes featured rubber cleats for the turn of the century golfer.

This coat would not only keep the golfer dry, it was sure to add strokes to his score.

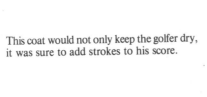

Though not very popular, golf gloves were available at the turn of the century.

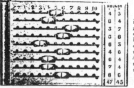

"THE BUNKER"
GOLF MARKER OR SCORER.

Golf says: "Not only is the marker ingenious, but it saves a vast deal of time at the putting greens. The marker is the *most useful and practical* we have yet seen."—March 24th, 1893.

Field says: "It is certainly an ingenious, yet simple, contrivance. We have every confidence in recommending it as the *best* of all the patent markers."— March 18th, 1895.

NO GOLFER SHOULD BE WITHOUT ONE.
Price 7s. 6d. each.   EXTRA CARDS, 2s. per 100.
To be had from all Dealers in Golfing Appliances, or

THE BUNKER MARKER COMPANY,
SWAN BUILDINGS, EDMUND STREET, BIRMINGHAM.
LONDON OFFICES: 115, PALMERSTON BUILDINGS, OLD BROAD STREET, E.C.

The Bunker mechanical scoring device "saved a vast deal of time at the putting greens."

An everlasting scorecard costing one penny. This company must not have been too keen on making repeat sales.

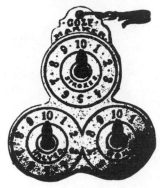

One of many scorekeeping devices.

This display of pencils from various golf clubs can be seen at the World Golf Hall of Fame Museum.

BAG TAGS

These plastic bag tags have been molded into unique shapes according to the product or event which they represent.

A display of souvenir bag tags from several U.S. Open Championships.

CLEANING AIDS

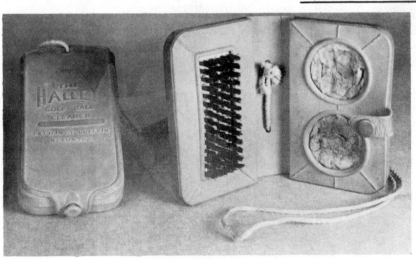

The most popular ball cleaners were those which had the sponges stored in a rubber case which could be secured to the golfer's bag of clubs. It was common for the units to be made by golf ball manufacturers such as Halley's.

NORTH BRITISH RUBBER
Company, Limited,
106, PRINCES' ST., EDINBURGH.
MOXON &
BRAND'S
Patent
GOLF BALL
CLEANER.
Made in the form of a
Tobacco Pouch.
Price 1s. each.

THE EDINBURGH GOLF BALL,
Made from Purest Gutta Percha.
PERFECT CONDITION.

North British Rubber Company was a large manufacturer of golf balls at the turn of the century.

"CLIP" GOLF CLUB CLEANER.
(Patent.)

Specially designed for cleaning iron clubs.

Price 2/6 each,

POST FREE. Weight, 3 oz.

Effective, cleanly, light, and cannot rust or get out of order. Will last a lifetime.

Refills of Emery to fit are supplied within the hollow handle of each machine, and extra boxes are supplied, when wanted, at a cost of 6d. per two dozen sheets. Each new sheet can be fixed into position in a few seconds, and the machine tightens it automatically in the operation. Anyone can do it.

SOLE LICENCEES—

HOME GOLF BALL PRESS CO.,

20, St. Vincent Lane, Glasgow.

In sending their Orders to Advertisers, our readers wil

One of the few advertisements for club cleaning tools. Before the electroplating of iron clubheads was standard practice, the heads had to be periodically cleaned of rust with emery paper. This miniature sanding block dates from 1892.

This sponge for ball cleaning was housed in an attractive container of plain or nickel plated brass.

PATENT GOLF NAILS WANTED.

To the Editor of GOLF.

SIR,—Could you inform me where the patent steel nails can be got for golfing boots, the kind that screw into the sole of the boot? A shoemaker at Carnoustie noticed them in my boots and wished to know where to get them. It might do a good turn to golfers here if they were to be had in the village.

I am, Sir, &c.,
WILLIAM GOURLAY.

Carnoustie, August 10th.

PATENT GOLF NAILS.

To the Editor of GOLF.

SIR,—In your issue of the 17th inst., I notice that a writer solicits information where to obtain patent steel nails, that screw into boots, for use in Golf. They can be obtained from Messrs. Lunn & Co., 257, Regent Street, W. The price is one shilling per dozen.

I am, Sir, &c.,
H. HARROW.

To the Editor of GOLF.

SIR,—In reply to your Carnoustie correspondent anent Golf nails, I may say that about twenty years ago, a Perth shoemaker (I do not now remember his name), supplied me with square-headed nails which screwed into the sole. They were not, however, satisfactory, and I, as well as some others who tried them, gave them up. We found it better to have four rows of ordinary nails, driven into the shoe, $\frac{3}{4}$ or $\frac{7}{8}$ of an inch apart. If it is afterwards desired to remove the nails, the holes can be efficiently filled up with the wooden pegs. What are our shoemakers about that they do not introduce aluminium nails for golfing shoes? For the sake of their lightness, they have already been introduced for the shoes of the German infantry.

I am, Sir, &c.,
TACKET.

PATENT GOLF NAILS.

To the Editor of GOLF.

SIR,—I think neither of the letters in last week's GOLF supply the information asked for in your issue of the 10th.

The screws for boots which I fancy your correspondent inquired about are made either by Nettlefold and Sons, 54, High Holborn, London, W.C.; or Nettlefold's (Limited), 11, Fenchurch Street, E.C., I forget which. The price is 3s. 6d. per gross, there are two kinds—square heads and round. The square are much the best, and half-inch the best size, in fact, perfect for shooting or Golf. They can be put in by anybody, cannot fall out or break off, as tackets do, and wear very much longer.

Not being pointed like ice nails, they don't tear up flooring and carpets.

I am, Sir, &c.,
C. D. J.

P.S.—The makers will not sell less than one gross.

In 1984, these four "letters to the editor" appeared in consecutive issues of *Golf* magazine. Their content provides an interesting insight into the early use of golf footwear.

Early golf attire.

The 15th Green at Cypress Point

CHAPTER 5 — PRINTS AND PAINTINGS

Prints and paintings related to golf have been created and treasured for many years. The artwork of the game is quite attractive and is desirable for decorating the walls of homes, offices and golf clubs. Most of the large collections are usually contained in museums, however there are a few private collections of noted quality.

One of the finest collections of golf art belonged to John W. Fischer of Cincinnati, Ohio. Fischer was noted for his golfing accomplishments such as being the United States Amateur Champion in 1936, a three-time playing member of the Walker Cup Team, and then Team Captain in 1965. Fischer was a longtime member of the Museum Committee of the United States Golf Association to which he had donated much of his collection. The various items can be seen at the Museum and Library located in Far Hills, New Jersey.

John Fischer recently passed away. He was an excellent source of information and provided the following account of his collecting experiences for inclusion in this chapter.

About forty years ago, a friend who was a dealer in the fine arts suggested to me that as a golfer, I should be interested in purchasing a volume of prints called A Golfers Gallery of Old Masters, *by Bernard Darwin, which he had recently obtained. After mulling the matter over for several days, I purchased the book.*

That was my first acquisition, and little did I realize what a wonderful new world of collecting would evolve in the ensuing years as I became interested in oil paintings, watercolors, mezzotint engravings, prints, bronzes and other art forms related to golf.

On trips to financial centers where my practice as a municipal bond attorney took me, I always found some spare time to frequent galleries where I could possibly find an addition for my collection. These interludes also represented a source of relaxation from the pressures and demands of the practice and were most welcome and beneficial. These were happy years of anticipation, finding, and acquiring many fine pieces of golf art which in themselves provided a historical background to the game, the championship courses, the players, and the humor associated with the playing of golf from its earliest times. It gave me a much greater respect, appreciation and understanding of the game and why it has captured the interest of so many people.

Among the favorites in my collection are the well known, original engravings of "The Blackheath Golfer", the portraits of James Balfour and John Gray, the etchings by Dendy Sadler, the humorous golf scenes from the British magazines, and the series of British golf courses by Cecil Aldin.

Of the modern golf art, I am particularly fond of the original paintings of championship courses by Arthur Weaver, the outstanding British watercolor artist. He has a wonderful ability to capture both the beauty of the picturesque greens of the American courses and the feel of the leaden skies and the often penetrating chill associated with the British courses.

My hobby of collecting golf art has been most pleasurable and I encourage all lovers of golf to explore the many types of golf art which are available. I would advise the beginning collector to deal with a reputable dealer or someone who is very familiar with golf art as a costly mistake can easily be made.

THE HISTORY OF GOLF PRINTS

The first golf print was published on November 22, 1790 and pictured William Innes, the Captain of the Society of Golfers at Blackheath, England in 1778. The original oil painting was by Lemuel Francis Abbott and less than fifty mezzotint engravings were done by Valentine Green. This picture of Innes was referred to as "The Blackheath Golfer" and is the most widely recognized golf print ever published since it has been copied many times in various sizes and techniques. The print was first reproduced in 1892 in black and white (size: 17" x 23¾"), while most of the later reproductions were done in color.

Four years later, J. Jones engraved a mezzotint after an oil of James Balfour which was painted by Henry Raeburn, the famous portrait artist. Balfour appears not as a golfer, but rather in his position as the Secretary and Treasurer of the Edinburgh Company of Golfers. The books on his table are titled "Record of Gentlemen Golfers" and "Bet Book". Historical references mention that the number of copies published was less than 50. It is assumed that there have been no reproductions except for small illustrations which have appeared in books. The size of the engraving is 14" x 17½" and is printed in black and white.

'James Balfour, Esq.' – painted by Henry Raeburn and printed in 1796.

'John Gray' — painted by Henry Raeburn and printed in 1806.

'The Blackheath Golfer' – painted by Abbott. In 1790, this became the first golf print to be published.

The third golf print also after a painting by Raeburn, featured John Gray, the Secretary of the Royal Company of Golfers. It was engraved in mezzotint by G. Dawe and was published on July 20, 1806 in black and white. This portrait is similar to the one of James Balfour in that there are no golf clubs in the picture and that fewer than fifty prints were published which were 13¾" x 17⅞" in size. The only other prints of this work have been in the form of book illustrations in the 1800's.

Another painting by Abbott was published in print form in 1812. This portrait of a prominent golfer was of Henry Callender, who was the Captain of Society of Golfers at Blackheath in 1790, 1801 and again in 1807. William Ward was the first to engrave this work in mezzotint which was printed in black and white; size 16⅞" x 23⅜". This portrait has been copied many times in different sizes and in color but only a few of the originals exist.

Thirty-eight years passed until another golf print was published. Artist Charles Lees, who had studied under Raeburn, featured an actual golf scene called "The Golfers — A Grand Match at St. Andrews". The scene, which shows a number of well known golf personalities, was engraved by Charles E. Wegstaffe in 1850 and printed in black and white. The exact number of prints made is not known, but the collector should be aware that several excellent reproductions were later published. The large original print measured 33¼" x 20¾" and was accompanied by an identification key to the many golfers shown in the picture.

It should be noted that the early golf prints discussed above were originally printed in black and white. Some may have been hand colored at a later time, so don't assume that a colored print is not an original. Many of the prints were published again at a later date by a different engraver. These later issues are still quite valuable as the art of an engraver or etcher is immensely more desirable than the same scene which was printed by modern photomechanical methods. A reputable dealer can assist the collector in determining the rarity and value of an original print.

During the period in which the early golf art was produced, golf was considered to be a sport for the aristocracy. It wasn't until the mid-1800's that golfers began to attain a level of expertise. Players such as Allan Robertson, Old and Young Tom Morris, the Dunns, the Parks and others began to play well publicized money matches and eventually the British Open Championship was played in 1860. The advent of the gutty ball and the appearance of expert clubmakers helped to create a different social class of golfers. These artisan golfers were more concerned with the game itself, rather than the fine arts which the upper class enjoyed so much. For this reason there was little demand for golf artwork, other than oils and watercolors, between the years 1850 and 1890, even though the number of golfers increased drastically during this period.

'Henry Callender, Esq.' – painted by Abbott
and first printed in 1812.

In 1890, *Vanity Fair* magazine began to publish stone lithographs of prominent golfers. It wasn't until 1897 that a truly great player was featured as the subject of a print when a photogravure of Tom Morris was made by H. J. Brooks. Then, in 1903, Sir George Reid was commissioned by the Royal and Ancient Golf Club of St. Andrews to paint a portrait of Morris. The four-time British Open champion had been a professional, clubmaker, ballmaker and greenskeeper for decades and finally had earned the recognition which had previously been reserved for the elite. These were the first of many prints of champion golfers which were to be published.

As golf periodicals and highly illustrated books came into being in the 1890's, the number of painters and illustrators ncreased. Artists such as Furniss, Frost, Crombie and Hodge began to produce golf works, some of which were published in print form. Golf course scenes, comical subjects, portraits of early golfers, and reproductions soon appeared on the market. Most, but not all, of the twentieth century prints are lithographs, some of high quality, and unfortunately, some of poor quality.

Until the 1970's, the publication of golf prints was sporadic and the majority of the dealing was in the older prints. As the interest in golf collecting expanded, so did the need for affordable art which featured historic golfers or incidents. The renewed American involvement in the British Open, commencing with Arnold Palmer's participation in the early sixties helped to develop the American golfer's fascination with the British links and the early players. As the interest began to grow, modern players such as Palmer, Nicklaus, Player and Trevino began to appear in prints. In addition to the British courses like St. Andrews and Turnberry, golfers began to want pictures of American courses like Pebble Beach and Augusta National. Quite a few humorous prints have also been produced in recent years.

Following an explanation of the various printmaking techniques used in making golf prints is a list of the prominent of golf artists along with illustrations of their works. Most of the artists have had their work published as prints, although a few are recognized only for their original works. Original oils, watercolors and sketches are discussed but have not been given market values since not that many fine works often change hands. A second listing contains the names of other artists who have made contributions to the field of golf art.

147

PRINTMAKING METHODS

There are numerous methods that have been used for the printing of golf prints. Most of the prints produced prior to 1890 required the talents of an engraver or etcher, for without these craftsmen, the printing plates could not be made. As the use of photomechanical printing processes became popular, prints became much easier to publish since a commercial printing concern was all that was required. The early platemakers would sometimes devote months to the creation of a single plate.

More often than not, the early golf paintings were life size. The engravers were required to transform the brush strokes from a five foot high painting into precisely placed incisions on a much smaller metal plate. These tremendous skills, combined with the small quantity prints produced, make the early prints highly desirable to the collector. Since most of the twentieth century prints have been produced by photomechanical methods, their value is derived primarily from the skills of the artist and the subject matter.

In the art world, an original print means that the actual printing plates were created with the skill and talents of an artist. Many of the subjects of original golf prints were initially produced as oil paintings. The subjects were subsequently engraved and original prints were produced. If the engraving was later reproduced by photomechanical means, it would be termed a reproduction golf print.

Most of the modern golf prints result from a painting being published in print form by a modern lithographic method. In this book, that print will be referred to as an original reproduction, since the mechanical skills of the printer were relied upon rather than the artistic talents of an engraver.

The following descriptions discuss the types of printing methods commonly employed in the production of golf prints. The serious collector should be familiar with these methods so that he can better understand the relative values of the prints he may come across.

INTAGLIO

Most of the early golf prints were printed using the intaglio method. After the design had been put into a metal plate by one of the processes listed below, printing ink was worked into the grooves with a roller. After the excess had been wiped clean, a sheet of dampened paper was placed on the inked plate, covered with blotters, and run through a roller type press under great pressure.

The paper then had the design inked upon it and could be dried. The embossed mark resulting from the edges of the plate remained on the print. Some engravings were trimmed and do not have the characteristic plate mark. It should be noted that modern lithographs are sometimes embossed to make them resemble intaglio prints, so the appearance of a plate mark does not necessarily mean that the print is an etching or engraving. Descriptions of intaglio printmaking are as follows.

AQUATINT — A copper or zinc plate is covered with rosin which creates a grain pattern on the plate. The design is put on in the form of an acid-resisting varnish, followed by immersion in an acid bath. The acid causes the rosin to be eaten away, thereby creating the areas which will receive the most ink. This technique is then repeated so that varying tones can be produced. Often the artist will incorporate some etching to achieve a particular result. Since aquatint is an intaglio method of printing, the prints will have a plate mark.

DRYPOINT — Drypoint is a method of engraving in which a copper or zinc plate is scratched with a sharp tool which results in a burr being left along the line. Often a steel facing or plating is applied to the finished plate which acts as a deterrent against wear. Drypoints can be distinguished by their velvety lines.

ETCHING — An etching begins with a polished printing plate which has a waxy compound applied to it. After the artist draws the design in the soft layer, the plate is immersed in an acid bath which then etches the exposed metal areas of the plate. A special varnisher is then applied to the lines which the artist desires to remain light and the plate is immersed in the bath again until the required amount of etching occurs. The varnishing and bathing continue until the artist is satisfied with the result. The plate is then cleaned off and is ready for printing.

LINE ENGRAVING — A sharp tool called a graver or burin is used to gouge a line in the copper plate. The varying depth of the line determines the width of the printed line. This intaglio process has been used for over 500 years. Under magnification, the beginning and end of an engraved line are noticeably pointed.

MEZZOTINT — A mezzotint starts with a copper plate which has been roughened with a special textured roller. The artist then burnishes the raised areas to create smooth surfaces which will not hold ink. The varying amount of scraping results in the tones that are characteristic of a mezzotint. Under magnification, the result of the raised burrs on the plate can be seen as a slightly irregular pattern of dots. Most mezzotints with color have been watercolored after being printed with black ink, although some have been made in color.

STEEL ENGRAVING — Steel engraving was practiced in the first half of the nineteenth century on printing jobs where a large number of prints were to be run and plate wear presented a problem. The engraving of the steel plates was extremely difficult and the prints which were run often exhibited the engraver's difficulty in working with the hard metal. Steel engraving was probably not used for the production of golf prints, although the term is often used incorrectly when describing a line engraving. The practice of steel facing the softer copper plates before printing began in 1857 and thereafter steel plates were rarely used.

RELIEF PROCESS

This method requires the artist to remove all areas of the plate which are to appear white when printed. The ink adheres to the raised portion prior to transfer to the paper.

WOOD ENGRAVING — These engravings are done in relief on the end grain of a wooden block. The nature of the wood allows for tonal variations in the print.

OTHER PRINTING METHODS

STONE LITHOGRAPHY — Originally lithographs were printed from designs drawn on a smooth slab of limestone with a greasy crayon. The amount of grease rubbed into the pores of the stone will vary the tones on the final print. Upon completion of the drawing, several steps are required before the stone, or possibly a metal plate, is ready for printing. The stone is moistened with water before the oily ink is applied. The ink will only adhere to the greasy areas of the plate while it is repelled from the watery areas. The paper is then set over the stone and rolled either manually or in a press. These lithographs have a fine grain which reflects the porosity of the stone and should not be confused with the screens evident in a lithograph printed by photomechanical means. Color printing can be accomplished by using several stones, each of which is designed to print a different color.

SILK SCREEN — This method usually consists of a stencil pasted onto a silk or synthetic textile which has been tightly stretched onto a frame. The frame is placed upon a piece of paper, ink is applied to the screen and squeegeed across, thus inking the area not covered by the stencil. Several screens can be used to apply different colors of ink to the paper.

SERIGRAPH — This is a type of silk screen in which the artists draws directly on the screen with a special crayon. A thin layer of glue is applied to the screen, followed by a washing with solvent. The solvent removes the design made with the crayon and leaves a stencil which can then be screened.

PROCESS PRINTS

These prints are a result of a photomechanical method and are not considered to be original prints since an artist is not directly involved in the creation of the printing plate.

LINE BLOCK — A line block is similar to a wood cut in that it is a relief type of plate, however the areas of the plate which are to appear white on the print are removed by means of light exposure through a photographic negative. A light sensitive emulsion is applied to the zinc plate before being exposured. Through a series of chemical processes, the plate is made ready for printing. The resultant print is a high contrast combination of black and white with no intermediate or gray tones.

LITHOGRAPHY — In this method, the continuous tones of a design are converted into small dots of different sizes by means of an optical method known as screening. This is similar to the process used for printing photos in newspapers. The newspaper method normally uses a screen of 65 lines per inch, whereas the method used in art prints makes use of a finer screen of up to 200 lines per inch. The finer screens have dots which are not visible to the casual observer and must be printed with more exacting procedures, otherwise the print will be distorted.

If the work is to be printed in color, the colors must be photographically separated into red, yellow, blue and black tones before a series of plates can be prepared. The plates, which are prepared through various chemical processes, will print the tiny dots in a specific color according to the separations. When all of the plates have been printed, the resulting combinations of dots will create a print that resembles the original. Color prints are normally run on printing presses which are capable of printing four plates, each with a different ink color.

OFFSET LITHOGRAPHY — This is the most common method of modern commercial printing. As with the method above, original artwork with halftones must be screened before a plate can be made. The offset method gets its name because the plate is attached to a curved cylinder which receives the ink, then transfers the inked image to a rubber cylinder called a blanket, which in turn prints the image onto the paper. The intermediate rubber blanket allows for a sharper image and enables the entire process to run at very fast speed.

PHOTOGRAVURE — A photogravure is a photomechanical process which is similar to aquatint. The copper plate is covered with a rosin followed by a light sensitive emulsion. The plate is exposed to a photographic transparency which usually contains gray tones. Following acid baths, the intaglio type of plate is created and is ready for hand printing. The photogravure print exhibits a fine grain and tones like a photograph and does not have the dots associated with most photomechanical processes.

ARTISTS AND THEIR WORKS

ABBOTT, LEMUEL FRANCIS

(1760-1803) One of the earliest golf portrait painters, Abbott's two works were engraved by Valentine Green, Will Henderson, W. A. Cox, William Ward and others. Both of Abbott's golf works have been reproduced many times through the years. Originally, less than fifty of each were printed in monotone. Later issues were in color in various sizes. (See illustration on page 146.)

'The Blackheath Golfer' is the earliest and best known golf print featuring William Innes in uniform as Captain of the Blackheath Golf Club. It was first printed in 1790 as a mezzotint engraving by Valentine Green.

(consult dealer)

Abbott's other work was of Henry Callender who was Captain of the Blackheath Golf club in 1790, 1801 and 1807. It was first engraved in 1812 as a mezzotint by William Ward. (See illustration on page 147)   (consult dealer)

ADAMS, DOUGLAS

(1853-1920) Adams is known for his British landscape scenes which included fishing and golf subjects. He painted three views of the Caernarvonshire Golf Club in Conway, Wales. One hundred and fifty signed artist's proofs were made as black and white photogravures of the first two scenes, 'The Putt' and 'The Drive' in 1893, while the third scene, 'A Difficult Bunker', was done at a later date with no known artist's proofs. The artist's proofs were printed on rice paper laid on India paper and were sometimes hand colored. The original plates are still in use in England for the production of hand colored restrikes. Several editions have been issued in recent years: hand colored lithographs, color lithographs, and black and white lithographs.

Original - $400 +; Restrike - $80-140; Reproduction - $15-40

Adams – 'The Putting Green'

Adams – 'A Difficult Bunker'

Adams – 'The Drive'

AIKMAN, GEORGE

(1830-1905) ARSA. Was trained as an engraver and did illustrations for the *Encyclopedia Britannica*. His hobby was golf. He engraved a series of views known as *A Round of the Links: A View of the Golf Greens of Scotland* which were painted by John Smart and published in book form in a limited edition of 10 sets in 1983 and later reprinted in the 1970's.

Entire book - $400 +; Reprint $80-140

ALDIN, CECIL

(1870-1935) An Englishman whose colorful illustrations appear in many books and also on Royal Doulton pottery. Well known subjects include animals, English inns, golf scenes and humorous items. An attractive series of views of six famous British golf courses were published in the early 1920's. His other golf illustrations are more representative of his characteristic style.

$140-400 (each)

Aldin – View of Royal St. Georges Golf Club in Sandwich, England

Advertisement from *Golf Illustrated* magazine offering Aldin's prints. Note the caption: 'These pictures will prove valuable as the plates have been destroyed'.

ALEXANDER, R.M.

(c 1890) Illustrated for the early British *Golf Illustrated* magazines.   No Known Prints

Alexander - 'A Beehive Incident on the Golf Course'

GOLF COLLECTIBLES

Original water color of Horace Hutchinson by SPY for the **Vanity Fair** series of prints.

"**The Triumvirate**" — British golfing greats J. H. Taylor, James Braid, and Harry Vardon are shown in this popular golf print.

Original oil painting by Douglas Adams of "**The Drive**," which measures six by four feet and is owned by a private collector in the United States. Several different prints of works by Adams have been issued since 1893.

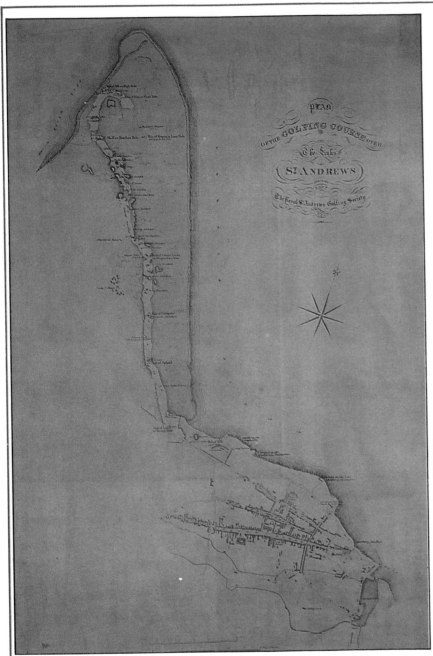

Very rare map of the Links at
St. Andrews issued in 1836.

Early twentieth century
American golfing game.

Many of the early golf magazines
featured attractive cover designs by
noted illustrators of the period.

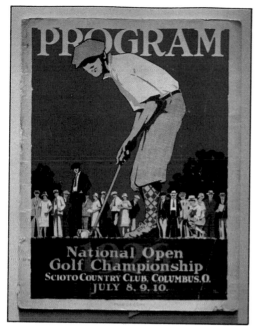

Illustrated calendar cover from 1900. Golf illustrations are shown throughout the year.

Program from the 1926 U.S. Open which was won by Bobby Jones.

Red golfing jackets were popular attire in the eighteenth and nineteenth centuries. This one was of the style used by the Innerleven Golfing Society in Scotland circa 1870.

An assortment of early gutta percha golf balls from the middle to late nineteenth century. **top row:** mesh patterned gutty for winter use, Paterson smooth gutty introduced in 1848, knife cut pattern. **middle row:** Eclipse composition ball, smooth gutty, hand hammered marking, Spalding factory made ball. **bottom row:** Exhibition brand, Allan Robertson hand hammered pattern, Ocobo mesh pattern.

This group of antique golf memorabilia features Copeland pottery.

Early twentieth century golf ball boxes make attractive additions to a display of golf memorabilia.

GOLF COLLECTIBLES

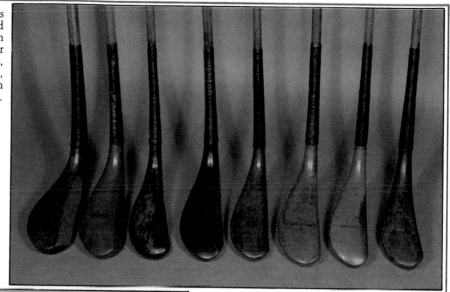

Early long nose golf clubs with heads hand crafted of apple, beech, and pear. **Makers, from left:** McEwan (1840), James Wilson (1860), maker unknown (1830), John Jackson (1845), Willie Park, Sr. (1855), Willie Dunn, Sr. (1850), McEwan (1850), and Hugh Philp (1840).

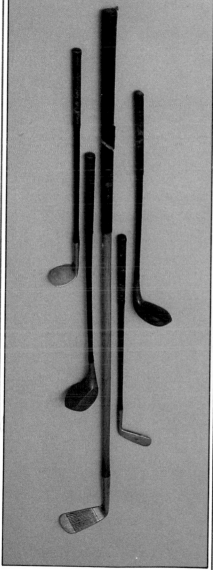

Several miniature clubs displayed along side a standard club. Miniature clubs were usually made by apprentice clubmakers as part of their learning process, however some were crafted by famous clubmakers as presentation pieces.

Antique clubs are appropriately displayed in old bags and club carriers.

These late nineteenth clubs are highly collectible due to their construction. The club shown on the left has its head and shaft constructed from only one piece of wood, while the other club has an unusual splice patented by A.H. Scott of Elie.

GOLF COLLECTIBLES

An attractive display of early clubs, pottery, and artwork shown in the den of a collector.

Harry Vardon is the subject of this bronze done by Henry Pegram in 1908.

An attractive display of golf collectibles consisting of pottery, early equipment, and books.

GOLF COLLECTIBLES

Bronze and marble bookends shown with some popular golf books.

Paper collectibles such as scorecards and commemorative envelopes can be found in almost every golf collection.

Since 1743, several thousand books on golf have been written. Collectors seek the old as well as the new ones for their informative contents.

GOLF COLLECTIBLES

"Attempting to Drive Off" by Victor Venner. One of a pair of colorful golf prints published in 1903.

"Narrow Fairway" by Gary Patterson. Patterson is known for his humorous depictions of golfers, tennis players, and other athletes.

Humorous print typical of the style of H.M. Bateman.

One of several fine golfing toys which are sought after by collectors. This tin toy was made in 1920 and features a clockwork mechanism which activates the golfer's swing.

ALLAN, DAVID

(1744-1796) Painted the well known portrait of Wm. Inglis. Allan is known for his portraits and humorous illustrations. He studied art in Italy and in 1786 became master of the Academy at Glasgow.

Allan – 'Wm. Inglis' — Inglis was a surgeon and a captain of the Honourable Company of Edinburgh Golfers from 1782 to 1784. Aquatint by Jossett $140-400

Ambrose – 'H.R.H. The Prince of Wales' — Published in 1932 as a supplement to *The Field* magazine. $80-140

AMBROSE, CHARLES EDWARD

(c 1905) He was primarily an illustrator for the earlier magazines, using oils, pen and ink and watercolors.

AUSTEN, JOE

Contemporary artist from the St. Andrews area.

Austen – 'The World of Golf' — Famous golf figures, past and present. Printed in 1978.   under $15

Austen – 'Action Portrait of Jack Nicklaus'   under $15

BARCLAY, JOHN

(1876-1923) An etcher from Edinburgh who was also a golfer, Barclay illustrated for *Golf Illustrated* in the 1920's. Barclay was awarded a WW I military cross. Several prints by Barclay can be found. $80-140

BARRIE, ERWIN

(1886-1983) Painted a series of thirty views titled 'Famous Golf Holes I Have Played'. He was the manager of the Grand Central Art Galleries in New York City.

BARROW, JULIAN

A modern artist from Great Britain.

BATEMAN, HENRY MAYO

(1887-1970) Bateman was an illustrator of golf and sporting scenes for *Punch*, Royal Doulton China and others. (See chapter on Pottery for examples.)

Barrow – 'The Maiden, Royal St. Georges' $80-140

Bateman Cartoon — (consult dealer)

BIRLEY, OSWALD

Birley painted a portrait of Horace Hutchinson in 1908.   Not Published

BLAIR, JOHN

Blair exhibited in London from 1885 to 1888.

Blair - 'St. Andrews, 1891' - Note the sheep which kept the links groomed.
$140-400; Reproduction - $15-40

BLAMPED, EDMUND

(1886-1966) An engraver, etcher and cartoonist. Also painted horses.

BRAUER, BILL

Painted 'The History of Golf', a series of eight memorable moments in 20th century golf history. $40-80/set

BRIGGS, CLARE

(c 1916) Briggs was a cartoonist and illustrator whose works can be seen in *The Book of a Thousand Chuckles* and several other humorous golf books.   No Known Prints

BRIL, PAUL

(1554-1626) Bril painted a scene depicting the playing of a game similar to golf in 1624. A limited edition of 350 prints titled 'Landscape with Golfers' has recently been published.
$400 +

Brauer – 'Gene Sarazen, Historic Double Eagle' — In the 1935 Masters Tournament, Sarazen scored an amazing two on the fifteenth hole which enabled him to tie Craig Wood and win in a playoff.

Brauer – 'Ben Hogan Takes British Open, 1953' — Hogan's win at Carnoustie was his first and only try at the British Open.

Brauer – '1960 U.S. Open, Arnold Palmer's First Charge' — Palmer began the last round seven shots behind and shot a 65 to beat a young Jack Nicklaus by two strokes.

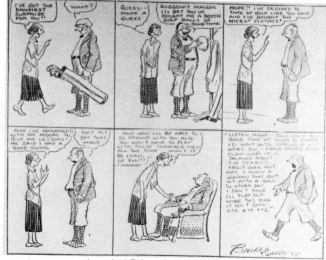

A typical Briggs Cartoon Strip

BROCK, CHARLES EDMUND

(1870-1938) Brock is listed as a member of the Royal Institute in 1909. His engravings were usually made by Frank Paton and some of the prints have been hand colored. His golf works consist of a series of three engravings in 1894: 'The Drive', 'The Putt', and 'The Bunker'. Artist's proofs exist.

$140-400

Brock – 'The Putt'

Brock – 'The Drive'

BROOKS, H. J.

(1865-　　　) Brooks is responsible for an excellent photogravure of Tom Morris which was printed in 1897. Some artist's proofs with Morris' signature can be found.

-Scarce

Brown – 'The Open Championship, St. Andrews 1895; - The original print is a photogravure done in sepia. Later lithographs are in color. A key is available which identifies the golfers in the background. J. H. Taylor, the winner, is shown addressing the ball.

Original - $400 +; Reproduction - $15-40

Brooks – 'Tom Morris'

Brown – 'Past Open Champions' — Morris, Hilton, Braid, Ball, and others.　　　　$140-400

BROWN, J. MICHAEL

Brown is best known for his illustrations for the calendars issued by the Life Association of Scotland between 1895 and 1916.

BROWNE, TOM

(1872-1910) Brown specialized in postcards, cartoons and illustrations primarily in London at the turn of the century.

Post Card Illustration by Tom Browne.　under $15

Chaiko - 'The Women's Amateur Championship, 1898' — Shown at the Ardlsey Club in New York when Beatrix Hoyt defeated Maude Wetmore for her third title. $15-40

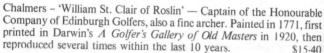

Chalmers – 'William St. Clair of Roslin' — Captain of the Honourable Company of Edinburgh Golfers, also a fine archer. Painted in 1771, first printed in Darwin's *A Golfer's Gallery of Old Masters* in 1920, then reproduced several times within the last 10 years. $15-40

CHAIKO, TED

CHALMERS, SIR GEORGE

(1720-1791) A portrait artist, Chalmers trained at the Royal Academy under Allan Ramsay. He was a member of the Honourable Company of Edinburgh Golfers.

CHAPMAN, LOYAL H. 'BUD'

A scratch golfer, Chapman has created a series of mythical 'Infamous Golf Holes' and then combined them into a view of the entire course. The captions on the prints are especially amusing $15-40

Chapman – 'Victoria Falls, No. 1'

Chapman – 'Grand Canyon, No. 4'

Chapman – 'Wall Street, No. 17'

CHRISTY, HOWARD CHANDLER

(1873-1952) Famous painter of the American girl who illustrated for Scribners and others. He was a member of the Roughriders in the Spanish-American War and acted as a correspondent for the press.

CLARK, RENE

(1886-1969) A founder of the Society of U.S. Illustrators. Illustrations were used by *McCalls, Collier's,* and for magazine ads.

COST, JAMES PETER

(1923-   ) A landscape artist from Monterey Peninsula, California who has done several golf pictures.

COX, WALTER A.

(1862-   ) Exhibited at the Royal Academy and in Paris. In 1926, he produced mezzotints in color of 'The Blackheath Golfer', 'John Taylor', and 'Henry Callender', all about 15" high. $80-140

CROMBIE, CHARLES

(1885-1967) Crombie illustrated for *Punch,* postcards, calendars, and books using several golf themes. Some of his original watercolors have sold in recent auctions.

Crombie — *The Rules of Golf* — A comical series on the rules of golf first published in book form by Perrier of France in 1905. The book was reprinted shortly thereafter. The earlier prints can be distinguished from modern reproductions by the Perrier advertisement on the reverse side. The original prints have English captions while the reproductions are done in both English and French.

Original set - $140-400; Reproduction set - $40-80

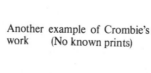

Crombie – Only the first edition has the copyright notice in this position.

Another example of Crombie's work   (No known prints)

CUYP, AELBERT

(1620-1691) Dutch painter from a family of artists. He painted mostly landscapes, seascapes, winter scenes and figures. Cuyp is recognized for his golf painting of a Dutch child which was first printed in 1908 as a photogravure on rice paper laid on India paper and signed as artist's proofs. The remainder of the first printing was done on India paper in sepia. Another printing was done for the *A Golfer's Gallery of Old Masters* in 1920 in color. A larger size lithograph and also a miniature were run in both color and in sepia in the 1970's.

Original - $140-400; Reproduction - $15-40

Cuyp – 'Young Dutch Golfer of the XVII Century' – This is actually a boy and not a girl as many believe.

Davis – 'The Hazard on the Ladies' Course'

Davison – 'Mac Donald Brothers' —First published in *A Golfer's Gallery of Old Masters*, the original hangs in the Scottish National Portrait Gallery in Edinburgh. $15-40

CYNICUS

Also known as Anderson Brothers, this is the artist of several postcards and prints published in the early 20th century.

DAVENPORT, I. BROMLEY

Davenport painted a series of golf course scenes which were published in 1954.

DAVISON (OR DAVIDSON), JEREMIAH

(1745-1795) His work can be seen at the National Portrait Gallery in London.

DAVIS, LUCIEN

(1869-   ) Davis won a bronze medal at the Universal Exposition in Paris in 1900. His only golf print was painted in 1890, first published in the *Illustrated London News* and reprinted in color in 1977.

Original Woodcut - $40-80; Reproduction - $15-40

DE GEEST, WYBRAND SIMONSZ

(1592-1659) De Geest was known to have painted Dutch golf scenes. He was Rembrandt's brother-in-law.

No Known Prints

DE HOOCH, PIETER

An early seventeenth century Dutch artist.

De Hooch – 'Golf Players' $15-40

Dickinsons - 'The Big Match' — Originally printed under the title, 'Royal St. Georges Cup'. It was painted in 1902 and features Harold Hilton. Hilton won the British Open twice, the British Amateur thrice, and the U.S. Amateur once. He was the last player from Great Britain to win the U.S. Amateur.

Original $400 +; Reproduction $15-40

DICKINSONS

Several prints have been published by Dickinsons and Foster such as 'Medal Day at St. Andrews' which shows A. J. Balfour playing in as Captain of the R & A in 1894. This print was published in 1898 and is scarce.

DOLLMAN, JOHN CHARLES

(1851-1934) His works are exhibited at the Royal Academy in London. Originally a black and white artist, he later used oils and watercolors. Dollman was known to spend his recreational time playing chess and fishing.

Dollman – 'The Sabbath Breakers' — John Henrie and Pat Rogie are shown being discovered by two clergymen while partaking of a round of golf on the Sabbath at the Leith Links in 1592. They were subsequently prosecuted for their violation. The Old Course at St. Andrews still remains closed to golfers for play on Sunday. The scene was painted in 1896 and printed as an engraving in black and white. Artist's proofs of this edition are rare. A color lithograph was printed in 1977.
Original - $140-400; Reproduction - $15-40

Dollman – 'The Stymie' — A black and white engraving done in 1899 with some artist's proofs. Note that the attire is reminiscent of golf in earlier days.
Original - $140-400; Reproduction - $15-40

DRAKE, STAN

(1923-   ) Drake is recognized for his illustrations in *Golf Digest* magazine and instructional books. He has won several national awards for his cartoon strips.   No Known Prints

DUNCAN, JOHN A.S.

This British artist painted a series of golf course scenes in the late 1970's which subsequently were published.
$40-80

DU MAURIER, GEORGE LOUIS PALMELLA BUSSON

(1834-1896) Made sketches showing women playing golf.

–Scarce

EARLE, L.

Two golf paintings were commissioned to be painted by one of the founders of the Stetson Shoe Company of South Weymouth, Massachusetts. In 1908, prints were produced and were distributed to Stetson's customers as a promotion. Both of the subjects were caddies at St. Andrews where they were painted on location.

(See illustration next page)   Original $80-140; Reproduction - $15-40

EDMONDSON, C.J.

Six golf sketches were done by Edmondson in color in 1894. They had quotations by Shakespeare and titles such as 'The Drive', 'A Bad Lie' and 'The Duffer'.

$80-140

Earle - 'St. Andrews Caddie' — Also known as the 'Old Scotch Caddie'. In 1928, a second edition was necessary, however they were produced from one of the earlier prints as the painting had been lost. A recent version, also in color, was printed in 1979 in a smaller size.

Earle - 'Bogey Man' — Originally published in 1908 and reproduced in a smaller size in 1980.

EDWARDS, LIONEL DALHOUSIE ROBERTSON

(1878-1966) English watercolor artist specializing in animals and landscape scenes. His style was similar to Aldin, Hassall and Venner. $140-400

ELLIS, RAY G.

(1921-   ) An American lecturer and artist whose golf works consist of landscape watercolors including Harbour Town and other courses.

$15-40

ELMORE, RICHARD

(1936-   ) A watercolor artist who started his career as a staff artist for *Stars and Stripes* in Korea, Elmore is known to golfers as the painter of the Robert Trent Jones Collection. The Jones Collection consists of paintings of six golf holes designed or remodeled by the famous golf architect. The courses depicted are: Baltusrol, Broadmoor, Hazeltine National, Mauna Kea Beach, Peachtree and Spyglass Hill. The prints were produced in the 1970's and included a limited edition of 250 signed by Jones and Elmore.

$15-40

Edwards – 'Stymied!'

EMERY, LESLIE

A well known artist who painted a series of eight golf clowns which were published in 1952.

under $15 (each)

FISHER, HARRISON

(1875-1934) Fisher was primarily an illustrator for the *Ladies' Home Journal*. He had a reputation as 'The King of Magazine Illustrators' and was famous for his glorification of the American Girl along with Gibson and Christy.

161

Elmore – 'Spyglass Hill Golf Course, Twelfth Hole'

Elmore – 'Broadmoor Golf Club, Fifth Hole, East Course'

Emery – 'Golf Shark'

Emery – 'Hand Niblick'

Emery – 'Nineteenth Hole'

A Fisher Illustration

Flagg – 'A Male-Female Golf Match'

FLAGG, JAMES MONTGOMERY

(1877-1960) An American illustrator who painted covers for *Judge, Life, St. Nicholas* and other magazines. His specialty was humor and satire. Flagg's most famous work was the World War I poster of Uncle Sam saying, 'I Want You For The U. S. Army'.

'The Triumvirate'

FLOWER, CLEMENT

Flower painted the Triumvirate in 1913 which shows J. H. Taylor, James Braid and Harry Vardon in their prime. Plans were made to publish prints in 1914, however due to lack of subscriptions only a few proofs were run. As time passed, the unequalled accomplishments of these three players were appreciated and there was a renewed interest in the painting. In 1978, a limited editon of 300 prints, copied from one of the original proofs, was issued and included facsimile signatures. This issue, marked 'Printed in England', was on heavy rag paper. In 1979, a similar edition of 750 was published by a different company on a different grade paper. Then in 1983, an edition of 350 prints on canvas were issued, however this edition was reproduced from the original painting in the possession of the Royal and Ancient Golf Club at St. Andrews. The actual painting has the players' names and records lettered directly on the canvas and is almost full life size.

$30-400 + (consult dealer)

FORBES, BART

Forbes has provided illustrations for present day American magazines and has also produced a limited edition lithograph in 1978 which featured Gary Player.

$40-80

FOX, FONTAINE

Fox is best known for his syndicated 'Toonerville Trolley' comic strip.

No Known Prints

FROST, A.B.

(1851-1928) An American, Arthur Burdett Frost began his career working in a wood engraving business and subsequently took up lithography. He went to England in 1877, but only stayed for one year. That was probably his first exposure to golf, which eventually became a common subject for his humorous watercolors. He illustrated for *Harpers Weekly* and also for the *Uncle Remus* books. Frost has been called 'The Mark Twain of Illustrators'. A number of his golf works were published in black and white at the turn of the century.

Black and White - $40-80; Modern Reproduction - under $15

Frost – 'Temper'

Frost – 'Stymied'

Frost – 'By Sheer Strength'

Frost – 'Twosome'

Frost – 'Leg Wrappings'

FUCHS, BERNIE

An illustrator for *Golf* magazine and *Sports Illustrated* whose painting of Arnold Palmer has been reproduced.
$40-80

FULLER, EDMUND G.

A set of six caricatures by Fuller were published in 1903. The series has recently been reproduced on paper which has been purposely stained to look old. The collector should be careful when purchasing these prints as the new ones exhibit the early date and are being sold as old.
$15-40

164

FURNISS, HARRY

(1854-1925) Furniss was primarily a cartoonist and illustrator for *Punch* who also illustrated for *The Badminton Library*. His original sketches have surfaced at auctions in Great Britain. The prints shown were published in 1973.

under $15

Furniss – 'A Bad Case'

Furniss – 'May-December'

Furniss – 'A Caddie's Duties'

Furniss – 'Teeing Off'

GALLEN, R. S. E.

(1800-1850) Gallen painted Alick Robertson (1756-1840) better known as 'Old Alick, the Holecutter', which was first printed in Bernard Darwin's *A Golfer's Gallery of Old Masters* in 1920. Alick caddied at the Blackheath Golf Club in London and was responsible for cutting new holes in the greens when it became necessary. This painting has been reproduced in various sizes and styles over the years. Most of the prints which exist are overruns from Darwin's book. A recent limited edition in a larger size has been issued.

Limited Edition - $400 +; Others $15-40

GIBSON, CHARLES DANA

(1867-1944) Gibson was a well known American illustrator best known for his drawings of women, the most famous of which was 'The Gibson Girl'. His golf art usually portrayed men and women on the course. The scenes were also reproduced on Royal Doulton pottery.

$15-40

GORDON, SIR JOHN WATSON

(1788-1864) RA, PRSA. Gordon is credited with the painting of a portrait John Taylor, Captain of the Honourable Company of the Edinburgh Golfers many times between 1807 and 1825. He founded the Royal Scottish Academy and was also the official painter for Queen Victoria.

Both Gordon and Henry Raeburn have been listed through the years as the artist of the Taylor portrait, however the authors of this book believe that the information provided by John Kerr in 1896 in *The Golf Book of East Lothian* is the most accurate. Kerr states that Raeburn started the painting and that it was finished by Gordon. The earliest print was engraved in mezzotint by Will Henderson in 1914. W. A. Cox made a later mezzotint in 1926. Several other lithographs of the work have been published including a print in *A Golfer's Gallery of Old Masters*.

Engravings - consult dealer; Reproduction - $15-40

Gallen – 'Old Alick'

Gordon – 'John Taylor'

Grant – 'John Whyte-Melville'

GRANT, SIR FRANCIS

(1803-1878) Grant originally was educated for the bar, but ended up as an artist with his first exhibition at the Royal Academy in 1834. His specialties were full length portraits and hunting meets. It is interesting to note that Grant was knighted for his social endeavors rather than for his artistic talent. Grant's contribution to golf art was a portrait of John Whyte-Melville who was captain of the Royal and Ancient Golf Club in 1823 and was again elected in 1883. Whyte-Melville died before entering office, thereby leaving a blank entry in his memory in the records of the R & A. The first print of this painting was published in an edition limited to 750 in the 1970's in London.

GREEN, VALENTINE
$80-140

(1739-1813) Green started his career as a line engraver and began to make mezzotints in London in 1765. Even though he had no formal training in the art of mezzotint, he became one of the best in the field and produced nearly 400 plates. Green's contributions to golf art were the mezzotints he made of the works painted by L. F. Abbott.

GREENWOOD, ERNEST

Greenwood created colored aquatints showing Wentworth and Moor Park Golf Courses in 1954. These were produced as lithographs in 1977.

Original - $40-80; Reproduction - $15-40

GUSTAVSON, LEALAND

(1899-1967) Gustavson illustrated for *McCalls,* the *Saturday Evening Post,* and other magazines as well as Tommy Armour's well known book, *How to Play Your Best Golf All The Time.* He was also talented as an athlete, having won four national badminton championships.

Gustavson painted a series of six scenes showing important moments in the history of golf in America which were later reproduced. The subjects were:

'The Old Apple Tree Gang'
'The First Clubhouse in America (Shinnecock Hills)'
'Awarding the First USGA Trophy'
'Ouimet Wins U.S. Open'
'Robert Tyre Jones Jr.'
'Playoff for Masters Championship (Hogan and Snead)'

Gustavson – 'Francis D. Ouimet Wins United States Open Title - 1913'

Gustavson – 'The Old Apple Tree Gang - 1888'

Harvey — 'Quail In The Rough' $40-80

Hassall — 'The Caddie'

Lastly The Caddie. Sans Teeth, Sans Eyes. Sans Everything!

HARVEY, BRUCE
Harvey is a modern artist who lives in New Zealand.

HASSALL, JOHN
(1868-1948) Hassall illustrated ads, prints, pottery and postcards in England. A portfolio of seven prints was published in 1899 in three different editions. The first consisted of 200 signed artists proofs. The second edition had only the first print signed and the third edition had no signatures.

Original - consult dealer; Reproduction - $15-40

HEARD, H. PERCY
(c 1920) An English artist, Heard painted watercolors and oils of the landscape around North Devon, including views of Westward Ho! Golf Course.

No Known Prints

HELD, JOHN, JR.
(1889-1958) Held was an illustrator for *The New Yorker, Life, Harpers,* and others. Along with F. Scott Fitzgerald, he has been credited for creating the flapper image of the Roaring Twenties. Held was an avid golfer and painted over twenty humorous golf scenes featuring his characteristic round faced people.

No Known Prints

HENDERSON, WILL
(c 1900) Henderson was an English artist and engraver who created the classic golf portraits of 'The Blackheath Golfer', 'Henry Callender', and 'John Taylor' in color between 1914 and 1917. Henderson's signature appears in pencil on his works. See listing under Abbott and Gordon.

$140-400

HEYWOOD, OLIVER
A limited edition of Heywood's uniquely abstract portrayal of Gleneagles Golf Course has been recently issued in Great Britain.

$15-40

HODGE, THOMAS

(1827-1907) Hodge did illustrations for *The Badminton Library* and other publications. A good athlete, he excelled at golf, cricket and lawn bowling. His golf victories included the spring meeting of the Royal and Ancient Club in 1861 and the King William IV Medal in 1866, 1867 and 1869.

HOPKINS, F. P.

(1830-1913) After his career in the military, Hopkins displayed his interest in golf both as a journalist and by painting golf course scenes, groups of golfers and individual golfers. He signed his oils 'F. P. Hopkins' and his watercolors 'Major Shortspoon' or Major S'. A biography of Hopkins has been recently published by Ian Henderson and David Stirk titled *Shortspoon: F. P. Hopkins, Golf Artist and Journalist*.

His painting of 'Medal Day at Blackheath' has appeared in several books and was recently published in a limited edition.

$400 +

HUMPHREY, MAUDE

(c 1890) Humphrey was primarily an illustrator of children's books, however her most important contribution to the arts was her son, Humphrey Bogart. Prints have been recently published.

$15-40 (each)

Hodge - 'Stymie' — Published in 1984.
$15-40

Humphrey – 'Ted'

(Bottom center) Humphrey – 'One Putt'
(Bottom right) Humphrey – 'Teeing Off'
(Bottom left) Humphrey – 'At The Turn'

HUNT, MICHAEL JOHN

(1941-   ) An Englishman specializing in landscape scenes, Hunt has recently issued a set of etchings of Royal St. Georges Golf Course in Sandwich, England. $40-80

IZATT, JAMES PATERSON

A Canadian golf course architect, Izatt has drawn numerous colorful maps of championship golf courses throughout the world. The routing of each of the holes is shown graphically.   under $15

Izatt – 'Pebble Beach Golf Links'

Izatt – 'The Old Course, St. Andrews'

JONES, DAVID

Jones was commissioned by the Augusta National Golf Club to paint several subjects. A view of the thirteenth hole has recently been published in England in a limited edition of 350. $400 +

Jones – 'Emperor Jones' — painted in 1971 and publsihed in 1977 in a signed and numbered limited edition. $40-80

JOSSETT, LAWRENCE

A modern English artist and engraver, Josset has reproduced the William Inglis painting in a hand colored aquatint which is pictured under the David Allan heading in this section. He has produced quite a few works with golfing themes.

KAY, JOHN

(1742-1826) A prolific portrait artist, Kay produced a book titled *Kay's Edinburgh Portraits,* which included golfers such as Alexander McKellar. Primarily an engraver, he produced more than 900 plates.

KELLER, ARTHUR IGNATIUS

(1866-1924) Keller was a well known illustrator of magazines and books such as *Ichabod Crane*. A member of the American Water Color Society, he painted 'A Mixed Foursome' in 1900. This watercolor was originally used on the cover of *Ladies' Home Journal* in March, 1900 and can now be seen at the World Golf Hall of Fame. A lithograph was published in 1973. $15-40

Kay – 'Cock of the Green' — Alexander McKellar is shown in 1803 on the Brunts-field Links. Kay was encouraged to produce this picture by Douglas Gourlay (the feather ballmaker) and Peter McEwan (the early clubmaker).   Scarce

Keller – 'A Mixed Foursome'

Top left: Josset – 'The Last Green' — Josset's fine attention to detail is also exhibited in this hand colored aquatint. $80-140

Center left: Josset – 'The Practice Shot' — An original hand colored aquatint showing a golfer in the early 1800's. $80-140

Bottom left: Josset – 'St. Andrews, 1800' — a hand colored print showing golfers in their old style attire. A limited edition of 75 signed colored etchings of the same scene were also published.
Limited edition - $140-400
Other edition - $40-80

KEMBLE, EDWARD W.

(1861-1933) Kemble illustrated with a style similar to Frost. Illustrated books including *Uncle Remus, Huck Finn* and *Uncle Tom's Cabin.*   (See illustration on next page)   No Known Prints

KENYON, ANN MANRY

Kenyon is a water color artist who lives in Florida. She produced a series of modern golf pros shown at famous courses. Her subjects which are not shown on the following pages include Snead, Player, Hogan and Nicklaus.
(See illustrations on next page) $15-40 (each)

KERNAN, J. F.

(c 1920) Kernan painted an oil of 'The Lucky Caddie'. He provided illustrations for *the Saturday Evening Post* and other publications.
No Known Portraits

KINSTLER, EVERETT RAYMOND

(1926-   ) Kinstler painted the portrait of Byron Nelson which hangs at the USGA Golf House and has only been reproduced in the book, *The Byron Nelson Story.* Outside of golfing circles, Kinstler is recognized for his many paintings of government officials. His portrait of President Ford is on display in the White House.
No Known Prints

KUBIK, KAMIL

Born in Czechoslovakia, Kubik painted scenes of the 1974 and 1976 U.S. Opens. $15-40

Kenyon – 'The 18th Hole at Pebble Beach — Arnold Palmer'

Kenyon – 'A Triumph At Sawgrass — Lee Trevino'

Kemble sketch

LAVERY, SIR JOHN

(1856-1941) RSA, RA, RHA. He painted a picture of the golf course at North Berwick in 1918.

LEES, CHARLES

(1800-1880) RSA. Lees painted portraits, landscapes and scenes from Scottish history after studying under Henry Raeburn. Lees painted 'The Golfers' in 1847, a popular work showing a match at St. Andrews with Sir David Baird and Sir Ralph Anstruther playing against Major Playfair and John Campbell. Dozens of other well known golfers are shown in the scene and can be identified on the accompanying key plate. Individual portraits of the different characters were made by Lees before he made the large painting. Some of these portraits can be seen in *A History of the Royal and Ancient Golf Club* by H.S.C. Everard published in 1907.

The first printing of the work was engraved by Charles Wegstaffe in 1850 in black and white (size 33¼" x 20¾"), some of which were hand colored. Reproductions have been published in various sizes at later dates.

Original - $400 +; Reproductions - $40-140 (consult dealer)

Lees – 'The Golfers'

LEUKART, SANDRA T.

Leukart has painted several scenes from resort golf courses which were reproduced in the 1970's.   under $15

'LIB' (Pseudonym for LIBERIO PROSPERI)

(c 1890) Known by his signature of 'LIB', this Italian artist was responsible for the John Ball caricature in the *Vanity Fair* magazine feature of prominent people of the day. (See illustration under the 'Spy' heading)

LOCKHART, BARBARA SHEENE

A cartoonist from Lexington, Kentucky, Lockhart painted these clowns in 1973 as a tribute to her father. Proceeds from the sale of this limited edition of 500 signed and numbered lithographs were earmarked for cancer research at the University of Kentucky. $15-40

Lockhart – 'Ironhead the Caddie'

Lockhart – 'Ironhead the Pro'

LUPO, DOM

Lupo is an illustrator for *Golf* magazine and others. During the past ten years, he has painted portraits of the inductees into the World Golf Hall of Fame in Pinehurst. These have been published in several different sizes. $15-40

Lupo - 'The Golf Immortals' — A montage of portraits of the first group of inductees into the World Golf Hall of Fame.

Mackenzie - 'Stone Bridge, Swilcan Burn' — Built over 800 years ago, this footbridge has been used by an untold number of golfers on the Old Course at St. Andrews.

Mackenzie - 'Allan Robertson' — Allan was reputed to be the finest golfer of the mid 1800's and also was one of the best makers of feather balls.

Mackenzie - 'The Putt' — Tom Morris and Allan Robertson are shown lining up a putt in a well publicized match against the Dunn brothers in 1849.

Mackenzie - 'Robert T. Jones Jr.' — Jones is featured playing at Merion Cricket Club at different points in his life. Merion was both the site of his first Amateur Championship at age fourteen and the finale of his 'Grand Slam' in 1930. This print was published in an edition of 1000.

Illustration by Broward Malouze · (No known prints)

Mackenzie · 'Tom Morris' — This famous St. Andrews professional is shown in is later years with his ever present pipe.

MACKENZIE, F. B.

(1912-   ) Primarily an illustrator, Mackenzie was commissioned by Old Golf Shop in the 1970's in Cincinnati to recreate moments in golf history. Lithographs of his works were limited to 500 copies except the Jones print.

(See illustrations previous page) $40-80 (each)

MALOUZE, BROWARD

(c 1920) Malouze was an illustrator specializing in art nouveau.

McIAN, R. R.

(c 1840) Mc Ian painted 'Grant of Glenmorrison', which was one of a collection of famous Scottish clans printed in book form. The print was first published in 1845 and later reproduced in 1977 in the United States.

Original - $80-140; Reproduction - $15-40

McQUEEN, JIM

A scratch golfer from North Carolina, McQueen is known for his illustrations of Jack Nicklaus which appear in instructional articles for *Golf Digest* magazine and in various books.   No Known Prints

MEO, DAVID

Meo painted a portrait of Gene Sarazen to commemorate his double eagle at the 1935 Masters Tournament. A print was later produced when Sarazen was honored at the 1979 Memorial Tournament.   under $15

MITCHELL, E. W.

(c 1900) Mitchell illustrated golf books by Bernard Darwin and also for British periodicals.

MORLAND, JOHN

Morland painted a series of 12 British golf courses in 1982. Small hand colored prints have been published.

$15-40 (each)

MOSS, DONALD

Moss is a modern painter who specializes in sports. His works can be seen in *Golf Digest* magazine and other publications. A painting of Arnold Palmer winning the 1960 U.S. Open at Cherry Hills has been reproduced. Moss also produced a modern lithograph showing Andy North winning the 1978 U.S. Open at Cherry Hills. $15-40

NEVILLE, A. MUNRO

Neville painted a series of six 'Famous Scottish Golf Courses' which were published in 1972. The courses featured were: Muirfield, St. Andrews, Carnoustie, Troon, Turnberry and Gleneagles. $40-80 (each)

A Mitchell Cartoon · No known prints

NICHOLSON, SIR WILLIAM

(1872-1949) Nicholson illustrated *An Almanac of Twelve Sports* in 1898 which was a bound calendar that featured a golfer as the October illustration. The calendar included verse by Rudyard Kipling. The golf illustration was subsequently reproduced in the 1970's.   Original Book - (consult dealer); Reproduction - under $15

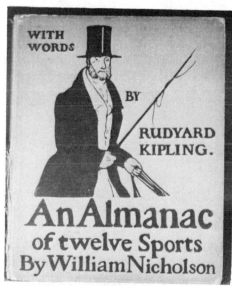

Nicholson - Cover of calendar

Golf.

Why Golf is Art and Art is Golf
  we have not far to seek —
So much depends upon the lie,
  so much upon the cleek .

Nicholson – Caption

Nicholson – Golf Illustration

NIEMAN, LEROY

(1926-   ) A contemporary artist with his own unique style, Neiman is probably America's most prominent sports artist. He has gained extensive television coverage on both ABC and CBS and also has been the official artist for the New York Jets and for Major League Baseball. His works can be found in oils, pen and ink, etchings and serigraphs. Bold, bright colors dominate his golf works.   Serigraph - $140-400; Reproductions - $15-40

Nieman - 'Poster of Six Golfers' — Featuring Hogan, Nicklaus, Palmer, Player, Snead and Trevino.

ORR, NORMAN

(1924-) One of Scotland's leading folklore and wildlife artists, Orr has painted a series of golf caricatures at his studio which is within 100 yards of the famous Leith Links. He is a leading glassware and crystal engraver and also a championship weight lifter. Orr's series consist of six different subjects and were published in two sizes.

under $15 (each)

Orr – 'Hole In One'

Orr – 'In The Rough'

Orr – 'Fresh Air Shot'

PALMER, WILLIAM

(1906-) Did the only known painting of Bobby Jones losing a match...the 1929 U.S. Amateur when he lost to Johnny Goodman.

PATON, FRANK

(1856-1909) Paton was an engraver, painter and illustrator. His most popular contribution to golf art was a small engraving of a match at the links at St. Andrews titled 'Royal and Ancient (St. Andrews, 1798)'. Eight humorous sketches surround the scene on the signed print. This print was published in 1894 and has been copied by Lawrence Josset in modern times under the title 'St. Andrews, 1800'. (See Jossett for illustration.) Paton also engraved golf scenes for Charles Brock.

$80-140

PATRICK, J. McINTOSH

This British artist did a scene of the Old Course at St. Andrews in charcoal and watercolor which was printed in 1977 as part of a series of golf course scenes.

$15-40

PATTERSON, GARY

Patterson's cartoons feature golfers, tennis players and other athlets and can be found on prints, greeting cards, etc.. 'Narrow Fairway.' (See color section for illustration.)

under $15

PHILLIPS, CHARLES G. L.
(1863-1944) Phillips was born in Uruguay of Scottish parents and spent most of his career as a painter and etcher in Dundee Scotland, where many of his works can be viewed in the Dundee City Art Gallery. His golf works consist primarily of etchings of golf in Scotland.
Consult Dealer

Phillips - This limited edition etching is unique in that it is numbered in Roman numerals.

PIPESHANK, GEORGE
(c 1890) Pipeshank's characteristic style can be found in his illustrations for Cope's Cigarette cards and advertisements. His real name was J. Wallace. (See illustrations in section on cigarette cards.)

PREISS, FREDERICK
An Austrian whose figures of golfing girls were printed in early 1900's.

PURDY, GERALD
(1930-   ) Purdy is an educator and artist who has had numerous exhibits throughout the country. His works consist primarily of aquatint etchings which he hand paints personally. His prints are truly originals and include several comical golf scenes. Purdy's biography lists some of his former occupations as pool hall rack boy, soda jerk, assistant tax assessor and haberdashery salesman.
$15-40

Pipeshank - Copes cigarette illustration $15-40

Purdy – 'Short'

RAEBURN, SIR HENRY

(1756-1823) RA. Raeburn studied in Rome and returned to Edinburgh in 1787 at which time he became the top portrait painter in Scotland. He was also a member of the Honourable Company of Edinburgh Golfers. A portrait of John Taylor has sometimes been attributed to Raeburn, but in all likelihood, it was actually started by Raeburn and completed by John Watson Gordon. Raeburn also painted a portrait of William Inglis, a captain of the Honourable Company of Edinburgh Golfers.

Two of Raeburn's paintings which have been reproduced are shown on page 146. They were both engraved in mezzotint and were printed in black and white. There have been no modern reproductions of these works except as illustrations in several golf history books.

James Balfour, the subject of Raeburn's first golf work, was the secretary and treasurer of Edinburgh Company of Golfers. This print was engraved by J. Jones in 1796 and less than fifty copies are believed to have been published.
$400 +

Raeburn's second golf work was a portrait of John Gray. Gray was the secretary of the Honourable Company of Edinburgh Golfers originally published in 1806. This engraving was done by G. Dawe.
$400 +

RAVIELLI, ANTHONY

His sketches can be found in many modern golf books and in *Golf Digest* magazine.   No Known Prints

REID, SIR GEORGE

(1841-1913) PRSA, HRSW. Reid was known for his portraits and landscapes. His works can be seen in museums in Edinburgh, Glasgow, London and Australia.

Reid - A gravure of Tom Morris published in 1903. A limited edition of fifty were signed by Old Tom. The original oil can be seen in the R&A Clubhouse at St. Andrews.
Limited edition $400 +; Other edition - $140-400

REMBRANDT

(1606-1669) Rembrandt made an etching in 1654 which has been referred to as a golf piece, however it is probably a depiction of another game. Several restrikes or reproductions are known to exist.
Original - $400 +; Restrike - $80-140

REYNOLDS, FRANK

(1876-1953) He was an illustrator, caricaturist, and water color artist who illustrated such works as *Punch* magazine and *David Copperfield*. Reynolds' golf works have been reproduced in *The Frank Reynolds' Golf Book*.
No Known Prints

RICHARDS, F. T.

(1864-1921) Richards published six prints in folio form in 1901 which featured golfers in period costume. Later issues have been published in a smaller size and are hand colored. He also was an illustrator for the old *Life* magazine of the 1800's.

Original Signed Edition - $400 + (set); Later Edition - $15-40

Richards – '1840'

Richards – '1682'

Richards – '1705'

ROBINSON, WILLIAM HEATH

(1872-1944) Robinson was a humorist painter, black and white artist and illustrator whose works can be viewed in the British Museum and the Victoria & Albert Museum. His unique drawings of inventions and contraptions earned him recognition as 'The Arch-Priest of Scatter-Brained Improvisation'. His style is often imitated. Robinson's prints are quite popular in Great Britain.

$40-80

ROCKWELL, NORMAN

(1894-1978) This famous American illustrator painted only a few golf subjects.

Robinson – 'Marvels of Golf'

Rockwell - 'Missed' — This group of young golfers was one of four illustrations for a calendar in 1951. A reproduction of the print was done in 1980.

Original - scarce
Reproduction - under $15

ROUNTREE, HARRY

(1880-1950) Rountree was born in New Zealand, however he is known as an English painter of landscapes. His golf course scenes were made famous in *The Golf Courses of the British Isles,* an excellent text written by Bernard Darwin in 1910. His original watercolors and oils can be seen in collections throughout the world. Prints have been published in some of Rountree's golf works. He also illustrated for *Punch* and other British magazines.

There are quite a few collectors who feel that Rountree's name is really spelled "Rowntree". The broad method in which he draws the "U" sometimes makes it appear as a "W". Most of the mispellings can be attributed to auction catalogs and dealer lists. However, the Royal Academy of Arts and an early directory of golfers confirm the "U" spelling. It is interesting to note that the cover of *The Golf Courses of the British Isles* shows the "W" spelling while the title page has the "U" spelling.   Original Prints - $80-140

Rountree oil of Royal North Devon Golf Club at Westward Ho!

RUSSELL, GENE

Russell specializes in painting golf courses. His works are done on location, usually following pen and ink sketches. Much of his work has been done in the Carolinas. $15-40

SADLER, W. DENDY

(1854-1923) Sadler liked to paint his figures attired in old world costume as can be seen in his five golf works. The first four of his golf paintings were engraved by James Dobie and were printed in black and white. A limited number of artist's proofs signed by Sadler and Dobie with a remarque were printed on rice paper and laid on India paper. Unsigned prints done in the same manner were published for Dewars Whiskey in 1926. Another series of early engravings was produced on plain paper. Restrikes from the original plates are still produced in England and are hand colored. A printing in larger format was made in 1972 as a line reproduction which contains the remarque and facsimile signatures.   Original - $140; Restrike - $40-80; Reproduction - $15-40

SANDBY, PAUL

(1725-1809) RA. Sandby painted a picture of the Bruntsfield Links in 1746 which hangs in the British Museum and is probably the oldest piece of artwork showing the game of golf as we know it today. Originally employed as a draftsman, he painted scenes while traveling on his surveying expeditions. He is credited with being the first to blend nature into topographical drawings.

Sadler – 'The First Tee' — A golfer and his caddy preparing to tee off, first published in 1917.

Sadler – 'A Little Practice' — A dedicated golfer practicing his putting indoors. Note the hole drawn on the floor. First published in 1915.

Sadler – 'A Winter Evening' — Off season club cleaning is the subject of this print which was done in 1914.

Sadler - 'The Stymie' — Originally published in 1915, this scene shows the negotiation of the stymie, a rule on the putting green which is no longer in force.

Sadler - 'This For A Half' — The familiar Sadler figures are seen in a match. This print has only been seen in color and has recently been reproduced in a limited edition of 1000 by the U.S. Golf Association.
Original prints - Scarce

SANDERS, CHRISTOPHER
Sanders painted an oil of the Sunningdale Golf Club in England which was published in 1977.　　$15-40

SEALY, ALLEN C.
In 1892 an edition of 300 proof copies were published of Sealy's picture of a match at Sandwich, England between H.S.C. Everard, the famous golf author, and Leslie Balfour. Tom Morris can be seen standing in the background.
Scarce

SHEARER, DONALD
A series of four British golf courses were painted by Shearer and published in print form in 1977.
$15-40 (each)

SMART, JOHN
(1838-1899) RSA. After an apprenticeship as an engraver, he became a landscape artist. He was an original member of the Royal Scottish Water Colour Society and is recognized for paintings of *The Golf Greens of Scotland*. (See Aikman listing.)

Smith – 'Just A Lucky Round'

Smith – 'Caught In The Rough'

SMITH, KEN

Smith is known for his illustrations which personify dogs. A set of four prints showing golfing dogs was published in the 1970's.

under $15 (each)

SPEIGLE, C.

Speigle painted 'Golf Boy' which was originally published in 1900 and later reproduced in 1978 in a smaller size.

Original $80-140; Reproduction - $15-40

Spiegle – 'Golf Boy'

'SPY' (Pseudonym for SIR LESLIE WARD)

(1851-1922) SPY is best known for his caricatures which appeared in *Vanity Fair* magazine. His works all contain the signature, 'SPY'. Besides being an artist, he also studied architecture. *Vanity Fair* was a weekly magazine published in London from 1869 to 1914. Each magazine contained a loose print which showed a caricature. These caricatures were painted by various artists and were also published in book form.

The early prints were stone lithographs while the later ones were chromolithographs. Some proof copies were issued without lettering. An amusing biography accompanied each print. Several other prints are associated with golf, but the subjects are not shown in a golfing manner. Most of the *Vanity Fair* prints which exist are originals, however some have been reproduced in other sizes. Not illustrated is a picture of H. Mallaby-Delley, "The Prince of Princes", printed in 1909.

'Horace G. Hutchinson' — 1890 - The original watercolor can be seen at the USGA Museum.

'John Ball, JNR.' — 1892. This print was done by 'Lib', the only Vanity Fair golfer not painted by 'Spy'.

'Muir' — 1903. Samuel Mure Fergusson.

'Hoylake' — 1903. Harold H. Hilton.

'North Berwick' — 1906. Robert Maxwell.

'John Henry' — 1906. J.H. Taylor.

'Jimmy' — 1907. James Braid.

'Honourable H. Lloyd George'—'Spy' also painted the Prime Minister with a golf club for *The World* magazine in 1910.

STEEN, JAN

(1626-1679) Steen painted Dutch scenes in the seventeenth century which showed a child holding a club and ball. The prints were originally published in 1920 in *A Golfer's Gallery of Old Masters,* a bound collection of golf art. The overruns from the initial printing are still available. Historians differ on whether or not this actually depicts golf.

$15-40

STEENE, WILLIAM

(1888-   ) Steene has produced many murals which can be seen in courthouses in Oklahoma, Texas and Arkansas. His portraits were mostly of southern public officials.   (See illustration on next page.)

STEVENS, THOMAS E.

Stevens painted the portrait of Bobby Jones which is exhibited at the USGA Museum in Far Hills, New Jersey. A limited edition of 1000 prints were published in 1952, some of which were signed by Jones. $40-80 (See following page for illustration.)

Stevens - Bobby Jones

Steene - 'Bobby Jones Concentration' — The top portion of the print was taken from a photo in Jones' book, 'Down The Fairway', while Jones himself posed for the lower part. The print was published in the 1970's. $15-40

Stewart - 'The First International Foursome' — A famous match played over the Leith Links in 1682. Stewart's original painting, which was done in 1919 hangs in the library at the USGA Museum. $40-80

STEWART, ALLAN
(1865-   ) Stewart made a painting called 'Memories of St. Andrews' in which he assembled famous golfers from different times and posted them in a match at St. Andrews. Another of his paintings which showed the Burgess Golfers on the Green in Edinburgh was published in 1927 with some artist's proofs. $80-140

STUDDY, GEORGE
In the early 1900's, Studdy showed dogs playing golf.

SWINSTEAD, GEORGE HILLYARD
(1860-1926) Swinstead painted an oil of a scene titled 'All Square and One to Play' which shows golfers in early costume. The same scene was reproduced as a bas relief bronze panel which was done especially for the South Herts Golf Club outside of London where Swinstead was a member. His works can be seen in the Sheffield Museum.   No Known Prints

TEPPER, SAUL
(1899-   ) Tepper illustrated for magazines and advertisements with a unique bold style. He is perhaps more famous as a songwriter for Ella Fitzgerald, Nat King Cole and others.   No Known Prints

THACKEREY, LANCE
(c 1900) Thackerey was an illustrator of humorous golf characters which appeared in *Punch* and on postcards.   No Known Prints

TIPPIT, JACK

Tippit is a contemporary cartoonist and has been a frequent contributor to publications such as the *New Yorker,*
Saturday Evening Post, and *Ladies Home Journal.* He is proud of the one time when he broke 80 on the golf course.

under $15

TITTLE, WALTER

(1883-1966) Tittle was an etcher who played golf and wrote for *American Golfer* magazine.

Scarce

van der NEER, AERT

(c 1600) This Dutch artist shows scenes of a game on ice which was probably related to golf. The prints were originally
published in 1920 in *A Golfer's Gallery of Old Masters,* a bound collection of golf art. The overruns from the initial
printing are still available.

$15-40

Van Der Neer - 'Winter Landscape'

Van Der Neer – 'River Scene in Winter'

Van De Velde – 'A Frost Scene'

van de VELDE, ADRIAEN

(1635-1672) Van De Valde painted this scene of men playing golf or kolven as it was known in Holland in 1668.
This print was originally published in 1920 in *A Golfer's Gallery of Old Masters,* a bound collection of golf art.
Most of the prints are overruns from the publication of the book, however two other issues are known. An engraving by J. Aliamet was done in France in the eighteenth century and was titled "Les Amusemens de L'Hiver" but
the scene was printed in reverse. A recent limited edition of this print has been done on canvas.

Engraving - $400 +; Canvas - $400 +; Lithograph - $15-40

van de VELDE, ESAIAS

(c 1600) Prints of a painting by the Dutch artist were originally published in 1920 in *A Golfer's Gallery of Old Masters,*
a bound collection of golf art. The overruns from the initial printing are still available.

$15-40

van LOO

From Holland, this artist painted a winter golf scene in 1780.

VENNER, VICTOR

Venner painted at the turn of the century. His golf pictures were printed in 1903 and are titled 'Looking for the
Ball' and 'Attempting to Drive Off'. All of the prints are signed and numbered by the artist. (See illustration on cover.)

Scarce

VORHEES, DONALD

A modern U. S. watercolor artist, Vorhees published series of views of championship golf courses.

$15-40

WAIN, LOUIS

(1860-1939) This British artist painted a series of cats playing golf.

Consult Dealer

WALLACE, HUGH R.

Wallace painted large watercolors in the style of the *Vanity Fair* caricatures.

No Known Prints

Watson - 'Turnberry' — A limited edition of 1000 prints of the course where Tom Watson edged out Jack Nicklaus for the 1977 British Open Championship. $80-140

Watson - 'St. Andrews' — A limited edition of 850 prints were published of the Old Course in 1977. $80-140

WATSON, JAMES FLETCHER

Watson is a landscape artist who exhibits regularly in London. He has painted views of Great Britain which have been reproduced on travel posters for the British Railways.

WEAVER, ARTHUR

(1918-   ) An Englishman, Weaver is best known for over 20 of his views of golf courses, many of which have been reproduced in limited quantities and are unique in that they all have hand drawn remarques which depict a golfer in action. Some of these sketches have been reproduced throughout this book at the chapter headings. Weaver has also been commissioned to paint Texas oil wells, cotton fields, and an African diamond mine. Three of his paintings which are ninety inches long are hanging in a bank in Dallas. $120 +

Weaver – 'View of the 18th Green - Pebble Beach, California'

Weaver – 'The 16th Green on the Old Course - St. Andrews, Fife'

WESTERN, JOHN

Western has spent much of his career designing postage stamps and first day covers. A print of the Ailsa Course at Turnberry, Scotland has recently been published in a limited edition of 850. $80-140

WHITMORE, M. COBURN

(1913-   ) Coby Whitmore has illustrated for many periodicals including *McCalls, Ladies Home Journal* and *Cosmopolitan*. He also enjoys painting racing cars. Whitmore annually paints a portrait of the Heritage Classic champion which hangs in the Harbour Town Clubhouse in Hilton Head, South Carolina.

Whitmore 'Arnold Palmer at Harbour Town'— A limited edition of signed and numbered prints. Also an unsigned edition.   Limited edition - $80-140; other edition - $40-80

Whydale Etching

Williamson – 'Robert Tyre Jones, Jr. winning the British Open Championship'

Ysasi Print

WHYDALE, E. HERBERT

(1886-   ) English painter and etcher.

Consult Dealer

WILLIAMSON, J.W.

(1899-   ) An illustrator for *Fortune* magazine, Williamson painted Jones winning the 1927 British Open. A print was published by Currier and Ives in 1930 in an un-numbered limited edition of 999. $80-140

WOOD, FRANK

(1862-1953) Wood painted landscapes and portraits.

No Known Prints

YSASI, RICARDO

Ysasi is a modern Spanish artist whose works have been reproduced. He exhibits primarily in Europe.

$15-40

OTHER GOLF ARTISTS

ARMOUR, G. D. ()1864-1949)
AYTON, SYMINGTON J. (c 1880)
BAUMER, LEWIS (1870-1963)
BECKHOFF, HARRY (1902-   )
BEARDSLEY, AUBREY (c 1880)
BENSING, FRANK (1893-   )
BIRLEY, OSWALD (c 1900)
BLACKLOCK, THOMAS BROMLEY (1863-1903)
BOOTH, FRANKLIN (1874-1928)
BOYD, A.S. (1854-1930)
BROWN, MARGARET FITZHUGH (c 1950)
BROWN, PAUL (1893-1958)
CADMAN, E.C.
CAMERON, JOHN (c 1900)
CHRISTY, F. EARL (c 1920)
CLEAVER, REGINALD
CUTLER, CECIL (c 1924)
DADD, S. T. (c 1880)
DOUGLAS, JAMES (c 1890)
DRUMMOND-FISH, CAPTAIN G.
EWING, LECKIE
FIRTH, L.
GILBERT, BERTRAM
GILBERT, F.
GILBERT, JOHN (c 1875)
GILLET, FRANK (1874-1927)
GRUBER, JACQUES
GRUGER, F. R. (1871-1953)
GUTHRIE, SIR JAMES (1859-1930)
HADDON, ARTHUR TREVOR (1864-1941)
HARDY, DUDLEY (1866-1922)
HARDY, HEYWOOD (1843-1933)
HARRISON, C.
HENRY, EVERETT (1893-1961)
HILTURN, JAMES (c 1900)
HINDLEY, GODFREY C. (c 1860)
HUTCHINSON, SIR WILLIAM
IMPIGLIA, GIANCARLO
JELLAND, H. C.
JENNINGS, F. NEVILL (c 1900)
KELLER, REAMER

KINSELLA, E. (c 1905)
LANDER, EDGAR
LORAINE, L. ARTHUR (c 1900)
LORIMER, JOHN HENRY (1856-1936)
LUDLOW, HAL S.
LUNT, WILMOT
MAY, P. W. (1864-1903)
MILLS, A. WALLIS (c 1890)
MITCHELL, CHARLES D. (1887-1940)
MONTGOMERY, JOHN
NEILL, J. R. (c 1880-1920)
ORPEN, WILLIAM (c 1922)
OWEN, WILL
PARTRIDGE, BERNARD (1861-1945)
PATRICK, JAMES (c 1890)
PEGRAM, FRED (1870-1937)
PETTIE, JOHN (1839-1893)
PHILLIPS, COLES (c 1920)
PRANCE, BERTRAM
PRICE, ALAN (c 1970)
RADLER, MIL (c 1975)
RAVEN-HILL, L. (c 1890)
RIDGEWELL, W. L.
SAVIGNE, MARIE (c 1900)
SHARP (c 1890)
SHEPARD, ERNEST (1879-1976)
SMITH, A. T.
STAMPA, G. L. (1875-1951)
STEVENSON, W. G. (c 1890)
TEMPLE, J. (c 1890)
TENNANT, DUDLEY
THOMAS, BERT
THORPE, J. H.
TOWNSEND, F. H. (1868-1920)
VAN WOLF, HENRY (c 1960)
WEINMAN, ADOLF (1870-1952)
WILSON, DAVID (1873-1934)
WILSON, JAMES (c 1856)
WOOD, STARR

Heywood Hardy, a well known British painter, produced this view of a mixed foursome on the 17th hole at North Berwick, Scotland. Painted in 1903, published as a photogravure, shortly thereafter, and recently reproduced in color.

French tourism poster with a golfing theme.

HERE'S ONE CUP HE DID NOT MIND LIP-PING. Illustrations such as this one of Walter Hagen after his 1924 British Open victory originally appeared in periodicals. Collectors may sometimes find the original drawings which make attractive decorations.

CHAPTER 6 — CERAMICS

Most of the pottery and porcelain with golf motifs was produced between 1890 and 1935. As golf equipment started to be mass produced and the number of golfers surged in the 1890's, so did the business of creating golf related items for the home. The early manufacturers of golf ceramics were: O'Hara Dial and the Ceramic Art Company (makers of Lenox China) in the United States; Royal Doulton, Copeland Spode, Minton and Wedgewood in England; Gerz in Germany; and Limoges in France. The early pieces were usually hand painted in limited quantities. The later pieces, many of which were produced in larger quantities, had decorations which were often printed by photomechanical means.

Since dining and social gatherings were popular forms of entertainment at the turn of the century, golfers found it desirable to bring golf related items into their homes for decorative purposes. Golf plates, mugs and pitchers, as well as golf related utensils made of silver were often on display. Many of the ceramics were awarded as tournament prizes.

By 1906, the majority of the firms had ceased production of their golf designs, with the exception of Royal Doulton which found that there was still a market for their huge variety of golf items. Finally by World War II, the production of golf ceramics was at a minimum. Only a few items of substantial value have been manufactured in recent years, with souvenirs comprising the majority of the offerings. Modern whiskey decanters with golf motifs are shown in Chapter 11 since they fall more into the advertising category as they tend to be commercial in nature.

Golf collectors acquire ceramics for various reasons. Some are serious collectors while others have only a few pieces for decorative purposes. Methods of collecting can include specializing in one manufacturer or in a single style as mugs or plates.

GUIDE TO CERAMICS VALUES

The following price ranges have been assigned to the various manufacturers of golf ceramics and to the items shown in the photographs. Prices are those which a collector should expect to pay to a dealer for pieces in good condition.

Value Ranges: over $500
$250-500
$100-250
$50-100
under $50

MAKERS OF GOLF CERAMICS

ARCADIAN CHINA — Stoke-on-Trent, Staffordshire, England
Cup and saucer combinations were made from 1904-1924   under $50

BEELEEK POTTERY Fermanagh, Ireland
A well known Irish company which produced only a few golf pieces. $250-500

SAMSON BRIDGEWOOD & SON - Longton, England
The Anchor pottery series by Bridgewood featured golfers.   under $50

CARLTON WARE by WILTSHAW AND ROBINSON - Stoke-on-Trent, Staffordshire, England
The registration numbers placed on the various pieces can be used for dating these pieces which were made from the 1890's until 1957. $50-100

Colorful Carlton Ware humidor.   Carlton Ware matchstick holder

COPELAND SPODE by W. T. COPELAND & SONS LTD. - Stoke-on-Trent, Staffordshire, England
Most of the golf items were made in the early 1900's with white raised designs on a background of either blue or green. $100-500 +

Copeland Spode: 6" jug, tea pot, 5" jug.

Copeland Spode mark.

CROWN STAFFORDSHIRE PORCELAIN COMPANY - Fenton, Staffordshire, England
Cups, saucers and plates with golf motifs were produced after 1930 using a transfer method of printing.

$50-100

Crown Staffordshire cup and saucer and mark.

DARTMOUTH POTTERY LTD. - Dartmouth, Devon, England
Dartmouth started up production in 1947.

$50-100

Dartmouth golf mug and mark.

ROYAL DOULTON

THIS ONE COMPANY HAS PRODUCED FAR MORE GOLF CERAMICS THAN ALL OTHER COMPANIES COMBINED. THE INFORMATION ON THE MAJOR CATEGORIES IS LISTED BELOW. DOULTON EARNED ITS ROYAL DESIGNATION IN 1902.

LAMBETH by DOULTON - Lambeth England

Although Doulton was in business in Lambeth in 1885, the Lambeth Studio actually began production of stoneware in the 1860's. The Lambeth golf items were produced in the early 1900's and are noted for their applied reliefs, which were created by applying several layers of slip.

The reliefs show golfing figures in a white color situated on tan backgrounds with borders of brown or blue. Some of the borders reflect an Art Nouveau influence. The designs were based on models by John Broad and were interchanged among the many jugs and mugs. The three scenes which have been used are "Lost Ball", "Putting" and "Driving".

$250-500 +

An assortment of Doulton Lambeth pottery in various sizes.

Lambeth 4½" beaker showing "Driving."

Lambeth mark.

All of Doulton's stoneware pieces were made at Lambeth, however some do not have the Lambeth mark and are only marked Royal Doulton. Many were used for advertising and trophies.

Advertising jug from 1904 by Royal Doulton for "Colonel Bogey Whisky"

Jug with a silver rim showing an illustration in the style of Charles Crombie.

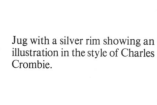

Lambeth humidor and pitcher by Royal Doulton made after 1902.

MORRISIAN WARE by DOULTON

This type of Royal Doulton was probably named after the William Morris type borders which were used. Morrisian Ware was made at Burslem from 1900 until 1924 and feature Bradley type golfers in 17th century costume. The shapes include vases, jardinieres and fern stands which were formal and sometimes large. The colors are either black on yellow or black on yellow and red. Some of the pieces are stamped "Morrisian". $250-500 +

One of the varying shapes of Morrisian Ware vases.

Large Morrisian fern stand on display at the USGA Golf House in Far Hills, New Jersey.

KINGSWARE by DOULTON

The process by which the scenes on Kingsware were decorated were quite unusual. Instead of painting the figures on a blank piece of pottery, the colors were applied to the interior of the plaster mold which already had the designs impressed in it in relief. After the mold was put together, the dark brown or pale yellow slip was poured which then fused with the already painted design. A transparent glaze was then applied which enhanced the pleasing tones. Most of the shapes were jugs and mugs except for the "Nineteenth Hole" dishes made from 1914 to 1930. The standard shapes of Kingsware were produced from 1899 until 1946. $250-500 +

An embossed low relief series was made in 1936 which appears similar to Kingsware, however the colors are lighter and the designs are applied to the surface in the traditional manner. This style can be distinguished from real Kingsware by its lighter inside color and D5716 series number.

Kingsware jug on the right as compared to a later Series Ware issue made by a different method.   (Kingsware valued higher)

Kingsware mug with silver lid.

Kingsware whiskey flask (decanter) with silver topped cork made in 1936.

Hand painted Doulton Burslem vase with an unusual shape.

DOULTON BURSLEM by DOULTON

Only a few rare pieces exist which bear the Doulton Burslem mark. These are usually made of bone china and were produced at Burslem between 1890 and 1902.   over $500

ROYAL DOULTON SERIES WARE

Series Ware was the idea of Charles J. Noke who joined Doulton in 1889 at Burslem and later became Art Director. Series Ware was based on standard blank shapes of white china or earthenware which were decorated in different series. The subject matter came from fields such as history, literature, pastimes, children's themes, legends, important events and the like. There were topics of interest to please everyone.

Various colors of glaze were used on Series Ware, the most common of which was the pale yellow or ivory. The designs were applied by the "print & tint" method of transfer printing followed by hand coloring.

Series Ware production was interrupted by World War II, and when resumed, the large variety of shapes was gradually reduced to the standard rack plate.

Large jug. $200-500

Vegetable bowl, platter, milk jug. $100-250 each

Most of the "Golfers" pieces show the D3395 series number, however the Royal Doulton mark will vary depending on the year made.

Royal Doulton punch bowl (over $500) and seldom seen vase. ($250-500)

THERE ARE SIX TYPES OF SERIES WARE WHICH HAVE GOLF THEMES:

1. Golfers. One of the more popular golf series, these figures resemble those painted by Charles Crombie in his humorous illustrations of the "Rules of Golf". $50-500 +

Shapes: Mugs, bowls, platters, jugs, candlesticks, bowls, vases, ash trays, etc.
Dates: 1911 to 1932
Pattern Numbers: D3394, D3395 and D5960

Designs: The pieces in the "Golfers" series ware line usually had one of the following sayings:

    A. *Give losers leave to speak &winners to laugh.*
    B. *He that complains is never pittied.*
    C. *All fools are not knaves but all knaves are fools.*
    D. *He hath good judgement who relieth not wholly on his own.*
    E. *Every dog has his day and every man his hour.*

2. Proverbs Plates. This art style has been attributed to Will Bradley (1868-1930) even though he was not responsible for the designs. $100-250

Designs: These rack plates have either stylized floral or grapevine borders with one of the following proverbs surrounding the golfers who are shown in Eastern attire:

    A. *If at first you don't succeed try again.*
       A miss is as good as a mile.

    B. *Fine feathers make fine birds.*
       Old saws speak the truth.

    C. *Hope springs eternal in the human breast.*
       Hope deferred maketh the heart sink.

    D. *An Oak is not felled by one blow.*
       Take the will for the deed.

    E. *Nothing venture nothing win.*
       Count not your chickens before they are hatched.

    F. *Fine feathers make fine birds.*
       Handsome is that handsome does.

    G. *Nothing venture nothing have.*
       A bird in the hand is worth two in the bush.

Dates: 1911 to 1928.
Pattern Numbers: D3391 and D3481.

Proverb plate.

3. Gibson. Charles Dana Gibson (1867-1944) illustrated for *Life, Harper's Weekly, The Century* and others. He is best remembered for his creation of "The Gibson Girl", an Edwardian beauty, which was used extensively for decorative purposes. $100-250

Pair of small Gibson vases.

Designs: Gibson's figures are accompanied by one of the following quotes:

- A. *Golf — a good game for two.*
- B. *Is a caddie always necessary?*
- C. *Don't watch the player, keep your eye on the ball.*
- D. *One difficulty of the game — keeping your eye on the ball.*
- E. *Fore.*
- F. *From 10 a.m. to 6:45 p.m. this dog has been kept out. Where is the S.P.C.A.?*
- G. *The last day of summer.*
- H. *Who cares?*

Shapes: Pin trays, small vases, cups and saucers.
Colors: Usually polychrome, although some monotones do exist.
Dates: Introduced in 1904 and probably withdrawn during World War I.
Pattern Numbers: E2766 and E2827.

4. Bateman. Henry Mayo Bateman (1887-1970) was an illustrator of humorous drawings for Punch and other magazines and was also known for his caricatures. The pottery pieces with his designs show a facsimile signature. under $100

Bateman's humorous figures are presented on this Series Ware mug. $50-100

Designs: Bateman's three golf designs are "An Irate Golfer", "The Laughing Caddies", and "The Smug Golfer".
Shapes: Octagon sweet dish, stein, playing card box, cigarette box, pin trays, etc.
Dates: First recorded in 1930, not marked until 1937 and withdrawn in 1950.
Pattern Number: D5813.

5. Diversions of Uncle Toby. Uncle Toby is a character taken from Laurence Sterne's novel, *Tristam Shandy*, written in the 18th century. A series of fifteen games which Uncle Toby was known to enjoy are depicted in various scenes by designer Walter Nunn and one scene shows Uncle Toby playing golf. $100-250

"Uncle Toby" tries his hand at golf.

Shapes: Rack plates and jugs.
Colors: Polychrome, Whieldon ware, Holbein glaze.
Dates: Introduced in 1909 and withdrawn by 1930.
Pattern Numbers: D3111, D3121 and D3197.

6. The Nineteenth Hole. This series features two men drinking at a table with a bag of golf clubs nearby and the golf course in the background.

Dates: 1914-1930.
Pattern Numbers: D3755 and D3770

OTHER DOULTON ITEMS

Bunnykins. This ware features personified bunny rabbits which were taken from water color paintings by Barbara Vernon. Made in the 1930's, a cup and saucer combination is most popular. $50-100

Bunnykins Series Cup and distinctive mark.

Golfer. This character jug, designed by David Biggs, was introduced in 1971 with a D6622 pattern number. The character jug range was first introduced in 1934.

FOLEY CHINA by E. BRAIN & CO. LTD. - Fenton, Staffordshire, England

Golf plates and cups were produced by Foley, which began business in 1903. $50-100

SIMON PETER GERZ - Hohr, Germany

Gerz crafted only a few golf pieces at the beginning of the twentieth century. Because of the inscription placed on bottom of the pieces, many collectors incorrectly assume that this pottery was made by "Gesch". The word "Gesch" is actually an abbreviation for "Gesetzlich Geschutzt" which translates to "protected by law" meaning that the design is copyrighted. $250-500

Stoneware pitcher and mark by Gerz.

WILLIAM HENRY GOSS LTD. - Stoke-on-Trent, Staffordshire, England

Goss was primarily a manufacturer of souvenirs, trinkets and tea cups, some of which featured golf themes.

under $100

GRIMWADES LTD. - Stoke-on-Trent, Staffordshire, England.

Grimwades golf ceramics can be found, but are generally not prized by collectors.

under $100

HAUBER & REUTHER - Freising, Bavaria, Germany.

"HR" manufactured steins of excellent quality in the late nineteenth century. Other steins of lesser quality are more common.

$250-500

LENOX by CERAMIC ART COMPANY - Lawrenceville, New Jersey.

Lenox was named for Walter Scott Lenox who co-founded this American company in 1889. When he took over full control of the company in 1896, he added his last name to the mark which consisted of a wreath encircling the letters, "CAC".

The attractive Lenox golf items of various shapes and sizes were produced between 1894 and 1906. Many of the artists responsible for the fine hand painting can be identified by their marks placed on the pottery.

$250-500 +

Three Lenox mugs in slightly different styles.

Lenox decanter with stopper.

Unusual oil lamp with silver trim.

LIMOGES - Paris, France

Limoges produced mugs with men and women in golf attire. $250-500

Limoges mug and mark.

MINTON - Stoke-on-Trent, Staffordshire, England.

This old, well known company was one of the first producers of golf pottery in the 1890's. $100-500

MINTONS
ENGLAND

Minton mark.

Minton plate painted in blue. $100-250

Minton pitcher. $250-500

O'HARA DIAL CO. - Waltham, Massachusetts.

Their principal business was the manufacture of enamelled dials for watches and meters, however they distributed porcelain mugs and the like which were made for them in Paris circa 1900. The mugs often had metal lids with enamelled decorations which were made by O'Hara. $250-500

O'Hara mugs showing some of the different enamelled lids which were used.

ROOKWOOD POTTERY COMPANY - Cincinnati, Ohio.

Rookwood only made a few golf pieces first in 1899 and then at later dates. The pieces were usually vases or trophies. $100-500 +

Rookwood golf trophy with silver plate dated 1899.   over $500

ROYAL BONN by FRANZ ANTON MEHLEM - Rhineland, Germany.

Royal Bonn golf mugs were made in the 1890's and are a rare find today. over $500

Royal Bonn mark.

SLEEPYEYE - Wisconsin, United States.

Mugs, mixing bowls and milk jugs were produced for use as advertising premiums for flower companies in the 1930's by the Sleepyeye Indians. $50-100

TEPLITZ - Germany

An unusual vase in the form of a caddy was offered by Teplitz in the early 1900's. $50-100

JOSIAH WEDGWOOD & SONS - Burslem, England.

Wedgewood produced Kenlock Ware golf pieces in the early 1900's and in 1931 made plates and other items with the Wedgewood name. They recently issued a pin tray with a modern golf theme. $100-500 +

This Kenlock Ware creamer was made by Wedgwood in 1900. Most of the pieces were made of basalt or terra cotta in various sizes and featured a woman golfer.   over $500

WELLER - Zanesville, Ohio.

Weller's stoneware at the beginning of this century depicted men, women and children golfers on many different pieces. $250-500

WILLOW ART CHINA by HEWETT BROTHERS — Longton, Staffordshire, England.

Willow Art cups, plates and saucers were offered in the 1920's with a golf theme. A small bust of Tom Morris, the famous St. Andrews golf figure, was also produced.   under $250

Willow Art mark in use from 1907 to 1926.

ARTHUR WOOD & SON - Longport, Staffordshire, England.

Wood sold a mug featuring a caddie some time after 1934. $50-100

WORCESTER PORCELAIN CO. - Worcester, England.

A cup and saucer combination was produced by Royal Worcester in the 1960's. $50-100

MISCELLANEOUS GOLF CERAMICS:

Numerous pieces of pottery have been hand made by hobbyists or produced by lesser known manufacturers than those listed. The Delft tiles with Dutch golf scenes were first made in Holland in the 17th century. The very early tiles are not too common, but inexpensive reproductions that have been made through the years are often seen.

Modern ceramics range from a plate made in Paris to a Disney character made in Japan.
Under $50 each

Various golf items have been made of glass such as these decanters which have been etched and then overlaid in silver.
$250-500 each

Other glassware has been manufactured by A. H. Heisey of Newark, Ohio; Cambridge Glass of Cambridge, Ohio; and T.G. Hawkes & Co. of Corning, New York. $250-500 each

Porcelain figures such as this have been recently produced by Lefton China in Taiwan.
Under $50

CHAPTER 7 — SILVER AND RELATED ITEMS

Trophies for golf competitions have been traditionally made of silver. Some early examples dating to the eighteenth century can be seen on display at golf clubs throughout England and Scotland. The trophies were usually presented to the clubs or golf associations by members, and many remain on permanent display at the clubs, in golf museums or in private collections.

The earliest known prizes were silver replicas of golf clubs to which were attached silver golf balls engraved with the name of each winner. The Honourable Company of Edinburgh Golfers was the first to use this method of presentation in 1744. Some of the other clubs which still use these trophies for ceremonial purposes are: Royal and Ancient Golf Club, Royal Blackheath Golf Club, Royal Burgess Golfing Society and Panmure Golf Club.

Other permanent trophies which appear in the trophy cases are in the form of loving cups, bowls, medals, trays and jugs. A championship belt with a large silver buckle was used as the first trophy of the British Open in 1860 and was retired in 1870 after Young Tom Morris won the event three times in succession. These silver and sometimes gold prizes were handmade by fine craftsmen and were usually elaborately engraved. As some of the golf societies were disbanded over the years, their silver possessions were either put up for sale or were given to the families of members. Many of these trophies are now in the possession of collectors of golf memorabilia.

Traditionally, the winner would receive a gold or silver medal for their accomplishment while their name was inscribed on the permanent trophy which was kept by the club or association which conducted the competition. The medals varied from simple engraved ones to those which were enamelled or elaborately adorned. Since each club would have at least six annual competitions, quite a few medals have been presented through the years and are sought after by golf collectors. Few trophies were presented to the winners until the 1890's when they became popular.

Most of the medals were struck in the Birmingham region of England, however Alex Kirkwood and Son, founded in 1826 in Edinburgh, produced many of the early golf medals and continue to do so today. Great skill was required to design and make the dies and also to strike the medals. Some medals were cast, but do not have the sharp images of the ones that were struck. Medals were not used as often for club tournament prizes in the United States, but continue to be used in major competitions.

Private collections contain medals which date from the mid-1800's to the present time. One of the most impressive collections is the display of Bobby Jones' championship medals which can be seen at the USGA Museum in Far Hills, New Jersey.

Prior to the 1890's, most of the silver golf items were made in Great Britain of standard silver, which was 97% pure. As golf increased in popularity in the 1890's, economical silver plated wares became more common in Britain and the United States. Gifts and prizes appeared in the form of: ink stands, cups, bowls, plaques in relief, toast racks, candle sticks, spoons, ash trays, flasks, card cases, jewelry, dresser sets, match safes, watches, clocks, etc. These items have become popular collectibles today. Buttons, badges and pins displaying club insignia were also produced in silver, silver plate, brass and some with enamelling.

The British silver pieces were stamped with a hallmark except for small items such as jewelry which may have been marked "sterling". The hallmark showed where, when, and often by whom, the piece was made. American silver, usually marked "sterling," was not quite as pure as the British silver. Most of the British plated golf wares were stamped with a mark similar to a hallmark to signify the type of plating process. The marks were:

EPNS – Electro Plated Nickel Silver
EPBM – Electro Plated Base Metal
EPC – Electro Plated Copper

The hallmarked British items are relatively easy to date whereas American items usually require the skills of an experienced collector or dealer. Most of the American silversmiths would mark their work with either their name or initials, but no indication for dating was used. Collectors will find it helpful to consult one of the many handbooks on hallmarks and silversmiths as an aid for dating and identification.

There are no general rules to follow when evaluating silver due to the many variables encountered. Silver content, age, design and the style and content of the engraving make each piece unique. Therefore, these prices are meant to be a general indication of value.

MEDALS AND TROPHIES

Two finely detailed silver medals of Scottish origin. $200-500

Beautifully engraved medal presented by the Aberdeen Golf Club, which was established in 1780. This medal dates from 1885. $200-500

Left: This medal was originally presented by the Royal North Devon Golf Club to the Ladies Champion in 1868, and is still being struck off the original dies as a modern day prize. $100-200

Below: Silver medal with an enamelled design, circa 1905. $50-100

Jack Nicklaus with the permanent British Open trophy. A three time winner of the championship, Nicklaus uses a likeness of the trophy in the logo of The Memorial Tournament and his Muirfield Village Golf Club in Dublin, Ohio.

Former captain, Donald Tindley, is shown with one of the silver clubs belonging to the historic Royal Blackheath Golf Club.

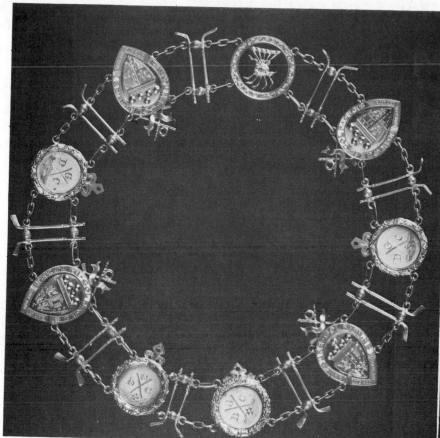

Necklace made of early golf medals, some of which are from the Panmure Golf Club in Scotland. over $1,000

The head of a silver club which was played for in Edinburgh from 1888 until World War I. Most of the silver club trophies were fashioned after long nose woods, however this one is a cleek because the competiton required the players to use only one club, namely a cleek. The extensive hand engraving exhibits the extraordinary talents of the engravers of the period. over $1,000

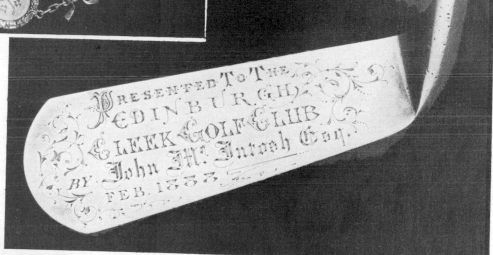

Left: This medallion, struck in both silver and polished pewter, was designed in 1980 and features Old Tom and Young Tom Morris. The four inch diameter version is believed to be the largest medal ever struck in Scotland. $50-100

Example of one of the silver hole-in-one trophies which were first offered by golf ball manufacturers in the 1920's. $50-100

Front and back views of a Blackheath Golf Club medal won in 1849 by the Rev. William Marsh, chaplain of Morden College in the Blackheath area of London. A view of this college can be seen in the background of the famous portrait of William Innes, titled "The Blackheath Golfer," painted by L.F. Abbott and first published as a print in 1790. $1,000 up

Front and back views of a Blackheath silver medal from 1870. By that time, the Club had been awarded the "Royal" designation. $500-1,000

GIFTS, JEWELRY, ETC.

Left: Club badges are also sought after by golf collectors along with blazer buttons.   under $50

Below: Inkstands were popular prizes and gifts for the golfer at the turn of the century. Most were made in silver plate, however some were silver. $200-500

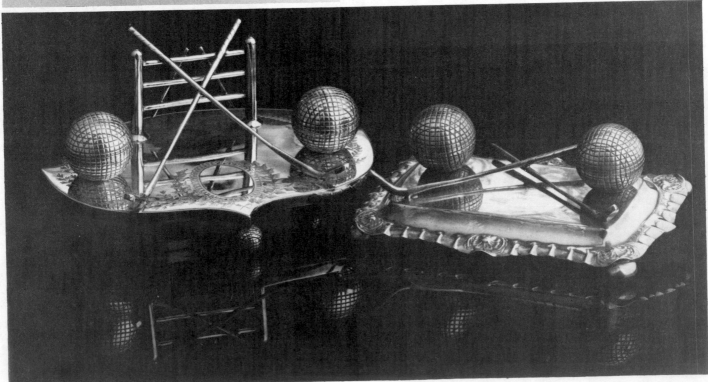

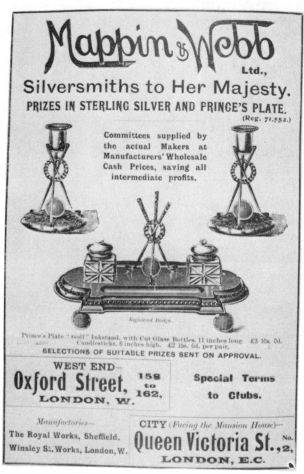

Ad from 1899 for silver golf items.

Above two photos: Several different styles of sterling match safes made in the United States. $100-500

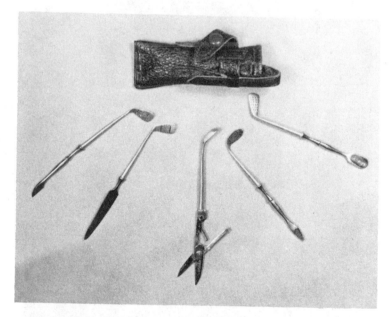

Golfer's manicure kit complete with a miniature golf bag.   under $50

Early silver cigarette case, the interior of which was later converted to hold family photographs for a former Master's champion. $200-500

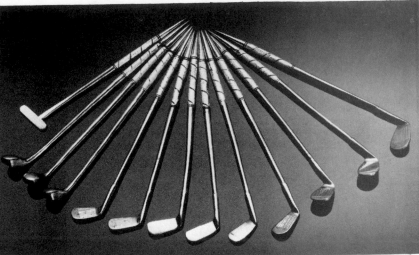

Above: Complete set of miniature golf clubs made as hors d'oeuvres picks. These are not antiques, but were handmade in Scotland in the 1970's. $200-500

Left: Gent's silver pocket watch, circa 1900. Gold watches can also be found.
$500-1,000

Early twentieth century brass clock of typical Scottish design. (approximately 6" high).
$500-1,000

Silver pin cushion in the shape of a driver, hallmarked 1908. $100-200

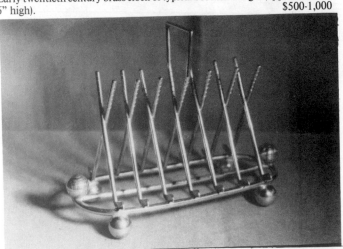

Example of one of many styles of silver plate toast racks with golf motifs which were made at the turn of the century.
$100-500

Three inch high desk calendar of silver plate with celluloid inserts. $50-100

211

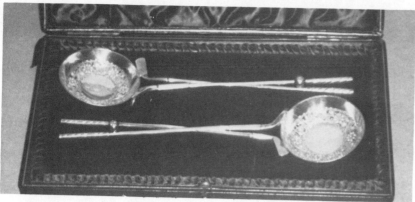

Above: Silver plate captain's spoons formerly used by golf club captains for ceremonial winetasting.
$200-500

Right: American sterling silver whiskey flask, circa 1915. $200-500

Early silver flask engraved with scenes of four sports: golf, hunting, fishing and curling. Dating from 1850, this Scottish flask features a removable cup from the lower portion. This is one of the earliest and finest silver golf items.
over $1,000

CHAPTER 8 — BRONZES AND OTHER STATUARY

As golf art became more prolific at the end of the nineteenth century, several well known golfers had their likenesses cast in bronze. The first of these golf figures appeared in 1890 when the backswing of Horace Hutchinson, an amateur champion and golf writer, was sculpted by William Tyler. Until that time most golf art was in the form of paintings and prints that featured portraits of golfers rather than depictions of their swings. So this idea of showing a golfer's swing was somewhat of a novel idea.

Sculptors were usually commissioned by golf associations, clubs, or members of a golfer's family to create these statues which were then used as presentation pieces or for decorations. Most of them were cast in bronze and bear the sculptor's signature and the date. Sometimes other materials were used such as silver, pot metal, silver plate, pewter, iron and wood.

The following list includes the most notable works in the field of golf statuary. Many miscellaneous golf statues have been manufactured over the years of inexpensive pot metal. The sculptors and producers of these items are difficult to identify and the articles are usually of relatively little value. Some of the miscellaneous works that are worth mentioning are: a set of bookends depicting Bobby Jones putting; a recent limited edition of a Ben Hogan figure; and bronzes of Chick Evans, Arnold Palmer and Jack Nicklaus.

The early bronzes were cast in limited quantities and are worth thousands of dollars. Since they are very seldom sold, it is difficult to establish a market price. There were quite a few bronzes of Harry Vardon done by both Henry Pegram and Hal Ludlow which sell for over $1000. The more ordinary statues generally cast of pot metal vary greatly in price with many valued under $100.

This 7½" by 5" bronze relief plaque shows King Charles I receiving news of the Irish Rebellion while playing golf on the Leith Links. The scene was taken from a painting by John Gilbert in 1875.

213

Here Is Something New

to solve the problem as to what to buy for that

Trophy, Christmas, New Year's or Birthday Present.

Useful   Ornamental   Worth While.
Made of Government Bronze, Fully Warranted

Price $24.00
Sent prepaid anywhere
in U. S. A.

Write for illustrated catalog, it contains many things of interest to the golfer.

GOLF SPECIALTY COMPANY

258 Broadway   New York

Left: Small statue of an unknown golfer cast in pot metal.
Right: This concrete caddy holds the lamp at the entrance to the Museum of the United States Golf Association.
Above: Advertisement from 1918 for a bronze inkstand.

These bronze and marble bookends of a golfer and his caddy date from the 1920's.

SOME OF THE BETTER KNOWN GOLF STATUARY
(LISTED IN CHRONOLOGICAL ORDER OF ISSUE)

Horace Hutchinson, by William Tyler

John Ball, by Alex Macleay

Male Golfer by Ed Wilson

Finish of the Swing by Frank Taubman

Harold Hilton by Cassidy

Glenna Collett by E. E. Codman

Cecil Leitch, by Sam Bugnatz

Harry Vardon, by Hal Ludlow

HORACE HUTCHINSON by William Tyler in 1890. (26" high)

Hutchinson (1859-1932) was the British Amateur Champion in 1886 and 1887. He is best remembered as the author of many fine books and articles.

JOHN BALL by Alex Macleay in 1893. (19½" high)

John Ball (1861-1940) was the first amateur golfer to win the British Open, a feat he accomplished in 1890. He dominated the amateur scene by winning the British Amateur eight times between 1888 and 1912. A replica of this bronze was also done in iron.

MALE GOLFER by Ed Wilson in 1898. (19" high)

The identify of this golfer is not known.

"AT THE TOP OF THE SWING" and **"FINISH OF THE SWING"** by Frank Taubman in 1895. (14" high)

Taubman sculpted two bronzes of a male golfer.

HARRY VARDON by Hal Ludlow in 1899. (Three sizes: 5", 10", 26")

One of the greatest players of all time, Vardon (1870-1937) was a six time winner of the British Open. Vardon was a member of the "Golf Triumvirate" with James Braid and J. H. Taylor.

This bronze was done in great detail by Hal Ludlow, who was also an accomplished artist, and was cast by Elkington in England. The smaller statues were usually mounted on a plinth and were often presented as tournament prizes. The 10" high figure was also cast in German silver. Ludlow was also a fine golfer, having won the 1904 Welsh Native Amateur Championship by a 13 and 11 margin in the 36 hole finals.

216

One of only ten *Golfer Medallions* cast by Benno Schotz.

HAROLD HILTON by Cassidy in 1901. (12" high)

Harold Hilton (1869-1942) was another famous amateur golfer to be honored with a bronze. He was a two time winner of the British Open, a four time winner of the British Amateur, and the only Briton ever to win the U.S. Amateur.

HARRY VARDON by Henry Pegram in 1908. (12" high)

Pegram featured Vardon in his backswing.

JOYCE WETHERED by Sir W. Reid Dick in 1925. (14½" high)

Joyce Wethered (1901-   ) is considered to be the finest woman player of all time in Great Britain. A winner of countless numbers of tournaments, she is now known as Lady Heathcoat-Amory.

CECIL LEITCH by Sam Bugnatz circa 1925. (19" high)

Cecil Leitch was the winner of twelve women's national golf championships in England, France and Canada.

GLENNA COLLETT Possibly by E. E. Codman circa 1930. (14" high)

Now known as Glenna Collett Vare, this American golfer won the U.S. Women's Amateur six times, the Canadian Women's Amateur twice and played on the Curtis Cup Team four times and was Captain twice. This bronze was cast by Gorham in the United States.

"THE CADDY" by Philip S. Sears circa 1930.

This caddy is featured attending the flagstick with a bag of clubs over his shoulder.

Rawcliffe Pewter golfers by P. Davis.

Putter Boy

Hudson Pewter Company golfers by Philip Kraczkowski.

BOBBY JONES by Rosario Fiore in 1931. (28½" high)

This statue of the great Bobby Jones (1902-1971) was done just after he completed his Grand Slam. Jones' major championship record set between 1923 and 1930 has only been surpassed by Jack Nicklaus.

Jones is featured posing with a club in this large bronze which is on display at the World Golf Hall of Fame.

SUNDIAL OF GOLFER by Laura Gardin Fraser circa 1934. (19" high)

As with other golfer sundials, the shaft of the player's club at address casts shadows upon the base of the statue. Fraser's golfer is an energetic youth with his sleeves rolled up.

SUNDIAL OF GOLFER by E. E. Codman circa 1935. (20" high)

This sundial stands in front of the pro shop at the Augusta National Golf Club. It was cast by Gorham and is thought to be of Bobby Jones addressing the ball.

"PUTTER BOY" SUNDIAL Sculptor not known. (26" high)

For many years this sundial was situated by the putting green at Pinehurst Country Club in North Carolina. It is now on display at the World Golf Hall of Fame. Since the mid 1970's, reproductions have been made in three sizes.

BEN HOGAN by Henry Van Wolf in 1954.

The familiar follow through of Ben Hogan is the subject featured on the Golf Writers Association of America Trophy. The original, standing thirty-two inches high, is one of the largest bronzes of a golfer and is on display at the USGA Museum in Far Hills, New Jersey. Each year a miniature replica is presented to the recipient of the award.

GOLFER MEDALLION by Benno Schotz in 1979. (6" diameter)

    This bronze medallion shows an 18th century golfer at the top of his backswing. Schotz (1890-1984) was a very talented sculptor and won numerous awards for his work. He lived in Glasgow and was the Sculptor to the Royal family.

MODERN PEWTER

    Several pewter golf figures have been cast in recent years which depict modern golfers of no particular fame. These pieces feature great detail and sell for under $150.

Bronze relief plaque of Freddie Tait, the British Amateur Champion in 1896 & 1898, produced in 1905.

WOOD CARVINGS

Modern hand carved Scottish golfers are currently made in Sweden by C.O. Trygg, one of the foremost woodcarvers in the world.

Wood golfer figures were also machine made in Italy in the 1970's.

220

CHAPTER 9 — BOOKS

While researching information for this chapter on golf books, thousands of books were found which were written for and about golfers. A majority of the books were written for the golfers who are always seeking ways to improve their games, regardless of how good they may already be. The remainder of the books can be attributed to the stories, competitions and personalities which have resulted from the hundreds of years in which the game has been played.

The first known reference to golf was in 1457, when King James II of Scotland issued his famous decree which prohibited the playing of golf because it interfered with the archery practice of his soldiers. It was not until 1566 that the printing technology could record the acts of parliament in book form. These early volumes are quite rare since only a few dozen different books were printed in Scotland in the 16th century. It is hard to believe that there were golfers before there were books!

Only a few short references to golf appeared in books during the next two hundred years. In 1743, a Scot, Thomas Mathison, wrote the first book, entirely dedicated to golf, which he titled *The Goff, An Heroi-Comical Poem in Three Cantos*. Only 24 pages long, this book was reprinted in 1763 and again in 1793. Since this amusing little book is so rare, it has been reproduced for the benefit of collectors by the United States Golf Association. A copy of the second edition recently sold at auction in St. Andrews, Scotland for over $15,000, which is by far the highest price ever paid for a golf book.

The next golf book to appear was also a poem called *Golfiana, or, Niceties Connected With the Game of Golf* written by George Fullerton Carnegie in 1833 and republished in 1842.

Finally, the first of over a thousand instruction books appeared in 1857. *The Golfer's Manual* by "A Keen Hand" (Henry B. Farnie) devotes almost a hundred pages to the mechanics of the swing and the proper use of the various clubs. Later editions appeared in 1862 and 1870, followed by reprinted versions.

Robert Chambers wrote the next golf book of interest in 1862, which included the rules of the game. This small volume was named *A Few Rambling Remarks on Golf*. Two later editions were also printed.

Following Chambers' book, approximately thirty more works were published before the rapid growth of golf in the 1890's. It was in 1895 that *Golf in America* by James Lee became the first American golf book. There had been catalogs and small pamphlets prior to Lee's work, but none were substantial. After the turn of the century, golf books regularly appeared on both sides of the Atlantic.

It should be mentioned that there are four books which have been written through the years which can give additional information as to the content of many of the golf books. The first extensive attempt at a golf bibliography was *Collecting Golf Books,* written by Cecil Hopkinson in 1938. A very informative bibliography, which includes a history of golf books, was later written by Joe Murdoch in 1968 and is called *The Library of Golf.* It was subsequently updated in a private edition in 1978. Murdoch and Janet Seagle collaborated in 1979 to produce *Golf – A Guide to Information Sources* which includes a section on golf literature. Both Murdoch and Seagle have contributed to the book reviews which are contained in this book.

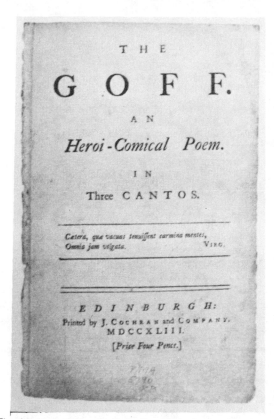

The title page of *The Goff*, the first book about golf which was published in 1743.

A selection of notable golf books from the early twentieth century.

A sampling of the astounding number of golf instructional books.

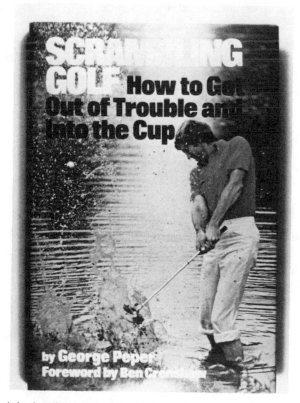

A book written by and containing a foreword by two of the contributors to this Encyclopedia.

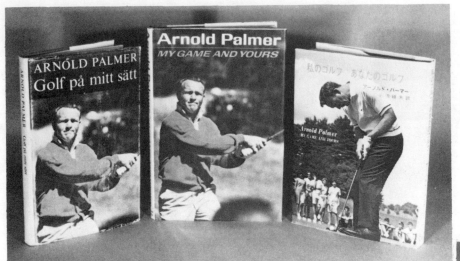

Golf is very much an international game as evidenced by the foreign language editions of this book by Arnold Palmer.

A number of books are written by women for women golfers.

These "action photo" books were the forerunners of today's television instant replay.

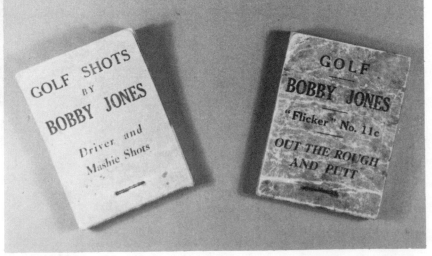

223

GOLF BOOK TITLES

The enormous time spent researching information for this chapter brought one amusing fact to light. The title of a golf book can be just as interesting as its content. Titles can be short and unimaginative such as *Golf* or they can be long and detailed like *Putting Analyzed: a book on a perplexing phase of golf covering half the game. Dedicated to the dubs, of whom the author is one, who go down to the Links with brave hearts, high hopes - and little more. Done for the purpose of adding a lot more - the clearance of the conflicting theories that make us fozzle our putts.*

Some authors assume that golfers must be relatively good with numbers, so often a number is included in the title: *295 Golf Lessons, Better Golf in 5 Minutes, 101 Ways to Win, Par Golf in 8 Steps, 12 Short Cuts to Better Golf, 80 5-Minute Golf Lessons,* and *73 Years in a Sand Trap.* If you think you might like the last book listed, then be sure to read Fred Beck's other book, *89 Years in a Sand Trap.*

Since rhythm is vital to the golf swing, maybe a golf book title should have rhythm too: *From 102 to 82 in a Month or Two.* There are over 90 books which have a title that incorporates the phrase *How to . . .* This gets so confusing that we wouldn't even know how to list them.

Quite a few authors have developed methods which are supposed to enable a player to attain a certain level of proficiency. The following books have a certain goal in mind: *How to Break 90 at Golf* and *How to Become a Scratch Golfer.* These authors have put a lot of faith in their methods, unlike this book which may be a bit more realistic in its goal: *How to Play Golf in the Low 120's.*

Joseph James wrote his first book with a question in mind: *So You're Taking up Golf?.* The following year, and several strokes later, he wrote a most interesting sequel which he called *How to Give up Golf!*

Even family golf has produced topics such as *Golf for Boys and Girls* and *Family Golf,* but *How to Play Golf With Your Wife and Survive* and *The Golf Lunatic and His Cycling Wife* are the prize winners.

As you can see, collecting golf titles can be an amusing and certainly inexpensive hobby. In fact, every owner of this book already owns one of the finest title collections in the world.

HOW TO USE THIS CHAPTER

The purpose of this chapter is to list as many titles of golf books as possible and to review some of the more notable works. Only the date of the first edition of a book will be shown in the main list. Important limited editions and reprints which are of importance to the collector have also been included.

The books on the main list are listed alphabetically by author. The first date of publication, content category and value is shown for each book. The values represent the price which a buyer would be expected to pay a dealer for a book in good condition. Foreign language books, many of which are written in or have been translated into Japanese, are not included in this chapter.

Brief reviews of some of the outstanding books in each category preceed the bibliography listings. These summaries have been written by recognized authorities in their respective fields. Each of the contributors was asked to make a selection of titles which they felt were particularly noteworthy with regard to both their content and value to the golf book collector. The books which have been selected are not necessarily the rare and expensive ones, since reviews of those books only would not be beneficial to the average collector.

GOLF BOOK CATEGORIES

ABBREVIATION	CATEGORY	CONTENTS	BOOK REVIEW AUTHORS
AN	ANTHOLOGY:	ANTHOLOGY COLLECTIONS	GEORGE PEPER
GC	GOLF COURSE:	ARCHITECTURE DESCRIPTION LISTING TRAVEL TURF	BEN CRENSHAW
CH	CLUB HISTORY		ALASTAIR JOHNSTON
EQ	EQUIPMENT		TOM WISHON
ES	ESSAYS		CHAS. "BUD" DUFNER
F	FICTION:	ARTWORK FICTION HUMOR POETRY	NEVIN GIBSON
H	HISTORY:	AUTIOBIOGRAPHY BIOGRAPHY HISTORY	JOSEPH S. F. MURDOCH
I	INSTRUCTION		
R	REFERENCE:	ANNUALS HANDBOOKS RECORDS REFERENCE YEARBOOKS	JANET SEAGLE
RU	RULES		

A "✓" NEXT TO A TITLE DENOTES THAT A REVIEW OF THE BOOK APPEARS IN THIS CHAPTER.

BOOK REVIEWS

COLLECTIONS AND ANTHOLOGIES
by George Peper

George Peper is the Editor of Golf Magazine and has authored several books on golf. He recently was one of a unique foursome that played golf at St. Andrews, Winged Foot and Pebble Beach . . . all in the same day!

Quite a few excellent anthologies have been written on golf by some of the game's finest authors. The books listed below are very entertaining and can be read a little at a time since the articles are generally not too lengthy.

Some of the books which are listed in the section on essays could possibly be classified as anthologies and vice versa. So, if you are interested in reading the great literature of the game, be sure to examine the listings in both areas.

A History of Golf in Britain, by Bernard Darwin, H. Gardiner-Hill, Sir Guy Campbell, Henry Cotton, Henry Longhurst, Leonard Crawley, Enid Wilson, and Lord Barbizon of Tara. (London; Cassell, 1952)

A distinguished group of contributors traces the game's history in entertaining style. Particularly interesting are the portraits of the game's finest players, by Darwin, Longhurst and Crawley. Illustrated with excellent photos.

Down the Nineteenth Fairway, compiled by Peter Dobereiner. (New York; Antheneum, 1983)

Every major golf writer of the last century is included in this wide-ranging collection of pieces. The group includes Alistair Cooke, Bernard Darwin, Paul Gallico, Dan Jenkins, Bobby Jones, Henry Longhurst, A. A. Milne, Ogden Nash, George Plimpton, Charles Price, Harry Vardon, Pat Ward-Thomas, Herbert Warren Wind, P.G. Wodehouse and two dozen others. With names like that, no defense of the content need be made.

The Royal and Ancient Game of Golf, edited by Harold H. Hilton and Garden C. Smith. (London; for Golf Illustrated by the London and Counties Press Association, 1912)

One of the treasures of golf collecting; the limited edition was lavishly produced, bound in red leather, embossed in gold and limited to a run of 900 copies. Hilton, a two-time British Open Champion, debunks the theory that golf had its origins in Holland, and includes much material on the early Scottish game. A special section lists all the courses in existence at the time, many of which are shown in excellent photographs. The head and tail illustrations of each chapter were drawn by famed golf artist, Harry Rountree.

Golf; The Badminton Library, by Horace G. Hutchinson, edited by His Grace, the Duke of Beaufort. (London; Longmans, Green & Company, 1890 and later editions)

A superbly comprehensive anthology of golf at the end of the 19th century, as delightful as it is informative. It includes sections on history, equipment, instructions, match and medal play, etiquette, handicaps, courses and rules. A wonderful chapter on the "Humors of Golf" includes whimsical instruction on how to break a club as well as a description of "that peculiar feeling of nervousness which occurs when one faces a putt of a club's length." Known as the "Badminton Library", this book is a must for any serious collector.

The American Golfer, edited by Charles Price. (New York; Random House, 1954)

A wonderful selection of articles which appeared in *The American Golfer,* the highly regarded magazine from the 1920's and 30's whose issues are collectors' items in themselves. Founded by Walter J. Travis and edited by Grantland Rice, *The American Golfer* produced some of the best writing the game ever saw. This book contains timeless instructional pieces from Tommy Armour, Bobby Jones, Ernest Jones and Harry Vardon, plus good reading from Rice and Red Smith, among others.

The Best of Henry Longhurst, compiled and edited by Mark Wilson with Ken Bowden. (New York; Simon and Schuster, 1978)

A marvelous collection of wry, sly, gently cynical essays by Britain's fine amateur golfer cum journalist cum television commentator. Longhurst holds forth on golf, golfers, golf equipment, golf courses and other aspects of what he calls "an entire, familiar exercise in human vanity." As Alistair Cooke writes in the foreword, "there is no one like Henry."

The Complete Golfer, edited by Herbert Warren Wind. Introduction by Robert Tyre Jones Jr. (New York; Simon and Schuster, 1954)

The finest of the modern golf anthologies, compiled by the finest of the modern golf writers. Wind's selections are diverse, but all reflect his superb taste and far-reaching knowledge of the game. There is plenty of good reading here, on instruction, on golf's great players and greatest moments, and just on "the spirit of the game." Also, perhaps owing to the editor's long association with *The New Yorker,* a delightful anthology of golf cartoons.

The Golf Omnibus, P. G. Wodehouse. (London; Barrie & Jenkins, Ltd. 1973)

In golf, humorous essays are as rare as double eagles, but fortunately one genius of 20th century humor, P.G. Wodehouse, turned his talent occasionally toward the fairway. This one-man collection is full of the foibles of golfers, beginning with the classic story from 1916, "The Clicking of Cuthbert." There may be other collections of golf humor, but this is probably the only one worth owning.

GOLF ARCHITECTURE BOOKS
by Ben Crenshaw

Ben Crenshaw, the 1984 Masters Champion, is an avid golf collector. He particularly enjoys reading books on golf history and golf course design. Ben's appreciation of the heritage of the game is unsurpassed.

My enthusiasm for the history of the grand game of golf is accompanied by an affection for the dignified settings of the game. How lucky I was to have as my maiden voyage, the USGA Junior Amateur at The Country Club in Brookline, Massachusetts! How guilty I felt taking divots from such lovely bent grass fairways, and how I marvelled watching the ball roll on such beautiful, slick greens! Such perilous bunkers with craggy, natural and bold outlines! What a gorgeous piece of land for golf that tumbled and rolled and tossed and turned and possessed such endless variety. I can still close my eyes and visualize an exciting second shot played over a cavernous bunker beyond the racetrack, which is now gone. I can see an inviting semi-punch bowl green framed by such stately trees, and the regal clubhouse so welcoming nearly. This is golf in its highest sense, so beautiful, so stimulating, so proper, so dignified.

Architecture happens to be one of the world's highest art forms. People get different impressions when they observe and study a particular building, home or other structure. The architect opens himself to constant criticism, as the end result is only a reflection of one man's particular opinion of his likes and dislikes. Nowhere can this be more evident than with the design of a golf course, as courses are generally loved or cursed.

The Old Course at St. Andrews is the supremely natural golf course which is certainly both loved and cursed. It has crossfire holes, double greens that are enormous, and bunkers completely hidden from the golfer's view, sometimes in the middle of the fairway! Preposterous you might say — only if you haven't experienced it! This course simply evolved with little or no help from man, and it has provided a special fascination for golfers that have constantly challenged throughout its existence. My fondness and respect for the Old Course are many: there are many ways to play it; each hole has an alternate route (or routes); every bunker or hazard is different from the last; the ground is firm and allows the ball to run, which is still another element in the general course of play; and, the whole course is sufficiently and wildly undulating, which adds immensely to one's strategy. Most importantly, you are required to attempt almost every conceivable golf shot, which makes every round unique and challenging.

As my all-time favorite author, Bernard Darwin, might say, "My pen has started to run away from me." I shall list some of my favorite books on the subject of golf course architecture, which is what the authors of this book requested. I might add at this moment there is precious little that has been written about this wonderful subject. A.W. Tillinghast and Donald Ross, both outstanding and prolific architects, never produced a book on the subject.

In addition to those listed, there are other fine books which have been written on the subject. One of the reasons for writing this brief article is to interest more people on the subject of golf course architecture. I think I am not too far out-of-bounds in saying that its importance is being far too overlooked.

The economics of land costs and maintenance techniques have changed along with our playing equipment, but our game is essentially the same. The real works of art, meaning the older classical courses, need to be studied more in detail, and their qualities should be stressed in our future works. The early courses tend to be more natural than some of the artificial looking courses which are found too often today.

I suppose at one time or another, all of us who play golf fantasize as to how we could change a bland hole, to do away with an ugly man-made water hazard or an ill-shaped circular bunker which occurs blithly on the landscape and adds nothing to our enjoyment. Hopefully, some of the modern day golf architects will come to be admired in the manner in which we revere the great designers of the past: Donald Ross, A. W. Tillinghast, and Alister Mackenzie.

The Golf Course by Geoffrey Cornish and Ronald E. Whitten. (New York; The Rutledge Press, 1981)
>An incredible text resulting from the most research by far of any architecture book published. An absolute must for every serious golfer.

The Golf Courses of the British Isles, by Bernard Darwin. (London; Duckworth, 1910) Second edition in 1925 titled *The Golf Courses of Great Britain.*
>This volume is illustrated handsomely by Harry Rountree and makes for wonderful reading. It may not help the aspiring architect, but the descriptions of the individual courses are most entertaining.

The Links, by Robert Hunter. (New York; Charles Scribner's Sons, 1926)
>Another great book with photos and diagrams, which substantiated his view as an impassioned symposium on links golf being the best test. Mr. Hunter also assisted Dr. Alister Mackenzie at Cypress Point. He absolutely believed in stressing natural features as much as possible, and providing a test for all classes of golfers.

Scotland's Gift; Golf, by Charles Blair MacDonald. (New York; Charles Scribner's Sons, 1928) Also a limited edition.
  MacDonald was the builder of Chicago Golf Club, National Golf Links of America, Yale Golf Club and Mid Ocean in Bermuda. I absolutely love this book which has, though rather opinionated, one of the best chapters on views and thoughts on architecture.

Golf Architecture, by Dr. Alister Mackenzie. (London; Simpkin, Marshall, Hamilton & Kent, 1920) Reprinted as *Dr. Mackenzie's Golf Architecure* (Droitwich, England; Grant Books, 1982)
  This is a great little book that is a must for would-be architects. An expert on camouflage in the Boer War, Dr. Mackenzie shows us how to work with nature and reflect her strong points, and above all to provide an interesting test for all classes of golfers. It is a little disappointing that this fine architect and writer did not provide us with more literature. Cypress Point, Royal Melbourne and Augusta National are some of his major works.

Golf Course Architecture in America: its Strategy and Construction, by George C. Thomas. (Los Angeles; Times-Mirror Press, 1927)
  A charter member of Pine Valley, that great course in New Jersey, Thomas gave the world such courses as Los Angeles Country Club (36 holes), Bel-Air Country Club, Riviera Country Club (one of my favorites), and collaborated on the present Philadelphia Cricket Club. A classic book with wonderful photos and diagrams, this work contains observations by many architects.

World Atlas of Golf, by Pat Ward-Thomas, Herbert Warren Wind, Charles Pirce, Peter Thomson and Donald Steel. (New York; Random House, 1977)
  This volume is very handsomely illustrated with some of the best photographs and diagrams of the world's most famous courses. The excellent text is preceded by a foreward by Alistair Cooke.

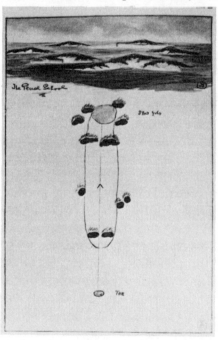

One of the attractive illustrations from *The Architectural Side of Golf.*

The Architectural Side of Golf, by H. N. Wethered and T. Simpson. (London; Longmans Green, 1929) Also a limited edition. Reprinted as *Design for Golf* (London; Sportman's Book Club, 1952)
  This book is complete with delightful diagrams and very sound thoughts. T. Simpson built Liphook, Chantilly in France, Walton Heath with James Braid, and Royal Lytham and St. Annes.

  The following two books contain quite informative chapters on golf architecture — both eminently sound:
The Complete Golfer, by Harry Vardon. (London; Methuen and New York; McClure, Phillips, 1905 and later editions)
Advanced Golf, by James Braid. (London; Metheun and Philadelphia; George Jacobs, 1908 and later editions)

GOLF CLUB HISTORIES
by Alastair J. Johnston

Alastair is associated with International Management Group and is responsible for managing the business affairs of several professional golfers. A native of Scotland, he literally travels to every corner of the world in his search for additions to his golf library.

The first step for someone interested in collecting golf club histories is to determine in one's own mind exactly what constitutes a golf club history book. Some clubs issue handbooks and/or member rosters, while others publish books which only relate to a description of the golf course itself. The books or booklets produced with the primary intention of describing the particular club's evolution and history are those which will be discussed in this article.

Unquestionably, many clubs have published historical records as a means of raising funds. Also, some clubs have been anxious to broadcast to the world the particular contribution that, in itself or through its members, it has made to various facets of our golfing heritage, be it on a local, national, or international basis. However, the prime motivation is usually to preserve for present and future generations of members, the activities of the founders and others charged with directing the club's destiny.

One of the attractions of collecting club history books is the uniqueness of each publication. However, there are several factors which are common to all of the books. The birth of the club is described with the acquisition of property, the introduction of the chartering members, and an assessment of the political and financial hurdles that had to be surmounted. In many of these books one can experience the flavour of the socio-economic climate of the times. Usually, a prominent club member was designated (or appointed himself) the authoritative historian and compiles the material for publication.

Some of these authors have been legendary club figures in their own right such as John Arthur Brown, author of *Short History of Pine Valley*. On occasions, a golf author who has had some associaton with the particular club was commissioned to compile the book. Among these I would include *History of the Royal & Ancient* by Pat Ward-Thomas, *History of Royal Perth Golfing Society* by Rev. T. D. Miller, *St. Andrews Golf Club 1888-1938* by H. B. Martin, and *75 Year History of Shinnecock Hills* by Ross Goodner.

The production and appearance of the club histories themselves varies widely. Some are extremely elaborate publications such as *Lakeside Golf Club of Hollywood: 50th Anniversary* or *Waialae Country Club: It's Half Century,* while others are somewhat nondescript. Some books are prepared as limited editions, perhaps with the original intention to restrict circulation to members only. Others are available to the general public and are therefore more readily available to the collector.

Several of the older club histories are in themselves classics of golf literature and are keenly sought by golfiana collectors, for example: *History of the Royal & Ancient; 1754-1900* by H. S. C. Everard, *The Aberdeen Golfers* by Charles Smith, and *Chronicles of the Blackheath Golfers* by W. E. Hughes. It is interesting to observe that the sense of pride that emanates from the pages of these volumes remains consistent from one history to the next.

The first club histories appeared about 1880 and throughout this century the process has gained momentum. The oldest clubs in the United Kingdom have all been charted (in several instances by more than one biographer): i.e., Honourable Company of Edinburgh Golfers, Royal & Ancient Golf Club of St. Andrews, Royal Blackheath, Royal Burgess, Royal Aberdeen, Royal Musselburgh, Glasgow and Bruntsfield. Outside of the home countries, Royal Calcutta claims to be the oldest golf club still in existence as documented in its history published in 1979.

In North America, Royal Montreal has been long regarded as the first to be established in the "New World". Its story was first recounted in 1923 and was then updated on its centenary in 1973. However, new evidence of the existence of clubs on the east coast of the United States in the late 18th century has rendered the previous suppositions suspect. For the historical record, it is now believed that the South Carolina Golf Club and the Savannah Golf Club, established in 1786 and 1795, respectively, were the first clubs formed outside the United Kingdom. Their administration and procedures were apparently consistent with the Scottish clubs of that era. However, they were abandoned and disappeared in the early 19th century (although the South Carolina Club was resurrected in 1968). No club histories per se have been published on these particular clubs although in 1980, salient aspects of their early activities were documented in a book entitled *Carolina Low Country: Birthplace of American Golf* by Charles Price and George Rogers Jr.

As the evolution of golf in the United States has not been as prolifically documented by scholars and scribes as it has been in the United Kingdom, the contents of the early club histories are somewhat more intriguing as a general information source. Most of the older established clubs have produced history books including four of the founding members of the United States Golf Association: The Country Club at Brookline, Chicago Golf Club, Shinnecock Hills and St. Andrews. Naturally the older clubs in the northeast of the country dominate the list of histories, but a review of the volumes on clubs such as Southern Hills, Oak Hill, Augusta National and Cherry Hills provides an understanding of the circumstances that inspired some of the golf courses which act as major tournament venues.

To the collector of golfiana, especially golf books, there is comfort in the fact that many of the books of recent vintage are readily available. Indeed, the clubs themselves are often flattered by direct inquiries and try to accommodate those enthusiasts who they believe show a genuine interest in learning about their particular club. Very often histories are published to coincide with specific commemorative celebrations. With so many clubs now reaching centenary status, or at least 75 or 50 year anniversaries, there should be a veritable plethoria of books coming available for enthusiasts in the forthcoming years. Perhaps from a collector's standpoint, there is the attraction in knowing that the opportunity still exists where one can uncover a history hitherto unknown to the general society of golfiana hunters.

Notwithstanding, with some degree of trepidation I have compiled a list of clubs that to date have been identified with the publication of a history. This list has been restricted to English language books, although various other countries such as Japan, Sweden and Norway have produced very attractive club histories.

The special list of club histories follows the regular bibliography and starts on page 268.

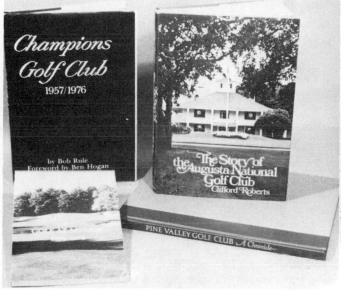

Scottish club histories showing one of the first such books which was published by the Glasgow Golf Club.

Club histories from some of the better known clubs in the United States.

GOLF EQUIPMENT BOOKS
by Tom Wishon

Tom Wishon is associated with The Golf Works, a major supplier of golf club making and repair equipment. He is involved daily with classic club refurbishing and new club design and enjoys playing with and collecting golf equipment.

Of the thousands of books written about golf, only a few have been devoted entirely to the equipment which has helped shape the game over hundreds of years. The rise in the popularity of the game in the mid 1800's was partially due to the demise of the feather ball and subsequent affordability of the gutty ball. The further advent of the rubber core ball and then the steel shaft continued to increase the growth of the game and even changed the styles of golf course design.

The improvements in golf clubs and balls since the 1890's have generally been written about in the many golf periodicals. Often instructional books will mention the importance of proper equipment selection, however they do not delve into the subject as well as the books listed below.

Classic Golf Clubs, a pictorial Guide, by Joe Clement. (Jackson, MS; Classic Golf Clubs Joint Venture, 1980)

In one of the only books of its kind, Clement presents a "who's who" of some of the most collectible and valuable playable golf clubs. Close-up photographs and accompanying text guide the reader through the study of these woods, irons, putters and wedges. Included with the book is an insert which shows the relative values of the clubs.

The Search for the Perfect Swing, by Alastair Cochran and John Stobbs. (London; Heinemann, 1968)

While much of this book deals with the study of the mechanics of the golf swing, there are several well researched chapters dealing with the equipment of the game. The interaction of the club and ball has been recorded by means of sophisticated scientific methods and the results reveal the modern truths of how the golf shot is produced.

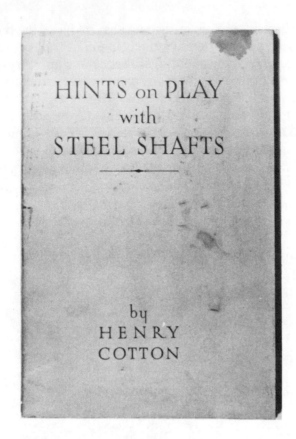

A small book about a very important matter to golfers...from 1934.

Better Golf in 5 Minutes, by J. Victor East. (Englewood Cliffs, NJ; Prentice-Hall, 1956)

This book is primarily instructional in content, however the author, a professional golfer, discusses many of his thoughts regarding golf club design and fitting. East explains the various components of the golf club and his experiences as a clubmaker. Of particular interest is the chapter in which the author discusses the duplication of a favorite driver for Bobby Jones.

Golf in the Making, by Ian Henderson and David Stirk. (Yorkshire; Manningham Press, 1979)

Through research taken from early records and writings, the authors have compiled a very interesting book about the evolution of the game of golf and its equipment up to 1914. Particular attention is paid to the evolution of the golf ball and the early clubmakers. Biographies of the craftsmen from the 17th, 18th and 19th centuries tell us much about their personal and golfing lives. Specifications and methods of the makers enable the collector to learn much about the early implements of the game.

The Compleat Golfer, by the same authors contains advertisements, illustrations, and excerpts from this book, but is presented in a much simpler form.

Golf: The Badminton Library, by Horace G. Hutchinson, edited by His Grace, the Duke of Beaufort. (London; Longmans, Green & Company, 1890 and later editions)

Hutchinson, a well known player and author, has written an interesting section on the clubs and balls of the 1800's. He discusses the types of equipment available to players in a style which resembles a consumer's guide. Early methods of fitting equipment are presented by this most informative source.

Golf Club Trademarks - American: 1898-1930, by Patrick Kennedy. (South Burlington, VT; Thistle Books, 1984)

Pat Kennedy has compiled over 400 registered golf club trademarks and related information for this guide. His fine illustrations and helpful text make this a handy reference for club collectors.

Golf Club Design, Fitting, Alteration and Repair, by Ralph D. Maltby. (Newark, OH; Faultless Sports, 1974) Revised edition (Newark, OH; Ralph Maltby Enterprises, 1982)

This most complete study leads the reader through every conceivable area dealing with golf clubs. Hundreds of photos and charts are presented in a step-by-step fashion in a manner that benefits anyone who works on golf clubs. Maltby has compiled an invaluable guide for those in the golf club business as well as an informative book for golfers who take their game seriously.

Maltby also compiled *Golf Repair in Pictures,* an instructional manual illustrated with over 1100 photographs which was first published in 1978.

231

The Curious History of the Golf Ball: Mankind's Most Fascinating Sphere, by John Stuart Martin. (New York; Horizon Press, 1968)

Martin's title is very appropriate for this informative and fun to read volume. His research, which traces the methods of manufacture of the feather, gutta percha, rubber wound and modern solid golf balls, has produced some amusing anecdotes.

ESSAYS
by Chas. "Bud" Dufner

Bud is very much interested in the printed word as evidenced by his vocation as a commercial printer and his hobby of collecting golf literature. He has made a great contribution to the field of golf collecting by providing valuable assistance with the editing of the bibliography included in this chapter.

It is through essays and articles that we become aware of many aspects of the game of golf. Essays appear in magazines, newspapers, annuals and also in book form. They are the primary reason that golf has acquired so much high quality literature that is unmatched by any other sport. Some of the great early golf essayists were Horace Hutchinson, Bernard Darwin, Andrew Lang, John Low and Henry Leach.

Although Hutchinson dominated the writing of early essays, Bernard Darwin was the model for other writers and also the most prolific, with over two dozen books to his credit. The grandson of evolutionist Charles Darwin, he was awarded the title of Commander of the British Empire for "services to literature and sport". He spent his career as a golf writer for *The Times* of London for forty-six years and was a frequent contributor to *Country Life* and other periodicals. Darwin lived from 1876 to 1961.

Some of the writers who have produced notable works in more recent times are: Henry Longhurst, Herbert Warren Wind, Pat Ward-Thomas, Charles Price and Peter Dobereiner, among others.

All of the authors mentioned in this review are known for their flowing prose, a command of the English language, and a thorough understanding of the game. The staid Victorian works of the early writers and the witty humor of the contemporary authors such as Dobereiner and Longhurst present a great variance in styles among the essayists. This makes for enjoyable reading since the essays can usually be read at one sitting because of their generally short length.

A Friendly Round, by Bernard Darwin. (London; Mills and Boon, 1922)

A collection of some of Bernard Darwin's golf columns from *The Times* of London. His graceful prose is, perhaps, unequaled and it has been said that to read a Darwin story is to be there.

For the Love of Golf — The Best of Dobereiner, by Peter Dobereiner. (London; Stanley Paul, 1981)

This is a collection of Dobereiner's finest works. Always controversial and a master of the tongue-in-cheek, he is undoubtedly one of the best golf writers today.

The Mystery of Golf, by Arnold Haultain. (Boston and New York; Houghton Mifflin and Lodon; Constable, 1908) Reprinted in 1965.

This is one of the finest books on the game which has withstood the test of time and is considered to be a golf classic. It is entertaining to the golf connoisseur as well as to any lover of literature.

The Spirit of the Links, by Henry Leach. (London; Methuen, 1907)

A book of charming essays by a man whose work is continually included in all of the "best of" lists. His books are in great demand and are still as interesting as when they were first written.

Talking About Golf, by Henry Longhurst. (London; MacDonald, 1966)

This is a selection of articles from *Golf Illustrated Magazine* in which Longhurst answers questions about golf. Longhurst's comments are typical of his witty and enlightening style that provide enjoyment for all lovers of the game.

Golfer-At-Large, by Charles Price. (New York; Atheneum, 1982)

This collection of articles, mostly from *Golf Magazine,* shows what an authoritative and often humorous writer Price can be. The book presents a wonderful insight into some of golf's great players and places. Price is also the author of *The World of Golf,* one of the masterpieces of golf literature.

Mostly Golf: A Bernard Darwin Anthology, edited by Peter Ryde. (London; Adam and Charles Black, 1976)

Books such as this allow us to enjoy and experience golf from an earlier era. A quote taken from the dust jacket says it best: "As golf correspondent for *The Times,* he transformed sports writing from a jumble of figures at the foot of a page into an established branch of literary journalism."

The Art of Golf, by Sir Walter G. Simpson. (Edinburgh; David Douglas, 1887)

This is a true masterpiece in the field of golf literature. Simpson, a friend of Robert Louis Stevenson, maintained the highest level of style in his writing, which became a model for many later golf writers. This was the first book to feature photographs of the golf swing as an instructional tool.

Simpson is known for his amusing quotes such as the following reference to golf: "Unlike the other Scotch game of whisky-drinking, excess in it is not injurious to the health."

Herbert Warren Wind's Golf Book, by Herbert Warren Wind. (New York; Simon & Schuster, 1971)

This is a 317 page collection of beautifully written articles and essays by the dean of American golf writers. His knowledge of the game is always evident in his graceful and sensitive prose. The interesting foreward was written by Bing Crosby, a true aficionado of the game.

FICTION BOOKS
by Nevin Gibson

Nevin Gibson is very familiar with golf books, having been an author of several and a collector of thousands. A retired Air Force Major, he is a golf writer and avid collector of golf memorabilia.

The following is a selection of nine golf fiction books which I consider deserving of a brief review. I would like to point out that the greatest golf fiction is not in book length except for golf mysteries, although recently the longer works are appearing. One of our greatest writers, P. G. Wodehouse, never wrote a book length golf novel, but he did indeed write many outstanding short stories such as *The Clicking of Cuthbert* and *Ordeal by Golf,* which, among others, were included in a single book.

There are also quite a number of humorous golf books which often include funny drawings and cartoons. Most of the books on golf poems are also collections except for some of the early books which consisted of poems which were hundreds of lines long.

Recently, an avid book collector from London visited and was amazed at my numerous shelves of golf novels. He soon realized that many golf mysteries and other golf fiction are not published by the leading publishers, but are privately printed. Therefore, many are not known to the general golf reader.

I hope that these reviews will enlighten some readers to the entertaining realm of golf fiction.

Two of the many fine fiction books which revolve around the game of golf.

Golf can be a funny game and there are dozens of books that can attest to the fact.

Murder on the Sixth Hole, by David Frome. (London; Methuen & Co., 1931)

A golf novel which takes place near Baltimore and Washington, D.C. on a golf course called South Forest Country Club on the South River. A most intriguing tale which will keep you on the edge of the chair or bed until the revelation unfolds.

The Long Green, by William Campbell Gault. (New York; E.P. Dutton & Co., 1965)

A novel about a professional, D. Shea, which traces his endeavor to reach the top. Almost succeeding, then failing and rising again. A story which reveals the realism, the lonely starkness and the popular glamour of the professional golf tour.

Dormie One and Other Golf Stories, by Holworthy Hall. (New York; The Century Club, 1917)

A book dedicated to Grantland Rice. Dormie One is one of seven stories contained in this great volume and it is indeed one of the greatest golf novels of all times. A most heartfelt revelation of an immortal amateur in a match-play contest who is on the verge of 'aging' out of the competition with the execution of every shot. Psychologically, he must retain that positive outlook, but then again he realizes that his physical being is really by-gone and that

233

this is really his very last duel. Or is it? Every shot becomes an agonizing ordeal in both the mental and physical sense. But with the tenacity of a cantankerous old golfer, he continues his march — to hell or heaven.

Your First Golf Game, by Gerald Hillinthorn. (London; Day and Son, 1891)

One of the first, if not indeed the very first, golf book to feature color cartoons which are definitely most humorous and in great detail. Although a novel contained in only twenty-seven pages, it must rank among the leaders of outstanding treatises on the subject of fiction. "The only way to excel is to practice. Practice therefore assiduously, and don't be discouraged upon finding that the more you practice, the worse you may play."

Golf in the Year 2000, or What We Are Coming To, by J.A.C.K., pseudonym for J. McCullough. (London; T. Fisher Unwin, 1892) Reprinted: (Cincinnati; Old Golf Shop, 1984)

In this amusing little book, the author tells of his experience with the future. He falls asleep for 108 years, awakens in the year 2000 and then relates to the reader how the world has changed. While the book revolves around his golf activities, some interesting forecasts into the future are presented.

The author refers to systems of electrically connected mirrors which enable spectators to sit in London and view a golf match between the champions of Scotland and the United States. High speed subways transport golfers to distant courses in just minutes so that they can play with a unique golf club that automatically records the number of strokes taken. He relates of how daily life revolves around the game of golf and how the destructive capability of an atomic bomb exists but is not necessary since all disputes are decided by a round of golf.

When reading this book, written in the author's own style, one needs to keep aware that it was written in 1892, when golf was at its infancy in the United States and the conveniences of modern day living were non-existent.

Fairway Challenge, by Jackson Scholz. (New York; William Morrow & Co., 1964)

The author, an enthusiastic amateur golfer, writes with authority of the people and situations a touring pro might meet and endure. Surrounded by a hostile gallery, Gary Cannon lined up his putt with difficulty. He was playing the third round of his first tournament as a professional with the golfing star, Sandy Miller. He fell apart under pressure. Only an unexpected turn of events gave Gary the perspective to make the difficult decision about his future.

The author served in the Naval Aviation during World War I, competed on the 1920 and 1924 Olympic Teams, and won two gold medals.

The Golf Course Mystery, by Chester K. Steele. (Cleveland; International Fiction Library, 1919)

Being somewhat of a different detective story. When Horace Carwell sinks the final winning putt on the last green of the Maraposa Golf Club to win the club championship, and then drops dead, this mystery begins. Another most exciting golf course mystery.

I'll Never Be Cured and I Don't Much Care, by Douglas Bertram Wesson. (New York; J. H. Sears, 1928)

The History of an Acute Attack of Golf and Pertinent Remarks relating to Various Places of Treatment. Illustrated with drawings by Wyncie King. Humor indeed with some most serious attention given to many of the most famed links of Scotland and England. This most heterogeneous collection of words all ends in two lines: "I'll never be cured and I don't much care'.

On Tour with Harry Sprague, by Herbert Warren Wind. (New York; Simon & Schuster, 1960)

A most hilarious novel. Harry Sprague, a young pro hits the Tour and reports his progress to his sponsors with letters. Harry's progress, if indeed it is progression, is usually hindered by some small incident. These are all minor hindrances which according to Harry, will not interfere with his successful venture towards stardom. Harry marches on from week to week at the expense of his sponsors who are beginning to doubt his reputed talent. Will any of the sponsoring tribe ever receive a single cent from this would-be great prodigy golf professional?

HISTORY BOOKS
by Joseph S. F. Murdoch

Joe Murdoch is the dean of golf book collectors. He was one of the driving forces behind the formation of the Golf Collectors' Society in 1970 and continues to display his interest in the history of the game as the first and only editor of the "Bulletin". Joe's golf bibliography, The Library of Golf *has become an invaluable reference for those interested in golf literature.*

Golf history books have been defined by my mentors, the Editors, as those which encompass "the history of the game, biography and autobiography." Of the latter, there are precious few for it is well known that if golfers could write, they would be writers, not golfers. The corollary of that statement is also true.

It may be repetitious to say that golf is a game that encourages the writing of literature and the game has been singularly blessed with veritable treasures of such writing. Over the last 130 years, there have been many talented writers who dedicated their skills to reporting and describing the events that have made golf history. There are so many that are excellent that it becomes a chore, (as was asked of this poor scribe), to list the books of golf history of notable importance and excellence. The chore becomes all the more pleasant, however, when one is forced to re-read portions or all of the many books that have been published on the subject.

While this is really a bound collection of art reproductions, the various golfers and scenes are of historic importance.

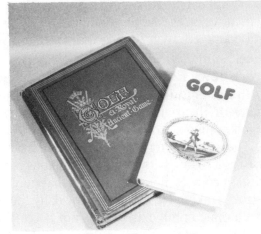

Quite a few of the early classic books have been reprinted in recent years. A very informative work by Robert Clark, *Golf: A Royal and Ancient Game* is seen in the limited edition version from 1875 the modern edition printed in 1975.

A History of Golf: The Royal and Ancient Game, by Robert Browning. (London; Dent and Den York; E. P. Dutton, 1955)
 Browning was editor of the British weekly "Golfing" from 1910 to 1955. He witnessed and reported the growth of the game during that period and, in addition, was a scholar who studied the known literature that had preceded him. This is an intelligent and well-written record of the game from its early beginning.

Ladies in the Rough, by Glenna Collett (Vare). (New York; Alfred A. Knopf, 1928)
 Although Miss Collett (Mrs. Vare) continued to represent a major force in ladies' golf long after this book was published, it represents one of the few records of golf, as played by ladies, in the early years of the game in America.

Five Open Champions and the Musselburgh Golf Story, by George M. Colville. (Musselburgh; privately published, 1890)
 The village of Musselburgh exerted an influence on the game that is still felt around the world. Told by a man who has lived long years and knew many of the early champions, this is a record of the game when it was still a game — not an industry.

A History of Golf in Britain, by Bernard Darwin et al. (London; Cassell, 1952)
 In addition to Darwin, one of the great golf writers, the "et al" represents a number of golf-writers who played the game well, loved it enough to study it and represent the most knowledgeable of golf historians of their time. This book, as a result, is a distillation of the (then) known history.

Golf Between the Two Wars, by Bernard Darwin. (London; Chatto & Windus, 1944)
 The "long weekend" between the two great wars was a period of tremendous growth in the game, in England and America. This finest of golf writers records his impressions of the period and the many fine golfers who made that "weekend" more enjoyable.

My Partner, Ben Hogan, by Jimmy Demaret. (New York; McGraw-Hill, 1954)
 One of the greatest golfers of his time and certainly one to be considered as one of the greatest of all time, Hogan is the subject of a biography by another golfing great, his frequent partner, Demaret.

The Glorious World of Golf, by Peter Dobereiner. (New York; McGraw-Hill, 1973 and later editions)
 Dobereiner is another in a long line of superb British golf writers who brings the game to life in prose that is a pleasure to read. Not the least of the charms this book offers is the host of beautiful illustrations which avoid being ordinary.

Chick Evans' Golf Book, by Charles (Chick) Evans Jr. (Chicago; Reilley and Lee, 1921) Also limited edition. Reprinted in 1978: (Cincinnati; Old Golf Shop)
 Just as Gene Sarazen came to represent the professional's role in golf, Chick Evans represented the role of the amateur. He was a dominant figure in the game during early years of this century and his story offers us an insight into golfing that no longer exists.

Golf's Greatest, by Ross Goodner, (Norwalk, CT: A Golf Digest Book, 1978)

Short informative biographies of those golfers who have achieved the most elusive of man's goals . . . immortality. Even though written rather recently, Goodner's profiles of golf's greatest players provide the reader with fresh and insightful information about these legendary figures.

The PGA: The Official History of the Professional Golfer's Association of America, by Herb Graffis. (New York; Thomas Y. Crowell, 1975)

The growth of the game of golf in America was inexorably tied in the development of the professional as an influential figure, first as a Club professional and later as the concept of the touring pro evolved. This definitive history of the PGA organization tells the story of that development.

Golf in the Making, by Ian Henderson and David Stirk. (Yorkshire; Manningham Press, 1979)

Supported by research that found sources of information that had never been explored before, this book explores the lives of the men who created the implements with which the game is played. As a result, it offers insights into the game that had not been reported in previous histories.

Fifty Years of Golf, by Horace G. Hutchinson. (London; Constable, 1919)

The author was as responsible as any one man in spreading the gospel of golf. In addition to the intelligence he offers as to the early days of the game, his autobiography has a virtue few such books can offer; it is well written.

Down the Fairway, by Robert T. Jones Jr. (New York; Blue Ribbon Books, 1927 and later editions) Also 1927 limited edition.

The man to whom all other golfers are compared wrote this record of his experiences in golf that were compressed, from a national reputation, in fourteen years. His record, within that period is incomparable. It is still a thrill to read of it.

The Golf Book of East Lothian, by Rev. John Kerr. (Edinburgh; T. and A. Constable, 1896) Regular edition limited to 500 copies; Large-paper edition limited to 250 copies.

This is the first of many books that recorded the history of the game in a particular area. It is a beautifully produced book and contains many reprints of the earlier "pieces" of literature that are so difficult to find.

Scotland's Gift: Golf, by Charles Blair MacDonald. (New York; Charles Scribner's Sons, 1928) Also a limited edition.

An early and dominant figure in the birth and growth of golf in the United States, MacDonald wrote this biography of his life in golf. It offers insights into the game as played in the latter half of the 19th century and the subsequent growth of the game in the early years of the 20th century.

Golfer's Gallery, by Frank Moran. (Edinburgh; Oliver and Boys, 1946)

This reporter (Moran) never achieved the status of his colleague, Bernard Darwin, although he covered the Scottish golfing scene for almost as long a period of time. His recollections of golf during the long years he covered the sport are incisive and always interesting.

The World of Golf, by Charles Price. (New York; Random House, 1962)

There is no other golf writer who brings such a breezy, fresh and original "turn of phrase" to the writing of golf. His touch is sure, his knowledge is authoritative and his irreverence is refreshing.

Thirty Years of Championship Golf, by Gene Sarazen, with Herbert Warren Wind. (New York; Prentice-Hall, 1950)

Sarazen is an important figure in American golf and has had the good fortune to live through an extended period of the game's growth in this country and around the world. His story is enhanced by his having the good sense to commission Herb Wind to write it.

The Life of Tom Morris, with Glimpses of St. Andrews and Its Golfing Celebrities, by W. W. Tulloch. (London; T. Werner Laurie, 1908) Reprinted as *The Life and Times of Tom Morris* (London; Ellesborough Press, 1982)

"Old Tom" is one of the true legends of golf and earned that label by being associated with the game through the three eras of golf that are represented by the ancient feather ball, the gutty ball and the modern ball. He is unique in that respect and his story should be known to anyone who professes an interest in golf history.

Early Golf, by Steven J. H. van Hengel. (Amsterdam; privately published, 1982)

A study, masterfully researched, of the games played in the Low Countries which may — or may not — have been golf. This book does not settle questions but explores ground that had never been explored before.

The Story of American Golf, by Herbert Warren Wind. (New York; Farrar, Strauss, 1948; subsequent editions in 1956 and 1975)

Wind is the great student of the game and writes with a style and grace that reminds us of the sweetest of swings. His work is a definitive study of the growth of the game in America.

REFERENCE BOOKS
by Janet Seagle

Janet Seagle is the Curator and Librarian of the Museum and Library of the United States Golf Association in Far Hills, New Jersey. She is one of the premier golf historians and has the wonderful ability to easily locate information in the USGA's collection of more than 8000 books pertaining to golf.

Whether it is a question to settle a wager, or to confirm facts for a soon-to-be published golf story, or to appease the statistic buff, the reference and records section of the United States Golf Association Library is heavily used. There is a surging interest in historical data and the books listed in this section can be of help for quick answers.

The following list of books includes information that covers competition results and facts from the nineteenth century to the present. An interesting sidelight is that almost all the annuals contain the Rules of Golf, so changes there can also be noted. There is a little bit of every facet of the game noted throughout all these books along with a certain amount of repetition. The duplication helps to confirm facts and figures, and can sometimes cause dismay when there are contradictions.

It should be noted that many of the books intended to be annuals did not appear more than once or twice. This is because either the sales did not warrant succeeding volumes or the authors realized how tedious and time consuming the updating of these books would be for them.

Most of the books listed are referred to regularly by our staff at the USGA as well as by authors, sportswriters and historians. Many of the early annuals are highly collectible, whereas later books such as the one on caddying have more of a utilitarian value to golfers.

How many facts can you come up with to stump your fellow golfers after studying these books? You may want to try testing yourself first on how much you absorbed with Herbert Warren Wind's *Golf Quiz* published by *Golf Digest Magazine*.

There have been numerous publishers of the rules of golf and, of course, there are the books which explain them.

The golf annuals published over the years can provide detailed facts about golf happenings in a particular year.

Reference Year Book of Golf, edited and published by John C. Alicoate. (Canoga Park, California; 1971 & 1972)
A general information source for tournaments, associations and instruction. It contains the first list of clubs to appear after many years.

237

Golfing Annual, edited by C. Robertson Bauchope, John Bauchope and David Scott Duncan. (London; Printed by Horace Cox, 1888-1910)

This was the first annual to be enjoyed and supported by the public. In addition to records of championships, it contains articles, poems and golf course descriptions replete with maps.

Golfers' Guide 1908: A Complete Handbook of Useful Information for Golf Clubs and Their Members, edited by C. C. Chattell. (Chicago; Lakeside Press, 1908 & 1909)

This guide is a good source for information on golf clubs in the United States in the first 20 years of active organization and construction.

Fraser's International Golf Year Book, edited by Leo D. Cox. (Montreal and New York; Fraser Publishing Co., 1923-1937)

A valuable source of information on club makers, professionals and a list of clubs in the United States.

Spalding's Official Golf Guide, edited by Charles S. Cox, Thomas Bendelow, Charles Kirchner and Grantland Rice. (New York; American Sports Publishing Co., 1897-1932)

A successful and popular annual or year book which provided each year a review of the preceding years' championships and winners, including sectional events. Also a valuable source of information on clubs and equipment made by Spalding.

Davies Dictionary of Golfing Terms, by Peter Davies. (New York; Simon & Schuster, 1980)

Besides providing definitions, Davies attempts to trace the origin of terms and words of the game and includes relevant quotations.

The Woman Golfer's Catalogue, by Jolee Edmondson. (New York; Stein and Day, 1980)

This is a general guide on the game for women which includes instruction tips from top women professionals.

Who's Who in Golf, by Len Elliott and Barbara Kelly. (New Rochelle, New York; Arlington House, 1976)

The title tells it all: contains brief accounts of players, officials and others associated with the game including birth and death dates, as well as other facts.

Encyclopedia of Golf, compiled by Webster Evans. (London; Robert Hale, 1971 & 1974) Also: (New York; St. Martins Press, 1971)

Evans covers a wide variety of information on the game.

Picadilly World of Golf, edited and compiled by Golf World Magazine. Contributors include Henry Longhurst, Pat Ward-Thomas, Ben Wright, Mark Wilson, Raymond Jacobs, George Houghton, John Jacobs, Herbert Warren Wind. (London; Wayland Publishers, 1972-1975)

This is a general compendium of golf tournaments, winners plus interesting review articles.

Collecting Golf Books, by Cecil Hopkinson. (London; Constable, 1938) Reprinted: (Droitwich, England; Grant Books, 1980)

Hopkinson compiled the first golf bibliography which has become a valuable guide for developing a golf library. Golf historian, Joe Murdoch, calls it "a definitive study of early golf literature".

Ladies Golf Union Annual, edited by the Hon. Secretary. (England; various publishers, has appeared annually since 1894 except for the war years. Title later changed to *The Ladies Golf Union Yearbook)*

The first volume contains an account of the organization and early beginnings of this oldest women's golf association.

Nisbet's Golf Year Book, edited by John L. Low and Vyvyan G. Harnesworth. (London; James Nisbet, 1905-1914)

Nisbet's is an early annual containing club listings, a who's who of players, various records, rules and miscellaneous historical accounts.

Golfer's Handbook, edited by Donald M. Mathieson, R. D. Mathieson and William C. Goldie. (Edinburgh and Glasgow; 1898-1941, 1946 to present)

This is the longest and most successful annual and is considered to be "the Bible" of golfing statistics and information, particularly on British events. Information is also provided on events in Europe and the United States.

World of Professional Golf, by Mark McCormack. (New York; World Publishing Co. and A. S. Barnes and Atheneum. London; Cassell and Collins. 1967 to present) Title varies.

A driving force in the promotion of international golf and its superstars, McCormack has been compiling this long running annual which reviews the previous year of professional golf.

Golf — A Guide to Information Sources by Joseph S. F. Murdoch and Janet Seagle. (Detroit; Gale Research, 1979)

Besides being a condensed bibliography of golf books, this book also provides sources of periodicals, organizations, schools and libraries, equipment and instruction.

Library of Golf 1743-1966, by Joseph S. F. Murdoch. (Detroit; Gale Research Co., 1968) An addendum was privately printed in 1978.

This is a comprehensive bibliography of golf books, complete with entertaining comments by the author, a most knowledgeable and delightful man who expresses in it his great pleasure in books. The books is invaluable to those interested in developing a library of golf books.

Official Golf Guide of America, by Joseph Newman. (Garden City, New York, 1899 & 1900)

This guide was the earliest to list pertinent information on golf courses in the United States, and also provides Rules of the game.

American Annual Golf Guide and Year Book, by various editors: P.C. Pulver, John G. Anderson, J. Lewis Brown. (New York; The Angus Co., 1916-1932)

Information on golf courses, rules and handicapping can be found in this early American guide.

Golfer's Year Book, edited by W. D. Richardson and Lincoln Werden, Grantland Rice and A. J. Morrison. (New York; Golfer's Year Book Co., 1930-33 and 1938-40. The seven volumes were in different sizes.)

Golf club and course listings as well as information on major tournaments appear in this yearbook.

Whole Golf Catalog, edited by Larry Sheehan. (New York; Atheneum, 1979)

A practical guide to important sources, resources and services in the world of golf.

The Encyclopedia of Golf, Edited by Donald Steel, Peter Ryde and Herbert Warren Wind. (New York; The Viking Press, 1975)

The volume is profusely illustrated with biographies as well as details of courses, articles on the Rules, terms, playing techniques and equipment. It is most valuable to anyone interested in the history of the game.

Guinness Book of Golf Facts and Feats, compiled by Donald Steel. (Enfield, Middlesex, England; Guinness Superlatives Ltd., 1980 & later updated editions)

Steel has compiled not only records to learn from but also many varied entertaining facts.

Official Tournament Records, edited by The Tournament Bureau. (Dunedin, Florida; Professional Golfers Association of America, 1941 with later supplements) Also issued *Tournament Player Catalog* annually since 1959, now titled *The Tour Book.*

An official media guide, this book contains brief biographies of all professional golfers who have played on the PGA Tour, as well as results of top finishers in all major tournaments.

Record Book of USGA Championships and International Events. (Far Hills, New Jersey; United States Golf Association, Two volumes: 1895-1959 & 1960-1980 with supplements)

Statistics on all USGA championships and international events with USGA teams are presented in these volumes.

Caddie Operations Manual, by The Western Golf Association. (Golf, Illinois; Western Golf Association, 1969)

The Western Golf Association, the organization which runs the largest caddie scholarship program in the country, has compiled information on caddie responsibilities, guidelines, qualifications and recruiting.

BIBLIOGRAPHY GUIDELINES

ABBREVIATION	CATEGORY	REVIEWS BEGIN ON PAGE
AN	ANTHOLOGY	225
GC	GOLF COURSE	227
EQ	EQUIPMENT	230
ES	ESSAYS	232
F	FICTION	233
H	HISTORY	234
I	INSTRUCTIONAL	
R	REFERENCE	237
RU	RULES	

See page 224 for "How To Use This Chapter"

BIBLIOGRAPHY

A.B.
Told at The 19th Hole: Humorous St. Andrews Golfing Stories: 1928, F, under $15

A.Q.
Swing in Golf: And How To Learn It, The: 1919, I, under $15

ABBOTT, B.R.
Golf Quiz: 1915, RU, $40-80
Also see listing under "C.G.C."

ACREE, EDWARD C. & HUTCHISON, JOCK & HUTCHISON, BILL
Golf Simplified: 1946, I, under $15

ADAMS, FREDERICK UPHAM
John Henry Smith, A Humorous Romance of Outdoor Life: 1905, F, $40-80

ADAMS, HERBERT
19th Hole Mystery, The: 1939, F, $15-40
Body in the Bunker, The: 1935, F, $15-40
Death off The Fairway: 1936, F, $15-40
Death on the First Tee: 1957, F, $15-40
Golf House Murder, The: 1933, F, $15-40
John Brand's Will: 1944, F, $15-40
Perfect Round: Tales of the Links, The: 1927, F, $15-40
Secret of Bogey House, The: 1924, F, $15-40

ADAMS, ROBERT WINTHROP
Timing Your Golf Swing: 1957, I, under $15

ADWICK KEN
Dictionary of Golf: 1974, R, under $15
Golf: 1975, I, under $15
Ken Adwick's Alphabet of Golf: 1973, I, under $15
X-Ray to Master Golf: 1970, I, under $15

AGENDA CLUB
Rough and the Fairway: An Enquiry by The Agenda Club etc...., The: 1912, R, $15-40

AIKMAN, GEORGE & SMART, JOHN
Round of the Links: Views of the Golf Greens of Scotland, A: 1983, GC, Scarce
Round of the Links: Views of the Golf Green of Scotland, A (reprint): 1980, GC, $80-140
Also see listing under "G.A."

AITCHISON, THOMAS S. & LORIMER, GEORGE
Reminiscences of the Old Bruntsfield Links Golf Club, 1866-1874: 1902, H, $140-400

ALFANO, PETER
Grand Slam: 1973, H, under $15

ALICOATE, JOHN C.
✓ Reference Yearbook of Golf: 1971, R, under $15

ALLEN, PETER
Famous Fairways: 1968, GC, $15-40
Play the Best Courses: Great Golf Courses in the British Isles: 1973, GC, $15-40

ALLERTON, MARK
Girl on the Green, The: 1914, F, $40-80
Golf Faults Remedied: Containing Also Rules Worth Remembering: 1911, I, $15-40

ALLERTON, MARK & BROWNING, ROBERT
Golf Made Easy: A Book for the Man Who Plays but Wants to Play Better: 1910, I, $15-40

ALLISON, WILLIE
First Golf Review, The: 1950, R, under $15

ALLISS, PERCY
Better Golf: 1926, I, under $15
Making Golf Easier: 1933, I, under $15

ALLISS, PETER
Duke: A Novel, The: 1983, F, under $15

More Bedside Golf: 1982, AN, under $15
Peter Alliss: An Autobiography: 1981, H, under $15
Peter Allis' Bedside Book: 1980, AN, under $15
Shell Book of Golf: 1981, AN, under $15
Who's Who of Golf, The: 1983, R, under $15

ALLISS, PETER & FERRIER, BOB
Alliss Through the Looking Glass: 1963, H, under $15

ALLISS, PETER & RAIDLAW, RENTON
Play Golf with Peter Alliss: 1977, I, under $15

ALLISS, PETER & SHANKLAND, CRAIG
Stroke Saving for the Handicap Golfer: 1979, I, under $15

ALLISS, PETER & TREVILLION, PAUL
Easier Golf: 1969, I, under $15

ALPERT, HOLIS & MOTHNER, IRA & SCHONBERG, HAROLD
How To Play Double Bogey Golf: 1975, I, under $15

ANDERSON, ROBERT
Funny Thing Happened on the Way To The Clubhouse, A: 1971, F, under $15
Heard at the Nineteenth: A Light-Hearted Look at the Game of Golf: 1966, F, under $15

ANDRE, RICHARD
Colonel Bogey's Sketch Book: etc...: 1897, F, $80-140
Golf Plays and Recitations: 1903, F, $80-140

ANDREASON, DALE
Simplified Golf: 1960, I, under $15

ANGAS, MAJOR L.L.B.
Golf Swings in the Plural: A Course For Professional Instructors etc...., The: 1962, I, under $15

ANONYMOUS
200 Funny Golf Stories, as Told at the 19th: 1931, F, $15-40
Business Man's Golf Course (Set of 6): 1924, ES, under $15
Friendly Fairways of Michigan: 1979, GC, under $15
Golf Know How: An Amazing Encyclopedia of Golf Tips: 1957, I, under $15
Golf Mind vs. Business Mind: The Neutro-Mental System for Golfer: 1924, ES, $15-40
Golf Professional's Handbook of Business: The Best of Pro Business Practices etc.....: 1932, R, $15-40
Gorham Golf Book, The: 1903, AN, over $400
Gregory's Guide for Golfers: A Complete Handbook Containing High Class Maps etc.....: 1947, R, under $15
How To Play the Old Course: 1932, GC, under $15
Know the Game: Golf: 1952, I, under $15
Laws of Golf: 1895, RU, $40-80
Links Book, The: 1900, GC, $80-140
Most Convenient Setting Forth of Much Interesting Information Regarding Golf, etc..., A: 1900, RU, $40-80
Official Year Book and Directory of Golf and Automobiling with Newman's Golf Guide: 1900, GC, under $15
Where to Stay and Where to Play: 1977, GC, under $15
Who's Who in Golf and Directory of Golf Clubs and Members: 1909, R, $40-80

ARGEA, ANGELO
Bear and I, The: 1979, H, under $15

ARMOUR, RICHARD
Golf Bawls: 1946, F, under $15
Golf Is A Four-Letter Word: The Intimate Confessions Of A Hooked Slicer: 1962, F, under $15

ARMOUR, TOMMY
How To Play Your Best Golf All The Time: 1953, I, under $15
Round of Golf with Tommy Armour, A: 1959, I, under $15
Tommy Armour's A.B.C.'s of Golf: 1967, I, under $15

ARNOLD, A.E.
Putting and Spared Shots: 1939, I, under $15
ASTLE, M.J.
Principles of Golf, The: 1924, I, under $15
AUGUSTA NATIONAL G.C.
Masters: The First Forty-One Years, The: 1978, H, under $15
AULTMAN, DICK
101 Ways to Win: 1980, I, under $15
Better Golf In Six Swings: 1982, I, under $15
AULTMAN, DICK & BOWDEN, KEN
Methods of Golf's Masters, The: 1975, I, under $15
AULTMAN, DICK & GOLF DIGEST, EDITORS OF
Learn To Play Golf: 1969, I, under $15
Square-to-Square Golf Swing: Model Method for the Modern Player,
The: 1970, I, under $15
AYTON, LAURIE
Golf as Champions Play It: 1925, I, under $15
BAERT, RAYMOND
Adventures of Monsieur DuPont, Golf Champion: 1913, F,
$40-80
BAILEY, C.W.
Brain and Golf: Some Hints for Golfers from Modern Mental
Science, The: 1923, ES, $15-40
Professor on the Golf LInks: Some Sidelights on Golf from Modern
Science, The: 1925, ES, $15-40
BAIRD, ARCHIE
Golf on Gullane Hill: 1982, H, under $15
BAKER, STEPHAN
How to Play Golf in the Low 120s: 1962, F, under $15
BALFOUR, J. STUART
Golf: Spalding Athletic Library: 1893, I, over $400
BALFOUR, JAMES
Reminiscences of Golf on St. Andrews Links: 1887, H, over $400
Reminiscences of Golf on St. Andrews Links: (reprint): 1982, H,
under $15
BALL, BRIAN
Death of a Low Handicap Man: 1974, F, under $15
BALLARD, JIMMY & QUINN, BRENNAN
How to Perfect your Golf Swing: Using 'Connection' and the
Seven Common Denominators: 1981, I, under $15
BALLESTEROS, SEVERIANO & DOUST, DUDLEY
Seve: The Young Champion: 1982, H, under $15
BANES, FORD
Right Down your Fairway: 1947, F, under $15
BANNON, GILLIAN
Good Golfing: 1978, I, under $15
BANTOCK, MILES
On Many Greens: A Book of Golf and Golfers: 1901, AN,
$140-400
BARBER, JERRY
Art of Putting, The: 1967, I, under $15
BARCLAY, ROBERT & LANG, ANDREW & OTHERS
Batch of Golfing Papers, A: 1892, I, $80-140
BARKER, REG
Eighteen For Ever: 1959, F, under $15
BARKOW, AL
Golf's Golden Grind: The History of the Tour: 1974, H, under
$15
BARLOW, COL. RAYMOND G.
Golf for the Beginner and the Confused: 1954, I, under $15
BARNES, JAMES M.
Guide to Good Golf: A: 1925, I, under $15
Picture Analysis of Golf Strokes: A Complete Book of Instruction:
1919, I, $15-40
BARNETT, TED
Golf is Madness: 1977, F, under $15

BARON, HARRY
Golf Resorts of the USA: 1967, GC, under $15
NBC Sports Golf Guide, 1967: 1967, R, under $15
BARRINGTON, JOHN
U.S. Golfer's Annual Handbook: 1958, R, under $15
BARRON, LEONARD
Lawn Making: Together with the Proper Care of Putting Greens:
1906, GC, $15-40
BARTLETT, CHARLIE
New 1969 Golfer's Almanac, The: 1969, R, under $15
BARTLETT, MICHAEL
Bartlett's World Golf Encyclopedia: 1973, R, under $15
Golf Book, The: 1980, AN, under $15
BARTON, PAM
Stroke a Hole: 1937, I, under $15
BASSLER, CHARLES T. & GIBSON, NEVIN H.
You Can Play Par Golf: 1966, I, under $15
BATCHELOR, GERALD
Golf Stories: 1914, F, $15-40
BATEMAN, H.M.
Adventures at Golf: 1923, F, $40-80
H. M. Bateman on Golf: 1977, F, under $15
BAUCHOPE, C. ROBERTSON & BAUCHOPE, JOHN & DUN-
CAN, DAVID SCOTT *ANNUAL*
✓ Golfing Annual, The: 1888 +, R, $40-400
BAUER, ALECK
Hazards: The Essential Elements in a Golf Course without which
the game etc. . . . : 1913, GC, $140-400
BAUER, DAVE
Golf Techniques of the Bauer Sisters: 1951, I, under $15
BAUGHMAN, ERNEST A.
How to Caddie: 1914, I, under $15
BAXTER, JOHN E.
Locker Room Ballads: 1923, F, $40-80
BAXTER, PETER
Golf in Perth and Perthshire: Traditional, Historical and Modern:
1899, H, over $400
BEARD, FRANK
Shaving Strokes: 1970, I, under $15
BEARD, FRANK, & SCHAAP, DICK
Pro: Frank Beard on the Golf Tour: 1970, H, under $15
BEARD, JAMES B.
Turf Management for Golf Courses: 1982, GC, $15-40
BEARD, JAMES B. & BEARD, HARRIET & MARTIN, DAVID
P.
Turfgrass: Bibliography from 1672 to 1972: 1977, GC, $15-40
BEATTIE, JAMES
Club Toter, The: N.D., I, under $15
BECK, FRED
89 Years in a Sand Trap: 1965, F, under $15
To H--- With Golf: 1956, F, under $15
BECK, FRED & BARNES, O.K.
73 Years in a Sand Trap: 1949, F, under $15
BECKER, HARLAND ALDRICH
Knack of Golf, The: 1952, I, under $15
BEGBIE, HAROLD
J.H. Taylor, or, The Inside of a Week: 1925, H, $40-80
BELDAM, GEORGE W.
Golf Faults Illustrated: 1905, I, $15-40
Golfing Illustrated: Gowan's Practical Picture Books, No. 2: 1908,
I, $15-40
Great Golfers: Their Methods at a Glance: 1904, I, $40-80
World's Champion Golfers: Their Art Disclosed by the Ultra-
Rapid Camera, The (11 Books): 1924, I, $15-40
BELL, PEGGY KIRK & CLAUSSEN, JERRY
Women's Way to Better Golf, A: 1966, I, under $15

BENEDICTUS, DAVID
 Guru and the Golf Club, The: 1969, F, under $15
BENNETT, ANDREW
 Book of St. Andrews Links: Containing Plan of Golf Courses,
 Description etc...., The: 1898, GC, over $400
BENSON, E.F. & MILES, E.H.
 Book of Golf: Imperial Athletic Library: 1903, I, $15-40
BERG, PATTY
 Golf for Women Illustrated: 1951, I, under $15
 Golf Illustrated: 1950, I, under $15
 Inside Golf for Women: 1977, I, under $15
BERG, PATTY & DYPWICK, OTIS
 Golf: 1941, I, under $15
BERKELEY, EARL OF
 Sound Golf: By Applying Principles to Practice: 1936, H, $15-40
BERNARDONI, GUS
 Golf God's Way: 1978, ES, under $15
BETINIS, JAMES
 Hit the Nail on the Head: 1961, I, under $15
BIDDULPH, MICHAEL
 Golf Shot, The: 1980, I, under $15
BISHER, FURMAN
 Augusta Revisited: An Intimate View: 1976, H, $15-40
BISHER, FURMAN & OLDERMAN, MURRAY
 Birth of a Legend: Arnold Palmer's Golden Year, 1960, The:
 1972, H, under $15
BLACK, ANDY
 Golf Courses of Scotland, The: 1974, GC, under $15
BLAKE, MINDY
 Golf: The Technique Barrier: 1978, I, under $15
 Golf Swing of the Future, The: 1972, I, under $15
BLALOCK, JANE & NETLAND, DWAYNE
 Guts to Win, The: 1977, H, under $15
BLATCH, WILLIAM DESMOND
 Law Relating to Golf Clubs: Being a Guide to the Varying Rates
 and Taxes etc...., The: 1943, R, $15-40
BLOGH, ARTHUR
 Crotchets and Foibles: Stories of Shooting, Cricket and Golf:
 1903, AN, $15-40
BLOS
 Fore! Forty Drawings by Mahood: 1959, F, under $15
BOARD, JOHN
 Right Way to Become a Golfer, The: 1948, I, under $15
BOLSTAD, LES & ROTVIG & GRIFFIN & MacDONALD
 Golf: 1964, I, under $15
BOLT, TOMMY & GRIFFITH, WILLIAM G.
 How to Keep Your Temper on the Golf Course: 1969, I, under
 $15
BOLT, TOMMY & MANN, JIMMY
 Hole Truth: Inside Big-Time Big-Money Golf, The; 1971, H,
 under $15
BOND, MICHAEL
 Paddington Hits Out: 1980, F, under $15
BOOMER, PERCY
 On Learning Golf: 1942, I, under $15
BOROS, JULIUS
 How to Play Golf with an Effortless Swing: 1964, I, under $15
 How to Play Par Golf: 1953, I, under $15
 Swing Easy, Hit Hard: 1965, I, under $15
BOSWELL, CHARLIE & ANDERS, CURT
 Now I See: 1969, H, under $15
BOTTOME, GEORGE McDONALD
 Golf for the Middle-Aged and Others: 1946, I, under $15
BOTTOME, GEORGE McDONALD & HERON, JOHN
 Modern Golf: 1949, I, under $15

BOVIS, JOHN L.
 It of Golf: Simplified Golf Demonstrated as Applied Mechanics,
 The: 1927, I, under $15
BOWDEN, KEN
 Golf Gazeteer, The: 1968, H, under $15
BOWLING, MAURINE
 Tested Ways of Teaching Golf Classes: 1964, I, under $15
BOY, DR. ANGELO V.
 Psychological Dimensions of Golf: 1980, ES, under $15
BOYNTON, H.W.
 Golfer's Rubaiyat, The; 1901, F, $40-80
BRAID, JAMES
 ✔ Advanced Golf, or Hints and Instruction for Progressive
 Players: 1908, GC & I, $15-40
 Golf Guide and How to Play Golf (Spalding Athletic Guide No.
 10): 1906, I, $15-40
BREEDEN, MARSHALL
 Us Golfers and Our California Links: Facts about all the Golf
 Links in California, etc....: 1923, GC, $40-80
BREWER, GAY
 Gay Brewer Shows You How to Score Better Than You Swing:
 1968, I, under $15
BREWER, GAY & GANEM, ROGER
 Gay Brewer's Golf Guidebook: 1980, I, under $15
BRIGGS, CLARE
 Golf: The Book of a Thousand Chuckles: 1916, F, $80-140
BRINTON, ALAN
 Mr. and Mrs. Golfer...Cut their Handicaps: 1954, I, under $15
BRITISH MASTERS
 How to Improve your Golf: Lessons by British Masters: 1925, I,
 under $15
BROADBENT, W. F.
 Golf: Fundamental Instructions: 1937, I, under $15
BRODY, SIDNEY 'STEVE'
 How to Break 90 Before You Reach It: 1967, I, under $15
BROOKS, DICK
 Offensive Golfer: A Handbook for Compulsive Golvers, The:
 1963, F, under $15
BROOME, J.E.
 Keep your Eye on the Ball: 1936, I, under $15
BROWN, ERIC
 Knave of Clubs: 1961, H, under $15
BROWN, ERIC & HERRON, ALAN
 Out of the Bag: 1964, H, under $15
BROWN, GENE
 Complete Book of Golf, The: 1980, AN, under $15
 New York Times Encyclopedia of Sports: Golf, The: 1976, R,
 under $15
BROWN, GEORGE S.
 First Steps to Golf: 1913, I, under $15
BROWN, HORACE
 Murder in the Rough: 1948, F, under $15

BIBLIOGRAPHY GUIDELINES

ABBREV.	CATEGORY	REVIEWS BEGIN ON PAGE
AN	ANTHOLOGY	225
GC	GOLF COURSE	227
EQ	EQUIPMENT	230
ES	ESSAYS	232
F	FICTION	233
H	HISTORY	234
I	INSTRUCTIONAL	
R	REFERENCE	237
RU	RULES	

See page 224 for "How To Use This Chapter"

BROWN, INNIS
  How to Play Golf (Spalding Athletic Library, No. 4B): 1931, I, $15-40
  Ready References to the Rules of Golf: 1924, RU, $15-40
BROWN, JAMES
  Songs of Golf: 1902, F, $80-140
BROWN, KENNETH
  Putter Perkins: 1923, F, $15-40
BROWN, M. GILLETTE
  Fell's Teen Age Guide to Winning Golf: 1963, I, under $15
BROWN, THOMAS
  Golfiana, or a Day at Gullane: 1869, F, over $400
BROWN, WILLIAM G.
  Golf: 1902, I, $15-40
BROWNE, TOM
  Game of Golf and Some other Sketches, That: 1902, F, $40-80
BROWNING, ROBERT H. K.
  Golf in the Sun All Year Round: 1931, GC, $15-40
  Golf with Seven Clubs: 1950, I, under $15
  Golfer's Catechism: A Vade Mecum to the Rules of Golf, The: 1935, RU, $15-40
  ✓ History of Golf: The Royal and Ancient Game, A: 1955, H, $40-80
  Moments with Golfing Masters: 1932, I, $15-40
  Stymie: A Miscellany of Golfing Humor and Wit, The: 1910, F, $15-40
  Super-Golf: 1919, H, $15-40
BRUCE, BEN & DAVIES, EVELYN
  Beginning Golf: 1962, I, under $15
BRUFF, NANCY
  Country Club: A New Novel, The: 1969, F, under $15
BRUTUS (Pseudonym for SPOONER, JOHN D.)
  Class: A Novel: 1973, F, under $15
BULGER
  Echoes from the Links: 1924, ES, $15-40
BURD, RON
  Ron Burd's Basic Principles of Golf: 1966, I, under $15
BURKE, JR., JACK
  Natural Way to Better Golf, The: 1954, I, under $15
BURKE, JR., JACK & NELSON & REVOLAT & RUNYAN & SMITH
  How to Solve Your Golf Problems: 1963, I, under $15
BURTON, RICHARD
  Length with Discretion: 1940, I, under $15
BUTLER, W. MEREDITH
  Golfer's Manual, The: 1907, AN, $80-140
C.B.C.
  Early Days of the Honourable Company of Edinburgh Golfers — 1744-1764 (Typed Manuscript): 1938, H, under $15
C.G.C.
  Quiz Book upon the USGA Rules of Golf, A: 1914, RU, $40-80 RU, $40-80
C.J.B. (Pseudonym for BILLSON, C.J.) - P.S.W. is CO-AUTHOR
  Horace on the Links: With Notes from Horace Hutchinson's Writings: 1903, F, $40-80
CAKE, PATRICK
  Pro-Am Murders: 1978, F, under $15
CAMERER, DAVE
  Improve Your Golf: 1958, I, under $15
  Golf With The Masters: The Secret to Better Golf: 1955, I, under $15
CAMP, WALTER & BROOKS, LILLIAN
  Drives and Putts: A Book of Golf Stories: 1899, F, $80-140
CAMPBELL, BAILEY
  Golf Lessons from Sam Snead: 1964, I, under $15

CAMPBELL, JOHN
  Greenkeeping: 1982, GC, under $15
CAMPBELL, PATRICK
  How to Become a Scratch Golfer: 1963, F, under $15
  Patrick Campbell's Golfing Book: 1974, AN, under $15
CAMPBELL, SIR GUY
  Golf at Prince's and Deal: 1950, GC, $40-80
  Golf for Beginners: 1922, I, under $15
CANAUSA, F.C.
  How to Win at Golf: 1956, I, under $15
CANHAM, PETER
  Introduction to Golf: 1975, I, under $15
CARL, HENRY M.
  Analytic Physical Culture Golf: Home Exercises for Automatic Correct Form, etc.... : 1928, I, under $15
CARMEL WORK CENTER
  Photographic Study of Pebble Beach Golf Links, Stroke by Stroke, A: 1952, GC, $15-40
CARNEGIE, GEORGE F.
  Golfiana, or Niceties Connected with the Game of Golf: 1833, F, Scarce
CARR, DICK
  You, Too, Can Golf in the Eighties: An Effective Strategy for Reducing Strokes: 1977, I, under $15
CARRELL, AL & JANUARY, DON
  Golf is a Funny Game: 1967, F, under $15
CASPER, BILLY
  Golf Shotmaking with Billy Casper: 1966, I, under $15
  My Million Dollar Shots: 1970, I, under $15
CASPER, BILLY & BARKOW, AL
  Good Sense of Golf, The: 1980, I, under $15
CASPER, BILLY & COLLETT, DON
  Chipping and Putting: Golf Around the Green: 1961, I, under $15
CASPER, BILLY & PUCKETT, EARL
  295 Golf Lessons: 1973, I, under $15
CAVANAGH, WALTER
  Art of Golf, The: 1928, I, $15-40
CHAMBERLAIN, FAUSTINA E.
  Charlie Emery, Pro: Biography of a Maine Golf Pro: 1982, H, under $15
CHAMBERS, CHARLES
  Golfing: A Handbook to the Royal and Ancient Game, With Lists of Clubs, Rule, etc.... : 1887, AN, $140-400
CHAMBERS, ROBERT
  Few Rambling Remarks on Golf, With the Rules, etc...., A: 1862, I, over $400
  Gymnastics, Golf and Curling: 1866, I, $140-400
CHAPMAN, HAY
  Law of the Links, Rules, Principles and Etiquette of Golf: 1922, RU, $15-40
CHAPMAN, RICHARD D. & SANDS, LEDYARD
  Golf as I Play It: Inside Golf by 28 Champions: 1940, I, under $15
CHARLES, BOB & GANEM, ROGER P.
  Bob Charles, Left-Hander from New Zealand: 1965, I, under $15
  Left Handed Golf: 1965, I, under $15
CHATTELL, C.C.
  ✓ Golfers' Guide, 1908; A Complete Handbook of Useful Information, etc...., The: 1908, R, $40-80
CHEATUM, BILLYE ANN
  Golf: 1969, I, under $15
CHERELLIA, GEORGE
  Tempo: The Heart of the Golf Swing: 1971, I, under $15

CHEVES, GEORGE
  Play Better Golf: 1966, I, under $15
CHINNOCK, FRANK
  How to Break 90 — Consistently: 1976, I, under $15
CHLEVIN, BEN
  Golf for Industry: A Planning Guide: 1957, R, under $15
  Golf Operator's Handbook: GC, under $15
CHRISTIE, AGATHA
  Murder on the Links: 1923, F, $15-40
CHRONICLES, JOE
  Uncle Jed, Caddie Master: 1934, F, $40-80
CHUI, EDWARD F.
  Golf: 1969, I, under $15
CLAPCOTT, C.B.
  History of Handicapping, The: 1924, RU, $140-400
  Rules of the Ten Oldest Golf Clubs from 1754-1848, The: 1935, R, over $400
CLARK, CLIVE & SAUNDERS, VIVIAN
  Young Golfer, The: 1978, I, under $15
CLARK, ROBERT
  Golf: A Royal and Ancient Game: 1875, AN, over $400
  Golf: A Royal and Ancient Game (Limited Edition): 1875, AN, Scarce
  Golf: A Royal and Ancient Game (Reprint): 1975, AN, $15-40
  Poems on Golf: 1867, F, over $400
CLARKE, CHARLES & GILBERT, MOTTRAM
  Commonsense Golf: 1914, I, $15-40
CLEMENT, JOE
  ✔ Classic Golf Clubs: A Pictorial Guide: 1980, EQ, under $15
CLEVELAND, CHARLES B.
  Approaching and Putting: The Key to a Lower Golf Score, etc...: 1953, I, under $15
CLIFFER, HAROLD J.
  Planning the Golf Clubhouse: 1956, GC, $15-40
CLOUGHER, T.R. *ANNUAL*
  Golf Clubs of the Empire: The Golfing Annual: 1926-1932, R, $40-80
CLOW, WILLIAM ELLSWORTH
  Good Golf: 1942, I, under $15
COBE, ALBERT & ELRICK, GEORGE & SIMON, R.E.
  Great Spirit: 1970, F, under $15
COCHRAN, ALASTAIR & STOBBS, JOHN & NOBLE, DAVID
  ✔ Search for the Perfect Golf Swing, The: 1968, EQ & ES, $15-40
COFFEY, MARTIN E.
  Golfing in Ireland: 1952, GC, under $15
COLES, NEIL
  Neil Coles on Golf: 1965, H, under $15
COLL, BEN
  Country Club, The: 1961, F, under $15
  I Love Golf: 1950, F, under $15
COLLETT, GLENNA
  Golf for Young Players: 1926, I, $15-40
  Golf for Young Players: (Reprint): 1984, I, $15-40
COLLETT, GLENNA & NEVILLE, JAMES M.
  ✔ Ladies in the Rough: 1928, H, $15-40
COLLIER, BASIL
  Local Thunder: 1936, F, under $15
COLONEL, THE
  Golfing by Numbers: One Action for Playing all Strokes (Except Putting): 1927, I, under $15
COLT, HARRY S. & ALISON, C.H.
  Some Essays on Golf Course
  Architecture: 1920, GC, $140-400

COLVILLE, GEORGE M.
  ✔ Five Open Champions and the Musselburgh Golf Story: 1980, H, under $15
COMER, JOHN L.
  Putting: a New Approach: 1961, I, under $15
COMPSTON, ARCHIE & ANDERSON, STANLEY
  Love on the Fairway: A Romance of the Open Championship: 1936, F, $40-80
COMPSTON, ARCHIE & LONGHURST, HENRY
  Go Golfing: 1937, I, $15-40
COMPTON, C.H.
  Antiquity of Golf, The: 1881, H, $80-140
CONGDON, ERNEST C.
  Golf Primer on Familiar Rules: 1915, RU, $15-40
CONNOLLY, BOB
  Carnaby Threep's Golf Class: 1971, I, under $15
  How to Become a Golfer and Have No One to Blame but Yourself: 1955, I, under $15
CORCORAN, FRED
  Golf Official Guide with the Official USGA Rules: 1949, R, $15-40
CORCORAN, FRED & HARVEY, BUD
  Unplayable Lies: 1965, H, $15-40
CORNISH, GEOFFREY, S. & WHITTEN, RONALD W.
  ✔ Golf Course, The: 1981, GC, $15-40
CORTISSOZ, ROYAL
  Nine Holes of Golf: 1922, ES, $15-40
COTTON, HENRY
  Game of Golf, This: 1948, I, under $15
  Golf: A Pictorial History: 1975, H, under $15
  Golf: Being a Short Treatise for the use of Young People, etc: 1931, I, under $15
  Henry Cotton Says...: 1962, I, under $15
  Henry Cotton's Guide to Golf in the British Isles: 1961, GC, under $15
  Hints on Play with Steel Shafts: 1934, EQ, $15-40
  History of Golf Illustrated, A: 1975, H, under $15
  My Golfing Album: 1959, AN, under $15
  My Swing: 1952, I, under $15
  Picture of the Golf Game, The: 1965, H, under $15
  Play Better Golf: 1973, I, under $15
  Study the Game with Henry Cotton: 1964, I, under $15
COTTON, HENRY & WHITE, JACK
  Golfing in Scotland at 100 Holiday Resorts: 1936, GC, $15-40
COUSINS, GEOFFREY
  Golf in Britain: 1975, H, under $15
  Golfers at Law: 1958, RU, under $15
  Handbook of Golf: A Guide to the Game and its Techniques, The: 1969, I, under $15
  Lords of the Links: 1977. H, under $15
COUSINS, GEOFFREY & POTTINGER, DAN
  Atlas of Golf, An: 1974, GC, under $15

BIBLIOGRAPHY GUIDELINES

ABBREV.	CATEGORY	REVIEWS BEGIN ON PAGE
AN	ANTHOLOGY	225
GC	GOLF COURSE	227
EQ	EQUIPMENT	230
ES	ESSAYS	232
F	FICTION	233
H	HISTORY	234
I	INSTRUCTIONAL	
R	REFERENCE	237
RU	RULES	

See page 224 for "How To Use This Chapter"

COUSINS, GEOFFREY & SCOTT, TOM
Century of Opens, A: 1971, H, under $15
COX, BILL
Can I Help You? The Guide to Better Golf: 1954, I, under $15
Improve Your Golf: 1963, I, under $15
Play Better Golf: 1952, I, under $15
COX, BILL & TREMAYNE, NICHOLAS
Bill Cox's Golf Companion: 1969, R, under $15
COX, CHARLES. *ANNUAL*
✔ Spalding's Official Golf Guide: 1897-1942, R, $40-80
COX, LEO D. *ANNUAL*
Fraser's International Golf Yearbook: 1923-1932, R, $15-40
COYNE, JOHN
Better Golf: 1972, I, under $15
CRAFTER, BRIAN
Winning Golf: 1984, I, under $15
CRAIGIE, JOHN C.
Golf Match Club: Record of Matches, 1897-1938: 1938, R, $15-40
CRAWFORD, PETER G.
Winning Touch in Golf: A Psychological Approach, The: 1961, ES, under $15
CRAWFORD, IAN
Open Guide to Royal St. George's and Sandwich, The: 1981, GC, under $15
Open Guide to Royal Troon & Kyle, The: 1982, GC, under $15
CRAWLEY, LEONARD
Playfair Golf Annual: 1950, R, under $15
CREAGH, JOHN
Golden Years of Australian Golf: 1977, H, under $15
CREHAM, WM.
Who's Who in Golf: 1971, R, under $15
CREMIN, ERIC
Par Golf: 1952, I, under $15
CROGREN, CORRINNE
Golf Fundamentals for Students and Teachers: 1960, I, under $15
CROMBIE, CHARLES
Rules of Golf Illustrated, The: 1905, F & RU, over $400
Some of the Rules of Golf (Reprint): 1966, F & RU, $15-40
CROMIE, ROBERT
Golf for Boys and Girls: 1965, I, under $15
New Angles on Putting and Chipping: 1960, F, under $15
Par for the Course: A Golfer's Anthology: 1964, AN, under $15
CROSBIE, PROVAN
Fairways and Foul: 1964, F, under $15
CROUCH, WILLIAM HH.
Guide to the Analysis of Golf Courses and Country Clubs: 1976, GC, under $15
CUMMING, GEORGE
It Goes Where You Hit It: 1948, I, under $15
CUNDELL, JAMES
Rules of the Thistle Club: 1824, H & RU, Scarce
Rules of the Thistle Club (Reprint): 1984, H & RU, $40-80
CUNNINGHAM, ANDREW S.
Golf Clubs around Largo Bay, The: 1909, GC, $80-140
Lundin Links, Upper and Lower Largo and Leven: 1913, GC, $80-140
CURRENTE, CALAMO
Half Hours with an Old Golfer: 1895, F, $140-400
DALRYMPLE, W.
Golfer's Referee, The: 1897, RU, $80-140
Golfer's Guide to the Game and Greens of Scotland: 1894, GC, $140-400
Golfer's Guide for the United Kingdom: 1895-1899, GC, $140-400
Hand Book of Golf: With Diagrams and Positions and Instructions, etc....: 1895, I, $80-140

DALY, FRED
Golf as I See It: 1951, I, under $15
DANTE, JIM & DIEGEL, LEO & ELLIOTT, LEN
Nine Bad Shots of Golf and What to do about Them, The: 1947, I, under $15
DANTE, JOE & ELLIOTT, LEN
Four Magic Moves to Winning Golf, The: 1962, I, under $15
Stop That Slice: 1953, I, under $15
What's Wrong with Your Game?: 1978, I, under $15
DARBYSHIRE, L. CLAUGHTON
Go Golfing in Britain: A Hole by Hole Survey of 25 Famous Seaside Courses: 1961, GC, under $15
DARO, AUGUST F. & GRAFFIS, HERB
Inside Swing: Key to Better Golf, The: 1972, I, under $15
DARSIE, DARSIE L.
My Greatest Day in Golf: 1950, H, under $15
DARWIN, BERNARD
British Clubs, 1947, H, under $15
British Golf: 1946, H, under $15
Every Idle Dream: 1948, ES, under $15
✔ Friendly Round, A: 1922, ES, $15-40
Golf: Pleasure of Life Series: 1954, AN, $15-40
✔ Golf Between Two Wars: 1944, H, under $15
✔ Golf Courses of the British Isles, The: 1910, GC, $140-400
✔ Golf Courses of Great Britain, The (2nd Edition of book above): 1925, GC, $80-140
Golf From The Times: A Reprint, etc....: 1912, ES, $40-80
Golfer's Gallery of Old Masters, A (Bound Art Prints): 1920, F, over $400
Golfing By-Paths: 1946, ES, $15-40
Green Memories: 1928, H, $15-40
✔ History of Golf in Britain, A: 1952, AN & H, $80-140
James Braid: 1952, H, $15-40
James Braid (Reprint): 1981, H, $15-40
Life is Sweet, Brother: 1940, H, under $15
Out of the Rough: 1932, ES, $15-40
Pack the Clouds Away: 1941, ES, under $15
Playing the Like: 1934, ES, $15-40
Round of Golf on the London & North Eastern Railway, A: 1924, GC, $15-40
Rubs of the Green: 1936, ES, $15-40
Second Shots: Casual Talks about Golf: 1930, ES, $15-40
Six Golfing Shots by Six Famous Players: 1927, I, $15-40
Tee Shots and Others: 1911, ES, $40-80
World that Fred Made: An Autobiography, The: 1955, H, under $15
DARWIN, BERNARD & OTHERS
Hints on Golf, With Supplement on Golfing Kit: 1912, I, $40-80
DAVIDSON, PETER
That's Golf: 1979, F, undeer $15
DAVIES, PETER
✔ Davies' Dictionary of Golfing Terms: 1980, R, under $15
DAVIS, WILLIAM
Punch Book of Golf, The: 1973, F, under $15
DAVIS, WILLIAM & GOLF DIGEST, EDITORS OF
100 Greatest Golf Courses — And Then Some! 1982, GC, $15-40
Great Golf Courses of the World: 1974, GC, $15-40
DAWKINS, GEORGE
Keys to the Golf Swing: 1976, I, under $15
DeAULA, W.
St. Andrews: Ancient and Modern: 1870, F, $40-80
DeGARMO, LOUIS
Play Golf and Enjoy It: 1954, ES, under $15
DeGUERRE, CHRISTIAN & FALLIOT, PATRICE
Europe's Golf Guide: 1982, GC, under $15

BIBLIOGRAPHY GUIDELINES

ABBREV.	CATEGORY	REVIEWS BEGIN ON PAGE
AN	ANTHOLOGY	225
GC	GOLF COURSE	227
EQ	EQUIPMENT	230
ES	ESSAYS	232
F	FICTION	233
H	HISTORY	234
I	INSTRUCTIONAL	
R	REFERENCE	237
RU	RULES	

See page 224 for "How To Use This Chapter"

ELLIOTT, LEN & KELLY, BARBARA
  Who's Who in Golf: 1976, R, under $15
ELLIS, WES
  All-Weather Golf: 1967, I, under $15
EMERY, DAVID
  Who's Who in International Golf: 1983, R, under $15
EMERY, FRED
  Colonel Bogey's Coloring Book for Golfers: 1983, F, under $15
ENGLISH GOLF UNION *ANNUAL*
  English Golf Union Yearbook (Title Varies): 1932 +, R, under $15
ESCRITT, J.R.
  ABC of Turf Culture: 1978, GC, under $15
EVANS, JR., CHICK
  ✔ Chick Evans' Golf Book: The Story of the Sporting Battles of
  the Greatest, etc. . . . : 1921, H, $15-40
  ✔ Chick Evans' Golf Book: The Story of the Sporting Battles
  Etc. . . . (Limited Edition): 1921, H, $140-400
  ✔ Chick Evans' Golf Book (Reprint): 1978, H, $15-40
  Golf For Boys and Girls: 1954, I, $15-40
  Chick Evans' Golf Secrets: 1922, I, $15-40
  Tee, Fairway and Green: 1926, I, $15-40
EVANS, JR., CHICK & PAYNE, BARRIE
  Ida Broke: The Humor and Philosophy of Golf: 1929, AN, $15-40
EVANS, WEBSTER
  ✔ Encyclopedia of Golf: 1971, R, under $15
  Rubs of the Green: Golf's Triumphs and Tragedies: 1969, AN,
  under $15
EVANS, WEBSTER & SCOTT, TOM
  In Praise of Golf: An Anthology for all Lovers of the Game: 1950,
  AN, under $15
EVERARD, H.S.C.
  Golf: In Theory and Practice: Some Hints to Beginners: 1896, I,
  $40-80
  History of the Royal and Ancient Golf Club, St. Andrews, From
  1754-1900, A: 1907, H, over $400
FALDO, NICK & PLATTS, MITCHELL
  Rough with the Smooth, The: 1980, H, under $15
FALL, R. G.
  Golfing in Southern Africa: 1958, GC, $15-40
  History of Golf at the Cape: In Which is also Treated the Origin
  of the Game, etc. . . . : 1918, H, $140-400
FARLEY, G. A.
  Golf Course Common Sense: 1931, GC, $40-80
FARRAR, GUY B.
  Royal Liverpool Golf Club: A History 1869-1932, The: 1933, H,
  $80-140
FARRELL, JOHNNY
  If I Were in Your Golf Shoes: 1951, I, under $15
  Weekend Golfer, The: 1952, I, under $15
FARRELL, MAJOR J.
  Golf: 1930, I, $15-40
FAULKNER, MAX
  Golf — Right from the Start: 1965, I, under $15
  Play Championship Golf all your Life: 1972, I, under $15
FAULKNER, MAX & STANLEY, LOUIS T.
  Faulkner Method, The: 1952, I, under $15
FENN, H.B.
  Box of Matches: Containing Forty Ways to Play Golf, or, the
  Handicapper's Hoyle, A: 1922, I, $15-40
FERGUSON, J.C.
  Royal and Ancient Game of Golf, The: 1908, AN, $80-140
FERRIER, JIM
  Low Score Golf, Little Sports Library: 1948, I, under $15
FINE, BENJAMIN & FINE, HOWARD
  Fine Method of Golf, The: 1957, I, under $15

FINGER, JOSEPH S.
  Business End of Building or Rebuilding a Golf Course, The: 1972,
  GC, under $15
FINSTERWALD, DOW
  Wedges, Pitching and Sand, The: 1965, I, under $15
FINSTERWALD, DOW & ROBINSON, LARRY
  Fundamentals of Golf: 1961, I, under $15
FISHMAN, LEW & GOLF, EDITORS OF
  Short Cuts to Better Golf: 1979, I, under $15
FITCH, GEORGE
  Golf for the Beginner: 1909, I, $15-40
FITZPATRICK, H.L.
  Golf Don'ts: Admonitions That Will Help the Novice to Play Well
  etc. . . . : 1900, I, $40-80
FLAHERTY, TOM
  Masters: The Story of Golf's Greatest Tournament, The: 1961, H,
  under $15
  U.S. Open, 1895-1965: The Complete Story of the United States
  Championship of Golf, The: 1966, H, under $15
FLANNERY, JEROME
  American Cricket Annual and Golf Guide: 1898-1901, R, $40-80
FLEMING, D. HAY
  Historical Notes and Extracts Concerning The Links of St.
  Andrews, 1552-1893: 1893, H, $140-400
FLETCHER, CHARLES
  How to Play Bad Golf: 1935, F, under $15
FLICK, JIM & AULTMAN, DICK
  Square-To-Squre Golf in Pictures: 1974, I, under $15
FLINT, VIOLET (Pseudonym for THOMPSON, COL. J.E.)
  Golfing Idyll, A: 1892, F, $140-400
  Golfing Idyll, A (Reprint): 1978, F, $15-40
FLOYD, CHANNING
  Little Golf Teacher, The: 1925, I, under $15
FLOYD, FRANK HARRIS
  Mechanics of the Golf Swing, The: 1927, I, under $15
FOLLOW THROUGH
  Essence of Golf, The: 1954, I, under $15
FORD, DOUG
  Brainy Way to Better Golf, The: 1960, I, under $15
  Getting Started in Golf: 1964, I, under $15
  How I Play Inside Golf: 1960, I, under $15
  Start Golf Young: 1955, I, under $15
  Wedge Book, The: 1964, I, under $15
FORGAN, ROBERT, JR. *ANNUAL*
  Golfers Handbook, Including History of the Game, . . . etc.:
  1881-1886, AN, $140-400
  Golfers Manual, The (New Title For Above): 1897 +, AN,
  $140-400
FORMAT PUBLICATIONS
  Fairways: A Detailed Graphic Description of All Los
  Angeles. . . Golf Courses: 1967, GC, under $15
FORREST, JAMES
  Basis of the Golf Swing, The: 1925, I, $15-40
  Golf Made Easy: 1933, I, $15-40
  Golf Stroke, The: 1930, I, $15-40
  Natural Golfer: Hand Action in Games, A: 1938, I, $15-40
FORSE, HARRY
  Seventy Second Hole, The: 1976, F, under $15
FOSTER, CY
  Golf is Easy: 1950, I, under $15
FOUR MASTERS, THE & SARAZEN & SHUTE & GULDAHL
  & REVOLTA
  From Tee to Cup: 1937, I, under $15
FOURTEEN CHAMPIONS
  Golfmasters: A Sure Way To Better Golf, 14 Champions Write A
  Book: 1940, I, under $15

FOWLIE, PETER
    Science of Golf: A Study in Movement, The: 1922, I, under $15
    Technique of the Golf Swing, The: 1934, I, under $15
FOX, G. D.
    Golfer's Pocket Tip Book, 1915, I, under $15
FOX, WILLIAM PRICE
    Doctor Golf: 1963, F, under $15
FRALEY, OSCAR
    Golf in Action: 1952, I, under $15
FRANCIS, JOE
    Dutch Open Champion, 1959, 'Papwa' Sewsunker Sewgoolum: 1959, H, under $15
FRANCIS, RICHARD S.
    Golf: Its Rules and Decisions: 1937, RU, $15-40
FRANKENBERG, H.X.M.
    Golf Made Easy: 1948, I, under $15
FRASER, GEORGE
    McAuslan in the Rough: 1976, F, under $15
FREDERICKS, VIC
    For Golfers Only: 1964, F, under $15
FROME, DAVID
    ✔ Murder on the Sixth Hole, The: 1931, F, under $15
FULFORD, HARRY
    Golf's Little Ironies: 1919, F, $15-40
    Potted Golf: 1910, F, under $15
G.A.
    Pen and Pencil Sketches on the Game of Golf: 1888, GC, over $400
G.B.W.
    Phraseology of Golf: Illustrated by Outlines and Adapted by G.B.W.: 1893, F, $80-140
GALIN, SAUL
    Golf in Europe: 1967, GC, under $15
GALLICO, PAUL
    Golf is a Friendly Game: 1942, F, $15-40
GALLWEY, W. TIMOTHY
    Inner Game of Golf, The: 1981, I, under $15
GALVANO, PHIL
    Secrets of Accurate Putting and Chipping: 1957, I, under $15
    Secrets of the Perfect Golf Swing: 1961, I, under $15
GAMBATESE, JOE *ANNUAL*
    Golf Guide: 1963 +, R, under $15
GAMBATESE, JOSEPH
    World Wide Golf Directory: 1977, F, under $15
GARDNER, DON
    Don Gardner's Golf Book: Three Point Method: 1947, I, under $15
GARRITY, J.T.
    Golfer's Guide to Florida Courses: 1973, GC, under $15
GASKELL, BUD
    Golf At A Glance: 1958: F, under $15
GAULT, W.K.
    Practical Golf Greenkeeping,: 1913, GC, $15-40
GAULT, WILLIAM C.
    ✔ Long Green,, The: 1965, F, under $15
GEDGE, MICHAEL
    Holiday Golf in Spain & Portugal: 1970, GC, under $15
GEIBERGER, AL & DENNIS, LARRY
    Tempo: Golf's Master Key: 1980, I, under $15
GENERAL, THE (Pseudonym for HEYWOOD, ERNEST)
    Golf and How to Play It: 1910, I, $15-40
GIBBINS, JAMES
    Sudden Death: 1983, F, under $15

GIBSON, NEVIN
    Encyclopedia of Golf: 1958, R, under $15
    Great Moments in Golf: 1973, H, under $15
    Pictorial History of Golf, A: 1968, H, $15-40
GIBSON, NEVIN & KOUZMENOFF, TOM
    Golf's Greatest Shots by the World's Greatest Golfers: 1981, AN, under $15
GILL, HOWARD
    Fun in the Rough from Golf Digest: 1957, F, under $15
    Golf Digest Annual: 1956 +, R, under $15
GILSON, C.J.L.
    Golf: Warne's 'Recreation' Books: 1928, H, under $15
GLADSTONE, DR. IRVING A.
    Confessions of a Golfer in Search of No-Fault Insurance: 1977, F, under $15
GLEASON, DAN
    Great, The Grand and the Also-Ran, The: 1976, H, under $15
GLYNES, MR. WEBSTER
    Maiden: A Golfing Epic, The: 1893, F, $80-140
    Windmill: A Golfing Poem, The: 1893, F, $80-140
GOLF DIGEST, EDITORS OF
    80 5-Minute Golf Lessons: 1968, I, under $15
    All About Putting: 1973, I, under $15
    Arnold Palmer: 1967, H, under $15
    Best of Golf Digest: The First 25 Years, The: 1975, AN, under $15
    Better Golf for Boys: 1965, I, under $15
    Golf: A Golden Pocket Guide: 1968, I, under $15
    How To Break 90 at Golf: 1967, I, under $15
    Instant Golf Lessons: 1978, I, under $15
    Rand McNally Golf Course Guide: 1966, GC, under $15
    Traveler's Guide to Golf: 1976, GC, under $15
GOLF FOUNDATION, THE
    Making Room for Golf: 1964, GC, under $15
GOLF MAGAZINE, EDITORS OF
    America's Golf Book: 1970, AN, under $15
    Golf Magazine's Handbook of Putting: 1973, I, under $15
    Tips From the Teaching Pros: 1969, I, under $15
GOLF RESEARCH INSTITUTE
    Guaranteed Golf Lesson: How to Hit Straight Shots, How to Hit Long Shots etc . . . . : 1974, I, under $15
    Guaranteed Golf Lessons: 1975, I, under $15
GOLF WORLD MAGAZINE (BRITISH) & VARIOUS CONTRIBUTORS
    ✔ Picadilly World of Golf, 1972-1975, The: 1972, R, under $15
GOLF WORLD, EDITORS OF & TAYLOR, DICK
    World of Golf 1973, The: 1973, R, under $15
GOLFER'S RECORD COMPANY
    Golfer's Record 1903, The: 1903, R, $40-80
GOLFER, A (Pseudonym for ROBB, GEORGE)
    Historical Gossip about Golf and Golfers: 1863, H, over $400

BIBLIOGRAPHY GUIDELINES

See page 224 for "How To Use This Chapter"

GOLFERS MAGAZINE
  Grip In Golf, The: 1922, I, $15-40
GOLFING MAGAZINE
  Golfing Yearbook: 1923, R, $15-40
GOODNER, ROSS
  ✓ Golf's Greatest: 1978, H, under $15
GORDIN, RICHARD D.
  Golf Fundamentals: 1973, I, under $15
GORDON, BOB
  Basic Golf: 1974, I, under $15
GORDON, CHARLES A.
  Gordon Caddie Guide, The: 1921, R, under $15
  Ten Commandments of the Golf Stroke: 1930, I, under $15
GORDON, HUGH M.
  Repair Your Own Golf Clubs: 1959, EQ, under $15
GORDON, JOHN
  Understandable Golf: 1926, I, $15-40
GOTTLIEB, HARRY
  Golf for Southpaws: 1953, I, under $15
GRAFF, STAN
  So You Want to Play Golf?: 1974,
  I, under $15
GRAFFIS, HERB
  Dictionary of Golf Information: 1960, R, under $15
  Easy Cures for your Ailing Golf: 1949C, I, under $15
  Esquire's World of Golf: 1965, AN, under $15
  Golf Lessons: The Fundamentals as Taught by Foremost Professional Instructors: 1960, I, under $15
  ✓ PGA: Official History of the Professional Golfers' Association of America, The: 1975, H, $15-40
  Planning the Professional's Shop: 1951, R, under $15
GRAHAM, A.S.
  Graham's Golf Club: 1965, F, under $15
GRAHAM, ALEX
  Please Sir, I've Broken My Arm: 1959, F, under $15
GRAHAM, LOU
  Mastering Golf: 1978, I, under $15
GRANT, ARTHUR
  Golf: The Pocket Professional: 1930, I, under $15
GRANT, DONALD
  Donald Ross of Pinehurst and Royal Dornoch: 1973, H, under $15
GRAVES, CHARLES & LONGHURST, HENRY
  Candid Caddies: 1935, F, $15-40
GRAY, MAXWELL
  Great Refusal: A Novel, The: 1906, F, $15-40
GREEN, MICHAEL
  Art of Coarse Golf, The: 1967, F, under $15
GREEN, SANDY
  Don'ts for Golfers: 1925, I, under $15
GREENE, KELL
  Golf Swing of Bobby Jones, The: 1931, I, $15-40
GREENSHAW, WAYNE
  Golfer, The: 1967, F, under $15
GREENWOOD, GEORGE W.
  Golf Really Explained: 1926, I, under $15
GREGSON, MALCOLM
  Golf With Gregson: 1968, I, under $15
GREGSTON, GREG
  Ben Hogan: The Man Who Played for Glory: 1978, H, under $15
GRESSWELL, PETER
  Week-End Golfer: 1977, I, under $15
GRIERSON, JAMES
  Delineation of St. Andrews: Being a Particular Account of Every Thing Remarkable etc.: 1833, H, over $400

GRIFFITHS, E.M.
  With Club and Caddie: 1909, F, $40-80
GRIMSLEY, WILL
  Golf: Its History, People and Events: 1966, H, $15-40
GROSS, MILTON
  Eighteen Holes in My Head: 1959, F, under $15
GROUT, JACK & AULTMAN, DICK
  Let Me Teach You Golf as I Taught Jack Nicklaus: 1975, I, under $15
GUINEY, DAVID
  Dunlop Book of Golf, The: 1973, R, under $15
GULDAHL, RALPH
  Groove Your Golf: Cine-Sports Library: 1939, I, $15-40
GULLICK, BILL
  Country Club Caper, The: 1971, F, under $15
GUNDELFINGER, PHIL, JR.
  Golf's Who's Who: 'Records of the Pros', 1958: 1958, R, under $15
GUNN, DR. HARRY E.
  How To Play Golf with Your Wife and Survive: 1976, F, under $15
GUSTAVSON, LEALAND
  Enjoy Your Golf: 1954, I, under $15
HAAS, HARRY J.
  Handbook for Caddies & Members: Teaching the Caddies by Illustration, etc. . . . : 1922, R, under $15
HABER, JAMES
  Golf Made Easy: How to Achieve a Consistently Effective Golf Swing: 1974, I, under $15
  Mastering the Art of Winning Golf: 1976, I under $15
HACKBARTH, JOHN C.
  Discipline System of Golf, The: 1928, I, $15-40
  Key to Better Golf: A Mental Plan, The: 1929, I, $15-40
HACKETT, BUDDY
  Truth About Golf: And Other Lies, The: 1968, F, under $15
HAGEN, WALTER & HECK, MARGARET SEATON
  Walter Hagen Story, The: 1956, H, $15-40
  Walter Hagen Story, The (Reprint): 1978, H, $15-40
HAHN, PAUL
  Paul Hahn Shows you How to Play Trouble Shots: 1965, I, under $15
HALIBURTON, THOMAS
  Rabbit Into Tiger: 1964, I, under $15
HALL, HOLWORTHY
  ✓ Dormie One, and Other Golf Stories: 1917, F, $15-40
HALLEM, A.E.
  Straight Road to Golf: How to Become an Accomplished Player, The: 1928, I, under $15
HAMILTON, DAVID
  Good Golf Guide to Scotland: 1982, GC, under $15
HAMILTON, EDWARD A. & PRESTON, CHARLES
  Golfing America: 1958, GC, $15-40
HAMMERTON, J.A.
  Mr. Punch's Golf Stories: Told by His Merry Men, No. 19 of etc. . . . : 1909, F, $15-40
  Rubaiyat of a Golfer, The: 1946, F, under $15
HAMMOND, DARYN
  Golf Swing: The Ernest Jones Method, The: 1920, I, under $15
HANDY, IKE S.
  How to Hit a Golf Ball Straight: 1967, I, under $15
  It's the Damned Ball: 1951, I, under $15
HARDCASTLE, MICHAEL
  Aim for the Flag (A Novel): 1969, F, under $15

HARE, BURNHAM
Golfing Swing Simplified and its Mechanism Correctly Explained, The: 1913, I, $15-40
HARNEY, PAUL
How to Putt: 1965, I, under $15
HARRIS, MARK G.
New Angles on Putting and Chip Shots: 1940, I, under $15
HARRIS, RICHARD
How to Take The Fun out of Golf: 1970, F, under $15
HARRIS, ROBERT
Sixty Years of Golf: 1953, H, $15-40
HART, AL
Golfun: A Humorous Approach to a Serious Subject: 1966, F, under $15
HATTSTROM, H.A.
Golf After Forty: 1946, I, under $15
In-Line Method of Putting and Approaching, The: 1959, I, under $15
HAULTAIN, ARNOLD
↙ Mystery of Golf: A Briefe Account of Games in General, etc...., The: 1908, ES, $140-400
↙ Mystery of Golf: A Briefe Account of Games in General, etc...., The (Reprint): 1965, ES, $15-40
HAWKES, KEN
BBC Book of Golf, The: 1975, R, under $15
HAWTREE, F.W.
Golf Course: Planning, Design, Construction & Maintenance, The: 1983, GC, $15-40
HAY, ALEX
Golf Manual, The: 1980, F, under $15
Mechanics of Golf: 1979, I, under $15
Skill & Tactics of Golf: 1980, I, under $15
HAYNIE, SANDRA & LYNCH, JAMES & COLLINS, CAROL
Golf: A Natural Course for Women: 1975, I, under $15
HAYWOOD, JOHN C.
Silver Cleek, The: 1910, F, $80-140
HAEGER, RONALD
Kings of Clubs: 1968, H, under $15
HECKER, GENEVIEVE & ADAIR, RHONA K.
Golf for Women: 1902, I, $80-140
HEISE, JACK G.
How you can Play Better Golf Using Self-Hypnosis: 1961, I, under $15
Super Golf with Self Hypnosis: 1962, I, under $15
HELME, ELEANOR E.
After The Ball: Merry Memories of a Golfer, etc....: 1925, H, $15-40
Best of Golf, by Some Best of the Golfers, The: 1925, I, $15-40
Family Golf: 1938, F, under $15
Lady Golfer's Tip Book: 1923, I, $15-40
HENDERSON, IAN T. & STIRK, DAVID I.
↙ Compleat Golfer: An Illustrated History of the Royal and Ancient Game, The: 1982, EQ & H, under $15
↙ Golf in the Making: 1979, GC & H, under $15
Shortspoon: F. P. Hopkins, Golf Artist and Journalist: 1983, H, $80-140
HENNING, HAROLD
Driving Around Southern Africa with Harold Henning: 1974, ES, under $15
HEPBURN, TOM & JACOBSON, SELWYN
America's Most Difficult Golf Holes: 1983, GC, under $15
Australia's Most Difficult Golf Holes: 1983, GC, under $15
Great Britain and Ireland's Most Difficult Golf Holes: 1983, GC, under $15
Great Golf Holes of New Zealand: 1981, GC, under $15

HERD, ALEXANDER & FOSTER, CLYDE
Golfing Life, My: 1923, H, $40-80
HERMANSON, ROGER H.
Rules of Golf in Programmed Form, The: 1968, RU, under $15
HERNDON, CHARLES
Golf Made Easier: 1930, I, $15-40
HEROLD, DONALD
Adventures in Golf or How to Golf Your Troubles Away: 1966, F, under $15
Love That Golf: It Can Be Better Than You Think: 1952, F, under $15
HEUER, KARLA L. & McKAY, JR., CECIL
Golf Courses: A Guide to Analysis and Valuation: 1980, GC, under $15
HEXTER, PAUL
You Can Play Golf Forever: 1979, I, under $15
HEZLET, MAY
Ladies Golf: 1904, I, $40-80
HICKS, ELIZABETH MARY & GRIFFIN, ELLEN J.
Golf Manual for Teachers: 1949, I, $15-40
HILL, DAVE & SEITZ, NICK
Teed Off: 1977, H, under $15
HILL, J. C. H.
Lyre On The Links and Other Verses, The: 1935, F, $15-40
HILLINTHORN, GERALD
↙ Your First Game of Golf: 1891, F, $140-400
HILTON, HAROLD H.
Golfing Remembrances, My: 1907, H, $80-140
Modern Golf: 1913, I, $15-40
HILTON, HAROLD H. & SMITH, GARDEN C.
↙ Royal and Ancient Game of Golf, The: 1912, AN, over $400
↙ Royal and Ancient Game of Golf, The (Limited Edition): 1912, AN, Scarce
HIME, MAURICE C.
Unlucky Golfer: His Handbook in Verse, The: 1904, F, $15-40
HITCHCOCK, JIMMY
Master Golfer: 1967, H, under $15
HOBBS, MICHAEL
50 Masters Of Golf: 1983, H, under $15
Golf for the Connoissieur: 1978, ES, under $15
Great Opens: Historic British and American Championships: 1976, H, under $15
In Celebration of Golf: 1982, AN, under $15
HOBBS, MICHAEL & ALLISS, PETER
Golf to Remember: 1978, H, under $15
HOBSON, WILLIAM G.
It Ain't Necessarily So: Letters from Willie Appleseed etc....: 1959, F, under $15
HOGAN, BEN
Power Golf: 1948, I, under $15
HOGAN, BEN & ARMOUR & MIDDLECOFF & SNEAD
Complete Guide to Golf, The: 1955, I, under $15

BIBLIOGRAPHY GUIDELINES

ABBREV.	CATEGORY	REVIEWS BEGIN ON PAGE
AN	ANTHOLOGY	225
GC	GOLF COURSE	227
EQ	EQUIPMENT	230
ES	ESSAYS	232
F	FICTION	233
H	HISTORY	234
I	INSTRUCTIONAL	
R	REFERENCE	237
RU	RULES	

See page 224 for "How To Use This Chapter"

HOGAN, BEN & WIND, HERBERT WARREN
Modern Fundamentals of Golf, The: 1957, I, under $15
HON, BILLY
Prominent Golfers in Caricature: 1930, F, $40-80
HONORABLE SECRETARY, THE *ANNUAL*
The Ladies Golf Union Annual (Title Varies): 1894 +, R, under $15
HOOPER, RICHARD W.
Game of Golf in East Africa, The: 1953, H, $80-140
HOPKINS, ANTHONY
Songs for Swinging Golfers: 1981, F, under $15
HOPKINS, FRANK
Golf Holes They Talk About: 1927, GC, $40-80
HOPKINS, JOHN
Beacon Golfing Handbook: 1983, R, under $15
HOPKINSON, CECIL
✓ Collecting Golf Books, 1743-1938: 1938, R, $80-140
✓ Collecting Golf Books, 1743-1938 (Reprint): 1980, R, $15-40
HORNABROOK, JOHN
Golden Years of New Zealand Golf, The: 1967, H, under $15
HORTON, CHESTER
Better Golf: 1930, I, under $15
HORTON, THOMAS
Golf: The Long Game: 1969, I, under $15
Golf: The Short Game: 1970, I, under $15
HOTCHKISS, HORACE L.
Origin and Organization of the Senior's Tournament: 1922, H, under $15
HOUGHTON, GEORGE
Addict in Bunkerland: 1962, F, under $15
Addict's Guide to British Golf: A County-by-County etc. . . . AN 1959, GC, under $15
Believe It or Not — That's Golf: A Miscellany, etc. . . . : 1974, R, under $15
Confessions of a Golf Addict: 1952, F, under $15
Confessions of a Golf Addict: An Anthology of Carefree etc. . . . : 1959, F, under $15
Full Confessions of a Golf Addict, The: 1966, F, under $15
Golf Addict Among the Irish: 1965, GC, under $15
Golf Addict Among the Scots: 1967, GC, under $15
Golf Addict Goes East: 1967, GC, under $15
Golf Addict in Gaucho Land: 1970, GC, under $15
Golf Addict Invades Wales: 1969, GC, under $15
Golf Addict Strikes Again: 1963, F, under $15
Golf Addict Visits the USA: 1955, F, under $15
Golf Addicts Galore: 1968, F, under $15
Golf Addicts on Parade: 1959, F, under $15
Golf Addicts Through the Ages: 1956, F, under $15
Golf on my Pillow: Midnight Letters to a Son in Foreign Parts: 1958, F, under $15
Golf With a Whippy Shaft: The Best of George Houghton: 1971, F, under $15
Golfer's Treasury: A Personal Anthology: 1964, AN, under $15
Golfers in Orbit: 1968, F, under $15
How To Be a Golf Addict: 1971, F, under $15
I Am a Golf Widow, A Frank Confession to George Houghton: 1961, F, under $15
Just a Friendly. . . A Book of Golf Addict Cartoons: 1973, F, under $15
More Confessions of a Golf Addict: 1954, F, under $15
Portrait of a Golf Addict: A Monograph in Words etc. . . : 1960, F, under $15
Secret Diary of a Golf Addict's Caddie, The: 1964, F, under $15
Truth About Golf Addicts: An Anthology of Carefree etc. . . . , The: 1957, F, under $15

HOUGHTON, GEORGE & SIMMONS, HUBERT
Golfer's A.B.C.: A Golfpabit for Addicts: 1953, F, under $15
HOVANESIAN, DR. ARCHIE
Golf is Mental: 1960, ES, under $15
HOWARD, ROBERT ENDERSBY
Lessons from Great Golfers: 1924, I, $15-40
HUDSON, D.C.N.
Your Book of Golf: 1967, I, under $15
HUGGETT, BRIAN & WHITBOURNE, JOHN
Better Golf: 1964, I, under $15
HUGGINS, PERCY
Golfer's Miscellany, The: 1971, AN, under $15
HUGHES, HENRY
Golf for the Late Beginner: 1911, I, under $15
Golf Practice for Players of Limited Leisure: 1913, I, under $15
HUGHES, W. E.
Chronicles of the Blackheath Golfers, with Illustrations etc . . . : 1897, H, Scarce
HUGMAN, ROBERT H.H.
Putting Know-How: 1963, I, under $15
HUMPHREYS, ERIC
Dunlop Golfer's Companion, The: 1977, AN, under $15
HUNT, ORRIN T.
Joy of Golf, The: 1977, ES, under $15
HUNTER, DAVID SMITH
Golf Simplified: Cause and Effect: 1921, I, under $15
HUNTER, MAC
Golf for Beginners: 1973, I, under $15
HUNTER, ROBERT
✓ Links, The: 1926, GC, $80-140
HUSTON, MERVYN J.
Golf and Murphy's Law: 1981, F, under $15
Great Golf Humor: 1977, F, under $15
HUTCHINSON HORACE
After Dinner Golf: 1896, F, $80-140
Aspects of Golf: 1900, F, $80-140
Bert Edward, The Golf Caddie: 1903, F, $80-140
British Golf Links: A Short Account of the Leading Golf Links of the United Kingdom: 1897, GC, over $400
British Golf Links: A Short Account of the Leading Golf Links etc. . . . (Limited Edition): 1897, GC, Scarce
✓ Fifty Years of Golf: 1919, H, $80-140
Golf: A Complete History of the Game, Etc.: 1900, H, $15-40
Golf Greens and Greenkeeping, The Country Life Library of Sport: 1906, GC, $80-140
Golfing Pilgrim on Many Links, The: 1898, F, $80-140
Golfing: The "Oval" Series of Games: 1893, AN, $40-80
Hints on the Game of Golf (14 Editions): 1886, I, $40-400 (varies)
HUTCHINSON, HORACE & EVERARD & LANG & OTHERS
Famous Golf Links: 1891, GC, $140-400
HUTCHINSON, HORACE & OTHERS
Book of Golf and Golfers, The: 1899, AN, $40-80
✓ Golf, The Badminton Library: 1890 +, AN & EQ, $40-80
✓ Golf, The Badminton Library (Limited Edition): 1890, AN & EQ, over $400
New Book of Golf, The: 1912, AN, $40-80
HUTCHISON, JOCK
Better Golf: 1928, I, $15-40
Twelve Golf Lessons: The Best Advice from Many of the Game's Most Famous Instructors: 1929, I, $15-40
HYSLOP, THEO B.
Mental Handicaps in Golf: 1927, ES, $15-40
I.P.C. BUSINESS PRESS
Guide to Golf Courses in the U.K.: 1973, GC, under $15

IDOUX, CLETE
Play Better Golf: 1966, I, under $15
IGNOTUS
Golf in a Nutshell: 1919, I, $15-40
IGOE, JR., JAMES
Hooks and Slices: A Parody on Golf: 1950, F, under $15
INGHAM, JOHN
Best Golfing Jokes: 1969, F, under $15
IRWIN, HALE & MACKIE, KEITH
Play Better Golf: 1980, I, under $15
IRWIN, J.F.
Golf Sketches: 1892, F, $80-140
ITO, CHO
Golfer's Treasures: Being an Alphabetical Arrangement of
Theories and Hints, . . . etc: 1925, AN, $140-400
J.A.C.K. (Pseudonym for J. McCULLOUGH)
⌐ Golf in the Year 2000, Or What We Are Coming To: 1892, F,
$140-400
⌐ Golf in the Year 2000, Or What We Are Coming To (Reprint):
1984, F, $15-40
J.F.T.
From a Hundred and Two to Eight-Two in a Month or Two:
1934, I, under $15
JACKLIN, TONY
Golf with Tony Jacklin: 1978, I, under $15
Jacklin: The Champion's Own Story: 1970, H, under $15
JACKLIN, TONY & DOBEREINER, PETER
Jacklin's Golf Secret: 1983, I, under $15
JACKLIN, TONY & REID, IAIN
100 Jacklin Golfstrips from The Daily Express: 1972, I, under $15
JACKLIN, TONY & WOOD, JACK
Golf Step by Step: 1970, I, under $15
Golf with Tony Jacklin: 1969, I, under $15
JACKSON, DAVID
Golf Songs and Recitations: 1886, F, $140-400
JACKSON, ROBERT B.
Supermex: The Lee Trevino Story: 1973, H, under $15
JACOBS, JOHN & AULTMAN, DICK
Golf Doctor: 1979, I, under $15
Quick Cures for Weekend Golfers: 1979, I, under $15
JACOBS, JOHN & BOWDEN, KEN
John Jacobs Analyses Golf's Superstars: 1974, I, under $15
Practical Golf: 1972, I, under $15
JACOBS, JOHN & STOBBS, JOHN
Golf: 1963, I, under $15
JAMES, JOSEPH
How to Give up Golf: 1970, F, under $15
Kill it Before it Moves: How not to Play Golf in Several etc. . .:
1961, F, under $15
Quiet on the Tee: 1963, F, under $15
So You're Taking Up Golf?: 1969, F, under $15
What it is, is Golf: 1965, F, under $15
JENKINS, DAN
Best 18 Golf Holes in America, The: 1966, GC, $15-40
Dead Solid Perfect: 1974, F, under $15
Dogged Victims of Inexorable Fate, The: 1970, ES, under $15
JEROME, OWEN FOX
Golf Club Murder, The: 1929, F, $15-40
JESSOP, J.C.
Teach Yourself Golf: 1950, I, under $15
JOHNSON, CAROL CLARK & JOHNSTONE, ANN CASEY
Golf — A Positive Approach: 1975, I, under $15
JOHNSON, W.O. & WILLIAMSON, N.P.
Whatta Girl: The Babe Didrickson Story: 1977, H, under $15

JONES, BOB
British Golf Odyssey: 1977, GC, under $15
Gulls on the Golf Course: 1975, F, under $15
Sherlock Holmes, the Golfer: 1981, F, under $15
JONES, ERNEST & BROWN, INNIS
Swinging into Golf: 1937, I, under $15
JONES, ERNEST & EISENBERG, DAVID
Swing the Clubhead: 1952, I, under $15
JONES JR., ROBERT TYRE
Bobby Jones on the Basic Golf Swing: 1969, I, under $15
Bobby Jones on Golf: 1930, I, $15-40
Bobby Jones on Golf (Different than above): 1966, I, $15-40
Golf is My Game: 1960, H, under $15
How to Play Golf: 1929, I, $15-40
My Twelve Most Difficult Shots: 1927, I, $40-80
Rights and Wrongs of Golf: 1936, I, $15-40
JONES, JR., ROBERT TYRE & KEELER, O.B.
⌐ Down The Fairway: The Life and Play of Robert T. Jones, Jr.:
1927, H, $15-40
⌐ Down The Fairway: The Life and Play of Robert T. Jones, Jr.
(Limited Edition): 1927, H, $140-400
JONES, JR., ROBERT TYRE & LOWE, HAROLD
Group Instruction in Golf: A Handbook for Schools and Colleges:
1939, I, $15-40
JONES, JR., ROBERT TYRE & OTHERS
Short Cuts to Par Golf: 1931, I, $15-40
JONES, REES L. & RANDO, GUY L.
Golf Course Development: 1974, GC, under $15
JONES, ROBERT TRENT
Golf Course Architecture: 1936, GC, $80-140
Great Golf Stories: 1982, AN, $15-40
KAHN, LIZ
Tony Jacklin: The Price of Success: 1979, H, under $15
KAPLAN, JIM
⌐ Hillerich & Bradsby: History — Catalogs: 1983, EQ, under $15
⌐ MacGregor Golf: History — Catalogs: 1980, EQ, under $15
⌐ Wilson Golf: History — Catalogs: 1981, EQ, under $15
KASKIE, SHIRLI
Woman's Golf Game, A: 1982, I, under $15
KAVANAGH, L. V.
History of Golf in Canada, The: 1973, H, $15-40
KAVANAUGH, JAMES EDWARD
Golf Made Easy: How to Play Without Stress or Strain: 1953, I,
under $15
KEANE, CHRISTOPHER
Tour, The: 1974, ES, under $15
KEELER, O.B.
Boy's Life of Bobby Jones, A: 1931, H, $15-40
KEELER, O.B.
Autobiography of an Average Golfer, The: 1925, H, $15-40
KEEN HAND, A (Pseudonym for FARNIE, HENRY

BROUGHAM)
Golfer's Manual, Being an Historical and Descriptive Account of the National Game, etc . . ., The: 1857, AN, Scarce
Golfer's Manual: Being an Historical and Descriptive Account of the National Game, etc. . . ., The (Reprint): 1947, AN, $140-400

KEENE, FRANCIS BOWLER
Lyrics of the Links: Poetry, Sentiment and Humor of Golf: 1923, F, $15-40

KELLEY, HOMER
Golfing Machine: The Star System of Golf, The: 1971, I, under $15

KELLEY, JAMES E.
Minnesota Golf: 75 Years of Tournament History: 1976, H, under $15

KELLY, G. M.
Golf in New Zealand: A Centennial History: 1971, H, under $15

KEMP, CHARLES F.
Smart Golf: A Study of the Mental and Emotional Side of Golf: 1974, ES, under $15
World of Golf and the Game of Life, The: 1978, ES, under $15

KENNARD, MRS. EDWARD
Golf Lunatic and His Cycling Wife, The: 1902, F, $80-140
Sorrows of a Golfer's Wife, The: 1896, F, $80-140

KENNEDY, DES & GEORGIADES, HARRY
Slice of Fun, A: 1965, F, under $15

KENNEDY, PATRICK
✔ Golf Club Trademarks - American: 1898-1930: 1984, EQ, under $15

KENNINGTON, DON
Sourcebook of Golf, The: 1981, R, under $15

KENT, JOHN HOYT
Rhythm Golf: 1958, I, under $15

KERR, JOHN
✔ Golf Book of East Lothian, The: 1896, H, over $400
✔ Golf Book of East Lothian, The (Limited Edition): 1896, H, Scarce

KIEHL, BOB
Duffer Golf: 1979, F, under $15

KIERNAN, THOMAS
Wood - Irons: 1981, I, under $15

KING, LESLIE
Master-Key to Success at Golf, The: 1962, I, under $15

KINGZETT, C. T.
Evolution of the Rubber-Cored Golf Ball, The: 1904, EQ, $40-80

KIRKALDY, ANDREW & FOSTER, CLYDE
Fifty Years of Golf: My Memories: 1921, H, $40-80

KIRKWOOD, JOE & FEY, BARBARA
Links of Life, The: 1973, H, under $15

KLEIN, DAVE
Golf's Big Three: 1972, H, under $15
Great Moments In Golf: 1971, H, under $15

KNEEDLER, ROBERT G.
Golfitis: 1965, F, under $15

KNIGHT, REG & SPICER, SYDNEY
Golf for Beginners: 1970, I, under $15
Learn Golf Backwards: 1965, I, under $15

KNIGHT, WILLIAM ANGUS
On the Links: Being Golfing Stories by Various Hands with Shakespeare on Golf etc . . .: 1889, F, $80-140
Shakespeare on Golf: With Special Reference to St. Andrews Links: 1885, F, $140-400

KNIGHT, WILLIAM ANGUS & OLIPHANT, T.T.
Stories of Golf: 1894, F, $40-80

KNOX, E. V.
Mr. Punch on the Links: 1929, F, $15-40

KOSTIS, PETER & DENNIS, LARRY
Inside Path to Better Golf, The: 1982, I, under $15

KRAETZ, REUBEN
Golf in Ten Lessons: With the Rules of Golf and 200 Golfing Tips, etc . . .: 1938, I, under $15

LADIES GOLF UNION . . . BY THE HON. SECRETARY
Ladies Golf Union Annual, The (Title Varies): 1894 +, R, under $15

LANCASTER, H. BOSWELL
Ridiculous Golf: In Story and Verse: 1938, F, under $15

LANGDON, DAVID
How to Play Golf and Stay Happy: 1964, I, under $15
How to Talk Golf: A to Z Glossary of Golf Terms: 1975, R, under $15

LAPHAM, ROBERT
Twenty Year of Life Begins at Forty: The Story of a Unique Golf Tournament: 1972, ES, under $15

LARDNER, GEORGE E.
Cut Your Score: The Book of Commonsense Golf: 1933, I, under $15
Golf Technique Simplified: 1933, I, under $15
How to Play Golf: 1920, I, under $15

LARDNER, REX
Downhill Lies and Other Falsehoods, or How to Play Dirty Golf: 1973, F, under $15
Great Golfers, The: 1970, AN under $15
Out of the Bunker and into the Trees, or The Secret of High-Tension Golf: 1960, F, under $15

LARIAR, LAWRENCE
Golf and Be Damned: 1954, F, under $15
You've Got Me in a Hole: A Collection of the Best Golfing Cartoons: 1955, F, under $15

LAW, JANICE
Death Under Par: 1981, F, under $15

LAWLESS, PETER & VARIOUS
Golfer's Companion, The: 1937, AN, $15-40

LAYARD, G.S.
His Golf Madness and Other "Queer Stories": 1892, F, $80-140

LAYER, A. P.
Simplicity of the Golf Swing, The: 1911, I, $15-40

LAZARO, JOE
Right Touch, The: 1978, I, under $15

LEACH, HENRY
Great Golfers in the Making: Being Autobiographical Accounts etc . . .: 1907, H, $40-80
Happy Golfer: Being Some Experiences, Reflections, etc . . . ., The: 1914, ES, $40-80
Letters of a Modern Golfer to his Grandfather: Being The etc . . . .: etc . . .: 1910, F, $40-80
✔ Spirit of the Links, The: 1907, ES, $40-80

LEE, JAMES P.
Golf and Golfing: A Practical Manual (2nd Printing of Title Below): 1895, I, $140-400
Golf in America: A Practical Manual: 1895, I, over $400

LEE, STAN
Golfers Anonymous: 1961, F, under $15

LEES, PETER W.
Care if the Greens: 1918, GC, $40-80

LEIGH, DELL
Golf at its Best on the L.M.S. (London, Midland & Scottish Railway): 1925, GC, $15-40

LEIGH-BENNETT, E.P.
Errant Golfer, An: 1929, F, $15-40
Some Friendly Fairways: 1930, GC, $15-40
Southern Golf (Golf in the South): 1935, GC, $15-40

LEITCH, CECIL
  Golf: 1922, I, $15-40
  Golf for Girls: 1911, I, $40-80
  Golf Simplified: 1924, I, $15-40
LEMA, TONY
  Inside Story of the Professional Golf Tour (British Edition of Golfer's Gold): 1964, H, under $15
LEMA, TONY & BROWN, GWILYM S.
  Golfer's Gold: An Inside View of the Pro Tour: 1964, H, under $15
LEMA, TONY & HARVEY, BUD
  Champagne Tony's Golf Tips: 1966, I, under $15
  Tony Lema, Champagne Golf (British Edition of Golf Tips): 1966, I, under $15
LEMMON, GEORGE J.
  About Golf: 1941, I, under $15
  Golf Bugs, N.D., F, $15-40
LENG, JOHN
  Leng's Golfer's Manual: 1907, R, $140-400
LIFE MAGAZINE
  Fore! Life's Book for Golfers: 1900, F, $80-140
LINSKILL, W. T.
  Golf: 1889, I, $80-140
LISS, HOWARD
  Masters Tournament, The: 1974, H, under $15
LISTER, DAVID
  I'd Like to Help the World to Swing: 1977, I, under $15
  Ultimate Simplification, The: 1981, I, under $15
LITTLER, GENE
  Long and Medium Irons, The: 1965, I, under $15
LITTLER, GENE & COLLETT, DON
  How to Master the Irons: 1962, I, under $15
LITTLER, GENE & TOBIN, JACK
  Real Score, The: 1976, I, under $15
LOCH, TONY
  Golf is my Mistress: 1981, F, under $15
LOCKE, BOBBY
  Bobby Locke on Golf: 1953, I, under $15
LOCKYER, SIR J. NORMAN & RUTHERFORD, W.
  Rules of Golf: Being the St. Andrews' Rules for the Game, The: 1896, RU, $140-400
LOFFELBEIN, ROBERT L.
  How to Goof-Proof your Game: 1971, I, under $15
LOGUE, JAMES
  Follow the Leader: 1979, F, under $15
LOHREN, CARL & DENNIS, LARRY
  One Move to Better Golf: 1975, I, under $15
LONGHURST, HENRY
  Eurogolf, 1974: 1974, GC, under $15
  Golf: 1937, I, under $15
  Golf Mixture: 1952, H, $15-40
  How to Get Started in Golf: 1967, I, under $15
  It was Good While it Lasted: 1941, H, $15-40
  My Life and Soft Times: 1971, H, $15-40
  Never on Weekdays: 1968, H, $15-40
  Old Course at St. Andrews, The: 1961, GC, under $15
  Only on Sundays: 1964, H, $15-40
  Round in Sixty-Eight: 1953, H, $15-40
  ✓ Talking about Golf: 1966, ES, under $15
LONGHURST, HENRY & COUSINS, GEOFFREY
  Ryder Cup, 1965, The: 1965, H, under $15
LONGO, PETER
  Simplified Golf: There's no Trick to It: 1980, I, under $15
LOOKER, SAMUEL J.
  On the Green: An Anthology for Golfers: 1922, AN, $15-40

LOPEZ, NANCY & SCHWED, PETER
  Education of a Woman Golfer: 1979, I, under $15
LORING, PHILLIP QUINCY
  Rhymes of a Duffer: 1914, F, $15-40
LOW, GEORGE & BARKOW, AL
  Master of Putting, The: 1983, I, under $15
LOW, JOHN L.
  F.G. Tait: A Record, being his Life, Letters and Golfing Diary: 1910, F, $40-80
LOW, JOHN L. & HARMSWORTH, VYVYAN G. *ANNUAL*
  ✓ Nisbet's Golf Year Book: 1905-1914, R, $15-40
LOW, JOHN L. & HILTON, HAROLD H.
  Concerning Golf: 1903, ES, $15-40
LOWE, W. W.
  Bedrock Principles of Golf: 1937, I, $15-40
LUCAS, LADDIE
  Five Up: A Chronicle of Five Lives: 1978, H, under $15
LUCOCK, E.
  Golf Mad: 1981, F, under $15
  Golfing with Lu: 1973, F, under $15
LUXTON, THEODORE
  Dynamics of Golf Correspondence Course, The: 1973, I, under $15
LYLE, SANDY & FERRIER, BOB
  Championship Courses of Scotland, The: 1982, GC, $15-40
LYONS, HARRY & JOHNSON, DICK
  Hazards of Golf, The: 1979, F, under $15
LYTTELTON, R. H.
  Outdoor Games: Cricket & Golf: 1901, AN, $40-80
MacARTHUR, CHARLES
  Golfer's Annual for 1869-70, The: 1870, R, $140-400
MacBETH, JAMES CURRIE
  Golf: Professional Methods, British and American: 1930, F, under $15
MacDONALD, CHARLES BLAIR
  ✓ Scotland's Gift: Golf: Reminiscences 1872-1927: 1928, GC & H, $140-400
  ✓ Scotland's Gift: Golf: Reminiscences 1872-1927 (Limited Edition): 1928, GC & H over $400
MacDONALD, ROBERT G.
  Golf: 1927, I, $15-40
  Golf at a Glance: The Pocket Pro: 1931, I, under $15
MacDONALD, ROBERT G. & BOLSTAD, LES
  Golf Instructor's Guide: 1952, I, under $15
  How to Improve your Golf: 1952, I, under $15
MacLAREN, MUIR
  Australian Golfer's Handbook, 1957, The: 1957, R, $15-40
  Golfer's Bedside Book, The: 1976, AN, under $15
MacLEAN, G.A.
  Golf Through the Ages, or, The History of the Game, From B.C. to 1975 A.D.: 1923, F, $15-40

BIBLIOGRAPHY GUIDELINES

ABBREV.	CATEGORY	REVIEWS BEGIN ON PAGE
AN	ANTHOLOGY	225
GC	GOLF COURSE	227
EQ	EQUIPMENT	230
ES	ESSAYS	232
F	FICTION	233
H	HISTORY	234
I	INSTRUCTIONAL	
R	REFERENCE	237
RU	RULES	

See page 224 for "How To Use This Chapter"

MacLENNON, R. J.
Golf at Gleneagles: 1928, GC, $80-140
MacNAMARA, DR. T. J.
Gentle Golfer, The: 1905, F, $80-140
MacPHERSON, DUNCAN
Golf Simplified: A Graphic Presentation of Practical Golf Instruction etc...: 1936, I, under $15
MacVICAR, ANGUS
Golf In My Galloweses: Confessions Of A Fairway Fanatic: 1983, F, under $15
MACBETH, JAMES CURRIE
Golf from A to Z: 1935, I, under $15
Golf Methods of the Masters: 1934, I, under $15
MACEY, CHARLES A.
Golf through Rhythm: 1957, I, under $15
MACKENZIE, ALISTER
↙ Dr. Mackenzie's Golf Architecture (Reprint): 1982, GC, $15-40
↙ Golf Architecture: Economy in Course Construction and Greenkeeping: 1920, GC, $80-140
MACKERN, MRS. LOUIS & BOYS, M.
Our Lady of the Green (A Book of Ladies Golf): 1899, I, $80-140
MAHONEY, JACK
Golf History of New England, The: 1973, H, under $15
MAIR, LEWINE
Dunlop Lady Golfer's Champion, The: 1980, AN, under $15
MALTBY, RALPH
↙ Golf Club Design, Fitting, Alteration and Repair:, etc...: 1974, EQ, $15-40
↙ Golf Club Repair in Pictures: 1978, EQ, under $15
Golf Club Assembly Manual: 1981, EQ, $40-80
MANGRUM, LLOYD
Golf: A New Approach: 1949, I, under $15
MANGRUM, LLOYD & DYPWICK, OTIS
How to Break 90 at Golf: 1952, I, under $15
How to Play Better Golf: 1954, I, under $15
MANION, JAMES S.
Culbertson's Contract Golf: 1932, F, $15-40
MANN, FREDERICK GEORGE
Lord Rutherford on the Golf Course: 1976, F, under $15
MANNING, REG
From Tee to Cup: 1954, F, $15-40
MAPPIN, MAJOR G. F.
Golfing You, The: 1948, I, under $15
MARIETTA
Six Golfing Stories: 1905, F, $40-80
MARKS, SARA W.
Fore! ...Women Only: An Anatomy of a Woman's Golf Club: 1966, R, under $15
MARR, DAVID
Woods from Tee and Fairway: 1965, I, under $15
MARSH, THOMAS
Blackheath Golfing Lays: 1873, F, over $400
MARSHALL, KEITH
Golf Galore: 1960, H, under $15
MARSHALL, ROBERT
Enchanted Golf Clubs, The (American edition of below): 1920, F, $15-40
Haunted Major, The (Many Editions): 1902, F, $15-40
MARTIN, H. B.
Fifty Years of American Golf: 1936, H, $140-400
Fifty Years of American Golf (Limited Edition): 1936, H. $140-400
Fifty Years of American Golf (Reprint): 1966, H, $15-40
Golf for Beginners: Easy Lessons for the Novice, etc....: 1930, I, under $15
Golf Made Easy: 1932, I, under $15

Golf Yarns: The Best Things about the Game of Golf: 1913, AN, $15-40
Great Golfers in the Making: 1932, I, $15-40
How to Play Golf: 1936, I, $15-40
Pictorial Golf: Practical Instruction for the Beginner etc...: 1928, I, under $15
What's Wrong with your Game: 1930, I, $15-40
MARTIN, JOHN STUART
↙ Curious History of the Golf Ball: Mankind's Most Fascinating Sphere, The: 1968, EQ, $15-40
↙ Curious History of the Golf Ball: Mankind's Most Fascinating Sphere, The (Limited Edition): 1968, EQ, $80-140
MASON, J. T.
Build Yourself a Golf Swing by the Seven Steps of the Mason Method: 1974, I, under $15
MASSY, ARNAUD & ALLINSON, A. R.
Golf: 1914, I, $15-40
MATHIESON, DONALD MACKAY & MATHIESON, R. D. & GOLDIE, WILLIAM C. *ANNUAL*
↙ Golfer's Handbook, The: 1898 +, R, $15-400 (varies)
MATHISON, THOMAS
Goff, An Heroi-Comical Poem in Three Cantos, The: 1743, F, Scarce
Goff, An Heroi-Comical Poem in Three Cantos, The (Reprint): 1981, F, $40-80
MATSON, GEOFFREY J.
Off The Tee: Favourite Golfing Stories and Anecdotes of the Famous: 1963, AN, under $15
MAUGHAN, WILLIAM CHARLES
Picturesque Musselburgh and its Golf Links: 1906, GC, $140-400
MAY, JOHN ALLAN
Bedside Duffer: 1969, F, under $15
Duffer's A.B.C.: 1970, F, under $15
MAYER, RICHARD
How to Think and Swing Like A Golf Champion: 1958, I, under $15
McADAM, CLIFF
How to Break 90/80/Par: 1973, I, under $15
McALISTER, ALEXANDER J.
Eternal Verities of Golf: A Study in Philosophy and the Ancient Game, The: 1911, AN, $80-140
McALLISTER, GEORGE
Golfercises: 1970, I, under $15
McANDREW, J.
Golfing Step by Step: 1910, I, $40-80
McBAIN, J. & FERNIE, W.
Golf: Dean's Champion Handbooks: 1897, I, $80-140
McCARTHY COLEMAN
Pleasures of the Game: The Theory-Free Guide to Golf, The: 1977, I, under $15
McCAUL, A.T.W. *ANNUAL*
Committee Year Book, The (3 Volumes): 1906-1908, R, $40-80
McCORMACK, MARK
Arnie: Evolution of a Legend: 1967, H, under $15
Golf '67: World Professional Golf: The Facts and Figures: 1967 +, R, under $15
World of Professional Golf, The (later edition of above - Title Varies) R, $15-40
Wonderful World of Professional Golf, The: 1973, H, under $15
McCORMICK, BILL
Complete Beginner's Guide to Golf, The: 1974, I, under $15
McCUE, CAROL
How to Conduct Golf Club Championships: 1964, R, under $15
McCULLOUGH, J.
Golf: Practical Hints and the Rules: 1899, I, $80-140

McDONNELL, MICHAEL
Golf: The Great Ones: 1971, H, under $15
Great Moments in Sport: Golf: 1974, AN, under $15
McDOUGAL STAN
101 Great Golf Jokes and Stories: 1968, F, under $15
McDOUGALL, DONALD
Davie: 1977, F, under $15
McGRAW, DONALD
Full Bag, or, The Golf Duffer's Own Handbook: How to Keep
from Breaking 100: 1962, F, under $15
McGURN, ROBERT & WILLIAMS, S.A. & EDITORS OF GOLF
DIGEST
Golf Power in Motion: 1967, I, under $15
McINERNY, RALPH
Lying Three: A Father Dowling Mystery: 1979, F, under $15
McLACHLAN, IAEN
Billy Dunk's "Five Under" Golf: 1972, I, under $15
One Hundred Golf Tips by Leading Australian and New Zealand
Golfers: 1973, I, under $15
Swing to Win: The Story and Techniques of Leading Proette,
Judy Perkins: 1975, I, under $15
McLEAN, JACK
Why not Beat Bogey: 1937, I, under $15
McLEAN, T. P. & WALLACE, A. J. *ANNUAL*
The DB Golf Annual: 1974 +, R, under $15
McLEOD, ROD
St. Andrews Old: 1970, GC, under $15
McMURTRIE, J. *ANNUAL*
Golfer's Guide, The: 1902-1903, R, $40-80
McPHERSON, REV. J. G.
Golf and Golfers, Past and Present: 1891, H, $140-400
McQUILLAN, EOIN
Fred Daly Story, The: 1978, H, under $15
McRAE, D. G.
Prinicple of Human Automation as Applied to Golf, The: 1945,
ES, under $15
McSPADDEN, JOSEPH WALKER
How to Play Golf, Compiled from the Best English and American
Authorities: 1907, I, $40-80
MEMBER, A (Pseudonym for STONE, DR.)
Duffers' Golf Club Papers, to Which is Added: A Day on the
Ladies' Links, The: 1891, F, $15-40
MENZIES, GORDON
World of Golf, The: 1982, R, under $15
MERRILL, ANTHONY F.
Golf Course Guide, The: 1950, GC, $40-80
MERRINS, ED & AULTMAN, DICK & EDITORS OF GOLF
DIGEST
Swing the Handle - Not the Clubhead: 1973, I, under $15
METZ, RICHARD
Graduated Swing Method, The: 1981, I, under $15
METZ, DICK
The Secret to Par Golf: Golf Made Easy for Men and
Women, 1940, I, $15-40
METZGER, SOL
Putting Analyzed, A Book on a Perplexing Phase of Golf
etc....: 1929, I, $15-40
MICHAEL, THOMAS & GOLF DIGEST, EDITORS, OF
Golf's Winning Stroke: Putting: 1967, I, under $15
MICHELMORE, CLIFF
Businessman's Book of Golf, The: 1981, I, under $15
MIDDLECOFF, CARY
Golf Doctor: 1950, I, under $15
MIDDLECOFF, CARY & MICHAEL, TOM
Advanced Golf: 1957, I, under $15
Golf Swing, The: 1974, I, under $15
Master Guide to Golf: 1960, I, under $15

MILLER, DICK
Triumphant Journey: The Saga of Bobby Jones and the Grand
Slam of Golf: 1980, H, under $15
MILLER, HELEN MARKLEY
Striving to be Champion: Babe Didrikson Zaharias: 1961, H,
under $15
MILLER, JOHNNY & SHANKLAND, DALE
Pure Golf: 1976, I, under $15
MILLER, REV. T. D.
Famous Scottish Links and Other Golfing Papers: 1911, GC,
$140-400
History of the Royal Perth Golfing Society: A Century of Golf in
Scotland etc..., The: 1935, H, $80-140
MILLER, RICHARD
America's Greatest Golfing Resorts: 1977, GC, under $15
MITCHELL, ABE & MARTIN, J.
Down to Scratch: 1933, I, $15-40
Essentials of Golf: 1927, I, under $15
Length on the Links: A Book for Players in all Stages Revealing
Secrets of Long Ball: 1935, I, $15-40
MONCADO, HILARIO CAMINO
360-Degree Power Swing: 1951, I, under $15
MONDAY, SIL
Golf in the Ohio Sun: 1970, GC, under $15
MONTAGUE, WILLIAM KELLY
Golf of our Fathers, The: 1952, H, $80-140
MOODY, ORVILLE & HISKEY, JIM
Golf by Orville Who?: 1972, H, under $15
MOONE, THEODORE
Golf from a New Angle: Being Letters from a Scratch Golfer to
his Son at College: 1934, I, under $15
MOORE, CHARLES W.
Mental Side of Golf, The: 1929, ES, under $15
MORAN, FRANK
Golfer's Gallery; 1946, H, under $15
MORAN, FRANK & OTHERS
Book of Scottish Golf Courses, The: 1947, GC, under $15
MORAN, SHARRON
Golf is a Woman's Game, or How to be a Swinger on the Fair-
way: 1971, I, under $15
MOREY, ALBERT A.
Tee-Time: Enjoy it and Live: 1952, F, under $15
MORGAN, JOHN
Golf: 1976, AN, under $15
MORLEY, DAVID C., M.D. & BOWDEN, KEN
The Missing Links: Golf and the Mind: 1976, I, under $15
MORLEY, MICHAEL E.
Art and Science of Putting, The: 1982, I, under $15
MORLEY, SAM
Start off Smashed: 1972, ES, under $15

BIBLIOGRAPHY GUIDELINES

ABBREV.	CATEGORY	REVIEWS BEGIN ON PAGE
AN	ANTHOLOGY	225
GC	GOLF COURSE	227
EQ	EQUIPMENT	230
ES	ESSAYS	232
F	FICTION	233
H	HISTORY	234
I	INSTRUCTIONAL	
R	REFERENCE	237
RU	RULES	

See page 224 for "How To Use This Chapter"

MORRIS, JOHN & COBB, LEONARD
   Great Golf Holes in Hawaii: 1977, GC, under $15
   Great Golf Holes of New Zealand: 1961, GC, under $15
MORRIS, WARREN E.
   Toltec Twist, or My Dad's Notebook on Golf, The: 1955, I, under $15
MORRISON, ALEX J.
   Better Golf without Practice: 1940, I, under $15
   New Way to Better Golf, A: 1932, I, under $15
   Pocket Guide to Better Golf: 1934, I, under $15
MORRISON, J.S.F.
   Around Golf: 1939, AN, $15-40
MORRISON, MORIE
   Here's How in Golf: 1950, F, under $15
   Here's How to Play Money Golf: 1953, F, under $15
   Life with Par: 1958, F, under $15
MORSE, CHARLES & MORSE, ANN
   Lee Trevino: 1974, H, under $15
MORTIMER, CHARLES G. & PIGNON, FRED
   Story of the Open Championship (1860-1950), The: 1952, H, $15-40
MORTON, CECIL W.
   Golf: The Confessions of a Golf Club Secretary: 1963, F, $40-80
MOSES, R. J. H.
   Fore!: 1937, F, $15-40
MR. X (Pseudonym for RUSSELL, ROBERT)
   Beginner's Buide to Golf: 1973, I, under $15
   Golf Monthly's Lessons with Mr. X: 1968, I, under $15
   More Golf Lessons with Mr. X: 1971, I, under $15
MULVOY, MARK
   Sports Illustrated: Golf: 1983, I, under $15
MULVOY, MARK & SPANDER, ART
   Golf: The Passion and the Challenge: 1977, AN, $15-40
MURDOCH, JOSEPH S.F.
   ✓ Library of Golf, 1743-1966: A Bibliography of Golf Books etc....: 1968, R, $15-40
   ✓ The Library of Golf, Updated: 1978, R, under $15
MURDOCH, JOSEPH S. F. & SEAGLE, JANET
   ✓ Golf— A Guide to Information Resources: 1979, R, $15-40
MURPHY, MICHAEL
   Golf in the Kingdom: 1971, ES, under $15
MURRAY, DR. C. M.
   Greenskeeping in South Africa: A Treatise on Scientific etc...: 1932, GC, $40-80
MURRAY, H. A.
   Golf Secret, The: 1953, I, under $15
   More Golf Secrets: Sequel to The Golf Secret: 1954, I, under $15
MURRAY, ROBINSON
   Are Golfers Human?: 1951, F, under $15
MUSSER, H. BURTON
   Turf Management: 1950, GC, $15-40
MYERS, EDWARD
   Experiences of a Caddy: 1927, F, $40-80
MYERS, WALTER
   Golf Notes: 1943, I, under $15
NADEN, C. J.
   Golf: 1970, AN, under $15
NAGLE, KEL & VON NIDA & FERRIER & THOMSON
   Secrets of Australia's Golfing Success, The: 1961, I, under $15
NAISMITH, TED
   Golf: 1947, I, $15-40
NANCE, VIRGINIA & ELWOOD, CRAIG
   Golf: 1983, I, under $15
NASH, GEORGE C.
   General Forcursue and Co.: More Letters to the Secretary of a Golf Club: 1937, F, $15-40
   Letters to the Secretary of a Golf Club: 1935, F, $15-40

   Whelk's Post Bag: Still More Letters to the Secretary of a Golf Club: 1937, F, $15-40
NATIONAL GOLF FOUNDATION
   Competitive Golf Events: 1968, I, under $15
   Easy Way to Learn Golf Rules: 1969, RU, under $15
   Golf Events: How to Organize and Conduct the Most Popular Golf Events: 1960, R, under $15
   Golf Instructors Guide: 1969, I, under $15
   Golf Lessons: 1968, I, under $15
   Golf Plan for Schools, A: 1960, R, under $15
   Golf Range Operator's Handbook: 1947, R, under $15
   How to Improve your Golf: 1968, I, under $15
   Planning and Building the Golf Course: 1954, GC, under $15
NEIL, MARK
   Awful Golfer's Book, The: 1967, F, under $15
NEILL, A.S.
   Booming of Bunkie, The: 1925, F, under $15
NELFORD, JIM
   Seasons in a Golfers Life: 1984, H, under $15
NELSON, BYRON
   Shape your Swing the Modern Way: 1976, I, under $15
   Winning Golf: 1946, I, under $15
NETLAND, DWAYNE
   Crosby: Greatest Show in Golf, The: 1975, H, under $15
NEWMAN, JOSEPH
   Newman's Guide to London Golf: 1913, GC, $15-40
   ✓ Official Golf Guide of America for 1900, The: 1900, R, $140-400
   Official Golf Guide to the United Kingdom, 1903-1904, The: 1903, R, $140-400
NIBLICK (Pseudonym for HANKS, CHARLES STEDMAN)
   Hints to Golfers: 1902, I, $15-40
NIBLICK (Pseudonym for KITCHING, R. L.)
   Introduction to Golf: 1932, I, under $15
NIBLICK (Pseudonym for SIGEL, REGINALD)
   Par Golf: Principles of the Natural Swing and Guides to Practice: 1926, I, under $15
NICHOLS, BOBBY
   Never Say Never: The Psychology of Winning Golf: 1965, I, under $15
NICKLAUS, JACK
   Best Way to Better Golf: 1967, I, under $15
   My 55 Ways to Lower Your Golf Score: 1964, I, under $15
   Take a Tip from Me: 1968, I, under $15
   Winning Golf: 1969, I, under $15
NICKLAUS, JACK & BOWDEN, KEN
   Golf My Way: 1974, I, under $15
   Jack Nicklaus' Lesson Tee: 1977, I, under $15
   Jack Nicklaus' Playing Lesson: 1977, I, under $15
   On & Off the Fairway: A Pictorial Autobiography: 1978, H, under $15
NICKLAUS, JACK & WIND, HERBERT WARREN
   Greatest Game of All: My Life in Golf, The: 1969, H, under $15
NIEPORTE, TOM & SAUERS, DON
   Mind Over Golf: What 50 Top Pros Can Teach You etc...: 1968, I, under $15
NOER, O. J.
   ABC of Turf Culture, The: 1928, GC, $15-40
NOLAN, JAMES
   Of Golf and Dukes and Princes: Early Golf in France: 1982, H, under $15
NORMAN, GREG
   Greg Norman: My Story: 1983, H, under $15
NORVAL, RONALD
   Gone to the Golf: 1965, H, under $15
   King of the Links: The Story of Bobby Locke: 1951, H, $15-40

NORWOOD, JOE & SMITH, MARILYN & BLICKER, STANLEY
Joe Norwood's Golf-O-Metrics: 1978, I, under $15
NOVAK, JOSEPH
Golf Can be an Easy Game: 1962, I, under $15
How to Put Power and Direction in Your Golf: 1954, I, under $15
Novak System of Mastering Golf, The: 1969, I, under $15
Par Golf in 8 Steps: 1950, I, under $15
NUNEVILLE, JACK
Illustrated Lessons in Golf: 1924, I, $15-40
NUNN, EDDY
Mechanics of Golf: 1962, I, under $15
O'BYRNE, ROBERT
Senior Golf: 1977, I, under $15
O'CONNOR, ANTHONY
Golfing in the Green: 1978, F, under $15
O'DONNELL, PADDY
South Africa's Wonderful World of Golf: 1973, GC, under $15
O'MALLEY, BILL
Fore — and Aft: 1969, F, under $15
Golf Fore Fun! A Book of Golf Cartoons: 1953, F, under $15
OBITZ, HARRY & FARLEY, DICK & TOLHURST, DESMOND
Six Days to Better Golf: The Secret of Learning the Golf Swing: 1977, I, under $15
OGG, WILLIE
Golf as I Know It: 1961, I, under $15
OLD GOLFER (Pseudonym for EVERAGE, L.)
Golf on a New Principle: Iron Clubs Superceded: 1897, I, $40-80
OLD PLAYER (Pseudonym for RIORDAN, COL. W.E.)
Golf and How to Play It: 1905, I, $40-80
OLMAN, JOHN M. & OLMAN, MORTON W.
Encyclopedia of Golf Collectibles, The: 1985, R, under $15
OLMAN, MORTON W.
Byron Nelson Story, The: 1980, AN, $80-140
OLSON, BILL & LINKERT, LO
Beat The Links: 1979, I, under $15
ORION (Pseudonym for TULLOCK, W. W.)
Lost and Won, or, Fresh Golfing Pastures: 1883, F, $80-140
OSBORN, ROBERT
How to Play Golf: 1949, I, under $15
OSTERMANN, H. T.
Golf in Europe: 1961, GC, under $15
OUIMET, FRANCIS
Game of Golf: A Book of Reminiscences, A: 1932, H, $15-40
Game of Golf: A Book of Reminiscences, A (Limited Edition): 1932, H, $140-400
Game of Golf: A Book of Reminiscences, A (Reprint): 1978, H, $15-40
Golf Facts for Young People: 1921, I, $15-40
Rules of Golf, (Revised), Illustrated and Explained, The: 1948, RU, under $15
OYLER, T. H.
Golfer's Glossary, or, Lexicon of the Links, The: 1920, R, $40-80
P. G. A. (EUROPEAN)
PGA 1980 Yearbook: 1980, R, under $15
P. G. A. TOUR *ANNUAL*
Tour Book, The: 1970 +, R, under $15
PA GOLF
Fore!: 1934, F, $15-40
PADGHAM, ALFRED
Par Golf Swing, The: 1936, I, under $15
PALMER, ARNOLD D.
Arnold Palmer Method, The: 1968, I, under $15

Arnold Palmer's Golf Book: Hit It Hard: 1961, I, under $15
My Game and Yours: 1965, I, under $15
Portrait of a Professional Golfer: 1964, H, $15-40
Situation Golf: 1970, I, under $15
PALMER, ARNOLD & DRUM, BOB
Arnold Palmer's Best 54 Golf Holes: 1977, GC, under $15
PALMER, ARNOLD & FURLONG, WILLIAM BARRY
Go For Broke: 1973, H, under $15
PALMER, ARNOLD & PUCKETT, EARL
495 Golf Lessons: 1973, I, under $15
PALMER, NORMAN & LEVY, WILLIAM V.
Five Star Golf: 1964, H, under $15
PARISH MINISTER (Pseudonym for LAWSON, ALEXANDER)
Letters on Golf: 1889, F, $140-400
PARK, WILLIE
Art of Putting, The: 1920, I, $80-140
Game of Golf, The: 1896, I, $80-140
PATEY, BOB
Welcome to the Club: 1981, R, under $15
PAZDUR, EDWARD F. *ANNUAL*
Private Country Club Guest Policy Directory: 1976 +, GC, under $15
PECK, SAMUEL MINTURN
Golf Girl, The: 1899, F, over $400
PERRY, PAUL D.
Billy Casper: Winner: 1969, H, under $15
PEILLE, PENTLAND
Clanbrae: A Golfing Idyll: 1908, F, under $15
PENDLETON, ALEXANDER
Better Golf With Brains: 1941, I, under $15
PENNA, TONEY & FRALEY, OSCAR
Wonderful World of Golf, My: 1965, H, under $15
PENNINK, FRANK
Frank Pennink's Choice of Golf Courses: 1976, GC, under $15
Golfer's Companion: 1962, GC, under $15
Homes of Sport: Golf: 1952, GC, under $15
PEPER, GEORGE
Golf's Supershots: How the Pros Played Them and How You Can Play Them: 1982, AN, under $15
Masters 1983, The: 1984, H, under $15
Scrambling Golf: How to Get Out of Trouble and into the Cup: 1977, I, under $15
PETER, H. THOMAS
Reminiscences of Golf and Golfers: 1890, H, $140-400
PETNUCH, ANDREW
Turn to Golf: 1969, I, under $15
PETTIT, ROY A.
Straight Line Golf Swing, The: 1946, I, under $15
PICKENS, ARTHUR E., JR.
Golf Bum: A Novel, The: 1970, F, under $15

BIBLIOGRAPHY GUIDELINES

See page 224 for "How To Use This Chapter"

PICKWORTH, H. O. & REEVE, JOHN
 Golf, The 'Pickworth' Way: 1949, I, $15-40
PIETZKER, GEORGE S.
 Eddy Williams: 1921, I, under $15
PIGNON, F. J. C.
 Spalding Golfers' Year Book, 1960: 1960, R, under $15
PIPER, CHARLES V. & OAKLEY, RUSSELL A.
 Turf for Golf Courses: 1917, GC, $15-40
PLATTE, JULES & GRAFFIS, HERB
 Better Golf through Better Practice: 1958, I, under $15
PLAYER, GARY
 Gary Player's Golf Secrets: 1962, I, under $15
 Grand Slam Golf: 1966, H, under $15
 Play Golf with Player: 1962, I, under $15
 Positive Golf: 1967, I, under $15
PLAYER, GARY & REID, IAIN
 124 Golf Lessons: 1968, I, under $15
 395 Golf Lessons: 1971, I, under $15
 Gary Player's Golf Class: 1967, I, under $15
 Golf Tips from Gary Player: 1967, I, under $15
 More Golf Tips from Gary Player: 1968, I, under $15
 Second Book of Gary Player's Golf Class: 1968, I, under $15
PLAYER, GARY & SULLIVAN, GEORGE
 Gary Player's Golf Book for Young People: 1980, I, under $15
PLAYER, GARY & THATCHER, FLOYD
 Gary Player — World Golfer: 1974, H, under $15
PLIMPTON, GEORGE
 Bogey Man, The: 1968, ES, under $15
PLUMON GUIDES *ANNUAL*
 Continental Golf Year Book, The: 1926 +, R, $15-40
PLUMRIDGE, CHRIS
 How to Play Golf: 1979, I, under $15
POET LAUREATE (Pseudonym for GRAHAM, WILLIAM)
 Songs of the Interleven Club: 1865, F, over $400
POLE-SOPPITT, CAPT. H. A.
 Eastern Counties Golf Links Guide, The: 1893, GC, $80-140
POLLARD, FRANK B.
 Golf on the Peninsula: An Illustrated Guide to the . . . Monterey
 Peninsula: 1973, GC, under $15
POLLARD, JACK
 Golf: The Australian Way: 1970, I, under $15
 Gregory's Australian Guide to Golf: 1963, GC, under $15
POLLOCK, WILLIAM H.
 You, The Golfer: 1937, I, $15-40
POND, HAROLD M.
 Guide to 1,870 North American Golf Courses: 1954, GC, under
 $15
POTTER, STEPHEN
 Golfmanship: 1968, F, under $15
PRAIN, ERIC M.
 Live Hands: A Key to Better Golf: 1946, I, under $15
 Oxford and Cambridge Golfing Society, 1898-1948, The: 1949, H,
 $15-40
PRATT, WILLIAM & JENNISON, KEITH
 Year-Round Conditioning for Part-Time Golfers: 1979, I, under
 $15
PRESTON, CHARLES
 Fore: Golf Cartoons from Wall Street Journal: 1962, F, under
 $15
PRICE, CHARLES
 ✓ American Golfer, The: 1964, AN, $15-40
 ✓ Golfer-At-Large, 1982, ES, under $15
 ✓ World of Golf: A Panorama of Six Centuries of the Game's
 History, The: 1962, H, $15-40

PRICE CHARLES & RODGERS, GEORGE C., JR.
 Carolina Low Country: Birthplace of American Golf, 1786, The:
 1980, H, under $15
PRICE, CHARLES & SARAZEN & DEMARET & SUGGS
 Pro Pointers and Stroke Savers: 1960, I, under $15
PROFESSIONAL GOLFERS ASSOCIATION OF AMERICA
 ANNUALS
 ✓ Official Tournament Record: 1934 +, R, $5-80 (varies)
 ✓ Tournament Player Catalog: 1950 +, R, $5-40 (varies)
PROFESSIONAL GOLFERS ASSOCIATION OF AMERICA &
 CARTER, EDWIN J.
 Tournament Sponsor's Guide: 1947 +, R, under $15
PUCKETT, EARL
 Golfer's Digest: The Encyclopedia for All Golfers: 1968, R, under
 $15
PULVER, P.C. & ANDERSON, JOHN G. & BROWN, J. LEWIS
 ANNUAL
 ✓ American Annual Golf Guide and Year Book: 1916-1932, R,
 $15-40
PUNCH MAGAZINE
 Funny Side of Golf, from the Pages of Punch, The: 1909, F,
 $40-80
QUANTZ, NANCY
 Tee Party (Fore Ladies Only): 1969, F, under $15
QUINN, BRENNAN
 How to Perfect your Golf Swing: 1981, I, under $15
R. A. S.
 Links: An Auld Kirk Allegory, The: 1895, F, $80-140
RAFTY, TOM & SMITH, TERRY
 Golfing Greats: 1984, F, under $15
 Tony Rafty Golfers: A Treasury of Stars in Caricature: 1975, F,
 under $15
RAGAWAY, MARTIN A.
 World's Worst Golf Jokes, The: 1973, F, under $15
RALSTON, W.
 North Again, Golfing This Time: 1894, F, $40-80
RAMSEY, LON W.
 Secrets of Winning Golf Matches: A Guide to Strategy and
 Tactics etc. . . . .: 1960, I, under $15
RAMSEY, TOM
 25 Great Australia Golf Courses: 1981, GC, under $15
 Golfer's Gift Book: 1984, R, under $15
 How to Cheat at Golf, or Know When your Opponent Does:
 1968, F, under $15
 Tom Ramsey's World of Golf: 1977, H, under $15
RAND McNALLY
 All About Golf: 1975, AN, under $15
RANKIN, JUDY & ARONSTEIN, MICHAEL
 Natural Way to Golf Power, A: 1976, I, under $15
RANKIN, STEVE
 Tournament Players' Championship, 1982: 1982, H, under $15
RAPPAPORT, MILT
 Oh, No! A Golf Duffer's Handbook: 1956, F, under $15
RASMUSSEN, REV. WALLY
 Preaching Pro, The: 1979, H, under $15
RAY, EDWARD
 Driving, Approaching and Putting: 1922, I, $15-40
 Golf Clubs and How to Use Them: 1922, I, $15-40
 Inland Golf: 1915, I, $15-40
RAY, TED
 Golf: My Slice of Life: 1972, F, under $15
READ, OPIE PERCIVAL
 Opie Read on Golf: 1925, I, $40-80
REDFORD, KEN & TREMAYNE, NICK
 Success in Golf: 1977, I, under $15

REDMOND, JACK
Golf Training: How to Play Golf in Simple Terms, Easy to Understand: 1930, I, under $15

REED, BETTY JANE
Golfin' with a Dolphin: 1968, F, under $15

REES, DAI
Dai Rees on Golf: 1959, I, under $15
Golf My Way: 1951, I, under $15
Golf Today: 1962, H, under $15
Key to Golf, The: 1961, I, under $15

REES, DAI & BALLANTINE, JOHN
Thirty Years of Championship Golf: 1968, H, under $15

REHLING, CONRAD HENRY
Golf for the Physical Education Teacher and Coach: 1954, I, under $15

REID, HASTINGS C.
Key to The Rules of Golf and Definitions: A Comprehensive Analysis etc..., The: 1946, RU, $15-40

REID, WILLIAM, F.J.I.
Golfing Reminiscences: The Growth of the Game, 1887-1925: 1925, H, $40-80

RENICK, MARION
Champion Caddy: 1943, F, $15-40

REVELL, ALEXANDER H.
Pro and Con of Golf: 1915, ES, $40-80

REVOLTA, JOHNNY & CLEVELAND, CHARLES B.
Johnny Revolta's Short Cuts to Good Golf: 1949, I, under $15

REYNOLDS, FRANK
Frank Reynolds Golf Book: Drawings from "Punch", The: 1932, F, $15-40
Hamish McDuff: 1937, F, $15-40

RHODES, HAL
Fundamental Principles of Golf: 1952, I, under $15

RHODES, LOUIS
Stop Action Golf: The Driver: 1971, I, under $15

RICE, GRANTLAND & BRIGGS, CLARE
Duffer's Handbook of Golf, The: 1926, F, $15-40
Duffer's Handbook of Golf, The (Limited Edition): 1926, F, $140-400

RICE, GRANTLAND
Bobby Jones Story: From the Writings of O. B. Keeler, The: 1953, H, under $15
Bobby Jones Story: From the Writings of O. B. Keeler, The (Reprint): 1980, H, $40-80
Fore...With a Glance Aft!: 1929, ES, $40-80

RICH, ENDICOTT G. & FOY, JOHNSON
You Can Think Ten Strokes off your Game, We Did! How Two Weekend Golfers etc...: 1931, I, under $15

RICHARDSON, DONALD H.
World Wide Golf Directory: 1973, R, under $15

RICHARDSON, W. D. *ANNUAL*
Barne's Official Golf Guide: 1947, R, under $15
✓ Golfer's Year Book, The (7 Volumes): 1930 +, R, $15-40 (each)

RICORNUS, C. A. P.
Goat Club Golf Book: The Rules of the Game as Played by the ... Order of Goats, The: 1911, F, $40-80

RIDDELL, GERVASE C.
Evolution of Golf in Victoria: 1982, H, under $15
Practical Golf Course Design and Construction: 1974, GC, under $15

REIDER, LAWRENCE
Beginning Golf: A Manual for Golf Class Instructors in High Schools and Colleges: 1934, I, under $15

RISK, ROBERT K.
Songs of the Links: 1904, F, $15-40

RISSELL, CAROL
U.S. Open Book, The: 1982, R, under $15

ROBB, GEORGE
Manual of the Bruntsfield Links: 1867, GC, over $400

ROBERTS, CLIFFORD
Story of the Augusta National Golf Club, The: 1976, H, $15-40

ROBERTS, HENRY
Green Book of Golf, The: 1914, R, $40-80

ROBERTS, PALMER W.
Fore: The Golfer's International Cookbook: 1978, R, under $15

ROBERTSON, A. J.
A. B. C. of Golf, The: 1904, I, $40-80

ROBERTSON, JAMES K.
St. Andrews: Home of Golf: 1967, H, $15-40

ROBERTSON, KOLIN
Some Yorkshire Golf Courses: 1935, GC, $40-80

ROBERTSON, MRS. GORDON
Hints to Lady Golfers: 1909, I, $15-40

ROBINSON, LAWRENCE
Golf Secrets of the Pros: 1956, I, under $15

ROBINSON, LAWRENCE & GRAHAM, JAMES & FINSTER-WALD, DOW
Golfer's Digests: 1966, AN, under $15

ROBINSON, W. HEATH
Humors of Golf: 1923, F, $15-40

ROBISON, NANCY
Nancy Lopez: Wonder Woman Golfer: 1979, H, under $15

RODRIGO, ROBERT
Birdie Book, The: 1967, AN, under $15

RODRIGUEZ, JUAN "CHI CHI"
Chi Chi's Golf Secret: 1964, I, under $15
Everybody's Golf Book: 1975, I, under $15

RODRIGUEZ, JUAN "CHI CHI" & STROIMAN, HARRY
Chi Chi's Secrets of Power Golf: 1967, I, under $15

ROSBERG, BOB
Putter Book, The: 1964, I, under $15

ROSE, WILLIAM GANSON & NEWCOMB, CHARLES MILTON
Cut Down That Score: The Psychology of Golf: 1925, I, $40-80

ROSS, A. C. GORDON
Mixed Bag of Golfing Verse, A: 1977, F, under $15

ROSS, CAMPBELL
More Fun of the Fairway: 1945, F, $15-40
The Fun of the Fairway: 1943, F, $15-40

ROSS, JOHN M. & GOLF MAGAZINE, EDITORS OF
Golf Magazine's Encyclopedia of Golf: 1979, R, $15-40

ROTELLA, ROBERT J. & BUNKER, LINDA K.
Mind Mastery for Winning Golf: 1981, I, under $15

ROWLAND, RALPH
Humours of Golf: 24 Pen Etchings of the Royal and Ancient Game, The: 1903, F, $40-80

ROYAL & ANCIENT GOLF CLUB
Decisions By The Rules of Golf Committee of The Royal and Ancient Golf Club (7 Volumes): 1909-1934, RU, $15-40 (each)
Golf Rules Illustrated: 1969, RU, under $15

RUDOLPH, MASON
Short Irons, The: 1965, I, under $15

RUNYAN, PAUL
Golf is a Game: 1939, I, $15-40
Paul Runyan's Book for Senior Golfers: 1963, I, under $15

RUNYAN, PAUL & AULTMAN, DICK
Short Way to Lower Scoring: 1980, I, under $15

RYAN, JOSEPH E. G.
Golfers' Green Book: 1901, R, $40-80

RYDE, PETER
Black's Picture Sports, Golf: 1976, I, under $15
✔ Mostly Golf: A Bernard Darwin Anthology: 1976, ES, under $15
Royal and Ancient Championship Records, 1860-1980: 1981, R, $15-40

SABIN, EDWIN L.
Magic Mashie and other Golfish Stories, The: 1902, F, $40-80

SALEY, DR. CLYNE & CRAWFORD, DAVID A.
How Well Should You Putt: A Search for a Putting Standard: 1977, I, under $15

SALMOND, D. S.
Reminiscences of Arbroath and St. Andrews: 1905, H, $80-140

SALMOND, DR. J. B.
Story of the R. & A.: Being the History of The First Two Hundred Years etc. . . . , The: 1956, H, $15-40

SAMPSON, HAROLD A.
Golf Instruction Simplified: 1950, I, under $15
Primer of Golf Instruction: 1932, I, under $15

SANDERS, DOUG
Compact Golf: 1964, I, under $15

SANDERS, DOUG & SHEEHAN, LARRY
Come Swing with Me: My Life On and Off the Tour: 1974, H, under $15

SANTEE, ROSS
Bar X Golf Course, The: 1933, F, $15-40

SAPPER
Uncle James' Golf Match: 1950, F, $15-40

SARAZEN, GENE
Gene Sarazen's Commonsense Golf Tips: 1924, I, $15-40
Want to be a Champion Golfer?: 1945, I, under $15

SARAZEN, GENE & DEMARET, JIMMY & BELL, PEGGY KIRK
Your Long Game: 1964, I, under $15

SARAZEN, GENE & DEMARET, JIMMY & SUGGS, LOUISE
Your Short Game: 1962, I, under $15

SARAZEN, GENE & GANEM, ROGER
Better Golf after Fifty: 1967, I, under $15

SARAZEN, GENE & MCLEAN, PETER
Golf: The New Horizons: 1966, GC, under $15

SARAZEN GENE & SNEAD & MANGRUM & FERRIER & VINES & OLIVER
Golf Clinic, The: 1949, I, under $15

SARAZEN, GENE & OTHERS
Winning Pointers from the Pros: 1965, I, under $15

SARAZEN, GENE & WIND, HERBERT WARREN
✔ Thirty Years of Championship Golf: The Life and Times of Gene Sarazen: 1950, H, $15-40
Thirty Years of Championship Golf: The Life and Times of Gene Sarazen (Reprint): 1979, H, $15-40

SAUCON VALLEY C.C.
Responsibilities of a Golfer, The: 1951, ES, under $15

SAUNDERS, VIVIAN & CLARK, CLIVE
Young Golfer, The: 1975, I, under $15

SAUNDERS, VIVIEN
Complete Woman Golfer, The: 1975, I, under $15

SAXE, JOHN GODFREY
Jones' Golf Swing and other Suggestions, The: 1948, I, $15-40

SCHAAP, DICK
Massacre at Winged Foot: The U.S. Open, Minute by Minute: 1974, H, under $15
Masters: The Winning of a Golf Classic, The: 1970, H, under $15

SCHARFF, ROBERT
Collier's Quick and Easy Guide to Golf: 1963, I, under $15
Encyclopedia of Golf: 1970, R, $15-40

SCHARFF, ROBERT & GOLF MAGAZINE, EDITORS OF
Great Golf Courses You Can Play: A Guide to Golf Courses Around the World: 1974, GC, $15-40
Handbook of Golf Strategy: 1971, I, under $15

SCHLEMAN, HELEN BLANCHE & HAYES, VIRGINIA
Group Golf Instruction: 1934, I, under $15

SCHMITT, CHUCK
My Golf Clinic: 1967, I, under $15

SCHOLZ, JACKSON
Fairway Challenge: 19674, F, under $15

SCHON, LESLIE
Psychology Of Golf, The: 1922, ES, $15-40

SCHRITE, J. ELLSWORTH
Divots for Dubs: 1934, F, $15-40

SCHULTZ, CHARLES M.
Snoopy's Grand Slam: 1972, F, under $15

SCOLLARD, CLINTON
Epic of Golf, The: 1923, F, $40-80

SCOT, A (Pseudonym for BALD, F.A.)
Consistent Golf, or How to Become A Champion: 1934, I, $15-40

SCOTCH GOLF SYSTEM
Golf Made Easy Through Golf Systems: 1936, I, under $15

SCOTT AND SONS, O. M.
Putting Green: Its Planting and Care, The: 1931, GC, $15-40
Seeding and Care of Golf Courses, The: 1922, GC, $15-40

SCOTT, TOM
AA Guide to Golf in Great Britain: 1977, GC, under $15
Club Golfers' Handbook: 1972, R, under $15
Concise Dictionary of Golf, The: 1978, R, under $15
Fifty Miles of Golf Around London: 1952, GC, under $15
Golf — Begin the Right Way: 1974, I, under $15
Golf: The Observer's Book: 1975, R, under $15
Golf Begins at 45: 1960, I, under $15
Golf with the Experts: 1959, I, under $15
Golfing Technique in Pictures: 1957, I, under $15
More Golf with the Experts: 1965, I, under $15
Sixty Miles of Golf around London: 1975, GC, under $15
Story of Golf: From its Origins to the Present Day, The: 1972, H, under $15

SCOTT, TOM & COUSINS, GEOFFREY
Golf for the Not So Young: 1960, I, under $15
Golf Immortals, The: 1969, H, under $15
Golf Secrets of the Masters: 1968, I, under $15
Ind Coope Book of Golf, The: 1965, AN, under $15
Wit of Golf, The: 1972, F, under $15

SCOTT, TOM & EVANS, WEBSTER
Golfers' Year, The: 1950, AN, under $15
Secrets of the Golfing Greats: 1965, I, under $15

SCRIBNER, ROMEYN B. & MATEY, FRANK
Senior Golf: Golf is More Fun after Fifty-Five: 1960, I, under $15

SEAGLE, JANET
Club Makers, The: 1980, EQ, under $15

SEAGRAVE, ALICE D.
Golf Retold: The Story of Golf in Cleveland: 1940, H, $15-40
SEITZ, NICK
Quick Tips from the CBS Golf Spot: 1982, I, under $15
Superstars of Golf: 1978, H, under $15
SELLECK, JACK & BERNARD, ART
Golf is a Trap: 1968, F, under $15
SENAT, PROSPER L.
Through the Greens and Golfer's Year Book, Philadelphia Section: Containing Maps Etc.: 1898, GC, $80-140
SERVOS, LAUNCELOT CRESSY
Practical Instruction in Golf: 1905, I, $40-80
SETON-KARR, SIR HENRY & OTHERS
Golf: Greening's Useful Handbook Series: 1907, AN, $80-140
SEYMOUR, BERT
All about Golf: How to Improve Your Game: 1924, I, $15-40
SHANKLAND, DALE & LUPO & BENJAMIN
Golfer's Stroke Saver Handbook, The: 1978, I, under $15
SHAPIRO, HAROLD & MAY, JOHN ALLAN
Get Golf Straight: 1972, I, under $15
SHAW, JOSEPH T.
Out of the Rough: 1934, F, under $15
SHAY, ARTHUR
40 Common Errors in Golf, and How to Correct Them: 1978, I, under $15
SHEEHAN, LARRY
Best Golf Humor from Golf Digest: 1972, F, under $15
Great Golf Humor: 1979, F, under $15
✔ Whole Golf Catalog, The: 1980, R, under $15
SHENSTONE, F. S.
Golf Rules and Decisions: A Summary of the Rules of Golf etc...: 1924, RU, $15-40
SHEPHERD, JAMES, JR.
Golf Shots: A Book for Beginners, Describing and Illustrating the Different etc...: 1924, I, $15-40
SHERIDAN, JAMES
Sheridan of Sunningdale: My Fifty-Six Years as a Caddie Master: 1967, H, under $15
SHERIDAN, JOHN DESMOND
It Stands to Reason: The Intelligent Rabbit's Guide to Golf: 1947, F, under $15
SHERMAN, JAMES W.
Joey Gets the Golf Bug: 1961, F, under $15
SHERWOOD, PETER
Arnold Snead's World's Best Golf Book Ever: 1982, F, under $15
SHOTTE, CLEEKE (Pseudonym for HOGBEN, JOHN)
Golf Craze: Sketches and Rhymes, The: 1905, F, $40-80
SILVEY, JIM
Golf: How to Learn the Total Game: 1982, I, under $15
SIMEK, THOMAS G. & O'BRIEN, RICHARD M.
Total Golf: Behavioral Approach to Lowering your Score & Getting More Out of your Game: 1981, I, under $15
SIMMS, GEORGE *ANNUALS*
Official Tournament Guide, 1973: 1973 +, R, under $15
World of Golf 1977, The: 1977 +, R, under $15
SIMMS, GEORGE & SCHOFIELD, KEN
John Player Golf Yearbook, 1973: 1973 +, R, under $15
SIMPSON, HAROLD
Seven Stages of Golf, and other Golf Stories in Pictures and Verse: 1909, F, $140-400
SIMPSON, S. R.
Green Crop, A: 1937, F, $40-80
SIMPSON, SIR WALTER G.
✔ Art of Golf, The: 1887, ES, over $400
✔ Art of Golf, The (Reprint): 1983, ES, $40-80

SLOCUM, HELEN
Easy Way to Learn Golf Rules, The: 1948, RU, under $15
SMARTT, PATRICK
Golf: Grave and Gay: 1964, H, under $15
If You Must Play Golf: 1963, F, under $15
SMITH, ALEX
Lessons in Golf: 1907, I, $40-80
SMITH, CHARLES
Aberdeen Golfers: Records and Reminiscences, The: 1909, H, over $400
Aberdeen Golfers: Records and Reminiscences, The (Reprint): 1982, H, $40-80
SMITH, DONALD
Young Sportman's Guide to Golf: 1961, I, under $15
SMITH, EMIL, M.D.
Golf Laffs: 150 Cartoons to Suit You to a Tee: 1964, F, under $15
SMITH, EVERETT M.
Synonym Golf: A New Indoor Game: 1931, F, under $15
SMITH, GARDEN C.
Side Lights on Golf: 1907, AN, $40-80
Golf: 1897, I, $80-140
World of Golf: The Isthmian Library, The: 1898, AN $40-80
SMITH, HORTON
Secret of Perfect Putting, The: 1963, I, under $15
SMITH, HORTON & BENTON, MARIAN
Velvet Touch, The: 1965, H, under $15
SMITH, HORTON & TAYLOR, DAWSON
Master's Secrets of Holing Putts, The: 1982, I, under $15
Secret of Holing Putts, The: 1961, I, under $15
SMITH, J.S.K. & WEASTELL, B. S.
Foundations of Golf: Dedicated to the Late Beginner, The: 1925, I, under $15
SMITH, LORAN
Masters 1978, The (Issued through 1982): 1978-1982, H, $15-40
SMITH, PARKER
Golf Techniques: How to Improve your Game: 1973, I, under $15
SMITH, R. CRAIG
Enjoy Golf and Win: 1981, I, under $15
SMITH, ROBERT HOWIE
Golfer's Year Book for 1866, The: 1867, R, over $400
SMITH, TERRY
Australian Golf - The First 100 Years, H, under $15
Complete Book of Australian Golf, The: 1975, R, under $15
SNEAD, SAM
Driver Book, The: 1964, I, under $15
How to Hit a Golf Ball from any Sort of Lie: 1950, I, under $15
How to Play Golf, and Professional Tips on Improving your Score: 1946, I, under $15
Natural Golf: 1953, I, under $15
Sam Snead on Golf: 1961, I, under $15
Sam Snead's Quick Way to Better Golf: 1938, I, $15-40

BIBLIOGRAPHY GUIDELINES

ABBREV.	CATEGORY	REVIEWS BEGIN ON PAGE
AN	ANTHOLOGY	225
GC	GOLF COURSE	227
EQ	EQUIPMENT	230
ES	ESSAYS	232
F	FICTION	233
H	HISTORY	234
I	INSTRUCTIONAL	
R	REFERENCE	237
RU	RULES	

See page 224 for "How To Use This Chapter"

SNEAD, SAM & AULTMAN, DICK
  Golf Begins at Forty: 1978, I, under $15
SNEAD, SAM & SHEEHAN, LARRY & BOWDEN, KEN
  Sam Snead Teaches You his Simple "Key" Approach to Golf:
  1975, I, under $15
SNEAD, SAM & STUMP, AL
  Education of a Golfer: 1962, H, under $15
SNEDDON, RICHARD
  Golf Stream, The: 1941, F, under $15
SOMERVILLE, JOHN
  Foursome at Rye, A: 1898, F, $140-400
SORENSON, GARY L.
  Architecture of Golf, The: 1976, GC, under $15
SOUTAR, DANIEL G.
  Australian Golfer, The: 1906, I, $80-140
SOUTH AFRICAN PGA
  1984 South African PGA Golf Annual: 1984, R, under $15
SOUTHERN CALIFORNIA GOLF ASSOCIATION
  History of Golf in Southern California: 1925, H, $15-40
SPALDING, ANTHONY
  Golf for Beginners: 1935, I, $15-40
SPENCE, JOHN & FRALEY, OSCAR
  Golf Pro for God: 1965, H, under $15
SPOONER, JOHN D.
  Class: A Novel: 1973, F, under $15
SPORTS ILLUSTRATED MAGAZINE
  Golf Lessons From The Pros: 1961, I, under $15
  Golf Tips from the Top Professionals: 1961, I, under $15
SPORTS ILLUSTRATED MAGAZINE & PRICE, CHARLES
  Golf: Black's Picture Sports: 1976, I, under $15
  Sports Illustrated Book of Golf: 1970, I, under $15
SPRINGMAN, J.F.
  Beauty of Pebble Beach, The: 1964, GC, $40-80
  Many Faces of the American Golf Course, The: 1963, GC,
  $40-80
STANCLIFFE (Pseudonym for CLIFFORD, STANLEY)
  Astounding Golf Match, AN: 1914, F, $15-40
  Autobiography of a Caddy-Bag, The: 1924, I, $15-40
  Golf Do's and Don'ts: Being a Very Little about a Good Deal
  etc . . . : 1902, I, $15-40
  Quick Cuts to Good Golf: 1920, I, $15-40
STANLEY, DAVE
  Treasury of Golf Humor, A: 1949, F under $15
STANLEY, DAVE & ROSS, GEORGE C.
  Golfer's Own Book, The: 1956, AN, under $15
STANLEY, LOUIS T.
  Book of Golf, The: 1960, H, under $15
  Fontana Golf Book: 1957, I, under $15
  Fresh Fairways: 1949, ES, under $15
  Golf with your Hands: 1966, I, under $15
  Golfer's Bedside Book, The: 1955, I, under $15
  Green Fairways: 1947, ES, under $15
  Master Golfers in Action: 1950, I, under $15
  Pelham Golf Year Book: 1981, R, under $15
  Style Analysis: 1951, I, under $15
  Swing to Better Golf: 1957, I, under $15
  This is Golf: 1954, I, under $15
  This is Putting: 1955, I, under $15
  Woman Golfer, The (British Edition): 1952, I, under $15
  How to be a Better Woman Golfer (American Edition): 1952, I,
  under $15
STARK, A.
  Physical Training for Golfers: Improve Your Game by "Jerks":
  1937, I, $15-40

STEEL, DONALD
  Golf Course Guide: 1968, GC, under $15
  ✔ Guiness Book of Golf Facts and Feats: 1980, R, under $15
  Golfer's Bedside Book, The: 1965, AN, under $15
STEEL, DONALD & RYDE, PETER & WIND, HERBERT
  WARREN
  ✔ Encyclopedia of Golf, The: 1975, R, $15-40
STEELE, CHESTER K.
  Golf Course Mystery, The: 1919, F, $15-40
STEIN, JENNETTE A. & WATERMAN, EMMA F.
  Golf for Beginning Players: 1934, I, under $15
STEWART, J. I. M.
  Michael Innes, An Awkward Lie: 1973, F, under $15
STEWART, JAMES LINDSEY
  Golfiana Miscellanea: Being a Collection af Interesting
  Monographs etc . . . : 1887, AN, $140-400
STEWART, EARL, JR. & GUNN, DR. HARRY E.
  Golf Begins at Forty: 1977, I, under $15
  Left-Hander's Golf Book: 1976, I, under $15
STEWART, T. ROSS
  Lays of the Links: A Score of Parodies: 1895, F, $80-140
STIBBENS, FRED
  Norfolk's Caddie Poet: His Autobiography, Impressions and Some
  of His Verses: 1923, F, $15-40
STINE, CHARLEY
  1984 Florida Golf Directory: 1984, GC, under $15
STIPE, FRANK M.
  Australian, The: 1980, F, under $15
STOBART, M. A.
  Won at the Last Hole: A Golfing Romance: 1893, F, $40-80
STOBBS, JOHN
  A.B.C. of Golf, AN: 1964, R, under $15
  Anatomy of Golf, The (American Edition): 1961, I, under $15
  Tackle Golf this Way (British Edition): 1961, I, under $15
  At Random through the Green: A Collection of Writing about
  Golf: 1966, AN, under $15
STODDARD, WILLIAM LEAVITT
  New Golfer's Almanac: Carefully Compiled and Computed
  etc . . . , The: 1909, R, $15-40
STOUTS, CARLTON
  Unsinkable Titanic Thompson, The: 1983, H, under $15
STRINGER, MABEL E.
  Golfing Reminiscences: 1924, H, $40-80
STUART, IAN
  Golf in Hertfordshire: 1972, GC, $15-40
SUGGS, LOUISE
  Par Golf for Women: 1953, I, under $15
  Golf for Women: 1960, I, under $15
SULLIVAN, GEORGE
  Champion's Guide to Golf, The: 1966, I, under $15
SUNSET MAGAZINE
  Golf Course Directory for California: 1964, GC, under $15
SUTPHEN, W. G. van T.
  Golfer's Alphabet, The: 1898, F, $140-400
  Golficide and Other Tales of the Fair Green, The: 1898, F,
  $80-140
  Harper's Official Golf Guide: 1900, R, $140-400
  Nineteenth Hole: Being Tales of the Fair Green, The: 1901, F,
  $40-80
SUTTON, MARTIN A. F. & SIMPSON & ALISON & HOBSON
  & ROSS & COLT
  Golf Courses: Design, Construction and Upkeep: 1933, GC,
  $140-400
SUTTON, MARTIN, H. F.
  Layout and Upkeep of Golf Courses and Putting Greens: 1906,
  GC, $140-400

SUTTON, MARTIN H. F. & RIDDELL & DARWIN & COLT & HALL
Book of the Links: A Symposium on Golf: 1912, GC, $140-400
SWARBRICK, BRIAN
Duffer's Guide to Bogey Golf, The: 1973, F, under $15
Every Duffer's Way to Good Golf: 1973, F, under $15
SWENY, HARRY ROY
Keep your Eye on the Ball and your Right Knee Stiff: A Short and Concise etc....: 1898, I, $40-80
TARBUCK, JIMMY
Tarbuck on Golf: 1983, H, under $15
TAYLOR, ARTHUR V.
Origines Golfianae: The Birth of Golf and Its Early Childhood etc...: 1912, F, $80-140
TAYLOR, BERT LESTON
Line O'Gowf or Two, A: 1923, F, $15-40
TAYLOR, DAWSON
Inside Golf: 1978, I, under $15
Masters: All about Its History, Its Records, etc..., The: 1973, H, under $15
Masters: An Illustrated History, The (2nd Edition of Above): 1981, H, under $15
St. Andrews: Cradle of Golf: 1976, H, under $15
TAYLOR, HUGH
Golf Dictionary: 1970, R, under $15
TAYLOR, J. H.
Golf, My Life's Work: 1943, H, $40-80
Taylor on Golf: Impressions, Comments and Hints: 1902, I, $40-80
TAYLOR, JOHN L.
Golf Collector's Price Guide: 1983, R, $15-40
TAYLOR, JOSHUA
Art of Golf, The: 1913, I, $15-40
Lure of the Links, The: 1920, ES, $15-40
TAYLOR, PAULA
Golf's Great Winner: Jack Nicklaus: 1977, H, under $15
TEEMAN, LAWRENCE
Consumer Guide: Complete Guide to Golf: 1975, EQ, under $15
TEEPLE, DAVID SHEA
Innermost Secrets of Golf, The: 1958, I, under $15
THOMAS, DAVID
Instructions to Young Golfers: 1959, I, under $15
THOMAS, DAVID & WRIGHT, BEN
Modern Golf: 1967, I, under $15
THOMAS, J. S.
Stepping Stones to a Golf Course, The:, GC, $40-80
THOMAS, GEORGE C., JR.
✔ Golf Architecture in America: Its Strategy and Construction: 1927, GC, $80-140
THOMPSON, KENNETH R.
Mental Side of Golf: A Study of the Game as Practised by Champions, The: 1939, ES, under $15
THOMPSON, PHILLIPS B.
Simplifying the Golf Stroke: Based on the Theory of Ernest Jones: 1928, I, under $15
THOMPSON, W. J.
Common Sense Golf: 1923, I, under $15
THOMSON, BERNARD
How to Play Golf: 1939, I, under $15
THOMSON, DAVID
Practical Golf: 1923, I, under $15
THOMSON, JAMES
Hit 'Em A Mile! How to Drive a Golf Ball: 1940, I, under $15
THOMSON, JOHN
Golfing and Other Poems and Songs: 1893, F, $140-400

THOMSON, PETER & ZWAR, DESMOND
Wonderful World of Golf, This: 1969, ES, under $15
TILLINGHAST, A. W.
Cobble Valley Golf Yarns and Other Sketches: 1915, F, $15-40
Mutt and Other Golf Yarns: A New Cobble Valley Series, The: 1925, F, $15-40
TOLLEY, CYRIL J. H.
Modern Golfer, The: 1924, I, $15-40
TOSKI, BOB
Beginner's Guide to Golf: 1955, I, under $15
TOSKI, BOB & AULTMAN, DICK
12 Short Cuts to Better Golf: 1975, I, under $15
Bob Toski's Complete Guide to Better Golf: 1977, I, under $15
TOSKI, BOB & AULTMAN, DICK & GOLF DIGEST, EDITORS OF
Touch System for Better Golf, The: 1971, I, under $15
TOSKI, BOB & FLICK, JIM & DENNIS, LARRY
How to Become a Complete Golfer: 1978, I, under $15
TOSKI, BOB & TARDE, JERRY
Golf for a Lifetime: 1981, I, under $15
TOW, KRISTIN
International Golf Directory: Resorts, Clubs, Courses around the World: 1974, GC, under $15
TOWNSEND, PETER & REID, IAIN
Golf: 100 Ways to Improve your Game: 1977, I, under $15
TOWNSHEND, R. B.
Inspired Golf: 1921, I, under $15
TRAINING & EDUCATION ASSOCIATION
Golf: 1974, I, under $15
TRAVERS, JEROME D.
Travers' Golf Book: 1913, H, $40-80
TRAVERS, JEROME D. & CROWELL, JAMES J.
Fifth Estate: Thirty Years of Golf, The: 1926, H, $15-40
TRAVERS, JEROME D. & RICE, GRANTLAND
Winning Shot, The: 1915, H, $40-80
TRAVIS, WALTER
Practical Golf: 1901, I, $40-80
TRAVIS, WALTER J. & WHITE, WALTER & BELDAM, GEORGE W.
Art of Putting, The: 1904, I, $15-40
TREMAYNE, NICHOLAS
Golf: How to Become a Champion: 1975, I, under $15
TRESIDDER, PHIL
Golfer who Laughed, The: 1981, F, under $15
TREVILLION, PAUL
Dead Heat: The '69 Ryder Cup Classic: 1969, H, under $15
Perfect Putting Method, The: 1971, I, under $15
Save Strokes with the Stars: 1970, I, under $15
Tony Jacklin in Play: 1970, I, under $15
TREVINO, LEE & AULTMAN, DICK
Groove your Golf Swing My Way: 1976, I, under $15

BIBLIOGRAPHY GUIDELINES

See page 224 for "How To Use This Chapter"

TREVINO, LEE & BLAIR, SAM
  They Call Me Super Mex: An Autobiography: 1983, H, under $15
TREVINO, LEE & FRALEY, OSCAR
  I Can Help your Game: 1971, I, under $15
TRIEFUS, PAUL
  Most Excellent Historie of MacHamlet, Hys Handicap, etc..., The: 1922, F, $40-80
TRIPP, WILLIAM A.
  Geometry of Golf, The: 1960, I, $15-40
TRISCOTT, C. PETTE
  Golf in Six Lessons: 1924, I, $15-40
TRUMBULL, L. W. BENHAM
  Golftique: A Price Guide to Old Golf Clubs & other Golf Memorabilia: 1977, R, under $15
TUCKER, CECIL FINN
  Nineteenth Hole Romances and the Devious Methods of Joseph Blotchford: 1927, F, $15-40
TUFTS, RICHARD S.
  Principles Behind the Rules of Golf, The: 1960, RU, under $15
  Scottish Invasion: Being a Brief Review of American Golf etc..., The: 1962, H, $15-40
TULLOCH, W. W.
  ↙ Life of Tom Morris, With Glimpses of St. Andrews and Its Golfing Celebrities, The: 1908, H, $140-400
  ↙ Life and Times of Tom Morris, The (Reprint): 1982, H, $80-140
TURGEON, A. J.
  Turfgrass Management: 1980, GC, $15-40
TURNESA, JIM
  12 Lessons to Better Golf (American Edition): 1953, I, under $15
  Low Score Golf (British Edition): 1953, I, under $15
TUTHILL, MEX
  Golf without Gall: 1938, F, under $15
TUTTLE, ANTHONY
  Drive for the Green: 1969, F, under $15
TWADDLER, A.
  Golf Twaddle: 1897, F, $15-40
TWO OF HIS KIND (Pseudonym for FOX, G. D.)
  Six Handicap Golfer's Companion, The: 1909, I, $40-80
TYLER, RALPH G.
  Handbook on Golf for Beginners, A: 1914, I, $15-40
TYNER, FREDERICK D.
  Golfer's Dream, The: 1936, F, $15-40
UNITED STATES GOLF ASSOCIATION *MOSTLY ANNUALS*
  Conduct of Women's Golf, The: 1940, R, under $15
  Decisions on the Rules of Golf: 1971, RU, under $15
  ↙ Record Book of the USGA Championships and International Golf: 1895 +, R, $15-40
  United States Golf Association Yearbook: 1897 +, R, $5-140 (varies)
UNIVERSAL GOLF COMPANY
  Universal Golf Directory: Summary of Golf and Golf Etiquette: 1934, R, under $15
UZZELL, THOMAS H.
  Golf in the World's Oldest Mountains: 1926, GC, $40-80
VAILE, P. A.
  Golf on the Green: 1915, I, $15-40
  How to Drive: How to Approach: How to Putt: 1919, I, $15-40
  How to Learn Golf: Spalding Primer Series: 1922, I, under $15
  Illustrated Rules of Golf and the Etiquette of the Game, The: 1919, RU, $15-40
  Modern Golf: 1909, I, $15-40
  New Golf, The: 1916, I, $15-40

Putting Made Easy: The Mark G. Harris Method: 1935, I, $15-40
  Short Game, The: 1929, I, under $15
  Soul of Golf, The: 1912, I, $15-40
VALENTINE, JESSIE
  Better Golf ... Definitely: 1967, I, under $15
VALLI, JIM
  Golf Guide: Central Otago-Southland: 1979, GC, under $15
VAN DAALEN, NICHOLAS
  International Golf Guide, The: 1976, GC, under $15
VAN EVERA, MAXINE & ALCOTT, AMY
  Building Your Golf Swing for Better Golf: 1981, I, under $15
VAN HENGEL, STEVEN J.H.
  ↙ Early Golf: 1982, H, under $15
VAN LOAN, CHARLES E.
  Fore: Golf Stories: 1918, F, $15-40
VANDER MEULEN, JOHN M.
  Getting Out of the Rough: 1926, ES, $15-40
VARDON, A. & WILSON, E. W. J.
  Golfing Hints: 1912, I, $15-40
VARDON, HARRY
  ↙ Complete Golfer, The: 1905, GC & I, $15-40
  Gist of Golf, The: 1922, I, $15-40
  Golfing Life, My: 1933, H, $40-80
  How to Play Golf: 1912, I, $15-40
  Progressive Golf: 1920, I, $15-40
VARDON, HARRY & OTHERS
  Success at Golf: 1912, I, $15-40
VENTURI, KEN & BARKOW, AL
  Venturi Analysis: Learning Better Golf from Champions: 1981, I, under $15
VENTURI, KEN & FRALEY, OSCAR
  Comeback: The Ken Venturi Story: 1966, H, under $15
VERBECK, FRANK
  Hand-Book of Golf For Bears, A: 1900, F, $140-400
VETERAN
  Secret of Golf for Occasional Players, The: 1922, I, $15-40
VICTIM, A (Pseudonymn for FALLS, D.W.C.)
  A.B.C. of Golf, AN: 1898, F, $140-400
VON NIDA, NORMAN
  Golf Isn't Hard: 1949, I, under $15
VON NIDA, NORMAN & MacLAREN, MUIR
  Golf is My Business: 1956, H, under $15
VROOM, JERRY
  So You Want to be a Golfer?: 1973, I, under $15
W.C.B. (Pseudonym for BRZOZA, WALTER C.)
  Putting Secrets of the Old Masters: 1968, I, under $15
W. E. F. (Pseudonym for FAIRLIE, WALTER E.)
  Old Course of St. Andrews: Plans, With Names of Holes and Bunker: 1908, GC, $40-80
WALKER, OSCAR W.
  Practical Golf Lessons from a New Angle: 1949, I, under $15
WALSH, LEIGH
  How to Teach Yourself the Perfect Golf Swing: 1956, I, under $15
  Teach Yourself the New Upright Golf Swing: 1972, I, under $15
WARD-THOMAS, PAT
  Long Green Fairway, The: 1966, ES, under $15
  Masters of Golf: An Autobiography: 1981, H, under $15
  Not Only Golf: An Autobiography: 1891, H, under $15
  Royal and Ancient, The: 1980, H, under $15
  Shell Golfers' Atlas of England, Scotland and Wales: 1968, GC, $15-40
WARD-THOMAS, PAT & PRICE & STEEL & THOMSON & WIND
  ↙ World Atlas of Golf: 1977, GC, $15-40

WATSON, A. CAMPBELL
Podson's Golfing Year: 1930, F, $15-40
WATSON, TOM & HANNIGAN, FRANK
Rules of Golf: Illustrated and Explained, The: 1980, RU, under $15
WATSON, TOM & SEITZ, NICK
Getting Up and Down: How to Save Strokes from Forty Yards and In: 1983, I, under $15
WEBB, WARREN H.
Lessons on Golf: 1907, I, $15-40
WEBBER, LOUIS & KENNEDY, DENNIS
Golf Manners: 1968, I, under $15
WEBLING, W. HASTINGS
Fore: The Call of the Links: 1909, F, $15-40
Locker Room Ballads: 1925, F, $15-40
On and Off the Links: 1921, F, $15-40
WEETMAN, HARRY
Way to Golf, The: 1953, I, under $15
WEETMAN, HARRY & BALLANTINE, JOHN
Add to your Golf Power: 1963, I, under $15
WEISKOPF, TOM
Go for the Flag: The Fundamentals of Golf: 1969, I, under $15
WEISS, MIKE
100 Handy Hints on How to Break 100: 1951, I, under $15
WELDON, OLIVER
Golfing in Ireland: 1971, GC, under $15
WENDEHACK, CLIFFORD C.
Golf and Country Clubs: A Survey of the Requirements of Planning, etc. . . .: 1929, GC, $80-140
Recent Golf and Country Clubs in America: GC, $80-140
WESSON, DOUGLAS BERTRAM
🖝 I'll Never Be Cured and Don't Much Care: The History of an Acute Attack of Golf, etc. . . .: 1928, H, $15-40
WEST, HENRY L.
Lyrics of the Links: 1921, F, $15-40
WESTERN GOLF ASSOCIATION
🖝 Caddie Operations Manual: 1969, R, under $15
WETHERED, H.N.
Perfect Golfer, The: 1931, ES, $40-80
WETHERED, H.N. & SIMPSON, T.
🖝 Architectural Side of Golf, The: 1929, GC, $140-400
🖝 Architectural Side of Golf, The (Limited Edition): 1929, GC, over $400
🖝 Design for Golf (Reprint of Above): 1952, GC, $15-40
WETHERED, JOYCE & WETHERED, ROGER
Game of Golf, Vol. IX, The Lonsdale Library, The: 1931, AN, $15-40
WETHERED, ROGER
Golf from Two Sides: 1922, I, $15-40
WHEATLEY, VERA
Mixed Foursomes: A Saga of Golf: 1936, F, $15-40
WHIGHAM, H.J.
How to Play Golf: 1897, I, $40-80
WHITCOMBE, CHARLES ALBERT
Charles Whitcombe on Golf: 1931, I, under $15
Golf: 1949, I, under $15
WHITCOMBE, ERNEST R. & HIRST, FRANCIS
Golf I Teach: A Book of Instruction in Two Parts for Beginners and Others, The: 1947, I, under $15
WHITCOMBE, REGINALD A.
Golf's No Mystery: A Book for Golfers and Beginners, 1938, I, under $15
WHITE, FAIRMOUNT RICHMOND
Golf in the Seventies for Those in the Sixties: Psychology of Golf: 1963, ES, under $15

WHITE, JACK
Easier Golf: 1924, I, $15-40
Putting: 1921, I, $15-40
WHITE, RONALD JAMES
Golf As I Play It: 1953, I, under $15
WHITE, STEWART EDWARD
Shepper-Newfounder, The: 1931, F, $15-40
WHITLATCH, MARSHALL
Golf for Beginners and Others: 1910, I, $15-40
WHITTON, IVO HARRINGTON
Golf: 1937, I, $15-40
WICKHAM, VERNE
Municipal Golf Course: Organizing and Operating Guide, The: 1955, GC, under 15
WILD, PAYSON SIBLEY & TAYLOR, BERT LESTON & WOODWORTH, LAWRENCE C.
Links of Ancient Rome: 1912, F, $40-80
WILD, ROLAND
Golf: The Loneliest Game: 1969, ES, under $15
WILL, GEORGE
Golf the Modern Way: 1969, I, under $15
WILLIAMS, DAVID
How to Coach and Play Championship Golf: 1962, I, under $15
Science of the Golf Swing, The: 1969, I, under $15
WILLIAMS, EVAN
You Can Hit the Ball Farther: 1979, I, under $15
WILLIAMS, LEWIS
Golf without Tears: 1940, I, $15-40
WILSON, ENID
Gallery of Women Golfers, A: 1961, H, under $15
Golf for Women: 1964, I, under $15
WILSON, ENID & LEWIS, ROBERT ALLEN
So That's What I Do: 1935, I, under $15
WILSON, HARRY LEON
So This Is Golf: 1923, F, under $15
WILSON, KENNETH
It's All in the Swing: Self Help for the Average Golfer: 1947, I, under $15
To Better Golf in Two Strides: 1938, I, under $15
WILSON, MARK & BOWDEN, KEN
🖝 Best of Henry Longhurst, The: 1978, AN, under $15
WIND, HERBERT WARREN
🖝 Complete Golfer, The: 1954, AN, $15-40
Golf Quiz: 1980, AN, under $15
🖝 Herbert Warren Wind's Golf Book: 1971, ES, under $15
🖝 On The Tour with Harry Sprague: 1960, F, under $15
🖝 Story of American Golf: Its Champions and Its Championships, The: 1948, H, $40-80
🖝 Story of American Golf: Its Champions and Its Championships (2nd Edition): 1956, H, $15-40
Tips From the Top: 1955, I, under $15
Tips From the Top, Book 2: More Golf Lessons from the Country's Leading Pros, etc. . . .: 1956, I, under $15

BIBLIOGRAPHY GUIDELINES

ABBREV.	CATEGORY	REVIEWS BEGIN ON PAGE
AN	ANTHOLOGY	225
GC	GOLF COURSE	227
EQ	EQUIPMENT	230
ES	ESSAYS	232
F	FICTION	233
H	HISTORY	234
I	INSTRUCTIONAL	
R	REFERENCE	237
RU	RULES	

See page 224 for "How To Use This Chapter"

WINGATE, ROLAND
 Saving Strokes: 1934, I, under $15
WIREN, GARY
 Golf: 1971, I, under $15
 Planning and Conducting Junior Golf Programs: 1973, R, under
 $15
WIREN, GARY & COOP, DR. RICHARD
 New Golf Mind, The: 1978, I, under $15
WISE, SIDNEY L.
 Carolina Golfer Directory, 1976: 1976, GC, under $15
WODEHOUSE, P.G.
 Divots: 1927, F, $15-40
 ✓ Golf Omnibus, The: 1973, F, under $15
 Heart of a Goof, The: 1926, F, $15-40
 Wodehouse on Golf: 1940, F, $15-40
WOMAN GOLFER (Pseudonym for HOSKINS, MABEL S.)
 Golf for Women: 1916, I, $15-40
WOOD, HARRY B.
 Golfing Curios and the Like: 1910, R, over $400
 Golfing Curios and the Like (Limited Edition): 1911, R, Scarce
 Golfing Curios and the Like (Reprint): 1980, R, $15-40

WOY, BUCKY & PATTERSON, JACK
 Sign 'Em Up, Bucky: The Adventures of a Sport Agent: 1975, ES,
 under $15
WRIGHT, HARRY
 Short History of Golf in Mexico and the Mexico City Country
 Club, A: 1938, H, $80-140
WRIGHT, MICKEY
 Play Golf the Wright Way: 1962, I, under $15
WYNN, ANTHONY
 Death of a Golfer: 1976, F, under $15
YOGI, COUNT
 Five Simple Steps to Perfect Golf: 1973, I, under $15
YOUMANS, THOMAS GRANT
 Play Golf with Greater Ease: The New Scientific Game of Golf,
 etc....: 1939, I, under $15
ZAHARIAS, MILDRED "BABE"
 Championship Golf: 1948, I, under $15
ZAHARIAS, MILDRED "BABE" & PAXTON, HARRY
 This Life I've Led: My Autobiography: 1956, H, under $15
ZANGER, JACK
 Exercises for Better Golf: The Champions Way to a Stronger
 Game: 1965, I, under $15

GOLF CLUB HISTORIES

AUSTRALIA

Australian	1982
Barwon Heads	1973
Cobran-Barooga	1978
Concord	1939
Cromer	1979
Elanora	1977
Geelong	1967
Killara	1966
Kooyonga	1983
Liverpool	
Manly	1946
Metropolitan	1973
Mount Lofty	1975
Oatlands	1981
Peninsula	1975
Pennant Hills	1959
Riversdale	1977
Royal Canberra	1976
Royal Melbourne	1941 & 1972
Royal Sidney	1949
Sorrento	1974
Yarra Yarra	1971

CANADA

Beaconsfield	1979
Brantford	1979
Calgary	1972
Capilano	1981
Dunany	1967 & 1981
Dundas Valley	1979
Essex	1983
Idylwylde	1972
Kanawaki	1964
Laval Sur Le Lac	1967
Maritime Seniors	1942
Mississaugua	1981
Mount Bruno	1978
Oakville	1981
Ottawa Hunt	1983
Royal Montreal	1923 & 1973
Royal Quebec	1974
St. Charles	1965
St. Georges	1979
Toronto	1976
Westmount	1981
Weston	1980

ENGLAND

Aldeburgh	1984
Army	1983
Ashridge	1982
Bath	1980
Brighton & Hove	1973
Brookmans Park	1980
Dunstable Downs	1931
Felixstowe Ferry	1980
Formby	1972
Furness	1972
Golf Match	1938
Great Yarmouth & Caister	1932 & 1982
Hayling	1983
Hertfordshire (Misc.)	1972
Home Park	1950
Leatherjackets	1949
Lindrick	1951 & 1980
Longridge	1977

Manchester	1908 & 1982
Minehead & West Somerset	1982
Newbury & Crookham	1973
Northumberland	1978
Old Manchester	1909
Oxford & Cambridge	1949
Prince's Deal	1950
Richmond	1932
Royal Ashdown	1973
Royal Birkdale	1939
Royal Blackheath	1897 & 1981
Royal Isle of Wight	1886
Royal Liverpool	1933, 1969 & 1983
Royal North Devon	1964
Royal Wimbledon	1929 & 1965
St. George's Hill	1983
St. Stephens	1893
Seaton Carew	1974
Sussex (Misc.)	1977
Sutton Coldfield	1939
Walton Heath	1979
West Cancashire	1973
West Sussex	1981
Worcestershire	1979
Worthing	1980

HONG KONG

Royal Hongkong	1960

INDIA

Royal Calcutta	1979

IRELAND

Royal Dublin	1963
Woodbrook	1976

MALAYSIA

Selangor	1953

MEXICO

Mexico City	1938

NEW ZEALAND

Christchurch	1973
Manawatu	1970
Titirangi	1951

NORTHERN IRELAND

Ardglass	1982
Dunmurry	1980
Knock	1982
Royal Belfast	1981
Royal Portrush	1980
Scrabo	1982

SCOTLAND

Aboyne	1983
Arbroath	1904
Broughty	1978
Bruntsfield	1902
Cochrane Castle	1980
Craigmillar Park	1974
Crail	1936 & 1983
Dalbeattie	1912
Dalhousie	1968
Deeside	1953
Douglas Park	1982
Dumfries & Galloway	1980
Dunbar	1980
Falkirk Tryst	1926
Forfar	1971
Glasgow	1907
Golf House	1925 & 1975

Gullane	1982
Hawick	1898
Hilton Park	1977
Honourable Company	1944, 1946 & 1972
King James VI	1912
Kingknowe	1983
Kingussie	1911
Liberton	1980
Machrihanish	1922 & 1976
Melrose	1981
Murrayfield	1947
New (St. Andrews)	1982
North Berwick	1980
Panmure	1926
Prestwick	1938
Prestwick St. Nicholas	1950
Royal Aberdeen	1909 & 1980
Royal & Ancient	1907, 1956 1980 & 1984
Royal Burgess	1906 & 1936
Royal Dornoch	1977 & 1978
Royal Musselburgh	1974
Royal Perth	1935
Royal Troon	1974 & 1978
St. Andrews	1944
Scottish Ladies	1929
Selkirk	1983
Stirling	1969
Stromness	1974
Thistle	1824
Western (Gailes)	1947
Williamwood	1981

SOUTH AFRICA

Bedford	1967
Clovelly	1974
East London	1968
Maritzburg	1961
Mowbray	1939
Pretoria	1977
Rand Park	1971
Royal Durban	1952
Royal Johannesburg	1951
Scottburgh	1976
Uitenhage	1966

SRI LANKA (CEYLON)

Royal Colombo	1979

UNITED STATES

California

Annandale	1981
Claremont	1960
Green Hills	1980
Kagero	1975
Lakeside	1974
Los Angeles	1936 & 1973
Monterey Peninsula	1975
Olympic	1960
Presidio	1964
Red Hill	1972
Richmond	1978
Riviera	1976
San Francisco	1958
Victoria	1978
Wilshire	1979

Colorado		**Kent**	1980	**Rhode Island**		
Cherry Hills	1972	Wawashkamo	1983	Rhode Island	1952	
Connecticut		**Minnesota**		Wannamoisset	1948	
Brooklawn	1955 & 1970	Town & Country	1948	**South Carolina**		
Fairfield	1966	**Montana**		Columbia	1952	
Hartford	1955	Butte	1945 & 1949	**Tennessee**		
Innis Arden	1973 & 1980	**New Hampshire**		Chattanooga	1961	
New Haven	1949	Bald Peak	1964	**Texas**		
Round Hill	1979	**New Jersey**		Champions	1966	
Stanwich	1972	Canoe Brook	1965 & 1976	Dallas	1913	
Wee Burn	1979	Deal	1973	**Vermont**		
Florida		Echo Lake	1956	Ekwanok	1937, 1949 & 1974	
Dunedin	1945	Pine Valley	1963 & 1982	Mount Anthony	1944	
John's Island	1979	**New York**		Mountain View	1976	
Ponte Vedra	1982	Apawamis	1940 & 1965	Woodstock	1959	
Georgia		Ardsley	1929 & 1955	**Virginia**		
Augusta National	1976	Bedford	1965	James River	1957 & 1982	
Peachtree	1978	Edgewood	1938	Washington	1947 & 1973	
Hawaii		Fairview	1929	**Washington**		
Oahu	1981	Garden City	1949 & 1974	Broadmoor	1983	
Waialae	1981	Glens Falls	1923	Manito	1972	
Illinois		Huntington	1981	Seattle	1959 & 1972	
Butterfield	1970	Inwood	1951 & 1976	Tacoma	1969 & 1981	
Chicago	1967	Knollwood	1969	**West Virginia**		
Exmoor	1946 & 1972	Mahopac	1980	Berry Hills	1952	
Flossmoor	1979	Maidstone	1941	**Wisconsin**		
Glen View	1982	McGregor Links	1921	Blue Mound	1976	
Hades	1919	Mohawk	1973	Dairymen's	1939	
Hubbard Trail	1975	NYAC	1969	**WALES**		
Indian Hill	1964	Oak Hill	1977	Glamorganshire	1950	
LaGrange	1949	Orange Country	1974	Southerndown Ladies	1958	
Olympia Fields	1923	Park (Buffalo)	1978	**ZIMBABWE (RHODESIA)**		
Sunset Ridge	1973	Powelton	1982	Livingstone	1928	
Indiana		Rochester	1945 & 1971	Royal Salisbury	1973	
Ulen	1949	Rockaway	1952			
Kansas		St. Andrews	1938, 1963 & 1973			
Wichita	1975	Scarsdale	1948			
Maine		Shinnecock Hills	1923 & 1966			
Kebo Valley	1948	Siwanoy	1976			
Maryland		Sleepy Hollow	1919			
Burning Tree	1948, 1962 & 1972	Southampton	1975			
Chevy Chase	1958	USSGA	1954 & 1980			
Columbia	1938	Westhampton	1955			
Congressional	1984	Winged Foot	1984			
Kenwood	1978	Wykagyl	1968			
Henry Stambaugh	1973	**Ohio**				
Massachusetts		Country (Cleveland)	1964			
Bass River	1974	Dayton	1976			
Brae Burn	1947	Miami Valley	1963			
Charles River	1946	Mill Creek	1977			
The Country Club	1932 & 1981	Oakwood	1955 & 1980			
Eastward Ho	1978	**Oklahoma**				
Essex	1941 & 1954	Southern Hills	1977			
Highland	1951	**Pennsylvania**				
Kittansett	1968	Gulph Mills	1976			
Myopia	1941 & 1975	Longue Vue	1970			
N.E.S.G.A.	1972	Meadville	1980			
Oak Bluffs	1914	Merion	1977			
Oakley	1948 & 1973	Merion Cricket	1965			
Tedesco	1953 & 1978	Niblick	1947			
Thorny Lea	1950	Oakmont	1980			
Wollaston	1945 & 1970	Ozone	1911, 1925, 1927, 1957			
Woodland	1952 & 1977	Philadelphia	1965			
Michigan		Philadelphia Cricket	1954			
Crystal Downs	1981	Yardley	1978			
Detroit	1939	York	1929 & 1975			

A collection of books written by pro tour players. This photo originally appeared on the cover of Bay Hill Classic program.

CHAPTER 10 — PERIODICALS

Although articles on golf appeared in *The Sporting Magazine* in England as early as the 1820's, the first periodical devoted to golf appeared in 1890, when *Golf* was first published. A weekly publication, it was full of announcements of forthcoming events, tournament results, golf course information, equipment innovations, letters to the editor, and advertisements for golf equipment and related products.

The number of golfers was increasing so rapidly in the 1890's that the publishers of *Golf* decided to issue the magazine twice a week: on Tuesdays and Fridays. Unfortunately, this idea only lasted for a few months during the summer of 1894. In the same period in 1894, *The Golfer,* the first American golf magazine, started production in New York. By World War I, there were over a dozen golf periodicals throughout the world and by the 1930's there were so many that it became difficult for the golf enthusiast to decide which ones to read.

Periodicals, whether from the 1890's or 1950's, contain a wealth of information for the golf collector. The articles and advertisements contain many facts that have not appeared elsewhere in golf literature. The reading of old golf magazines is most enjoyable for the golf collector since he knows that he will invariably discover a new bit of trivia about a player or an ad for a club in his collection. Other revealing articles might discuss golf course openings and new theories on the golf swing. The cover illustrations, sketches and photos from the older magazines are also collectible.

Today, there are many fine golf periodicals available on the newsstand. The successful ones are generally those which have withstood the test of time. Most of the popular magazines in print today have been in existence for over twenty-five years.

The following list includes as many golf periodicals as could be found as a result of library research and queries to golf collectors. Wherever the beginning or ending dates of publication are not known, a question mark (?) has been inserted. The appearance of a plus (+) next to the ending date of publication denotes that there probably were later issues, but the authors of this book could not find a record of any. Major title changes are also accounted for since changes in ownership or format often resulted in a new name for the periodical. Therefore the notes about each magazine link it to its previous or subsequent title, if any. Of the numerous local, state and association publications, only the early or more notable ones have been listed.

The values of these golf periodicals vary from a dollar or less for the majority of the modern publications up to the fifteen dollar range for the ones issued prior to the 1940's. The earlier periodicals are so rarely traded that they have no set value. However, complete volumes of the turn of the century publications are valued into the thousands of dollars.

REMINDER: If any readers have additional information or corrections to this or any other chapter in this book, please contact the authors in the manner described in the introduction, so that revisions can be made in future editions of *The Encyclopedia.*

Golf magazine was the first periodical totally devoted to the game of golf. First appearing in London in 1890, it was published every Tuesday and Friday, weekly, and in modern times, on a monthly basis. In 1899, the title was changed to *Golf Illustrated*.

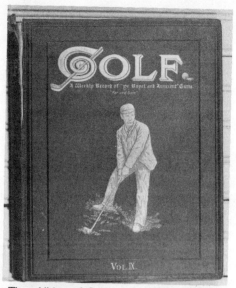

The publishers of *Golf* made hard bound volumes of the magazines available to readers for a reasonable fee. These volumes can still be found and are superb reference books for any golf library.

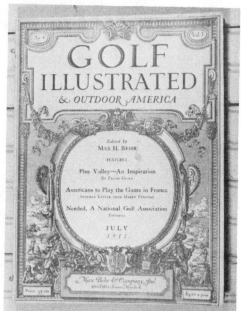

From 1914 to 1935, American *Golf Illustrated* featured articles, photos, and advertisements for the well-to-do golfer. There was more emphasis on high society happenings than on genuine golf competition. The content differs greatly from the British periodicals of the same period.

Golfers Magazine, The American Golfer, and *Golf* were some of the fine periodicals which provided an immense amount of reading material for golfers in the early twentieth century. Since there were no televised golf tournaments to keep the golfers entertained on rainy or cold weekends, they had plenty of time to read articles by the many fine golf writers of the period.

The American Golfer was the instructional magazine for the golfer who played the game for reasons other than social interaction. In production from 1908 to 1936, the first editor was champion golfer Walter Travis, who was succeeded by writer Grantland Rice.

This announcement from the publisher of *The Golfer* in 1898 firmly states his feelings about the golf magazine business.

The Golfer

Established 1894

An Official Organ of the United States Golf Association
An Official Organ of the Intercollegiate Golf Association
An Official Organ of the Central New York State League
184 Pearl Street, Boston, Mass., U. S. A.

Boston, July 1, 1898.

Gentlemen: The Golfer opened Volume Seven with its May number. It is three years older than any other Golf publication and has been under the same ownership and management since its first number. It has witnessed the demise of a number of golf publications, both weekly and monthly. It is not an experiment and your subscription is solicited to a well-established magazine. The price is one dollar a year and we would be pleased to receive a subscription of yourself and Club if agreeable.

Very truly yours,

THE GOLFER, Boston.

Edited by
JAMES SHIELDS MURPHY.

The cover of this hard to find publication does a good job of explaining its contents. *The Golfer* was one of several magazines which were simultaneously the official organ of the United States Golf Association. The magazine began in 1894 when golf was still in its infancy in America.

Harper's Weekly published many articles and illustrations about golf. This cover from 1897 features a scene by the prolific golf artist A. B. Frost.

Jack Nicklaus is featured on this cover of Japan's *Golf Magazine*.

LIST OF GOLF PERIODICALS - (1890 TO PRESENT)

10,000 Lakes Golfer And Outdoor Magazine - Minneapolis
Published from June, 1927 to March, 1928.
>Title changed to 'Amateur Golfer and Outdoor Magazine', then 'Amateur Golfer and Sportsman', and then 'Golfer and Sportsman'.

19th Hole, The - Philadelphia
Published from 1939 to October, 1946.
>Merged into U.S. 'Golf World'

19th Hole, The - St. Louis
Published from 1929 to ?

Amateur Golfer And Outdoor Magazine - Minneapolis
Published from April, 1928 to August, 1929.
>Formerly '10,000 Lakes And Outdoor Magazine'. Title changed to 'Amateur Golfer And Sportsman', Then 'Golfer And Sportsman'.

Amateur Golfer And Sportsman - Minneapolis
Published from September, 1929 to December, 1932.
>Formerly '10,000 Lakes And Outdoor Magazine' and 'Amateur Golfer and Outdoor Magazine'. Title then changed to 'Golfer And Sportsman'.

American Golf - New York
Published from March, 1900 to April, 1902.
>Merged with 'The Golfer' in 1902. Subtitle may vary.

American Golfer - New York
Published from November, 1908 to January, 1936.
>Monthly October to June & biweekly July to September until September 15, 1909. Edited by Walter Travis until April 3, 1920 when Grantland Rice took over. It then became weekly, biweekly and then monthly. From February, 1936 until 1937 when it was included as part of 'Sports Illustrated' and was then phased out.

Bridle And Golfer - Detroit
Published from November, 1921 to April, 1932.
>Early issues titled 'Detroit Bridle' and 'Bridle'.

Bulletin Of The Green Section Of The USGA
Published from 1921 to 1933.
>From 1936 to 1942 published as 'Turf Culture' or similar title. It was later revived in 1963 as the 'Green Section Record'.

California Golfer - Long Beach
Published from September, 1982 to ?

California Golfer, The - San Mateo & Other Locations
Published from July, 1949 to 1951.
>Title changed to 'The Golfer' in 1951, then 'The National Golfer' in 1957.

Canadian Golfer - Brantford, Ontario
Published from May, 1915 to 1936 +.
>Early issues can be found in the Hamilton, Ontario Public Library.

Car Illustrated And Golf - London
Published from June, 1922 to December, 1928.
Formerly 'The Car Illustrated Incorporating Golf'.

Car Illustrated Incorporating Golf, The - London
Published from March, 1922 to April, 1922.
Title changed to 'Car Illustrated And Golf'. A weekly publication.

Carolina Golfer - Charlotte
Published from 1964 to present.
Issued six time per year.

Chicago Golfer - Chicago
Published from 1925 to ?

Country Club Magazine & Pacific Coast Golf & Motor - Los Angeles
Published from 1925 to 1932.

Country Club Golfer - Irvine, CA
Published from 1971 to Present.

Country Club Life - Philadelphia
Published from May, 1914 to ?
Issued weekly.

Course And Clubhouse - New York
Published from January, 1919 to July, 1921.
Formerly 'The Pro'.

Delaware Valley Golfer - Philadelphia
Published from 1961 to 1963.
Issued monthly from March to December.

Dutch Golf - Holland
Published from 1952 to ?

El Golfista Mexicano - Mexico
Published from 1949 to ?

English Golf - London
Published in the 1950's.
Merged with 'Golf In Britain'.

Fairway - San Francisco
Published from September, 1924 to 1929 +.
Later titled 'Game And Gossip'. The University of California at Berkley Library has all issues.

Fairway And Hazard - London
Published from 1928 to 1963.
Official organ of the Ladies' Golf Union. Title changed to 'The Women's Golf Magazine' in 1963.

Fairways - Hialeah, FL
Published from February, 1962 to ?

Fairways Of New England - Boston
Published from 1925 to ?
Name changed to 'The Six States Golfer'.

Florida Golf Week - Winter Haven
Published from 1975 to present.
Issued weekly.

Florida Golfer - Miami
Published from 1968 to 1976.

Fore - Los Angeles
Published from Summer, 1968 to present.
Published quarterly by The Southern California Golf Association.

Fore - Evansville, IN
Published from July, 1958 to ?

Golden State Golfer - Oakland, CA
Published from December, 1947 to ?

Golf - New York
Published from September, 1897 to May, 1917.
Absorbed 'Golfing' in 1899 and 'American Golf' in 1902. It was one of the official bulletins of the United States Golf Association.

Golf - London
Published from September, 1890 to June, 1899.
This was the first magazine devoted entirely to golf. Bi-weekly only for the period from May 29 to July 24, 1894. Title changed to 'Golf Illustrated' June, 16, 1899.

Golf
Published from April, 1938 to November, 1941.
Formerly called 'National Golf Review'. Grantland Rice was the editor.

Golf - Madrid, Spain
Published from ? to ?
Published by The Federacion Espanola De Golf.

Golf - Canton, OH
Published from January, 1959 to ?
Monthly except no issue in October or December.

Golf & Club - Santa Monica, CA
Published from January, 1968 to ?

Golf And Lawn Tennis - Cambridge, MA
Published from 1900 to 1901 +.
Originally titled 'American Lawn Tennis'.

Golf And Social Sports - Montreal
Published from March, 1927 to June, 1929 +.

Golf Business - New York
Published from 1978 to August, 1981.
Originally titled 'Golfdom'. Name changed with change in ownership.

Golf Canada - St. Lambert, Quebec
Published from April, 1967 to ?
Issued ten times per year.

Golf Club News - England
Published from ? to January, 1979.
Titled changed to 'Golf News'.

Golf Collectors' Society Bulletin - Lafayette Hill, PA
Published from 1970 to Present.
> Editor Joe Murdoch has compiled almost eighty of these fact filled bulletins for members of the Golf Collectors' Society. A somewhat informal publication issued on a somewhat irregular basis, it contains articles which are most enjoyable for the diehard collector.

Golf Course Management - Lawrence, KS
Published from January, 1979 to Present.
> Formerly called 'Golf Course Superintendent'. Published by the Golf Course Superintendents Association of America.

Golf Course Reporter - St. Charles, IL
Published from March, 1951 to December, 1965.
> Name changed to 'Golf Course Superintendent'. Formerly titled 'Greenkeeper's Reporter'.

Golf Course Superintendent, The - Des Plaines, IL and Lawrence, KS
Published from January, 1966 to December, 1979.
> Title changed to 'Golf Course Management'. Formerly 'Golf Course Reporter'. A Golf Course Superintendent's Association of America Publication.

Golf Course, The - New York
Published from January, 1916 to 1923.
> Published by Carter's Tested Seeds. Volume 5 is the last known issue, although the Library of Congress shows 1923 as end of publication.

Golf Digest - Evanston, IL & Norwalk, CT
Published from 1950 to Present.
> First issue titled 'Arrowhead Golf Digest'. They moved to Norwalk, Connecticut in the mid 1970's. the magazine became monthly in 1962.

Golf Et Le Golfeur - Paris
Published from 1925 to 1937 +.

Golf Guide - Santa Monica, CA
Published from 1974 to ?
> Continues 'Golf Guide And Golf Club'.

Golf Illustrated - London
Published from June, 1899 to Present.
> A weekly, started as 'Golf' in 1890.

Golf Illustrated - New York
Published from January, 1914 to August, 1935.
> Title changed from 'Golf Illustrated And Outdoor America' in January, 1923. Merged with 'American Golfer' in 1935.

Golf Illustrated - Temecula, CA
Published from Summer, 1973 to ?
> Issued quarterly.

Golf Illustrated And Outdoor America - New York
Published from April, 1914 to January, 1923.
> Title changed to 'Golf Illustrated' in January, 1923. Then merged with 'American Golfer' in 1935.

Golf In Australia - Sydney
Published from 1929 to 1962 +.

Golf In Britain - London
Published from August, 1952 to ?
> Incorporating 'English Golf'.

Golf Industry - Miami
Published from October, 1975 to Present.
> A trade journal for golf professionals, retailers, etc.

Golf Journal — New York and Far Hills, NJ
Published from Spring, 1948 to Present.
> An official publication of the United States Golf Association. Initially six issues, then eight issues, then 10 issues for a while in the 1970's, and now back to eight issues per year.

Golf Life - Los Angeles
Published from August, 1949 to April, 1966 +.

Golf Magazine - New York
Published from April, 1959 to Present.
> Frequency varied initially with twelve issues per year starting 1963.

Golf Magazine - Tokyo, Japan
Published from 1953 to ?
> Text in Japanese.

Golf Monthly - Glasgow
Published from 1910 to Present.

Golf News - Johannesburg, South Africa
Published from December, 1978 to 1982 +.

Golf News - Hove, England
Published from February, 1979 to Present.
> Formerly 'Golf Club News'.

Golf Review - Swampscott, MA
Published from 1983 to Present.
> This informative publication is issued in a monthly newspaper format.

Golf Score - Santa Monica, CA
Published from 1977 to ?
> Issued eight times per year.

Golf Shop Operations - Norwalk, CT
Published from 1981 to Present.
> Supercedes 'Pro Shop Operations'.

Golf Traveler, The - Ft. Lauderdale, FL
Published from 1976 to Present.
> Issued six times per year.

Golf World - Southern Pines, NC
Published from 1974 to Present.
> Formerly titled 'Golf World Newsweekly'. They moved to Southern Pines in 1968 and publish weekly except bimonthly from October to December.

Golf World - London
Published from 1962 to Present.
> Absorbed 'Golfing' in 1970.

Golf World Newsweekly - Pinehurst, NC
Published from June, 1947 to 1974.
> The title was changed to 'Golf World' in 1974 and continues to be the authoritative weekly golf news source in the United States. It incorporated 'The National Golfer' in 1968.

Golfdom - Chicago
Published from February, 1927 to 1978.
> Title changed to 'Golf Business' in 1978. There were several owners during the period from 1968 to 1978.

Golfer And Sportsman - Minneapolis
Published from January, 1933 to February, 1943.
> Formerly known as '10,000 Lakes And Outdoor Magazine', 'Amateur Golfer And Outdoor Magazine' and 'Amateur Golfer And Sportsman'.

Golfer And Sportsman - California
Published form 1949 to ?

Golfer, The - San Mateo, CA
Published form 1951 to 1957.
> Titled 'The California Golfer' from 1949. Title changed to 'The National Golfer in 1957.

Golfer, The - Edinburgh
Published from August, 1894 to 1898.
> Became 'The Golfer's Magazine' in 1898.

Golfer, The - New York
Published from 1894 to October, 1903.
> Subtitle may vary. Originally started as 'Outdoors, A Magazine Of Country Life'. This publication was the oldest golf magazine in America and served as the official organ of the United States Golf Association, Intercollegiate Golf Association, and Central New York State League. It Merged into 'Field And Stream' in 1903.

Golfer, The - Pittsburgh
Published from 1925 to ?

Golfers Delight - Sacramento
Published from 1980 to ?
> Issued ten times per year.

Golfer's Magazine - Edinburgh
Published from 1898 to ?
> Formerly titled 'The Golfer'.

Golfers Magazine - Chicago
Published from May, 1902 to September, 1931.
> Chick Evans, the champion golfer turned author, was the editor. The magazine was known for its beautiful covers done by the famous illustrators of the day. It probably was not monthly at its inception.

Golfing - Chicago
Published from April, 1933 to 1968.
> Five issues per year. Publication suspended between July, 1942 and March, 1947.

Golfing - London & Glasgow
Published from June, 1895 to February, 1897.
> This weekly changed its title to 'Golfing and Cycling Illustrated' on February 4, 1897, then 'Golfing and Cycling' in November, 1898.

Golfing - New York
Published from 1899 to 1902.
> Another of the "Official" United States Golf Association Magazines, it merged with 'Golf' of New York in 1899.

Golfing - London
Published from 1898 to 1970.
> Combined into 'Golf World' in 1970.

Golf And Cycling - London & Glasgow
Published form November, 1898 to 1910 +.
> Formerly 'Golfing' and 'Golfing And Cycling Illustrated'.

Golfing And Cycling Illustrated - London & Glasgow
Published from February, 1897 to November, 1898.
> Formerly 'Golfing'. Title changed to 'Golfing And Cycling' in November, 1898.

Golfing Gentlewomen - London
Published from 1913 to May, 1916.
> A supplement to and continued as a department of 'Gentlewomen'.

Green Section Record - New York and Far Hills, NJ
Published from 1963 to Present.
> A United States Golf Association Publication. Originally published until 1933 as the 'Bulletin of the Green Section of the USGA'. Until this publication was revived in 1963 the USGA issued regional turf newsletters.

Greenkeeper's Reporter - Cleveland
Published from July, 1933 to February, 1951.
> July issue called 'Greenkeeper's Bulletin'. Formerly 'The National Greenkeeper'. Title changed in September, 1933 to 'Golf Course Reporter'. A publication of the Golf Course Superintendents Association of America.

Gulf Coast Golfer - Houston
Published from February, 1984 to Present.
> A newspaper tabloid.

Irish Golf - Dublin
Published from 1929 to ?

Irish Golfer, The - Ireland
Published from September, 1899 to ?
    Originally a weekly publication.

Journal Of Board Of Greenkeeping Research - Bingely,
  England
Published from November, 1921 to 1949 +.

Junior Golfer - New York
Published from 1966 to 1969.
    Published quarterly by The United States Golf
    Association Junior Golf Foundation.

Kansas City Golfer - Kansas City
Published from July, 1922 to 1924.
    Title changed to 'The Western Golfer'.

Le Golf - Paris
Published from 1929 to 1936 +.

Met Golfer, The - New York
Published from 1983 to ?

Metropolitan Golfer - New York
Published from July, 1923 to October, 1929.
    For the Christmas number 1923-27 combined with
    'Southern Golfer' as 'Southern Golfer And
    Metropolitan Golfer'.

Michigan Golfer - Ypsilanti
Published from April, 1983 to Present.
    Monthly April to September.

Midwest Golfer And Club (Sports) Review - Wilmette, IL
Published from 1921 to 1935 .
    Published by the Chicago District Golf Association.
    Title may vary.

National Golf Review
Published from November, 1936 to February, 1938.
    The title was changed to 'Golf' in April, 1938,
    Grantland Rice was the editor.

National Golfer, The - San Mateo, Etc.
Published from 1957 to 1968.
    Titled 'The California Golfer' from 1949, then
    changed to 'The Golfer' in 1951. Merged into 'Golf
    World' in 1968.

National Greenkeeper, The - Cleveland
Published from January, 1927 to June, 1933.
    Some issues have 'And Turf Culture' added to the
    title. Title changed to 'Greenkeeper's Reporter'.

Nebraska Golf - Nebraska
Published from 1983 to ?

New England Golf News - Worcester, MA
Published from April, 1916 to ?
    Also titled 'Golf News, New England'.

New Zealand Golf Illustrated - Auckland
Published from 1929 to 1962 +.

Northwest Golfer And Country Club - Seattle
Published from 1930 to ?

On The Green - Orlando
Published from 1979 to ?

On The Green - Myrtle Beach
Published from 1977 to Present.
    South Carolina Regional Magazine.

Pacific Coast Golfer - Seattle
Published from 1926 to 1942 +.

Par Golf - London
Published from January, 1974 to December, 1976 +.

PGA Magazine - New York, then Palm Beach Gardens,
F L
Published from 1920 to Present.
    The official publication of the Professional Golfers
    Association of America.

Philadelphia Golfer - Philadelphia
Published from 1924 to June, 1929.
    Became 'Philadelphia Golfer And Sportsman'.

Philadelphia Golfer And Sportsman - Philadelphia
Published from July, 1929 to ?
    Formerly the 'Philadelphia Golfer'.

Popular Golf - London
Published from April, 1954 to ?

Pro Shop Operations - Norwalk, CT
Published from ? to 1981.
    Combined with 'Golf Shop Operations'.

Pro, The - New York
Published from May, 1917 to December, 1918.
    Title changed to 'Course And Clubhouse' in 1919.

Professional Golfer, The - London
Published from 1929 to ?

Score - Toronto
Published from spring, 1981 to Present.
    Published quarterly.

Senior Golf - Myrtle Beach
Published from 1983 to Present.
    Issued six times per year.

Senior Golfer Journal - Myrtle Beach
Published from 1981 to ?
    Issued quarterly.

Six States Golfer - Boston
Published from ? to ?
    Formerly titled 'Fairways of New England'.

South African Golf - Capetown
Published from June, 1926 to Present.

South Florida Golfer - Palm Beach Gardens
Published from 1983 to Present.
  A weekly publication of golf happenings.

Southern Golfer
Published in the 1920's.
  See 'Metropolitan Golfer'.

Southern Golfer And Metropolitan Golfer
Published in the 1920's.
  See 'Metropolitan Golfer'.

Svensk Golf - Sweden
Published from 1975 to Present.

Tee It Up - Atlanta
Published from 1971 to ?
  A short lived publication of the National Junior
Golf Association.

Tee Time - Decatur, GA
Published from 1978 to Present.
  Publication of the Georgia State Golf Association
  and the Georgia PGA.

Tee Topics - London
Published from 1929 to 1936 +.

Texas Golf - Austin
Published from October, 1978 to Present.

Towne And Fairway - Los Angeles
Published from 1923 to ?

Western Golf Topics - Los Angeles
Published from 1948 to 1949 +.

Western Golfer, The - Kansas City
Published from 1924 to September, 1927.
  Formerly 'Kansas City Golfer'.

Western New York Golfer - Buffalo
Published from January, 1925 to ?

Woman Golfer, The - Greensboro, NC
Published from July, 1946 to ?

Women's Golf Magazine - London
Published from 1963 to ?
  Official organ of the Ladies' Golf Union. Title
  changed from 'Fairway And Hazard' in 1963.

World Of Golf, The - England
Published from April, 1905 to November, 1906 +.
  A weekly. They claimed to have the largest circula-
  tion of any golf paper.

CHAPTER 11 — PHOTOGRAPHS

Many golfers have certain mental images of famous golfers or golf occurrences. Since most of us have not been able to personally witness the great happenings in the game of golf, we must often depend on the talents of a photographer. Therefore the images etched in our minds result from pictures seen in newspapers, golf magazines, books, and of course, on television. As a result of many fine photographs, golfers usually have an easy time recalling particular moments in golf history such as: Arnold Palmer holing putts at The Masters; Tom Watson chipping in on the 71st hole of the 1982 U.S. Open at Pebble Beach; Sam Snead wearing his everpresent straw hat; Bobby Jones at the finish of his classic swing; the determined look of Jack Nicklaus as he lines up a crucial putt (and the resulting jubilation after he makes the putt!!); and, the rear view of Ben Hogan's famous one iron shot in the 1950 U.S. Open at Merion.

The aforementioned are just a few of the better known golf happenings which have been preserved through photography. While the modern golf photographs are generally not collectible, they are certainly important to the game. The photos of particular value are most often the early ones, the unusual ones, the fantastic views of golf courses, and those that have been autographed.

Photographs pertaining to golf existed as early as the mid nineteenth century. These photos, which were usually portraits or group pictures of golfers, are sought after by golf collectors. Some of the photos which the collector may find are actually reproductions made at a later date, so one should seek expert advice before investing substantial sums of money in old pictures.

The first professional photographer with an interest in golf is believed to have been Thomas Rodger, who was active in St. Andrews from 1849 to 1883. His full length portraits of prominent golfers were usually done in his studio and have appeared in some of the early golf books. Since photographs could not be reproduced by means of a printing press in the mid nineteenth century, engravings of the scenes in the early photos would be made for use in books. This was done with Rodger's portrait of golfer Allan Robertson which was taken circa 1855. At a later date, an engraver transferred the image of Robertson to a wooded setting. It is this engraving that readers of history books are most familiar with today.

Golf history buffs would be interested in knowing that Sir Hugh Lyon Playfair was a close friend of Rodger and was very much interested in the photographic experiments being conducted in Scotland at the time. Playfair was an avid golfer and can be seen in various early golf photographs.

Fine golf photos can be seen in several golf books which portray a pictorial history of the game. *British Golf Links,* written by Horace Hutchinson in 1897, is known for its fine views of golf courses as are many of the modern guides to golf courses. Peter Dobereiner's *The Glorious World of Golf,* is known for its superb collection of old and modern golf subjects, many of which are in color. Many of the modern photographs of players, tournament play and golf courses have been taken for use in the various golf periodicals, rather than for inclusion in books.

The earliest known golf photograph taken in the United States dates to 1888 and shows John Reid and his companions playing golf in a pasture in Yonkers, New York. Later that year, they established the St. Andrews Golf Club which not only moved several times, but grew from three holes to six, and finally, eighteen. There was a large apple tree at the course which served as a common meeting place thereby causing these early golfers to be known as "The Apple Tree Gang."

The photos of the early British golfers from the nineteenth century are most interesting to study. This time period produced many changes in the game and much can be learned from the photos about the equipment, styles of play and lifestyles of the players. The collector is frequently faced with the challenging task of identifying the golfers in the early photos.

Early negatives, as well as some in the 1920's, were made of glass. Over the years, reproduction photographs have been produced from either the original negatives or from an original print in good condition. These photos are priced from ten to thirty dollars and are much more affordable for the average collector as compared to the actual antique photographs which can be over a hundred years old and worth hundreds of dollars. There are also several modern golf photographers who are marketing actual photographic prints of their works to the golfing public. These photos are carefully printed under strict supervision and sometimes sell for hundreds of dollars.

An early photograph image printed on glass. This scene may have been printed in this manner for the purpose of projecting with a lantern, similar to a modern slide show.

These members of Richmond Park Golf Club, near London, did not mind a little discomfort on their journey to the golf course in 1925. Their course had been opened two years earlier when the Prince of Wales (later King Edward VIII) drove off the first ball.

Watty Alexander, an early caddie, is shown on the job. The style of clubs helps to determine that the date of this photo is in the 1860-1880 period.

An interesting family portrait from the 1890's.

Tom Morris poses in a bunker. Several of these pictures exist, some of which have been autographed.

Tom Morris looks out of the window above his shop along the eighteenth hole at the Old Course in St. Andrews.

Bobby Jones was fond of this photo which he would often send to admirers. This one was autographed to one of the authors in the 1960's, a time when Jones' crippling condition made it difficult for him to write.

This scene from 1888 is famous for being the first golf photo taken in the United States. John Reid (at the far right) is shown playing golf in a pasture near his Yonkers, New York home. His first golf clubs were provided by his friend Robert Lockhart who had purchased them from Tom Morris in St. Andrews, Scotland. Shortly after this photo was taken, Reid was one of the founders of the St. Andrews Golf Club. He was also instrumental in the formation of the United States Golf Association in 1894.

Freddie Tait is shown watching his brother, Alec, putting on the links at St. Andrews. Tait was a superb amateur champion in the latter part of the nineteenth century.

Arnold Palmer playing from the rough at Royal Birkdale in the 1961 British Open. He went on to win which resulted in a renewed American interest in the championship. Notice that the scorer's standard does not show the scores as related to par but rather to "4's".

Tom Rodger was responsible for taking this portrait of Allan Robertson in the 1850's. Robertson was known both as the finest golfer of his day and as a talented feather ball maker.

The finest players of their era pose for the camera. Alex Herd and J. H. Taylor are shown standing, while James Braid and Harry Vardon are seated. From 1892 through 1920, these professionals combined for seventeen British Open Victories and seventeen second place finishes. To say that they dominated British golf would be an understatement.

This photo shows a team of amateurs from the United States which played Great Britain in 1921. This match, held at Hoylake, was the forerunner of The Walker Cup and was the first overseas tournament appearance of Bobby Jones. Tommy Armour played for the British side which lost 9 to 3.

From left to right: William C. Fownes, Jones, Wood Platt, Fred Wright, Francis Ouimet, Paul Hunter, Jesse Guilford. Chick Evans was a member of the team but was not present for the photo.

This photo is one of a series recently printed from original glass negatives dating from the 1870's.

Peter Alliss, member of numerous British Ryder Cup Teams and now a television commentator, is shown at age fifteen in the British Boys Open Championship. On the back of this photo is a handwritten comment by Henry Cotton, a three time winner of the British Open, golf historian and teacher. Cotton writes: "This could not be Young Peter's grip of the club . . . all sloppy, left thumb 'outside', clubhead twisted. Must have been a swing for the camera."

This 2 page series documents one of the most memorable golf shots in the history of the game. Tom Watson is shown chipping in for a birdie on the 17th hole of the final round of the 1982 U.S. Open at the Pebble Beach Golf Links in California. British photographer Lawrence Levy is credited for this series which not only captures Watson's reaction, but also shows the ball going into the hole. A birdie on the finishing hole enabled him to win the Championship by two strokes over Jack Nicklaus.

1

2

5

6

3

4

7

8

CHAPTER 12 — POSTAGE STAMPS

Golf postage stamps are relatively modern collectibles as the first stamp that actually showed a golfer was issued by Cape Verde in 1962. Most of the stamps have been issued to promote tourism such as the Caribbean countries have done, while some countries, such as Ras Al Khaima, primarily produce stamps for the collector. Golf collectors tend to be interested in the commemorative stamps which feature a golf course opening, tournament or a great player.

Although Cape Verde's stamp showed a golfer, it was not the first golf stamp issued. In 1958, French West Africa produced a stamp which showed some golf clubs among other sports equipment. There are now thirty-five countries which have offered golf related stamps.

Some stamps included in this chapter require a little imagination to include them in the golf category. For instance, in 1953, Japan showed a view of Mt. Unzen as seen from the Sasebo Golf Course. Without previous knowledge of this fact, one would not consider it a golf stamp. It is some of these unknowns that add to the fun of collecting golf stamps.

First day covers, cachets, post office posters and corner cards of golf manufacturers and resorts are all collected and are often very attractive. Some of the major tournaments have temporary post offices at the course and will issue special postmarks. There has been a colorful cachet issued at the British Open for many years and is a welcome addition to any collection.

Although golf stamps and covers are relatively inexpensive, some items may be difficult to obtain. This requires the collector to have both patience and perseverance. Those new to stamp collecting will soon find that a familiarity with world geography is very helpful.

Some stamps are issued in sets and are usually sold in that manner by dealers. Often the non-golf stamps that have been included in the sets are sports related and may also be of interest to the buyer.

THE PRICES OF GOLF STAMPS RANGE FROM $2 TO $5 FOR INDIVIDUAL STAMPS AND FROM $5 to $30 FOR SETS. FIRST DAY ISSUES USUALLY SELL FOR LESS THAN $5. IT IS ADVISABLE TO CONSULT A DEALER FOR SPECIFIC PRICES.

THE STAMPS LISTED ARE SHOWN WITH THE DATE OF ISSUE AND *SCOTT'S CATALOG* NUMBER WHICH WILL ASSIST THE COLLECTOR IN MAKING PURCHASES. IN A FEW INSTANCES, A *MINKUS CATALOG* NUMBER WILL BE USED INSTEAD OF *SCOTT'S*.

ALDERNEY (GREAT BRITAIN)
6/14/83 Part of the first set of stamps issued by Alderney. (Minkus set AK1-12)

AUSTRALIA
7/24/74 (592 out of set 590-596)

BAHAMAS
8/68 (272 out of set 272-275)

BERMUDA
11/1/71   A series featuring golf courses of Bermuda:

Ocean View (284)

Port Royal (285)

Castle Harbour (286)

Belmont (287)

BOPHUTHATSWANA

12/5/80 Sun City Hotel
Casino Country Club. (64)

12/5/80 Sun City Gary Player
Country Club. (65)

CAPE VERDE
1/18/62 (325 out of set
320-325)

CHRISTMAS ISLAND
2/12/80 Commemorating 25 years of golf on the island:

Ninth green. (93)

Clubhouse. (94)

COLUMBIA
12/9/80 Issued for the
1980 World Cup Golf
Championship. (C695)

COOK ISLANDS
7/7/69 One of the prettiest golf stamps (263
out of set 254-263)

DOMINICAN REPUBLIC
10/24/74 Set of four stamps commemorating the World Amateur Golf Championship:

Golfers. (730)

World Amateur Golf
Council. (C222)

Emblems. (729)

Dominican Golf
Association. (C223)

FRANCE

EQUADOR
9/11/75 One of a series on
sports. (922 out of set
912-929)

9/3/62 Promoting golf,
tourism and the resort of
Le Touquet. (1027)

10/18/80 French Golf
Federation. (1714)

FRENCH POLYNESIA

9/8/71 Issued for the 1971 South Pacific Games. (C75 out of set C74-C77)

2/27/74 A typical tourism stamp. (275)

2/27/74 View of the golf course. (276)

FRENCH WEST AFRICA
3/15/58 Commemorates 100th anniversary of Dakar with a sports theme. (C27)

GAMBIA
2/18/76 The Banjul Golf Course is shown in this series celebrating the independence of Gambia:

The President playing golf. (334)

Woman golfer. (332)

Man golfer. (333)

GREECE
11/24/79 Commemorating the World Golf Championship. (1325 out of set 1319-1327)

GRENADA

IRELAND
6/26/75 Issued for the 9th Annual European Amateur Team Championship:

Chipping. (371)

Putting. (372)

2/ 25/76 St. Georges Golf Course. (704)

11/2/79 One of a series of Disney characters (954 out of set 950-958)

JERSEY (GREAT BRITAIN)
2/28/78 A native of Jersey, Harry Vardon is featured in this commemorative of the centenary of the Royal Jersey Golf Club:

Golf course plan. (183)

Vardon's grip and swing. (184)

JAPAN
11/20/53 Shows view of Mt. Unzen from the Sasebo Golf Course. This is the earliest stamp related to golf. (592)

Vardon's grip and putt. (185)

Vardon's accomplishments. (186)

JAMAICA
11/26/79 (466 out of set 465-470)

LUXEMBOURG
4/28/80 A sports issue with a barely recognizable golf club and ball. (643)

MOROCCO
2/8/74 A golf tournament commemorative. (310)

MALI
10/25/73 Astronaut Alan Shepard on the moon with a golf club. (C200)

NICARAGUA
12/12/63 Part of a set commemorating the 1964 Olympics. (C535 out of set C523-C535)

12/29/67 A tourism issue. (192 out of set 189-192)

11/30/70 (251 out of set 248-251)

MONTSERRAT

RAS AL KHAIMA
1971 Alan Shepard shown hitting the first golf ball on the moon. (Minkus 539 out of set of five)

SAMOA
8/31/83 Issued for the 1983 South Pacific Games. The artist obviously was not familiar with the golf swing.

SHARJAH
1971 The same illustration was also issued with a value of 35 DH.

ST. VINCENT
7/31/75 Aquaduct Golf Course. (431)

ST. KITTS (ST. KITTS, NEVIS, ANGUILLA)

11/1/75 Commemorating the opening of Frigate Bay Golf Course: Action swing. (310) Other denominations with same design but different colors: 4¢ (308) 25¢ (309), $1 (311)

9/8/78 Royal St. Kitts Hotel and Golf Course. (364 out of set 355-369)

SINGAPORE
8/25/81 Golfer shown in lower right hand corner. This is probably the tiniest golf illustration in existence. (375)

SOUTH AFRICA

12/2/76 Gary Player. (459)

10/4/79 A rose named in honor of Gary Player for the World Rose Convention. (525) out of set 525-528)

UMM AL-QIWAIN
10/17/68 Some collectors feel that one of the objects in the painting is a miniature golf club. (188 out of set Minkus 188-192)

4/7/77 A first day cover of an envelope which was offered in two sizes in conjunction with a tennis issue. (U583)

9/22/81 Bobby Jones. (1933)

9/22/81 Babe Zaharias. (1932)

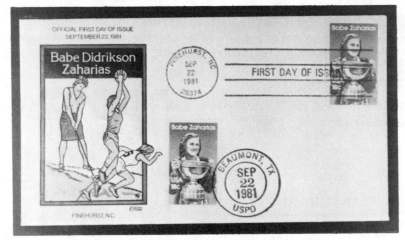

This first day issue of the Babe Zaharias stamp was postmarked both at Pinehurst, where it was issued, and in Texas where Zaharias resided. It is amusing to note that Babe is shown playing golf lefthanded, when she actually played righthanded.

A commemorative cover is issued at the British Open each year by The Royal Mail.

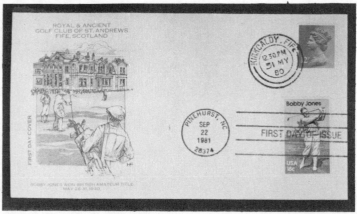

This set of five covers was issued in commemoration of the fiftieth anniversary of Bobby Jones' grand slam and his subsequent retirement from competition. The covers were postmarked in each of the cities where Jones won his major titles and also in Pinehurst where the U.S. postal service issued the Jones stamp.

CHAPTER 13 — CIGARETTE CARDS

Although the collecting of cigarette cards is not a new hobby, it has recently become of greater interest to golf collectors. Cigarette cards were patterned after the trade cards which promoted many commodities such as tea, candy and cosmetics and first appeared in the United States in 1879 and in Great Britain in 1885. The small cards, which are no longer used to stiffen cigarette packs, have illustrations which feature personalities such as royalty, actors and athletes and usually appear in sets of from twelve to fifty cards. The tobacco companies periodically issued new series of cards to encourage the sale of their products through the collecting of the cards. The hobby of cigarette card collecting, also known as cartophily, has been popular in Great Britain, although some Americans are becoming quite amused with the little cards which collectors display in albums or picture frames.

The cards were printed by various methods in color, monochrome and by photographic processes. Captions and text on the reverse side usually accompanied the tobacco company's advertisement. It is interesting to note that the same series of illustrations sometimes appeared on cards that were issued by different tobacco companies.

Golf themes were first used on cigarette cards produced by Ogden's Limited and Cope Brothers, both of Liverpool, England. Most of the records regarding the production of these early cards were lost during the Second World War, but it is believed that the first golf cards appeared in 1897. Ogden's used photographs for their cards while the Cope's cards were printed in color. The original illustrations for Cope's still exist in a private collection. They were painted in watercolor by J. Wallace, also known as George Pipeshank, in 1897 in the size of the actual cards.

The following list shows all known golf cigarette cards series and the many sets of non-golf cards which may have only a few golf topics. It is particularly gratifying to the collector to discover a previously unknown golf card among the non-golf sets. The dimension and color designations used in the list are standards in the trade and the approximate valuations have been assigned by the authors. Cards are shown in their actual size.

GUIDE TO CIGARETTE CARDS

DIMENSION:		COLOR:	
A — 36mm x 68mm		C — color	
B — 62mm x 80mm		P — photograph	
D — 37mm x 62mm		U — monochrome	
		B — black and white	

APPROXIMATE VALUES

PER EACH	E1:	$2-20
	E2:	UNDER 2
PER SET	S1:	OVER $300
	S2:	$100-300
	S3:	$50-100
	S4:	$20-50
	S5:	UNDER $20

NOTATIONS:
1 — Slightly larger size
2 — Slightly smaller size
* — Denotes an approximation
✓ — Set is not devoted entirely to golf subjects

COMPANY	SET QTY.	SIZE/COLOR	DATE	VALUE	
ARDATH CORK	50✓	A/C	1935*	E2	Cricket, Tennis & Golf Celebrities
FELIX BERLYN Manchester	25	A/C	1902*	S1	Humorous Golfing Series
	25	Postcard	1902*	S1	Humorous Golfing Series
ALEXANDER BOGUSLAVSKY LTD. London	25✓	A/C	1924*	E2	Sports Records (second series)
	50✓	A/U	1935*	E2	Sports Series No. 1
CARRERAS LTD. London	50✓	D/C	1936	E2	The Nose Game
	50✓	B/C	1936	E2	The Nose Game
W.A. & C.A. CHURCHMAN Ipswich	50	A/U	1927	S4	Famous Golfers
	12	B/U	1927	S4	Famous Golfers (first edition)
	12	B/U	1928	S4	Famous Golfers (second edition)
	50	A/C	1931	S4	Prominent Golfers
	12	B/C	1931	S4	Prominent Golfers
	50✓	A/C	1931	E2	Sporting Celebrities
	25✓	A/C	1931	E2	Sporting Trophies
	50✓	A/C	1931	E2	Men of the Moment in Sport
	36	A/C	1934	S4	Three Jovial Golfers In Search of the Perfect Golf Course (English issue)
	72	A/C	1934	S3	Three Jovial Golfers In Search of the Perfect Golf Course (Irish issue)
	55	A/C	1934	S4	Can You Beat Bogey at St. Andrews? (first edition)
	58	A/C	1934	S4	Can You Beat Bogey at St. Andrews? (second edition)
WM. CLARKE & SON Dublin	12	D2/C	1902	E1	Golf Terms (Part of a set of 50 Sporting Cards)
COPE BROS. & CO. LTD. Liverpool	50	A/C	1897*	S1	Cope's Golfers
	50	A2/C	1897*	S1	Cope's Golfers (cut narrow)
	32	B/B	1923	S3	Golf Strokes
	50	A/C	1983	S4	Cope's Golfers (reprint)
JOHN COTTON LTD. Edinburgh	50	A/U	1936	S3	Golf Strokes: A & B
	50	A/U	1937	S3	Golf Strokes: C & D
	50	A/U	1938	S2	Golf Strokes: E & F
	50	A/U	1939	S1	Golf Strokes: G & H
	50	A/U	1939	S1	Golf Strokes: I & J
MAJOR DRAPKIN & CO. London	40✓	A/C	1938	E1	Sporting Subjects
W. & F. FAULKNER London	12	A/C	1901*	E1/S2	Golf Terms

GALLAHER LTD. London	75✓	D/C	1924	E2	British Champions of 1923
	48✓	D/C	1934	E2	Champions
	100✓	D/C	1934	E2	Sports Series
	48✓	D/U	1936*	E2	Island Sporting Celebrities
T.P. & R. GOODBODY Dublin & London	25✓	D/C	1935	E2	Sports and Pastimes
HIGNETT BROS. & CO. Liverpool	50✓	A/C	1937	E2	Champions of 1936
IMPERIAL TOBACCO CO. Canada	50	A/B	1925	S2	How to Play Golf
	127	A/C	1926	S2	Smokers Golf Cards
MARSUMA LTD. Congleton	50	A/B	1914	S1	Famous Golfers and Their Strokes
MECCA CIGARETTES New York	6	60x75/C	1930	E1	Champion Golfers
J. MILHOFF & CO. LTD. London	27	A/P	1928	S3	Famous Golfers
	36✓	A2/P	1930	E2	In The Public Eye
STEPHEN MITCHELL & SONS Glasgow	50✓	A/C	1936	E2	A Gallery of 1935
	50✓	A/C	1936	E1	Humorous Drawings
	25✓	A/C	1937	E1	Sports
	50✓	A/U	1938	E1	Wonderful Century: 1837-1937
MORRIS & SONS LTD. London	25	D/U	1923	S4	Golf Strokes Series
OGDEN'S LIMITED Liverpool	18	D2/P	1897*	S2	"Guinea Gold" Series - Golfers
	420✓	D/P	1897*	E1	"Tabs" Series - Golfers (A subset of 15 golfers)
	25✓	A/C	1930*	E2	ABC of Sport (Letter "G")
	50✓	A/C	1937	E2	Champions of 1936
J. A. PATTREIOUEX Manchester	50✓	A/C	1936	E1	Celebrities in Sports
GODFREY PHILLIPS LTD. London	54✓	A2/C	1936*	E2	In The Public Eye
JOHN PLAYER & SONS Nottingham	25	B/C	1936	S4	Championship Golf Courses
	25	B/C	1939	S4	Golf
	25	B/C	1939	S5	Golf (Same as above but without Imperial Tobacco notation)
NICHOLAS SARONY & CO. London	50✓	A/C	1934*	E1	Origin of Games

F. & J. SMITH Glasgow	46✓	D/B	1902	E1	Champions of Sport (contains six un-numbered golfers)
STATE EXPRESS	50✓	A/C	1935*	E2	Sports Champions
W.D. & H.O. WILLS Bristol	50✓	A/C	1900	E2	Sports Of All Nations
	25	B/C	1924	S4	Golfing
	25	B/C	1930	S4	Famous Golfers
	48✓	B2/B	1937	E2	British Sporting Personalities

Some of the first cigarette cards issued by Copy Brothers in 1897:

"Fiery" — a well known caddie of the 19th century. (With trimmed borders.)

A typical pose of "Old Tom" Morris. (With untrimmed borders.)

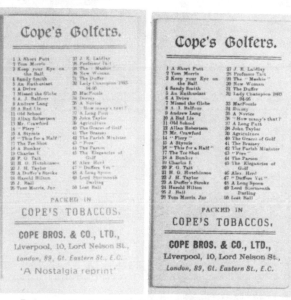

Reverse sides of a Cope's Golfers original and a reprint.

Ogden's photographic cards from 1897:

Other Ogden cards:

Guinea Gold series. These have no printing on the reverse side.

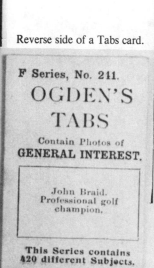

Reverse side of a Tabs card.

Ogden's Tabs series. James Braid was mistakenly listed as John Braid.

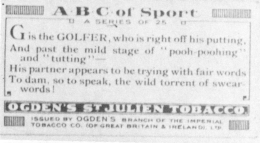

Above two cards:
Ogden's "ABC of Sport" featuring "G" for golf.

Mitchell's "Gallery of 1935". A non-golf series featuring Alfred Perry, the 1935 British Open champion.

Two issues by Alexander Boguslavsky:
Left: Turf Cigarettes. Henry Cotton is shown on this card from 1935 in honor of his first British Open win.
Right: "Sports Records" series, showing D. Chambers, winner of the 1923 English Ladies' Close Championship.

One of many cards issued by Churchman.

Gallaher "Champions" from 1934, front and back.

Phillips' "In the Public Eye" featuring Lawson Little. After winning both the U.S. and the British Amateur titles in 1934 and 1935, this American was certainly in the public eye.

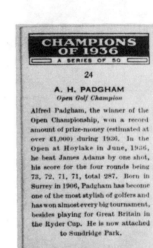

Reverse side of Hignett's card. (shown below)

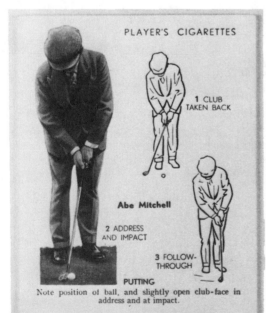

British professional Mitchell shows his style of putting on a Player's card.

Both Ogden's and Hignett's issued the same series of "Champions of 1936".

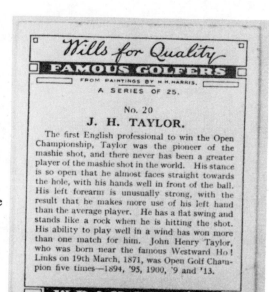

Some of the larger size cigarette cards:

An example of the front and back of the "Famous Golfers" issue by Wills in 1930.

Reverse side of a Mecca cigarette card, the only American golf series.

CHAPTER 14 — OTHER COLLECTIBLES

There are many golf collectibles which are not covered by any of the other chapters in this book. Paper items, games, advertising objects and other items are pictured in this chapter in order to make their presence known to the collector. These items have been listed together because they usually complement a golf collection rather than form the basis for one. Values have not been shown because many of these items can have great sentimental value and can range in price for almost nothing for a scorecard to thousands of dollars for a rare document.

PROGRAMS, PAMPHLETS AND BROCHURES

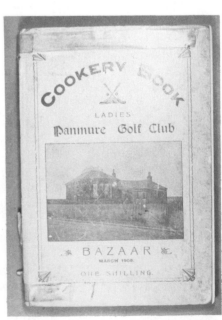

Spalding issued their first golf related brochure in 1893 which contained an explanation of the game and advertisements for golf supplies. Old, as well as new, equipment catalogs are valuable to collectors for dating and identification purposes.

The Ladies' Panmure Golf Club issued this cookbook in 1908.

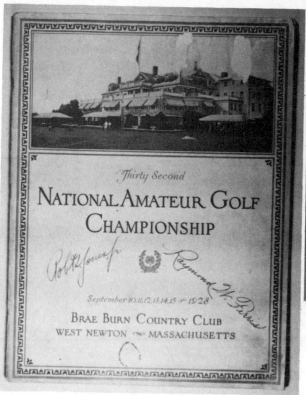

Tournament programs autographed by the winner are prized by collectors such as this 1928 U.S. Amateur program signed by Bobby Jones.

Examples of programs from major championships.

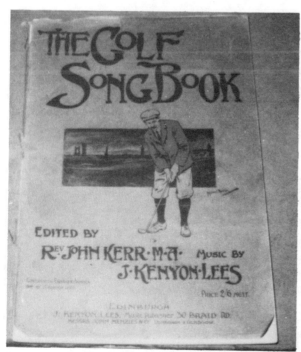

Many songs have been written with a golf theme, the best known being "Straight Down the Middle" which was made popular by Bing Crosby. This book of golf songs dates to 1903 and was edited by Reverend John Kerr, author of the famous *Golf Book of East Lothian.*

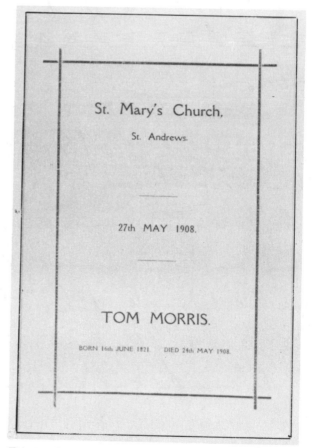

This rare piece of golf memorabilia is from the funeral service of Tom Morris, the great Scottish golfing figure of the nineteenth century.

J. H. TAYLOR, CHAMPION GOLFER.

JH Taylor.

TRADE MARK.

CANN & TAYLOR LIMITED

DIRECTORS:
G. H. CANN. J. H. TAYLOR.

GOLF GOODS MANUFACTURERS

EAST SHEEN & RICHMOND
—— SURREY ——

J. H. TAYLOR.
  OPEN CHAMPION   1894, 1895, 1900, 1909, 1913.
  RUNNER UP   1896, 1904, 1905, 1906, 1907, 1914.
  FRENCH CHAMPION 1908, 1909.
  RUNNER UP AMERICAN OPEN CHAMPIONSHIP 1900.

REGISTERED OFFICE & WORKS:

37, GROSVENOR AVENUE
EAST SHEEN, S.W. 14

Mid Surrey G Club
Richmond
24/12/23

Messrs Rowan & Co Ltd
70 Buchanan St.
Glasgow.

Dear Sirs

Replying to yours of Dec 19th. I shall be very pleased to visit Glasgow for the purpose of your Golf week, from Monday March 3rd to Sat 8th March next, and for the Terms you name viz 8 Guineas per day plus Hotel and travelling expenses. Should you be able to arrange an Exhibition match on Sat afternoon it would add to the pleasure of the visit. Except I hear to the contrary I will consider this a definite engagement.

Faithfully Yrs

JH Taylor

Messrs Rowans & Co

70 Buchanan Street
Glasgow

Memorandum from **JAMES BRAID,**

30th Jan. 1925

WALTON HEATH GOLF CLUB,
STATION — WALTON-ON-THE-HILL
TADWORTH S.E.Ry. Surrey.

Telegrams:—"BRAID, GOLF, WALTON-ON-THE-HILL."

PARCELS:—Tadworth Station, S.E.Ry.

OPEN CHAMPION, 1901
" " 1905
" " 1906
" " 1908
" " 1910

GOLF CLUB and

BALL MAKER.

Speciality : DRIVERS and BRASSIES.

Dear Sirs/ I have secured Vardon Taylor Ray & Herd for a week can only manage two days myself Monday & Tuesday, 23rd & 24th march You can let me know later if you intend arranging a match, if you dont I should finish on the Friday as there is very little buisness on the Saturday

yours faithfully

Jas Braid

Autographs of famous golfers are much more desirable when they appear on a letter, scorecard or other document. This letter and the one on the preceding page from British Open Champions J.H. Taylor and James Braid were written to Rowans, a store in Glasgow, regarding "golf week" promotions in 1924 and 1925.

SCORECARDS

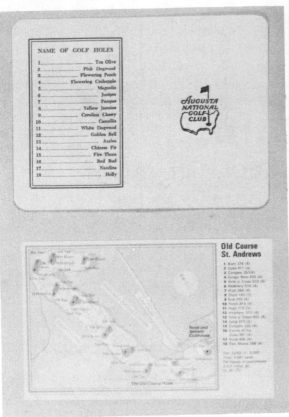

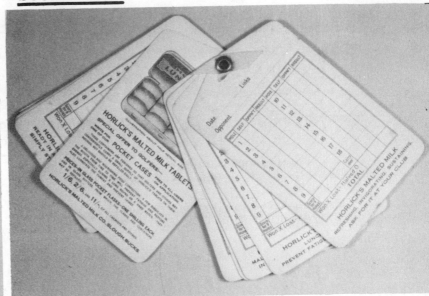

This early twentieth century pack of scorecards was issued by a company as an advertisement for their malted milk tablets.

Avid scorecard collectors and just interested golfers enjoy looking at scorecards from famous golf courses such as these.

GAMES, ETC.

This slot machine pays off in golf balls.

The above two yard games were popular at the turn of the century. Note the description of the "Marine Golf" version for use on the seas.

"After Dinner Golf" was one of many parlor games which were eventually replaced in modern times by the television.

Several golf games involving cards or dice have been devised over the past one hundred years.

Golf themes have been applied to the promotion of all types of products such as tobacco and candy.

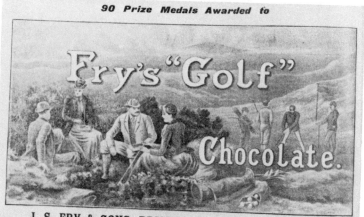

Since golfing societies were first formed in the eighteenth century, there have been buttons for clothing with a golf motif. Some are engraved with a crest or design while others have enamelled scenes.

Several styles of chairs with golf designs are known to exist. Some are captain's chairs with engraved silver plates and others have carved golf clubs as part of their structure.

All types of commemorative objects are issued in conjunction with golf tournaments. The ceramic items on the left are actually whiskey flasks.

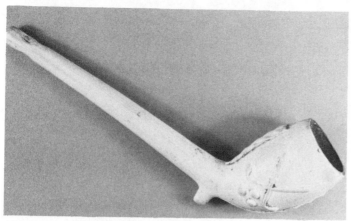

This old clay pipe is marked with the name of Prince Leopold of Belgium who was once Captain of the Royal and Ancient Golf Club. Perhaps it once belonged to Old Tom Morris?

Right: This does not appear to be a golf item, however it is actually a ballot box once owned by the Honourable Company of Edinburgh Golfers which now makes its home at Muirfield. The box is constructed so that a member could drop his small voting ball on either the "yes" or "no" side without anyone seeing his choice. Additionally, there are baffles on the interior of the box so that the votes could not be altered.

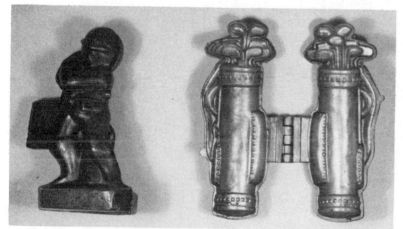

These contraptions are molds for forming ice cream in the shape of a golfer and a bag of clubs, probably used by a country club at the beginning of the century.

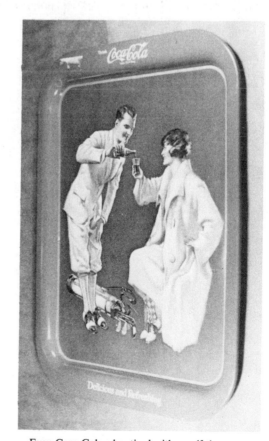

Even Coca Cola advertised with a golf theme.

Post cards, such as these, and other paper goods are often placed in picture frames for decorations.

NOTES

NOTES

NOTES